THE CORRESPONDENCE OF JEAN SIBELIUS AND ROSA NEWMARCH, 1906–1939

THE CORRESPONDENCE OF JEAN SIBELIUS AND ROSA NEWMARCH, 1906–1939

Edited and translated by
Philip Ross Bullock

THE BOYDELL PRESS

Editorial matter © Philip Ross Bullock 2011

Unpublished letters of Jean Sibelius © the Estate of Jean Sibelius
Unpublished letters of Rosa Newmarch © Renée Bodimeade

All Rights Reserved. Except as permitted under current legislation no part of this work may be photocopied, stored in a retrieval system, published, performed in public, adapted, broadcast, transmitted, recorded or reproduced in any form or by any means, without the prior permission of the copyright owner

First published 2011
The Boydell Press, Woodbridge

ISBN 978 1 84383 683 4

The Boydell Press is an imprint of Boydell & Brewer Ltd
PO Box 9, Woodbridge, Suffolk IP12 3DF, UK
and of Boydell & Brewer Inc.
668 Mount Hope Ave, Rochester, NY 14620, USA
website: www.boydellandbrewer.com

A catalogue record for this book is available
from the British Library

The publisher has no responsibility for the continued existence or accuracy of URLs for external or third-party internet websites referred to in this book, and does not guarantee that any content on such websites is, or will remain, accurate or appropriate.

Papers used by Boydell & Brewer Ltd are natural, recyclable products made from wood grown in sustainable forests

Printed in Great Britain by
CPI Group (UK) Ltd, Croydon, CR0 4YY

CONTENTS

Acknowledgements	vi
Illustrations	ix
Chronology	xi
Editorial conventions	xxi
Introduction	1
The Correspondence	49
Appendix A: Bibliography of publications by Rosa Harriet Newmarch pertaining to Jean Sibelius	247
B: Rosa Newmarch, *Jean Sibelius: Symphony No. 4 in A minor, Op. 63: Analytical Notes* (London, [1913])	249
Bibliography	267
Index	277

ACKNOWLEDGEMENTS

During the conception and preparation of this edition, I have received invaluable support and inspiration from a large number of individuals and organisations, without whom my work would have been quite impossible, and certainly a lot less enjoyable.

Peter Franklin, Glenda Dawn Goss and Daniel M. Grimley have all guided me expertly through the Sibelius literature, as have Laura Gray and Timo Virtanen. Gitta Henning not only pointed out crucial archival sources, but generously checked my translations from Finnish and Swedish sources with a remarkable combination of tact and enthusiasm (Marion Lafouge and Dora Osborne advised on matters relating to French and German). Liisa Byckling has been an expert guide to Helsinki, and to Finnish history and culture more generally. Charlotte Purkis provided a number of crucial leads and ideas, Catherine Maxwell helped to identify a number of troublesome quotations, Leanne Langley shed light on the British music scene, and Richard Davies of the Leeds Russian Archive shared details relating to Konstantin Saranchov. I am grateful to Lewis Stevens for showing me a version of his biography of Newmarch, as well as letting me consult Newmarch's papers. Jim Farrington of the Sibley Music Library at the Eastman School of Music, University of Rochester, generously provided copies of a number of rare bibliographical items. Julian Littlewood skilfully prepared the musical examples reproduced in the appendix. At Boydell & Brewer, Bruce Philips took a decisive early interest in this project, and Michael Middeke, Catherine Larner, and Vanda Ham dealt expertly with the complexities of seeing the manuscript into print.

Work on this book has taken me to many places. My thanks are due to the staff of the National Archives of Finland (especially Marja Pohjola and Kenth Sjöblom), the National Library of Finland, the British Library, the Royal College of Music, the

Acknowledgements

Bodleian Library, the Taylor Institution and the BBC Written Archives Centre. Trips to Finland have been made possible by Wadham College and the Faculty of Medieval and Modern Languages, University of Oxford, and Wadham College covered the cost of reproducing the images. That I have been able to complete this edition at all is in large measure due to the award of a Philip Leverhulme Prize by the Leverhulme Trust, which, together with a Major Award from the John Fell OUP Research Fund and further support from Wadham College, allowed me to take an extended period of research leave. My thanks are due to these institutions, and to Muireann Maguire who ably looked after my teaching.

I have been gratified by the support and interest shown in this project by the descendants of both correspondents: Pertti Virkkunen gave permission to reproduce Sibelius's letters on behalf of the composer's estate; likewise, Renée Bodimeade has not only sanctioned the publication of her grandmother's letters, but also answered my constant questions with good humour and patience. In addition, I should like to acknowledge the following institutions and individuals for permission to cite unpublished archival material: the National Archives of Finland (for material in the Sibelius Family Papers); the National Library of Finland (for material in the Sibelius and Aino Ackté papers); the Royal Academy of Music (letters of Sir Henry J. Wood); the Harry Ransom Humanities Research Centre, University of Texas at Austin (letters of Rosa Newmarch to John Lane); the Tertis Foundation (letter of Lionel Tertis); Dr Cuillin Bantock (letters of Sir Granville Bantock); Mark and Edward Brewer (letters of Sir Herbert Brewer); and the Elgar Birthplace Museum, Lower Broadheath (letters of Rosa Newmarch to Sir Edward Elgar). Individual letters from Otto Kling and Joseph Williams to Sibelius are reproduced by kind permission of Chester Music Limited, London, and Stainer & Bell Limited, London, respectively. As Newmarch died in 1940, her published works are no longer in copyright (I am grateful to for Breitkopf & Härtel for confirming this, and for assenting to the publication of Newmarch's note on Sibelius's Fourth Symphony as an appendix to the present volume). The author and publishers would be happy to acknowledge any other copyright holders inadvertently omitted in any future editions of this book.

It is hard to express how much I owe to Stefano Evangelista, whether for living with Rosa Newmarch for longer than he could ever have imagined possible, for sharing his expertise in Scandinavian languages and cultures, or for consenting to a memorable holiday in Karelia that took us to many of the places visited by Sibelius and Newmarch during their expedition of summer 1910. Whilst translating these letters, I have been thankful for the grounding in French and German given to me by my teachers both at school and university, without whose labours my subsequent studies in Russian (and tentative first steps in Sibelius's own languages of Swedish and Finnish) would have been unthinkable. My greatest debt, though, is to my parents. My love of Sibelius's music dates back to the teenage discovery of a recording of the Second Symphony in my father's LP collection (by Eugene Ormandy and the Philadelphia Orchestra, if memory does not deceive me). My current work on aspects of British, Russian and Finnish music history is in large measure due to the education that my parents provided for me. It was they who unconditionally encouraged my first aspiration to be a performing musician, yet never questioned my subsequent decision to pursue the study of modern languages instead. Although it can be no material recompense for all the sacrifices they have made (and, indeed, continue to make), this book is dedicated to them with love and admiration.

Philip Ross Bullock
Wadham College
University of Oxford

ILLUSTRATIONS

1. Postcard to Aino Sibelius signed by Rosa Newmarch, Jean Sibelius, Otto Kling and Granville Bantock, London, 27 February 1908. (courtesy of the National Archives of Finland) — 62
2. Photograph of Jean Sibelius (Atelier Nyblin, Helsinki, 1912). (courtesy of the Sibelius Museum, Turku/Åbo) — 89
3. Signed photograph of Rosa Newmarch, inscribed to Jean Sibelius (Klary, Brussels [April–May 1909]). (courtesy of the Sibelius Museum, Turku/Åbo) — 93
4. (a) 'Sibelius at Lake Saïma', in Rosa Newmarch, *Jean Sibelius: A Short Story of a Long Friendship* (Boston, 1939) — 115
   (b) 'Mr. and Mrs. Jean Sibelius in their Garden at Jarvenpää', in Rosa Newmarch, *Jean Sibelius: A Short Story of a Long Friendship* (Boston, 1939) — 115
5. Jean Sibelius to Rosa Newmarch, 2 May 1911. (courtesy of the National Archives of Finland) — 129–130
6. Rosa Newmarch to Jean Sibelius, 7 September [1912]. (courtesy of the National Archives of Finland) — 154
7. Jean Sibelius to Rosa Newmarch, 3 May 1919. (courtesy of the National Archives of Finland) — 195
8. Rosa Newmarch to Jean Sibelius, Wednesday [9 February 1921, not 1912 as annotated]. (courtesy of the National Archives of Finland) — 207
9. Rosa Newmarch to Jean Sibelius, 3 March 1930. (courtesy of the National Archives of Finland) — 231

CHRONOLOGY

Year	Sibelius's life and career	Newmarch's life and career	Contemporary events
1857		18 December: born Rosa Harriet Jeaffreson into an affluent middle-class family in Leamington Spa	
1865	8 December: born into a Swedish-speaking family in Hämeenlinna (Tavastehus)		
1883		marries Charles Henry Newmarch	
1885		birth of a son, John	
1888		publishes translation of Hermann Deiters, *Johannes Brahms: A Biographical Sketch*	
		birth of daughter, Elizabeth ('Elsie')	
1892	10 June: marries Aino Järnefelt		
1895		publishes translation of Alfred Habets, *Borodin and Liszt*	
			August 1895: establishment of Promenade Concerts at Queen's Hall
1897		first visit to Russia, works with Vladimir Stasov at the Imperial Public Library in St Petersburg and meets leading representatives of the Russian arts	
		meets Henry J. Wood	

Correspondence of Jean Sibelius and Rosa Newmarch

Year	Sibelius's life and career	Newmarch's life and career	Contemporary events
1900		publishes *Tchaikovsky: His Life and Works*	
1901		second visit to Russia	
	26 October: Henry Wood gives first performance of a work by Sibelius in Britain at Queen's Hall (Suite from *King Christian II*)		
1903		publishes *Horae Amoris: Songs and Sonnets*	
	13 October: first British performance of First Symphony by Henry Wood at Queen's Hall		
1904		publishes *Henry J. Wood*	
	27 May: invited by Granville Bantock to conduct concert of own works at Liverpool on 18 March 1905		
	September: moves into villa ('Ainola') at Järvenpää		
1905	2 March: Hans Richter gives first British performance of Second Symphony with the Hallé Orchestra in Manchester		
	March: cancels visit to Liverpool, leaving Bantock to conduct First Symphony and *Finlandia*		
	November–December: first brief visit to Britain, conducting First Symphony and *Finlandia* at Liverpool (2 December)		
1906		publishes *Songs to a Singer and Other Verses* and translation of Modeste Tchaikovsky, *The Life and Letters of Peter Ilich Tchaikovsky*	

Chronology

Year	Sibelius's life and career	Newmarch's life and career	Contemporary events
		15 January: first writes to Sibelius	
	8 February: first replies to Newmarch		
		22 February: gives lecture on Sibelius at the Concert-Goers' Club, subsequently published as Jean *Sibelius: A Finnish Composer*	
	3 April: first British performance of Suite from *Pelléas et Mélisande*		
		December: embarks on long trip to France and Italy	
1907		publishes *Poetry and Progress in Russia*	
	1 October: first British performance of Violin Concerto		
1908	February: second visit to Britain, conducts British premiere of Third Symphony (dedicated to Bantock) with Philharmonic Society in London (27 February)		
	May: treatment for throat tumour in Berlin, as a result of which, he gives up alcohol and tobacco		
		becomes programme-note writer for the Promenade, Symphony and Sunday Concerts at Queen's Hall	
1909	February–April: third visit to London. London, conducting *En saga* and *Finlandia* at Queen's Hall (3 February), attending reception at Concert-Goers' Club (16 February) and working on String Quartet		

· xiii ·

Correspondence of Jean Sibelius and Rosa Newmarch

Year	Sibelius's life and career	Newmarch's life and career	Contemporary events
	29 September: first British performance of suite from *Swanwhite*		
1910		Publishes translation of Vincent d'Indy, *César Franck: A Study*	
		April–June: third visit to Russia, returning via Finland with her companion, Elisabeth Johnson	
		16 September: death of Mary Wakefield	
		October: meets Rachmaninov	
		December: meets Aino Ackté	
1911	3 April: first performance of Fourth Symphony in Helsinki		
		June: her husband's financial problems force the sale of the family home	
	21 October: first British performance of 'Autumn Night' at Queen's Hall by Aino Ackté		
	October–December: visits Paris (Newmarch visits 19–30 November)		
1912		publishes *Mary Wakefield: A Memoir*	
	17 January: offered chair of composition in Vienna		
		August: publishes 'Chauvinism in Music' in *The Edinburgh Review*	
	September–October: fourth visit to Britain, conducting first British performance of Fourth Symphony at Birmingham Festival (1 October)		

Chronology

Year	Sibelius's life and career	Newmarch's life and career	Contemporary events
1913		expanded version of analytical note on the Fourth Symphony published as *Jean Sibelius: Symphony No. 4 in A minor, Op. 63: Analytical Notes*	
	4 March: first British performance of *Voces intimae* by Leeds Bohemian Quartet		
			June: visit to London by *Suomen laulu*
		2 September: death of Newmarch's sister, Marie Thérèse	
	10 September: world premiere of *Luonnotar* at Gloucester Festival performed by Aino Ackté		
	18 October: Dan Godfrey gives second British performance of Fourth Symphony at Bournemouth		
1914		publishes *The Russian Opera*	
	May–June: visits America to conduct the world premiere of *The Oceanides*		
			August: outbreak of World War I
1915		May–July: fourth and final visit to Russia, travelling via Finland with her daughter, Elsie, and Otto Kling	
1916		publishes *The Russian Arts*	
1917			March: abdication of Tsar Nicholas II
			November: Bolsheviks seize power in Russia
			6 December: declaration of Finnish independence

Correspondence of Jean Sibelius and Rosa Newmarch

Year	Sibelius's life and career	Newmarch's life and career	Contemporary events
1918			January–May: Finnish civil war
		publishes *The Devout Russian*	
		31 December: Newmarch's first post-war letter to Sibelius	
1919	3 May: Sibelius's first post-war reply to Newmarch		
		July: first visit to Czechoslovakia	
1920	20 March: first London performance of Fourth Symphony		
1921	3 January: accepts professorship at the Eastman School of Music, Rochester		
	January–March: fifth and final visit to Britain, giving five concerts in London (including first British performances of the Fifth Symphony and *The Oceanides* on 12 and 27 February respectively), plus further engagements in Birmingham, Bournemouth and Manchester, and a visit to Oxford		
		April: publishes 'Sibelius' in *The Chesterian*	
	May: finally declines the Eastman professorship		
	August: *Suite mignonne* accepted by Chappell		
1922	2 July: death of brother, Christian		
1925	August: due to conduct British premiere of Sixth Symphony at Gloucester Festival, but withdraws		

Chronology

Year	Sibelius's life and career	Newmarch's life and career	Contemporary events
1926	February: accepts invitation to conduct at Manchester, but withdraws in August		
		April–May: visit of Leoš Janáček to London	
			4 November: death of Robert Newman
	20 November: first British performance of Sixth Symphony		
1927	January–April: visits Paris with wife		
		July: death of Newmarch's husband	
		becomes President, Society of Women Musicians (until 1930)	
			BBC takes over the running of the Proms
	8 December: first British performance of Seventh Symphony		
1928	1 September: first British performance of *Tapiola*		
1930	26 February: first British performance of *Nightride and Sunrise* and the Prelude from *The Tempest* at the Hastings Festival		
1931			publication of Cecil Gray, *Sibelius*
		30 May and 12 December: lectures on Sibelius for the Society of Women Musicians	
1932			establishment of Sibelius Society in Britain
1934			publication of second edition of Cecil Gray, *Sibelius*

Correspondence of Jean Sibelius and Rosa Newmarch

Year	Sibelius's life and career	Newmarch's life and career	Contemporary events
1935			publication of Constant Lambert, *Music Ho! A Study of Music in Decline* publication of Cecil Gray, *Sibelius: The Symphonies*
1936	extensive celebrations to mark Sibelius's seventieth birthday		publication of English translation of Karl Ekman, *Jean Sibelius: His Life and Personality*
1937			publication of Bengt de Törne, *Sibelius: A Close-Up*
1938	August–September: Henry Wood performs all of Sibelius's symphonies at the Proms	9 September: Newmarch's brief memoir of her friendship with Sibelius published in Proms programme	September: Munich Agreement
1939	October–November: 'Sibelius Festival' in London organised by Sir Thomas Beecham	March: death of Newmarch's sister, Caroline	
			15 March: German invasion of Czechoslovakia
		publishes *Jean Sibelius: A Short Story of a Long Friendship* in America	
	24 July: Sibelius's last letter to Newmarch		
			3 September: Britain declares war on Germany

Chronology

Year	Sibelius's life and career	Newmarch's life and career	Contemporary events
		13 October: Newmarch's last letter to Sibelius	
			30 November: Soviet Union attacks Finland
1940			12 March: peace treaty signed with Moscow, bringing end to the 'Winter War'
		9 April: dies in Worthing	
1942		posthumous publication of The *Music of Czechoslovakia*	
1944		posthumous publication of *Jean Sibelius* in Britain	
1945		8 September: Elsie Newmarch writes to Sibelius, informing him of Newmarch's death in 1940	
1956	August: Sibelius's letters to Newmarch returned to the Sibelius family		
1957	20 September: dies at Ainola		

EDITORIAL CONVENTIONS

Printed letter heads are designated by the use of small capitals and are right justified; dates are generally reproduced in the format given in the original document (although Sibelius's distinctive manner of writing the date has been partially rationalised). Where addresses or dates have been conjectured, this information appears in square brackets, as does editorial information about the medium and language of communication (e.g. postcard or telegram, French, German or English). New paragraphs are indented, even if this is not the case in the original. Missing or illegible portions of documents are indicated thus: <...>. Postscripts are placed after the signature, as are the afterthoughts that Newmarch would often add up the left-hand side of the first page of a letter. The correspondence between Sibelius and Newmarch was almost entirely handwritten (typed letters are noted): underlinings have been retained, rather than being replaced by italics; single inverted commas have been preferred throughout, even where the author uses double. Where Newmarch included her own translations of Sibelius's letters in her 1939 memoir of the composer (republished in Britain in 1944), these have been used, although omitted material has been silently reincorporated, a few minor corrections made and Sibelius's punctuation and paragraphs have been restored. In her own translations of extracts of this correspondence, Newmarch retained Sibelius's 'chère Madame', a policy reflected here (even where the remainder of a letter is written in French). Newmarch's custom of signing her letter 'à vous de cœur' poses different problems. 'With all my heart' or other such renderings are clearly far too intimate, whilst 'cordially' is stiff and formal in comparison; accordingly, the original French has been retained. Other phrases have been retained in their original language where this differs from the main language of the letter (with a translation given in the notes). Newmarch, like most British writers of the time, tended to refer to Finnish towns by the Swedish names, and these are retained in the translation of her letters (therefore Helsingfors rather than Helsinki, Åbo rather than Turku etc.), although Finnish names are preferred elsewhere. Errors and inconsistencies in the spelling of proper names have not been corrected (hence, Newmarch usually gives Sibelius's address as Jarvenpää, etc.).

INTRODUCTION

FIRST ENCOUNTERS

When, on 4 December 1905, Jean Sibelius set off for Paris after his first brief trip to Britain, he left behind him a small but influential coterie of individuals who were to play a crucial role in encouraging the cause of his music in the English-speaking world over the next three and a half decades or so.[1] At Queen's Hall in London, Henry Wood had been the first British conductor to programme Sibelius's works in his concerts, rapidly followed in both Birmingham and Liverpool by the composer Granville Bantock. Ernest Newman had written some of the earliest and most enthusiastic reviews of these concerts, and Sibelius was to find a durable place in his criticism thereafter. As London representative of Sibelius's German publisher, Breitkopf & Härtel, Otto Kling also laboured to promote Sibelius's compositions with the concert-going (and music-buying) public. It was, though, with Rosa Harriet Newmarch that Sibelius enjoyed the closest and most sympathetic of all his British friendships. They met frequently during his five trips to Britain (in 1905, 1908, 1909, 1912 and 1921), and Newmarch visited him twice in Finland (in 1910 and 1915) and once in Paris (in 1911). As well as programme notes, journal articles and translations of his songs, Newmarch published three short books about the composer and his music: *Jean Sibelius: A Finnish Composer* (1906, also translated into German), *Jean*

[1] For a general survey of British responses to Sibelius and his music, see Peter Franklin, 'Sibelius in Britain', in *The Cambridge Companion to Sibelius*, ed. Daniel M. Grimley (Cambridge, 2004), pp. 182–95. Vesa Vahtola's study of Sibelius's visits to Britain – *Sibeliuksen konserttimatkat Englantiin* ([Tampere], 2008) – contains a wealth of documentation, including letters and an impressive number of reviews, although it is available in Finnish only.

Sibelius: Symphony No. 4 in A minor, Op. 63 (1913, also translated into German) and *Jean Sibelius: A Short Story of a Long Friendship* (US edition 1939; UK edition 1944, under the title *Jean Sibelius*). Their relationship lasted until Newmarch's death in May 1940 and was expressed in the more than one hundred and thirty letters, notes and telegrams that are published here for the first time in their entirety.

The exact details of how and where Newmarch and Sibelius first met are not entirely clear. In his preface to Newmarch's account of her friendship with Sibelius, Bantock suggests that the three of them first met in London in December 1905, from where they travelled on to Liverpool:

> I met Sibelius on his arrival at Victoria Station, London, and as the great man could then speak little English, and my knowledge of Finnish was *nil*, our conversation was limited to a polyglot combination of French and German words. Knowing that Rosa Newmarch was a fluent Russian linguist and an accomplished translator I sought her aid, happily not in vain. How well I remember that eventful railway journey from Euston to Liverpool, during which we three were the sole occupants of the compartment! I can still recall the pungent odour of those enormous cigars, which Sibelius procured from a gigantic cigar-case, and smoked incessantly.[2]

In Erik Tawaststjerna's slightly different version, they met 'on the train from London to Birmingham'.[3] Newmarch's own recollection is, though, at variance with both of these:

> the Bantocks invited me to meet him at their house at Moseley near Birmingham ... I was put next to him at dinner with a vague idea that as nobody knew what language he spoke, a little Russian might come in handy. I had been long enough in Russia and over the Finnish borders to know that

---

[2] Granville Bantock, 'Foreword', in Rosa Newmarch, *Jean Sibelius: A Short History of a Long Friendship* (Boston, 1939), pp. 7–11 (p. 8), reprinted in Rosa Newmarch, *Jean Sibelius* (London, 1944), pp. 5–7 (p. 5). Hereafter, Newmarch's memoir is referred to as *Jean Sibelius*, with page numbers given to both American and British editions, separated by a slash.

[3] Erik Tawaststjerna, *Sibelius*, trans. Robert Layton, 3 vols (London, 1976–97), vol. 2, p. 162.

the Finns were not too keen to speak the language of their big neighbour, but we soon effected a compromise: a sort of sandwich between French and German, to which, looking over our correspondence which has lasted over thirty years, I found to my amusement we always adhered.[4]

What is certain, however, is that Newmarch's linguistic facility, organisational abilities and keen feeling for Sibelius as both an artist and an individual meant that she was ideally placed to become a prominent and effective advocate of his music over the years to come.

Sibelius first visited Britain at the instigation of Bantock, who, in May 1904, had invited him to direct a concert of his works in Liverpool on 18 March the following year.[5] Plans were made for Sibelius to conduct the First Symphony, *Finlandia* and three of his songs (as well as *Finlandia* and the Suite from *King Christian II* in Birmingham),[6] but he cancelled at the last minute in order to finish the music for a production of Maurice Maeterlinck's play, *Pelléas et Mélisande*, at the Swedish Theatre in Helsinki, leaving Bantock to conduct the concert himself. Fortunately, Sibelius was able to accept Bantock's subsequent invitation to come to Liverpool later that year, and a concert was arranged for 2 December 1905, at which he would conduct the First Symphony and *Finlandia*.[7] Quite what stimulated Bantock's astute and prescient interest is not known, but it coincided with a period when Sibelius's music was beginning to be performed in Britain. The first work by Sibelius to have been heard in Britain appears to have been the Suite from *King Christian II*, Op. 27, conducted by Wood at a Promenade Concert in London on 26 October 1901; Wood subsequently gave the British première of the First Symphony in London

---

[4] Newmarch, *Jean Sibelius*, p. 16/pp. 8–9.
[5] Bantock to Sibelius, 27 May 1904, National Archives of Finland, Sibelius Family Papers Box 16 (hereafter NAF SFP, followed by the relevant box number). Bantock's letter was forwarded by his publishers, Breitkopf & Härtel, who subsequently wrote to Sibelius, urging him to accept the invitation (Kling to Sibelius, 17 June 1904, NAF SFP Box 42).
[6] Bantock to Sibelius, 28 February 1905, NAF SFP Box 16.
[7] Bantock to Sibelius, 13 and 25 September, 13 and 20 November 1905, NAF SFP Box 16.

on 13 October 1903.[8] The first British performance of the Second Symphony took place in Manchester on 2 March 1905, with Hans Richter conducting the Hallé Orchestra.

Britain was a destination that Sibelius was particularly keen to visit for himself. Although much of his early reputation was based on works associated with aspects of Finnish nationalism (in particular the *Kalevala*), he was equally committed to establishing himself as a major European symphonist outside of any one particular tradition. Yet his appearances during the 1900 World Fair in Paris, as well as in Germany and Austria, revealed to him that critics were still inclined to view him as a specifically nationalist composer. By contrast, much of the appeal of Britain for Sibelius lay in his discovery of a keen set of influential advocates who seemed willing to listen to his music in a less narrowly nationalistic spirit than had been the case elsewhere. As he later told his biographer, Karl Ekman, Britain appeared to promise more by way of sympathy and understanding:

> I had looked forward to my journey to England with great expectations. Busoni had spoken many times with rapture of England and had praised its audiences as remarkably receptive to anything new in music, and I had made a solemn vow to myself: I shall go there! . . . Bantock played the first symphony, 'Finlandia' and the 'King Christian' suite, and to judge by the critiques they were very successful. I noticed then already that Englishmen understood certain features in my music that were dismissed by the German critics of that time as mere mannerisms.[9]

Turn-of-the-century Britain was remarkably responsive to a wide range of musical influences from other European traditions. Despite undergoing an intense search for a musical culture of its own (what has been referred to by some as the 'English Musical Renaissance'), it seemed to lack some of the ingrained prejudices

---

[8] Arthur Jacobs claims that an earlier performance had been anticipated: 'What had been planned as the first *London* performance of Sibelius's first symphony on 13 October 1903 turned out to be . . . the first in Britain, a previously planned performance at the Three Choir's Festival in Gloucester having been cancelled' (*Henry J. Wood: Maker of the Proms* (London, 1994), p. 89 (emphasis original)).

[9] Karl Ekman, *Jean Sibelius: His Life and Personality*, trans. Edward Birse (London, 1936), p. 168.

about what exactly might constitute modern symphonic music that were characteristic of the German context. So widespread did interest in Sibelius's compositions become, and so closely was he bound up with figures central to the so-called 'renaissance', that one conductor even appears to have believed he was in fact a British composer. In February 1912, Michael Balling wrote to Percy Pitt to ask: 'Would you be so kind and give me the names (and publishers) of a few young English composers who have written some Concert music? – of course I don't mean the names of already famous composers Elgar, Bantock, Sibelius etc.'[10] Sibelius's music found a ready home in Britain because it seemed to offer answers to the very questions that critics and composers were asking about the nature and development of British music in the early twentieth century, particularly with respect to nationalism and modernism.[11]

Yet that moment was still some way off, and the earliest performances of Sibelius's works aroused both curiosity and a degree of bewilderment. Of the 1901 performance of the Suite from *King Christian II*, one critic wrote:

> The music is not in any sense remarkable, although, certainly, there are one or two memorable contrasts, and the last

---

[10] Lewis Foreman, ed., *From Parry to Britten: British Music in Letters 1900–1945* (London, 1987), p. 50, cited in Tomi Mäkelä, 'Towards a Theory of Internationalism, Europeanism, Nationalism and "Co-Nationalism" in 20th-Century Music', in *Music and Nationalism in 20th-Century Great Britain and Finland*, ed. Tomi Mäkelä (Hamburg, 1997), pp. 9–16 (p. 15).

[11] The influence of Sibelius on British composers in the interwar period has been the subject of a considerable amount of recent study. See, in particular: Daniel M. Grimley, 'Music, Ice, and the "Geometry of Fear": The Landscapes of Vaughan Williams's *Sinfonia Antartica*', *Musical Quarterly* 91 (2008), 116–50; J. P. E. Harper-Scott, '"Our True North": Walton's First Symphony, Sibelianism, and the Nationalization of Modernism in England', *Music and Letters* 89 (2008), 562–89; David Stern, '"One Thought Grows out Another": Sibelius's Influence on Ralph Vaughan Williams's Fifth Symphony', in *Sibelius in the Old and New World: Aspects of His Music, its Interpretation, and Reception*, ed. Timothy L. Jackson et al., Interdisziplinäre Studien zur Musik 6 (Frankfurt, 2010), pp. 383–400; and Gunnar Sundberg, 'National Parallels in the Orchestral Works of Jean Sibelius and Arnold Bax: Focusing on their Symphonic Language', in *Music and Nationalism in 20th-Century Great Britain and Finland*, ed. Mäkelä, pp. 59–66. For a related study of the American context, see Howard Pollack, 'Samuel Barber, Jean Sibelius, and the Making of an American Romantic', *Musical Quarterly* 84 (2000), 175–205.

movement is vigorously effective. The whole Suite makes a tolerably pleasing impression, but that impression is not in any sense due to the existence of individuality, nor to strength of feeling.[12]

The First Symphony fared somewhat better, with the same author suggesting that:

> the music is extraordinarily original. The composer particularly shews his individuality in his orchestration. Yet it is far from being a strong symphony in a constructive sense. It would really seem that Sibelius's music is a little too independent in style. Not often can one say that! He is well equipped as a contrapuntist. It is true he takes refuge in his power somewhat too frequently. But his counterpoint, happily enough, is not essentially dry: it has indeed considerable colour and fire at times. Altogether an interesting work, and I should not be at all surprised if Sibelius – who was born in 1865 – gave us something far stronger in the future.[13]

At its performance in Liverpool, however, the First Symphony met with a more tepid reaction:

> a first hearing of this symphony as well as a fantasia on Finnish airs did not convince me particularly. Perhaps a second hearing may modify this opinion, but such is the impression as far as your Liverpool correspondent is concerned. Perhaps when we have become more conversant with the peculiar orchestral dialect employed by him, Sibelius may obtain a vogue in this country, but at present he addresses us in a strange tongue and is consequently to a certain extent unintelligible.[14]

Performances of *The Swan of Tuonela* in London and Liverpool later that year did little to clarify matters. At its London performance, the work elicited the following dismissive response:

---

[12] J. H. G. B[aughan]., 'Music in London', *Musical Standard*, 2 November 1901, 279–81 (280).
[13] J. H. G. B[aughan]., 'Some Events of the Week', *Musical Standard*, 17 October 1903, 240–41 (240).
[14] W. J. B[owden]., 'Liverpool', *Musical Standard*, 25 March 1905, 187–8.

Introduction

> Not much need be written concerning Sibelius' orchestral composition, 'The Swan of Tuonela,' London's first performance of which occurred at the Promenade Concerts of August 31 ... The music has been described as picturesque. If we agree that is true, we also have to agree it is very monotonously picturesque. As composition pure and simple 'The Swan of Tuonela' is without strength. Its close is ridiculously tame. The *cor anglais* melody – 'obviously that of the swan's song' – is heard a great deal: unfortunately it is far from being an inspiration, nor do the modifications it undergoes materially effect the situation. Up to a certain point the orchestral colouring interests the listener; then that interest decreases rapidly. What variety there is comes all too late.[15]

Reactions to the work in Liverpool were yet more indifferent: 'Jan Sibelius's dismal Legend, "The Swan of Tuonela," ... as an example of musical pessimism, is about the most doleful effort I can remember.'[16] Although far from representative of the whole range of responses to early performances of Sibelius's works, such ambivalent reactions are particularly useful in amplifying and even challenging the usual story of Sibelius's British reception, which tends to see this initial period as a premonition of the later Sibelius 'cult' and emphasises, for reasons that are understandable enough, Newman's early and enthusiastic reviews over less penetrating and more sceptical analyses.[17]

With Sibelius's appearance in Liverpool, however, something began to change in the tone of these reviews, as if Sibelius were himself teaching the British audience how to understand his 'peculiar orchestral dialect' and his 'strange tongue'. W. J. Bowden, Liverpool correspondent of *The Musical Standard*, now warmed to Sibelius's music, not just because it seemed better performed than under Bantock's direction, but also because Sibelius was perceived as an ideal interpreter of this still alien idiom:

---

[15] 'Comments and Opinions', *Musical Standard*, 9 September 1905, 159–60.
[16] W. J. B.[owden]., 'Liverpool', *Musical Standard*, 11 November 1905, 313.
[17] See, for instance: E[rnest]. N[ewman]., 'The Hallé Concerts', *Manchester Guardian*, 3 March 1905, 7; 'Sibelius in Liverpool', *Manchester Guardian*, 4 December 1905, 7; and 'Liverpool Orchestral Society's Concert', *Manchester Guardian*, 26 March 1906, 6.

> The second Ladies' Concert of the Liverpool Orchestral Society on Saturday evening, December 2, was rendered peculiarly interesting by the presence of Jan Sibelius, of Helsingfors, whose First Symphony and tone-poem, 'Finlandia,' were again submitted. These two items had been prepared for the final concert of last season, when Sibelius was expected to visit England, but the political troubles in Finland prevented this and necessitated a postponement; a fact, however, that may, after all, not have been a disadvantage as far as the orchestra was concerned. At all events, the traces of unfamiliarity noticed on the last occasion had entirely disappeared under the personal influence of the composer, who conducted with manifest appreciation of the forces at his command. I must confess that I was not particularly struck by the Symphony last season, but must revise that decision on a second experience.[18]

Sibelius's first trip to Britain may have been brief, yet it was decisive in dispelling something of the ignorance that necessarily surrounded perceptions of his music at that time. To hear Sibelius's works in what audiences could take to be definitive and authoritative performances helped them to overcome their lack of familiarity with music from a part of the world that few understood, let alone knew at first hand. To see the composer himself in person gave them a personality to identify with the music.

This, then, was the context of Newmarch's encounter with Sibelius in late 1905. Like many, Newmarch had comparatively limited knowledge of his music (she mentions having been present at the first British performance of the First Symphony in 1903, and attended Sibelius's concert at Liverpool in December 1905).[19] Yet on 22 February 1906, barely three months after Sibelius's visit to Liverpool, she gave a public lecture about his music in London in which she daringly attempted to educate the British public about this new musical phenomenon. Published later that year by Breitkopf & Härtel as *Jean Sibelius: A Finnish Composer*, her lecture

---

[18] W. J. B[owden]., 'Liverpool', *Musical Standard*, 9 December 1905, 377–8 (377).

[19] Newmarch, *Jean Sibelius*, p. 15/p. 8. Wood's erroneous assertion that Newmarch 'was directly responsible for my interest in Sibelius' illustrates the extent to which she would subsequently become associated with the composer's music. See Henry J. Wood, *My Life of Music* (London, 1938), p. 302.

became the first book-length treatment of his music in any language, and did much to influence his reception, not just in Britain, but also in Europe more widely (it was published simultaneously in German translation).[20] Aside from any personal sympathy she felt for Sibelius and his music, Newmarch was perhaps as qualified as anybody to undertake this task. A prolific author and proficient linguist, she had a particular interest in musical nationalism. By the time of Sibelius's arrival in Britain, she had already established for herself a reputation as a pioneering authority on Russian music: she visited the country four times between 1897 and 1915, where she met leading cultural figures and gathered material for the vast range of original and translated works on Russian music (as well as on literature and the visual arts) that she would publish in the years leading up to the October Revolution. By 1905, she had already translated Alfred Habets's *Borodin and Liszt* (1895), published the first biography of Tchaikovsky in any language (*Tchaikovsky: His Life and Works*, 1900), given a series of five lectures on 'The Development of National Opera in Russia' to the Musical Association, and embarked on writing countless entries on Russian composers for the second edition of *Grove's Dictionary of Music and Musicians* (1904–10). Over the next decade or so, she would translate Modeste Tchaikovsky's *The Life and Letters of Peter Ilich Tchaikovsky* (1906), write a trilogy of books on Russian culture – *Poetry and Progress in Russia* (1907), *The Russian Opera* (1914) and *The Russian Arts* (1916) – and edit *The Devout Russian* (1918), a series of extracts from Orthodox spiritual texts and modern writers on religious and philosophical questions, whose relevance was overtaken by political events. After the October Revolution of 1917, her interest shifted to the music of Czechoslovakia, and in particular that of Leoš Janáček.[21] She

---

[20] Rosa Newmarch, *Jean Sibelius: A Finnish Composer* (Leipzig, 1906), trans. Ludmille Kirschbaum as *Jean Sibelius: ein finnländischer Komponist* (Leipzig, 1906) (in order to avoid confusion with Newmarch's later memoir, the English edition is hereafter referred to as *Jean Sibelius: A Finnish Composer*). At just twenty-four pages, Newmarch's booklet is hardly extensive, but it is still longer than the six pages devoted to Sibelius in Walter Niemann's *Die Musik Skandinaviens: Ein Führer durch die Volks- und Kunstmusik von Dänemark, Norwegen, Schweden und Finnland bis zur Gegenwart* (Leipzig, 1906).
[21] Their letters have been published as Zdenka E. Fischmann, ed., *Janáček–Newmarch Correspondence* (Rockville, 1986).

visited the country yearly, becoming closely involved with its musicians and other cultural figures; her history of the country's music – *The Music of Czechoslovakia* (1942) – was published only after her death. As well as writing about Slavonic music for British audiences, Newmarch was closely involved in British musical life itself. From 1908, she provided the programme notes for the Promenade, Symphony and Sunday Concerts at Queen's Hall. Her hagiographic 1904 biography of Wood was the first in a series of popular books about contemporary musicians that she edited for the publisher John Lane under the title *Living Masters of Music* (interestingly, she deemed that Sibelius was not yet well established enough to merit a volume in his own right, as he 'was still rather a composer of promise than fulfilment').[22] Her biography of Mary Wakefield, the founder of the Competition Festival Movement in Britain, was published in 1912. She even found time to publish two volumes of original poetry (*Horæ Amoris: Songs and Sonnets* in 1903, and *Songs to a Singer and Other Verses* in 1906).

SIBELIUS AS NATIONALIST

In retrospect, it seems evident that Newmarch's artistic convictions, personal and professional connections, and seemingly infinite energy would make her an ideal advocate of Sibelius's music in Britain. However, as an avowed Russophile, Newmarch would first have to deal with the question of his reputation as a patriot. Russian measures to curb Finnish independence – the February Manifesto of 1899, the Language Manifesto of 1900 and the Conscription Act of 1901 – evoked considerable resistance within Finland itself, and Sibelius's music came to symbolise the cause of Finnish resistance to Russian oppression, both at home and abroad. Early performances of *Finlandia* in Britain were tinged with ideological meaning that had more to do with the political situation than any understanding of the music (just as Sibelius's cancellation of his first visit to Britain in March 1905 was often incorrectly attributed to political circumstances). If the first British performance of the First Symphony in Liverpool in March 1905

---

[22] Newmarch, *Jean Sibelius*, p. 43/p. 29.

had left the audience perplexed, then *Finlandia* proved to be a more accessible proposition, and largely on extra-musical grounds. As the reviewer of that performance noted: 'The fantasia "Finlandia" . . . was redemanded and repeated, a compliment which I think owed more to Russophobism than an overweening admiration for the piece itself.'[23] After a performance of *Finlandia* in Birmingham in February 1906, another reviewer was quite carried away by the work's perceived political significance:

> Whether Sibelius, the Finn, is a great composer or not I cannot say – I know so little of his work – but his 'Finlandia' Symphonic Poem is great music – the most terrible music I have ever heard . . . The opening bars suggest the awful groans of a suffering people; but before the end of the piece the hearer is aware of a terrible, irresistible current of stern resolve which must finally triumph over tyranny; and of a sense of divine faith which reveals a certainty of ultimate love and peace. These three emotional suggestions – suffering, grim determination, and faith – intermix in this work in such a significant way that 'tis no wonder the Russian bureaucracy forbid its performance in Finland! Even I, an Englishman, was moved (at the very end of a concert) to an intense pitch of sympathetic excitement.[24]

Even works that had no such significance were read, however incongruously, through the prism of the political situation, which, for one reviewer, was the key to understanding the melancholy of *The Swan of Tuonela*:

> By all means let us sympathise with the down-trodden Finns, but if this is the kind of thing in which their premier composer persists in producing I fail to see that the cause of freedom can thereby advance. Perhaps, however, now that Finland has to some extent shaken off the intolerable yoke of the Muscovite, the tone of Sibelius' muse may assume a more cheerful mood.[25]

---

[23] W. J. B[owden]., 'Liverpool', *Musical Standard*, 25 March 1905, 187–8.
[24] Rubato, 'Birmingham', *Musical Standard*, 24 February 1906, 124.
[25] W. J. B[owden]., 'Liverpool', *Musical Standard*, 11 November 1905, 313.

Patriotic associations would prove to be an ambiguous feature in Sibelius reception thereafter; a supposedly political subtext might guarantee a work's immediate popularity, but it risked limiting its artistic significance in the longer term.

Newmarch had little time for such Russophobia, and her earliest writings on Sibelius show a deliberate attempt to qualify the political narrative that characterised many contemporary reviews. In her 1906 lecture, she alludes to Finland's 'recent struggle with Russia for the restitution of its constitutional rights',[26] before widening the historical perspective to include Finland's long history as part of Sweden: 'Situated between Sweden and Russia, Finland was for centuries the scene of obstinate struggles between these rival nationalities . . . Whether under Swedish or Russian rule, the instinct of liberty has remained unconquerable in this people.'[27] Strikingly, Newmarch then goes on to argue that Finnish cultural and political self-realisation was in fact a direct result of benign Russian rule:

> However we may regard the recent attempts on the part of an autocracy at bay to curtail the constitutional rights of the Finns, it must be obvious to an impartial mind that the renascence of the Finnish nation dates from the Act of Assurance granted to it by Alexander I in March 1809. His humane and liberal policy enabled Finland to develop from a mere province into an independent European state.[28]

The expression of what, at the time, was a potentially controversial opinion may well have been related to the fact that her familiarity with Finland itself was largely limited to her experience of 'one or two flying visits to a Russian friend who lived over the Finnish border in Karelia, and how deeply he had interested me in the history and temperament of this people'.[29]

Once Newmarch had dispensed with the Russophobic account of Finnish national identity, she was then free to draw on the

---

[26] Newmarch, *Jean Sibelius: A Finnish Composer*, p. 4.
[27] Ibid., p. 7.
[28] Ibid.
[29] Ibid., p. 3. The friend in question may well be Vladimir Stasov, who had a dacha at Pargolovo. For an account of one such trip to Stasov's dacha, see Rosa Newmarch, 'Rimsky-Korsakov: Personal Reminiscences', *Monthly Musical Record* 38 (1908), 172–3.

Introduction

growing body of studies dealing with Finnish history, society and culture, and which she used to illuminate 'the relation of his works to Finnish literature and the national idea'.[30] This 'national idea' could take a number of different forms. In part, it was a product of 'influences climactic and historical' that gave rise to the 'innate gravity and restrained melancholy of the Finnish temperament'.[31] For all its reputation as one of Europe's most recent nations, Finland was seemingly untouched by modernity:

> That the Finns still live as close to Nature as their ancestors, is evident from their literature, which reflects innumerable pictures from this land of granite rocks and many-tinted moorlands; or long sweeps of melancholy fens and ranges of hills clothed with dark pine-forests; the whole enclosed in a silver network of flashing waters – the gleam and shimmer of more than a thousand lakes.[32]

In musical terms, the national idea was expressed by the proximity of Sibelius's music to folksong:

> From his novitiate, Sibelius's melody has been stamped with a character of its own. This is due in a measure to the fact that it derives from the folk-music and the *runo*: – the rhythm in which the traditional poetry of the Finns is sung . . . In some of Sibelius's earlier works, where the national tendency is more crudely apparent, the invariable and primitive character of the rune-rhythm is not without influence upon his melody, lending it a certain monotony which is far from being devoid of charm.[33]

Like many early commentators, Newmarch found an explanation for her inability immediately to account for the originality of Sibelius's music in the alleged primitivism and lack of sophistication of Finnish art.

Here, however, Newmarch stumbled upon a particular problem. In his letter to her of 8 February 1906, Sibelius quickly moved to dispel what he saw as a common misconception about his music,

---

[30] Newmarch, *Jean Sibelius: A Finnish Composer*, p. 4.
[31] Ibid., p. 5.
[32] Ibid., p. 8.
[33] Ibid., p. 11.

and Newmarch cited his words directly in her lecture: '"There is a mistaken assumption among the press abroad", he has assured me, "that my themes are often folk-melodies. So far I have never used a theme that was not of my own invention. Thus the thematic material of 'Finlandia' and 'En Saga' is entirely my own."'[34] Newmarch would, of course, have been unable to verify the veracity of Sibelius's statement for herself, but it accorded with some of her own later reservations about the use of folksongs in other, more modern contexts. Writing about the English folksong revival, for instance, she wrote critically of 'our long neglected treasures of folk-song which have been, and are being, resuscitated with miraculous and suspicious rapidity in every corner of the kingdom'.[35] Even the Russian nationalist tradition which she so admired had its own shortcomings in this regard: 'The obligation . . . to model every melody on the folk-tune pattern, gave to some of the later music of the nationalists an air of monotony and perfunctoriness.'[36] Nonetheless, Newmarch continued to discern the imprint of folksong on Sibelius's musical language. Even if he avoided 'the crude material of the folksong', he was, she argued, 'so penetrated by the spirit of his race that he can evolve a national melody calculated to deceive the elect'.[37]

Given her interest in Russian music, it was perhaps inevitable that Newmarch's first reaction to Sibelius would be to present him as a nationalist composer along cognate lines. In Newmarch's account, the establishment of a properly nationalist school is prefigured by a similar anticipatory phase in both countries: 'Ehrström, Ingelius and Kollan contributed their quota to the musical development of their country, just as in Russia Alabiev and Verstovsky, by their pseudo-national operas and songs, paved the way for a higher manifestation of native genius in Glinka and his followers.'[38] A comparison between Sibelius and both Borodin and Tchaikovsky is based on the inability of some listeners to hear in

---

[34] Ibid., p. 15.
[35] Rosa Newmarch, 'Chauvinism in Music', *Edinburgh Review* 216 (1912), 95–116 (97).
[36] Rosa Newmarch, 'Scryiabin and Contemporary Russian Music', *Russian Review* 2 (1913), 153–69 (154).
[37] Newmarch, *Jean Sibelius: A Finnish Composer*, p. 15.
[38] Ibid., p. 8.

Introduction

them 'the spirit of an unfamiliar race', and a tendency to see them as purely cosmopolitan figures.[39] Newmarch discerns a resemblance between Sibelius and Glinka as composers able to avoid 'the crude material of the folksong', whilst arguing that each is 'so penetrated by the spirit of his race that he can evolve a national melody calculated to deceive the elect'.[40] In the Overture from the *Karelia Suite*, 'the use of the interval of the fourth ... reminds us of a precisely similar figure which recurs persistently in Borodin's First Symphony and seems to have some almost local significance'.[41] Such comparisons not only challenge the explicit Russophobism that had characterised early reactions to *Finlandia*, but also serve to situate Sibelius in relation to a nationalist tradition with which audiences were more likely to be familiar (Russian music then being a prominent feature of British concert life, and one, moreover, with which Newmarch was particularly associated).

Newmarch's nationalist rhetoric was also directly related to a strongly anti-German strain in her criticism (and which was to be repeatedly expressed in her letters to Sibelius). Although she had translated Hermann Deiters's biography of Brahms in 1888 and wrote notes on a vast range of German works for the Queen's Hall concerts, Newmarch was impatient with the perceived superiority of German music. As she prepared to give her lecture on Sibelius, she expressed her views to the conductor Vasily Safonov, who was to chair the event: 'Before the lecture Safonoff was my guest at dinner, and during a lively musical discussion I chanced to remark that to me personally a Mozart Symphony was more precious than all the music that had been made in Germany since Schubert's death in 1828.'[42] Yet it was not so much German music itself that offended Newmarch, as its influence on modern music elsewhere. Conscious of the way in which German music was held up as a model for younger composers in British universities and colleges, Newmarch deliberately spoke out against it:

> She believes that British music has entered upon a period of great activity and development. As to the influence exerted by

---

[39] Ibid., p. 12.
[40] Ibid., p. 15.
[41] Ibid., p. 16.
[42] Rosa Newmarch, 'Wassily Safonoff', *Musical Times* 57 (1916), 9–12 (10).

foreign music on the revival, she thinks that some of our composers have submitted too much to the influence of Brahms, who, although a sincere and natural composer, produces on his disciples the curious effect of making them wearisome, even though he gives them academic responsibility.[43]

The point, then, of promoting Sibelius as a Finnish nationalist was to distance him from the Austro-German tradition in the minds of British audiences and critics, to associate him instead with what Newmarch perceived as the newer and more vital Russian school, and ultimately to establish him as a model for British composers to emulate.

SIBELIUS AS SYMPHONIST

Newmarch's recourse to nationalism is predictable enough and may suggest that her writings on Sibelius are indebted to an outdated ideology that has come in for considerable scrutiny and criticism (a number of passing comments in her letters to Sibelius also reveal that she was not immune to the kind of casual anti-Semitism that was widespread in intellectual circles at the time). Yet her 1906 lecture effects at least one important intellectual manoeuvre out of which much of her subsequent thinking on Sibelius's music was to grow. At the time of the first performances of Sibelius's works in Britain, a debate was taking place about the viability of the symphony as a contemporary genre.[44] To Newmarch, Sibelius's symphonies proved not only that he 'possessed the large structural style and sustained eloquence which alone could entitle him to a place in the front rank of the

[43] M., 'Mrs. Rosa Newmarch', *Musical Times* 52 (1911), 225–9 (226).
[44] For a thorough survey of the symphony in early twentieth-century Britain with respect to Sibelius, see Laura Gray, '"The Symphonic Problem": Sibelius Reception in England Prior to 1950' (Unpublished PhD thesis, Yale University, 1997). See also her 'Sibelius and England', in *The Sibelius Companion*, ed. Glenda Dawn Goss (Westport and London, 1996), pp. 281–95, and '"The Symphony in the Mind of God": Sibelius Reception and English Symphonic Theory', in *Sibelius Forum: Proceedings from the Second International Jean Sibelius Conference, Helsinki, 25–29 November, 1995*, ed. Veijo Murtomäki, Kari Kilpeläinen and Risto Väisänen (Helsinki, 1998), pp. 62–72.

symphonists', but also provided an answer to a question 'of far wider significance, namely – is the symphony really an obsolete form?'[45] Given her interest in Slavonic music, Newmarch might well have been expected to espouse the kind of programmatic symphonic works favoured by Russian composers, but her description of Sibelius's symphonies (and he had written just two at the time she gave her lecture) makes clear that the source of her appreciation was rooted in her aesthetic response to their abstract and formal qualities: 'They bear no indication of any literary basis; they are not fettered to the expression of any particular sentiment, heroic, pathetic, pastoral, or even domestic.' Newmarch's chosen epithets – 'heroic, pathetic, pastoral, or even domestic' – deliberately allude to symphonies by Beethoven, Strauss and Tchaikovsky, but what separates Sibelius from all of these composers is what she sees as 'the sheer originality, beauty and vigour of the musical idea'.[46] Newmarch's admiration of Sibelius's music is based primarily on its formal and structural qualities, rather than any ability to convey extra-musical narrative or national character (very much characteristics of the Russian tradition with which she was so associated). Although the language of nationalism would continue to inform all of her subsequent writings on Sibelius, it is important to discern here her overriding commitment to him as a symphonist above all else.

A sideways digression into Newmarch's relationship with Edward Elgar sheds considerable light on her advocacy of Sibelius's symphonies. The development of a British tradition of symphony writing was an important theme in early twentieth-century musical criticism and was, moreover, closely related to the discovery of Sibelius's works, as Laura Gray observes: 'The rise of the national symphony, signalled by the historic premier of Elgar's First Symphony on December 8 1908, coincided precisely with Sibelius's ascendancy in English concert halls.'[47] One of Newmarch's most important contributions to the debate about the nature of the modern British symphony took the form of the detailed

---

[45] Newmarch, *Jean Sibelius: A Finnish Composer*, p. 19.
[46] Ibid.
[47] Gray, 'Sibelius and England', p. 288. In fact, Elgar's First Symphony received its première in Manchester on 3 December 1908 (it was first heard in London on 7 December).

programme note that she wrote for performances of Elgar's First Symphony at Queen's Hall. Through a series of comparisons with Tchaikovsky, she argued that the modern symphony should both adhere 'to the broad outlines of the classical model' and incorporate 'elements of the symphonic poem, with its concrete programme':

> Like the last three symphonies of the Russian composer, the work now before us seems to have a clear, but wordless, psychological programme. The composer of to-day – even while keeping his respect for classical tradition – cannot ignore what the symphonic poem has done to make his language richer and more supple. It becomes more and more probable that the musician who has music to express will be equally attracted to both forms, and will only be able to reveal himself completely by alternating between the symphonic poem and the emotional symphony. There is nothing blameworthy in this fluctuation, for it is easy to realize that a composer may feel at one period of his life that an ebullient and roving fancy works better within the restrictive limits of a settled programme, while at another phase of his career he may know himself able to give expression to ideas and feelings which cannot be referred to any definite subject. Nor can we quarrel with a seeming inconsistency which has endowed the world with such contrasting utterances of individual temperament as Tchaikovsky's 'Francesca da Rimini' and his 'Pathetic Symphony', or Elgar's 'In the South' and the A flat Symphony.[48]

By proposing Tchaikovsky as Elgar's most influential precursor, Newmarch was rejecting interpretations which related his new symphony to the German tradition. Arthur Nikisch, for instance, had traced Elgar's genealogy back to Beethoven and Brahms:

---

[48] Extract cited in M., 'Mrs. Rosa Newmarch', 228. Newmarch's complete note, first written for a performance of the symphony at a Queen's Hall Promenade Concert on 17 August 1909 (British Library (hereafter BL) shelf number h.5470), is reprinted in Rosa Newmarch, *The Concert-Goer's Library of Descriptive Notes*, 6 vols (London, 1928–48), vol. 1, pp. 25–35. Newmarch also wrote a note on the symphony for a performance at a Symphony Concert on 9 April 1909 (BL shelf number d.484.a), which, although considerably shorter, does contain a number of musical examples.

> I consider Elgar's symphony a masterpiece of the first order, one that will soon be ranked on the same basis with the great symphonic models – Beethoven and Brahms . . . You will remember . . . that when Brahms produced his first symphony it was called 'Beethoven's tenth,' because it followed on the lines of the nine great masterpieces of Beethoven. I will therefore call Elgar's symphony 'the fifth of Brahms.'[49]

Richter – who had conducted the first performance of the work – also emphasised this same tradition, and in a letter written shortly thereafter, Newmarch wrote to Elgar to dispute his interpretation:

> A young friend of mine told me Richter had said to him of the Symphony: 'es ist Beethoven'. Of course it was his supreme word of praise and appreciation. But that was the one drawback to his interpretation, because it is another voice altogether. Something perfectly individual and a century later than Beethoven, therefore expressing thoughts and feelings undreamt of in his philosophy. It is a beautiful, penetrating, complex creation such as could only be written nowadays, and, what is best of all, such as could only have been written by <u>you</u> – yourself.[50]

At the end of 1909, Newmarch wrote again to Elgar, returning to the question of the symphony's place within the wider European tradition:

> Franck is to me remarkably interesting, because in a period that was dazzled by Wagner, he saw the end of that brilliant cul-de-sac. When he decided that the high-road of the symphony was still the way of progress, he also discovered intuitively the kind of material from which symphony could be renewed. I think it is impossible to say that this intuition, or inspiration, for the right kind of symphonic material was inherited by his followers. Dukas certainly has not got it, not Vincent d'Indy, nor Chausson. But, following him chronologically, <u>you</u> have it. You have caught up the silver

---

[49] 'Occasional Notes', *Musical Times*, 50 (1909), 446–7 (446). Also cited in Jerrold Northrop Moore, *Edward Elgar: A Creative Life* (Oxford, 1984), p. 548.
[50] Newmarch to Elgar, 2 January 1909, Elgar Birthplace Museum (L 3804).

thread that links all the true symphonists together, and woven into it fresh strands of individual feeling and gleams of a new psychology.[51]

Although her emphasis here is on the French tradition rather than the Russian one, Newmarch's belief that the renewal of the symphony would take place outside of the German heartlands is the most striking feature of her version of musical history.

Although she does not mention him by name in her programme note on Elgar's First Symphony, Newmarch must also have realised that Sibelius too was a composer whose genius inclined equally to the modern symphony and the symphonic poem. Newmarch wrote appreciatively of Elgar's Second Symphony (1911) and the Violin Concerto (1910), but by the time of the first British performance of Sibelius's Fourth Symphony in Birmingham in October 1912, his music had begun to disappoint her. The work by Elgar that had been premiered at Birmingham alongside Sibelius's Fourth Symphony was his setting of an ode by Arthur O'Shaughnessy, *The Music Makers*. Although not a religious work like *The Dream of Gerontius* (1900), *The Apostles* (1903) or *The Kingdom* (1906), all of which had been commissioned for performance at previous Birmingham festivals, it was nonetheless redolent of a tradition which Newmarch held in particularly low regard:

> After the English musicians of the eighteenth and nineteenth centuries had set the Bible several times over to music of a colourless and tepid kind, there arose a generation who craved a secular renaissance. They realised that sacred music, like a sand-storm from the desert, had overwhelmed and choked nearly all that was bright and promising in our native talent. The religious spirit which animated our Church music until the time of the Restoration was altogether a different thing from the dry, semi-sacred, stolidly Protestant ideals which were Handel's legacy to the country of his adoption. In other countries Opera has balanced Church Music and supplied a wholesome, secular corrective which has kept musical art in a sane and progressive condition. In England –

---

[51] Newmarch to Elgar, 19 December 1909, Elgar Birthplace Museum (L 3804).

half-Puritan still in musical feeling – we accepted Oratorio as a compromise and became atrophied on the secular side.

There was of course some excuse for the men of promise and the men of incapacity who wrote their innumerable 'Hezekiahs,' 'Jeremiahs,' 'Jonahs' and 'Joshuas,' and celebrated all the prophets, virgins and martyrs in oratorio during the nineteenth century; it was almost the only form in which, by the medium of some festival performance, they could hope to reach the ears of the British public. To look into the catalogues and dictionaries which hold, like so many sarcophagi, all that remains of these countless oratorios and cantatas, is to shiver with depression. How came the England of Shakespeare, Ford and Webster to give birth to such an anæmic and passionless musical art, and to be satisfied with it for nearly two centuries? The fact is our musical works were not of true English birth. They were cuckoo eggs, imported from Germany by Handel and Mendelssohn and hatched in British nests to the detriment of our native singing-birds, who might otherwise have developed a distinct note of their own.[52]

After a period in which Elgar's symphonic works had marked him out as a leading representative of modern European orchestral music, the juxtaposition of *The Music Makers* with Sibelius's Fourth Symphony suggested that he had remained loyal to a form that Newmarch held to be anodyne and outmoded.

Sibelius, by contrast, inspired her ever more; in particular, the discovery of his Fourth Symphony marked an important development in her thinking. As programme-note writer for the Promenade Concerts at Queen's Hall, Newmarch's general practice was to stimulate the imaginative faculties of ordinary listeners by producing evocative summaries of works without musical examples. In her note for the Fourth Symphony, however, she employed a more self-consciously formal approach (as she also occasionally did for the Symphony Concerts at Queen's Hall, especially for performances of important new works). After a sizeable introduction to what she perceived to be the 'general characteristics of Sibelius's

---

[52] Rosa Newmarch, *Henry J. Wood* (London, 1904), pp. 14–15.

style',[53] Newmarch moves on to a pithy summary of the score that contains very little by way of subjective interpretation. Moreover, her summary is accompanied by a number of short musical examples (sixteen in the original note, twenty-six in the revised version published the following year). There are, to be sure, a number of observations linking the symphony to questions of landscape and national identity: 'much of it was thought out and written in the isolation of hoary forests, by rushing rapids, or wind-lashed lakes. There are moments – especially in the first movement – when we feel ourselves "alone with nature's breathing things".'[54] Yet in her conclusion, Newmarch distances the work from such interpretations, arguing that although the symphony 'takes us at times into shadowy regions of mystical idealism', this is 'something quite different from the vague Nature-worship – the "delirious animism" of the "Kalevala" – which is the inheritance of the essential Finn'.[55] If there is a vestigial sense of natural inspiration behind the symphony, then the finished result is something else altogether: 'he has developed a ruthless determination to refine and clarify every musical thought; to prune and concentrate; to avoid all useless display of orchestral luxury; all garrulous emotionalism – in a word "to cut the cackle" and deal only with essentials'.[56] Prefiguring the later reception of Sibelius's works in Britain, Newmarch identifies the main achievements of the symphony as 'simplicity of means', 'form for its own sake' and 'ellipsis, curtailment and condensation'.[57] For Newmarch, it was the Fourth Symphony that most clearly embodied 'the sheer originality,

---

[53] Rosa Newmarch, *Jean Sibelius: Symphony No. 4 in A minor, Op. 63* (London, [1913]), p. 7. All further citations are given from this published edition of Newmarch's note, which is a revised and expanded version of the note she originally wrote for the 1912 Birmingham Festival (a copy of which can be found at the Centre for Performance History of the Royal College of Music). As with her 1906 lecture, Breitkopf & Härtel were keen to use Newmarch's note to promote Sibelius's music more widely, issuing it both in English and in Ludmille Kirschbaum's German translation (*Vierte Sinfonie von Jean Sibelius (A moll, op. 63): Kleiner Konzertführer* (Leipzig, [1913])). Because it has barely figured in the critical literature on Sibelius, the original English text of Newmarch's published analysis is reproduced in an appendix to the present volume.

[54] Newmarch, *Jean Sibelius: Symphony No. 4*, p. 5.

[55] Ibid., p. 15.

[56] Ibid., p. 5.

[57] Ibid., pp. 6 and 7.

beauty and vigour of the musical idea' that she had singled out as Sibelius's chief characteristic in her 1906 lecture, and her interpretation of the work constitutes a profound modification of the nationalist paradigm with which she is most usually associated.

Newmarch's interpretation of the Fourth Symphony is all the more valuable when it is set aside German criticism of the same period. In the very year that her note was published both in English and in German translation, Walter Niemann gave the following assessment of Sibelius that continued to confine him to the nationalist school:

> Sibelius has the breadth and warmth of the true and essential musical innovator, the invincible power of popular inspiration. As both an ardent patriot and a musician, who prefers to take his poetic models from the ancient national epic of the *Kalevala*, from the melancholy beauty of his country's nature with its four-fold sounds of forest, moorland, lake and rocky outcrops, he is the purest and most noble embodiment of the national spirit in modern music. But when compared with Chopin or Grieg, his art is neither rich nor varied. For in his most important works the main ideas are repeated over and over again: tales of brave and grizzly ancient times, of nature, of the deep suffering and meagre joy of the people, of the sorrow of a country violated by the Russian bear and of the long-desired and radiant dawn of freedom. Thus his music is all too monotonous in its moods of grey on grey, all too exotic and provincial in its emphasis on antiquated elements from ancient-Finnish folk and church music, and in recent times it has been unmistakably influenced by Russia (Tchaikovsky) and French impressionism (Debussy). But overall, his remains thoroughly individual, thoroughly national, thoroughly developed on the model of nature's grandeur, and therefore we must hope that his name, even now great, will also come to find its place amongst our great names.[58]

Little appears to have changed in Niemann's analysis since 1906, when he first described Sibelius's music as 'reine Heimatkunst'.[59]

---

[58] Walter Niemann, *Die Musik seit Richard Wagner* (Berlin and Leipzig, 1913), pp. 266–7.
[59] Niemann, *Die Musik Skandinaviens*, p. 137.

By the time he published his *Jean Sibelius* in 1917, his patronising attitude to the symphonies had become yet more categorical. Devoting just three out of fifty-six pages of text to these works, Niemann argued that their content was 'from first to late the same: the soul of Finland as represented by nature and the people'.[60] He traced their failure to adhere to the cardinal virtues of the genre – 'monumentality and coherence, organic and logical inner development and construction'[61] – to Sibelius's alleged use of folksong: 'In order to understand Sibelius properly as a symphonist . . . one must realise that, fundamentally, short-winded Nordic folk melodies are ill suited to symphonic treatment as we understand it.'[62] The crucial phrase is, of course, 'symphonic treatment as we understand it': Niemann's conception of the symphony is so wedded to Germanic principles that it cannot accommodate works that do not appear to conform to them; moreover, so committed was Niemann to the view of Sibelius as a nationalist that he seemed unable to discern just how far the composer had moved away from that aesthetic in works such as the Third and Fourth Symphonies.

The irony is that Niemann's attitude may well have been influenced by the German edition of Newmarch's 1906 lecture, with its almost exclusive emphasis on landscape, myth and national character.[63] Yet where Niemann's rigid interpretation of the symphonies changes little between his publications of 1906, 1913 and 1917, Newmarch's approach was far more responsive to Sibelius's evolving handling of symphonic form. Although she had, by her own admission, failed to appreciate the Third Symphony at its first performance in Britain in 1908,[64] by the time of the Fourth Symphony, she had gained a deeper understanding of Sibelius's development from his earlier nationalist works towards a kind of purity and abstraction that placed him at the heart of the wider European tradition. Newmarch had visited Sibelius in the summer of 1910, when he was at work on the new symphony, and saw him again in Paris in late 1911, when he was checking the proofs before

---

[60] Walter Niemann, *Jean Sibelius* (Leipzig, 1917), p. 49.
[61] Ibid, pp. 47–8.
[62] Ibid., p. 47.
[63] Gray, '"The Symphonic Problem": Sibelius Reception in England Prior to 1950', p. 104.
[64] Newmarch, *Jean Sibelius*, pp. 20–21/pp. 11–12.

its publication. Although she claims never to have pressed him for details of his current compositions, their letters and conversations would surely have revealed to her the extent to which the Fourth Symphony was in part the product of Sibelius's ongoing attempt to resolve his complex relationship to European modernism. Part of the closeness of their friendship at this time is surely based on her ability to grasp the profound significance that the Fourth Symphony held for him, and which was so little understood by audiences and critics at the time.[65]

SIBELIUS AS MODERNIST

Newmarch's advocacy of the Fourth Symphony can also be seen as a contribution to the debate about modernism in early twentieth-century British music.[66] Its performance at Birmingham in 1912 coincided with a number of other important British premières of works by contemporary European composers in the years before the Great War, and which contributed to a long-standing debate about the role played by the latest in continental music within Britain itself. As Percy Scholes wrote in May 1914:

> In these present days the storms rage most fiercely, perhaps, around the heads of the three S.'s of the most modern music – Schönberg, Scriabin, and Stravinsky. Here are the men who have apparently cast aside all the accepted canons of musical art and evolved, each in his own way, something new and strange.[67]

---

[65] Sibelius would later use British enthusiasm for his music to counteract negative German stereotypes. Writing to Cecil Gray in 1930, Sibelius gave the following description of Niemann's work: 'Niemann's book is incorrect in many respects and has done much damage to me. Particularly my symphonies. Please ignore the book' (Sibelius to Gray, 14 April 1930, BL Add Ms 57786, fol. 49).
[66] On the question of British musical modernism, see Byron Adams, ed., *British Modernism*, special issue of *The Musical Quarterly* 91 (2008), and Matthew Riley, ed., *British Music and Modernism, 1895–1960* (Farnham, 2010).
[67] Percy A. Scholes, 'Stravinsky at Close Quarters', *Everyman*, 1 May 1914, 86–7 (86), cited in Glenda Dawn Goss, *Sibelius: A Composer's Life and the Awakening of Finland* (Chicago and London, 2009), p. 373.

Through her work at Queen's Hall, Newmarch was familiar with all of these figures. She had written the notes for the world première of Schoenberg's *Five Orchestral Pieces* on 3 September 1912 (the work was repeated under the direction of the composer on 17 January 1914).[68] Scriabin's *Prometheus* had been scheduled for performance alongside Sibelius's Fourth Symphony at the 1912 Birmingham Festival, but was withdrawn because of insufficient rehearsal time; it was given instead in London on 1 February 1913 (and repeated, with the composer taking the solo piano part, on 1 March 1914). His Third Symphony – *The Divine Poem* – was heard in London on 18 October 1913. Performance of Stravinsky's *Petrushka*, *The Firebird* and *The Rite of Spring* by the visiting Ballets Russes in 1912 and 1913 provoked considerable discussion in the press.[69]

Although Newmarch was sympathetic to Scriabin, and was fair-minded in her treatment of Schoenberg and Stravinsky, her writings nonetheless make it clear that she was sceptical about the direction of modern European music and regarded Sibelius as a welcome exception. In her note on the Fourth Symphony, for instance, she makes the following unflattering comparison:

> Too often in the work of the 'modernists' the short-winded, scrappy motives which serve as 'subjects' have to be disguised from their first appearance under some elaborate garb. They remind us of puny babies decked out in imposing christening robes; for they are often merely dwarfed and abortive ideas, disguised under brilliant orchestral tissues. But Sibelius undoubtedly retains an old-fashioned respect for the theme and regards the melodic material as the inspired word on which the whole message of the music depends.[70]

Writing after Sibelius's performance of the symphony in London in 1921, and after the October Revolution had put a decisive end to

---

[68] On the reception of Schoenberg's music in early twentieth-century Britain, see John Irving, 'Schönberg in the News: The London Performances of 1912–1914', *Music Review* 48 (1988), 52–70, and David Lambourn, 'Henry Wood and Schoenberg', *Musical Times* 128 (1987), 422–7.

[69] Lynn Garafola, *Diaghilev's Ballets Russes* (New York and Oxford, 1989), pp. 300–29.

[70] Newmarch, *Jean Sibelius: Symphony No. 4*, p. 7.

her interest in modern Russian music, Newmarch was more explicit about the identity of these so-called 'modernists':

> Sibelius is not a pugilistic colourist. His orchestration reacts against the gaudy and shouting colour spaces of the quasi-easterns, and the heavy superfluities of the neo-German school. But the war has given us a surfeit of noise, and most of us are also getting heartily tired of the sham gorgeousness, the extravagance and decadent trickery, which is the aftermath of the first truly great movement of the Russians towards self-expression. That movement, like the revolution, passed into the wrong hands. It is good to see our younger generation showing some respect for Sibelius, even though he disdains to parade in Joseph's coat of many colours.[71]

In her various writings on Sibelius, Newmarch juxtaposes his music – rooted in the past yet innovative in its own way, connected with the national life of the Finnish people yet aware of the supra-national traditions of European art music – with 'the neo-German school' and 'the quasi-easterns' (by whom Newmarch undoubtedly means younger Russian composers such as Prokofiev and Stravinsky, but also French composers who had fallen under the influence of the Ballets Russes).

Somewhat ironically, Newmarch's espousal of Sibelius even led her to agree with earlier critics of the craze for Russian music who had objected to the harmful influence of its emotional intensity and superficial orchestral brilliance on contemporary British composers. As early as 1908, Charles MacLean had described Sibelius as 'an austere Muse' and as 'something titanically elemental . . . forcing its way among sensuousness and decadence'.[72] Readers at the time would most likely have associated the latter characteristics with Tchaikovsky, as Newmarch herself admitted:

> Of late years English critics have expended a good deal of censure upon the morbid and melancholy tendencies of

[71] Rosa Newmarch, 'Sibelius', *Chesterian* n. s. no. 14 (April 1921), 417–21 (419). Apart from a number of small omissions, Newmarch incorporated this article almost entirely verbatim into her later memoir, where the above paragraph occurs on p. 75/pp. 53–4.
[72] [Charles MacLean], 'Sibelius in England', *Zeitschrift der internationalen Musikgesellschaft* 9 (1907–08), 271–3 (271).

modern composers. Death and sorrow, unhappy passion – all kinds of impolite and indiscreet tragedy – have incurred their displeasure and caused much shaking of heads over the decadence and pessimism of the younger generation. The influence of Tschaïkowsky has not altogether unjustly been held accountable for some of this wilful melancholy.

Evidently responding to growing awareness of Tchaikovsky's homosexuality, Newmarch sought to defend her interest in Russian music by putting forward Rimsky-Korsakov as 'a composer who combines in his music poetic interest with a vigorous and manly optimism'.[73] In the wake of the Fourth Symphony, however, Sibelius became a more suitable model for British composers to emulate, precisely because he espoused a kind of symphonic music that was progressive without being avant-garde, national without being nationalistic, and was – moreover – free from the accusations of degeneracy that had long been a feature of the reception of Russian music in Britain. In an article published in the summer of 1912, just before the British première of the Fourth Symphony, Newmarch confessed that 'a warning to avoid in our music the riotous excess of colour and the violent emotionalism of some of the Slav composers is fully justified', and recommended Sibelius as a figure who 'may possibly lead the way to a more chastened and sober taste in the art of music'.[74] Although her description of the Finnish school as 'more chastened and sober' suggests a potential debt to the moralistic tone of much criticism at the time, it is unlikely that Newmarch actively subscribed to the view of much modern European music as effeminate and unmanly; whether as a married woman who enjoyed at least one intimate relationship with another woman, or as a multilingual, cosmopolitan and well-travelled friend of a number of leading contemporary European composers, she must have viewed the gendered and xenophobic language of much contemporary musical criticism with more than a degree of scepticism. Nonetheless, her use of vocabulary such as 'chastened and sober' (in the case of Sibelius) or 'vigorous and manly' (in the case of Rimsky-Korsakov) shows an

[73] Newmarch, 'Rimsky-Korsakov: Personal Reminiscences', 173.
[74] Newmarch, 'Chauvinism in Music', 112 and 114.

Introduction

astute appeal to a number of widespread British views that was designed to facilitate the positive reception of musicians who were important to her.[75]

Yet it is important not to see Newmarch as espousing a vision of Sibelius as a straightforwardly conservative figure, isolated from and even resistant to developments in European modernism. Unlike subsequent generations of 'his more emphatically traditionalist Anglo-American champions',[76] Newmarch remained committed to Sibelius's music as the most important manifestation of artistic modernity (or progress, as she preferred to term it):

> Already we are accustomed to hear Sibelius described by the full-bodied realists of the day as reactionary. But reaction is often progress in disguise . . . Noting his tendency to shed much of the extravagant luxury of means employed by contemporary composers; his omission of much that is superfluous, or merely reiterative; his restraint in the matter of temperamental explosions, and his dislike of violent and noisy orchestration; his choice of themes which are not merely flashlights but sufficiently sustained and luminous to be the guiding stars of his movements; and his susceptibility to the undertones of nature – we are justified in feeling that Sibelius is no reactionary, but that perhaps on the contrary he has stepped ahead out of the dust and din of the blatant and motley pageantry which at the present moment occupies the high-road of musical progress.[77]

---

[75] Compare, for instance, reviews by Neville Cardus in *The Guardian*, which illustrate how the gendered language of much British criticism continued well past the early part of the twentieth century, especially as interest in Sibelius continued to grow. Discussing the Fifth Symphony, for instance, Cardus writes that: 'A more manly music than Sibelius's has never been heard since Beethoven' (25 October 1929). Similarly, a performance of the Seventh Symphony led him to wonder: 'my own feeling about the Seventh Symphony is not that Sibelius has lost his true masculinity but that in this Symphony he is dealing it out to us on a surface too small for his natural freedom of stride' (cited in *Cardus on Music: A Centenary Collection*, ed. Donald Wright (London, 1988), pp. 219 and 222).

[76] James Hepokoski, 'Structural Tensions in Sibelius's Fifth Symphony: Circular Stasis, Linear Progression, and the Problem of "Traditional" Form', in *Sibelius Forum*, ed. Murtomäki, Kilpeläinen and Väisänen, pp. 213–36 (p. 216).

[77] Newmarch, 'Chauvinism in Music', 115–16.

Newmarch was always more sensitive to the peculiar nature of Sibelius's modernism than other British critics. Sharing both his disenchantment with the categories of nineteenth-century romantic nationalism and his scepticism about the new music of the European avant-garde, Newmarch never advocated a view of Sibelius as a retrograde figure, whose music could be evoked as a defence against the influence of modernism on British music. As musicologists broaden their view of what might constitute modernism (often inspired by Carl Dahlhaus's interpretation of 'die Moderne' to cover music from the period 1890–1910),[78] it is not just Sibelius who takes on renewed significance, but Newmarch's advocacy of him too.

NEWMARCH AND SIBELIUS IN THE 1930s

Newmarch's fondness for the Fourth Symphony stemmed in part from the fact that it was the work that represented the period of her most intense friendship with Sibelius; they saw each other yearly between 1908 and 1912, and she considered 1912 as 'perhaps the culmination of our friendly relations'.[79] After a period following the Great War in which their relationship seems to have taken some time to re-establish itself, they met again during Sibelius's trip to Britain in 1921, when he gave the first British performance of the Fifth Symphony (as well as what appears to have been only the fourth performance of the Fourth). This trip promised to mark a period of renewed interest in Sibelius's music after the disruptions brought about by the war. Not only did Sibelius undertake more conducting engagements than during any of his other trips to Britain, but his visit was organised in collaboration with the Finnish Legation; the authorities clearly understood

---

[78] Carl Dahlhaus, *Nineteenth-Century Music*, trans. J. Bradford Robinson (Berkeley, Los Angeles and London, 1989), p. 334. Dahlhaus's writings have been particularly central to attempts to position Sibelius's music (especially the Fourth Symphony) in relation to European modernism more generally. However, as Matthew Riley points out, Dahlhaus's use of 'die Moderne' to qualify this period was intended to replace the widespread notion of 'late romantic' and does not map entirely accurately onto the English term 'modernism' ('Introduction', in *British Music and Modernism*, pp. 1–11 (p. 4)).

[79] Newmarch, *Jean Sibelius*, p. 48/p. 33.

Introduction

Sibelius's potential to represent the country abroad now that it had gained its independence. However, despite persistent attempts by Bantock, Wood and Newmarch herself, Sibelius was never to visit Britain again. Neither did Newmarch and Sibelius see each other again elsewhere, despite tentative plans to meet in Paris in 1927 or during one of her regular cures at Karlsbad.

Newmarch's and Sibelius's sporadic correspondence during the 1920s mirrors the way in which interest in his music in Britain appears to have declined during that decade. The economic situation led to a degree of retrenchment in British cultural life; in particular, problems with the financing of concerts at Queen's Hall meant that Sibelius no longer had access to one of his principal British performing venues. His supporters elsewhere in Britain (Bantock in Birmingham, Dan Godfrey in Bournemouth, as well as Donald Francis Tovey in Edinburgh) likewise found it difficult to arrange concerts for him, not least because of the expense of obtaining new scores. In May 1921, Bantock wrote to Sibelius, begging him to arrange preferential terms for the purchase of the Fifth Symphony, or even to let him have it directly in return for a copy of his own *Hebridean Symphony*.[80] Thereafter, Bantock would ask permission to lend the score and parts for performance of the work by Tovey in Edinburgh and Hamilton Harty in Manchester (often with a reduced performing-rights fee as well).[81] Sibelius's cancellation of his appearance at what would have been the British première of the Sixth Symphony at the 1925 Gloucester Festival meant the loss of a further opportunity to promote his reputation. It is also the case that the rise of 'ultra-modern' music (especially under the aegis of the British Broadcasting Company, founded in 1922) began to give credence to those who were inclined to see him as a conservative, even reactionary, figure. Nonetheless, important performances did take place in the 1920s, including British premières of his Sixth and Seventh Symphonies and the tone-poem *Tapiola*. The British Women's Symphony Orchestra, for

---

[80] Bantock to Sibelius, 3 May 1921, NAF SFP Box 16.
[81] Bantock to Sibelius, 14 October 1921 and 9 June 1922, NAF SFP Box 16. In 1927, Bantock would attempt to come to a similar arrangement with respect to the Seventh Symphony (Bantock to Sibelius, 9 January 1927, NAF SFP Box 16).

instance, gave his Third Symphony on 27 November 1928 (and would continue to feature his music in its programmes throughout the 1930s, including an all-Sibelius concert on 25 March 1933).

Ultimately, however, the 1920s were to be overshadowed by the burgeoning Sibelius 'cult' of the next decade, led by critics such as Cecil Gray, Constant Lambert and Donald Francis Tovey, conductors such as Basil Cameron and Thomas Beecham, and – as recording became an important way of promoting a composer's cause – by the producer Walter Legge. Sibelius's works were programmed more and more frequently in concerts, especially in London (it is interesting to note that the first phase of Sibelius's British reception in the first two decades of the twentieth century was strongly associated with such provincial centres as Birmingham, Bournemouth, Liverpool and Manchester). Robert Kajanus – one of the leading Finnish champions of Sibelius's music – launched the Sibelius Society on 2 July 1932 at Queen's Hall at a London Symphony Orchestra concert featuring the Third and Fifth Symphonies, *Tapiola, Pohjola's Daughter* and *Finlandia*. Between 29 May and 4 June 1934, Georg Schnéevoigt conducted four concerts (three at Queen's Hall and one in Hull) consisting primarily of works by Sibelius. This burst of concert activity was accompanied by a rapid increase in the amount of criticism designed to promote Sibelius as a contemporary symphonist who could renew a genre that was felt by some to be in crisis. In his *Sibelius* (1931, second edition 1934) and *Sibelius: The Symphonies* (1935), Cecil Gray made a number of audacious claims that were to characterise much writing on Sibelius in the 1930s: 'There is nothing in modern symphonic literature that can be placed by the side of Sibelius's achievements in this direction. I would even venture farther and say that the symphonies of Sibelius represent the highest point attained in this form since the death of Beethoven.'[82]

The zeal and intensity of the British cult of Sibelius in the 1930s had a number of unexpected consequences. As Matti Huttunen argues, by the 1930s, Finnish scholarship still largely regarded Sibelius as a nationalist. Yet awareness of British attempts to deal with his symphonies in formal terms gave rise to a native school of analysis that built on the work of Gray, Lambert and Tovey (Gray's

---

[82] Cecil Gray, *Sibelius* (London, 1931), pp. 186–7.

Introduction

book on the symphonies was translated into Finnish by Jussi Jalas in 1945, 'supplemented with lengthy comments and corrections'.[83] More deleterious was Theodor Adorno's infamous response to British enthusiasm for Sibelius. Although his *Glosse über Sibelius* has generally been read in the context of German avant-garde hostility to Sibelius as a figure of reactionary nationalism (it was first published in the *Zeitschrift für Sozialforschung* in 1938), it was in fact directly provoked by Adorno's experience of musical life in Britain, where he was exiled between 1934 and 1938. As a number of scholars have pointed out, Adorno seems to have been particularly affronted by the lack of British interest in Mahler's music, as well as by unflattering comparison between Sibelius and Mahler made by Sibelius's pupil, Bengt de Törne, in his *Sibelius: A Close-Up* of 1937.[84] As Laura Gray has convincingly demonstrated, Adorno's article is so profoundly influenced by terms common in British writing on Sibelius in the 1930s that it can be seen as 'a compendium of these catchphrases, which he viciously mocked and distorted in his richly allusive writing'.[85]

Perhaps the most visible manifestation of British interest in Sibelius in the 1930s took the form of the 1938 Sibelius Festival, a series of six concerts conducted by Sir Thomas Beecham with the London Philharmonic Orchestra that ran from 27 October to 12 November at Queen's Hall and Aeolian Hall. The festival was given unprecedented coverage in the press, not least because it enjoyed considerable patronage by members of society and the royal family. Such was the success of the 1938 festival that earlier phases of British interest in Sibelius appeared to have been

---

[83] Matti Huttunen, 'How Sibelius Became a Classic in Finland', in *Sibelius Forum*, ed. Murtomäki, Kilpeläinen and Väisänen, pp. 73–81 (p. 78).

[84] See, for instance, Bengt de Törne's assement of Mahler: 'The scores of the Viennese composer, although characteristic specimens of true symphonic music, will sink into oblivion because they lack intrinsic life' (*Sibelius: A Close-Up* (London, 1937), p. 75). On Adorno and Sibelius, see in particular Erik Tawaststjerna, 'Über Adornos Sibelius-Kritik', in *Adorno und die Musik*, ed. Otto Kolleritsch (Graz, 1979), pp. 112–24, and Tomi Mäkelä, 'Sibelius and Germany, *Wahrhaftigkeit* beyond *Allnatur*', in *The Cambridge Companion to Sibelius*, ed. Grimley, pp. 169–81.

[85] Gray, '"The Symphonic Problem": Sibelius Reception in England Prior to 1950', p. 8. For Gray's textual analysis of how Adorno derives his argument from the 'catchphrases' of British critics, see pp. 112–31.

forgotten.[86] Most articles and reviews tended to subscribe to the widespread view that Sibelius had been discovered only recently, and despite direct connections between British Sibelians of all generations (Newmarch knew both Basil Cameron and Harriet Cohen, for instance), the younger generation were careless in acknowledging the pioneering work of their precursors.

It is not difficult to adduce reasons for the decline of interest in the earlier generation of Sibelius's British acolytes. It was Cameron and Gray who visited him in Finland in the early 1930s, and even before the festival of 1938, Beecham had claimed the reputation of being Sibelius's leading British interpreter. Discussing the state of his reputation in Britain with Karl Ekman (whose biography appeared in English in 1936), Sibelius singled out the work of Beecham rather than Wood:

> In later years Great Britain came to signify more and more in confirming the position of my art in the international world of music. I have been fortunate in gaining many new friends. I need only mention the name of Sir Thomas Beecham to give an idea of the keen understanding that the musical life of Britain has shown for my art.[87]

Sibelius was familiar with Beecham's interpretations of his orchestral work through the recordings issued by the Sibelius Society, and he would have been aware of the success of the 1938 festival both through reports from his daughter, who attended it in person, and through the vast collection of press cuttings and reviews that were forwarded to him.[88] By contrast, financial and administrative difficulties at Queen's Hall in the 1920s meant that Wood and Robert Newman were less free to exercise the kind of patronage they once had (even if Sibelius had felt inclined to visit, which is itself far from certain). Bantock too found it difficult to

---

[86] Compare too Harriet Cohen's belief that Eva Turner's performance of *Luonnotar* during the festival was 'only the second performance in England' (*A Bundle of Time: The Memoirs of Harriet Cohen* (London, 1969), p. 277). There had, in fact, been a number of earlier performances of the *scena*, including one at a Promenade Concert on 4 September 1934, sung by Helmi Liukkonen and conducted by Wood.

[87] Ekman, *Jean Sibelius*, pp. 171–2.

[88] These are located in the National Library of Finland (hereafter NLF), Coll.206.81.

Introduction

realise his aspirations to bring Sibelius to Britain again. As for Newmarch, a particular reason for the absence of her name from many studies in the 1930s may be that, whereas writers like Gray and Lambert were keen to reclaim him as a symphonist in the Beethovenian tradition, she was still primarily associated with musical nationalism; her crucial writings on the Fourth Symphony were almost certainly unavailable, leaving only her early and outdated lecture of 1906 to represent her thought (the extent to which the contents of her lectures on Sibelius for the Society of Women Musicians in 1931 were known more widely is unclear).[89] Understandably enough, it must have seemed to Sibelius as though a new generation of supporters was now responsible for advancing the cause of his music in Britain.

The 1938 Festival was not, however, the first time that a major cycle of Sibelius's works had been heard in London. The previous year, in that summer's run of Promenade Concerts, Wood had given performances of all the symphonies, as well as a number of other orchestral works.[90] Privately, Wood was offended by the coverage given to Beecham's festival:

> It is very extraordinary to me to day, to scan the papers here and see that Sir Thomas Beecham – in large letters – is giving a so-called 'SIBELIUS FESTIVAL'. The fact seems to have been unaccountably overlooked, that during the strenuous Season of Promenade Concerts in 1937, I gave – <u>what was indeed a SIBELIUS FESTIVAL, and through the Season did your Seven symphonies</u>. It seems to me, because this great undertaking was carried out in the stride of these 'Series of Concerts['] that it may have passed un-noticed and un-recognised. This has hurt your friend extremely.[91]

---

[89] Newmarch first lectured on Sibelius to the society on 30 May 1931 ('Society of Women Musicians: Composers' Conference', *Musical Times* 72 (1931), 646. Her lecture of 12 December 1931 was summarised in 'Society of Women Musicians', *Musical Times* 73 (1932), 174–5.

[90] Sibelius concerts had been an annual feature of the Proms for some time already, taking place on 26 September 1933, 4 September 1934, 26 September 1935 and 10 September 1936. Two Sibelius concerts were also given in 1938 (23 August and 20 September).

[91] Wood to Sibelius, 29 October 1938, NAF SFP Box 32, cited in Tawaststjerna, *Sibelius*, vol. 3, pp. 324–5. Wood's copy of the letter is at BL Add Ms 56421, fol. 193.

When it came to publishing his memoirs, Wood took the opportunity to remind readers of his prior claim to have organised what was, in effect, a Sibelius festival in all but name:

> Granville Bantock and I have always been the champions of Sibelius, but now that I have performed all his seven symphonies in one season (1937) I look back with pride and satisfaction when I remember I was the first to have helped popularize the music of this deep and original thinker.[92]

Newmarch too noted that 'Sir Henry J. Wood was the first to give the entire series of symphonies at the Promenade Concerts in 1937.'[93] Wood's indignation was not without justification; he had kept Sibelius fully informed of plans for the cycle of his symphonies and other works at the Promenade Concerts,[94] and had even given the first British performance of the long-suppressed numbers from the *Lemminkäinen Suite* ('Lemminkäinen and the Maidens of the Island' and 'Lemminkäinen in Tuonela') at Bournemouth that February (replacing an indisposed Georg Schnéevoigt).[95]

Where Wood was offended by what he saw as Beecham's presumption (as well as by Sibelius's public recognition of his conducting), Newmarch was more astute and constructive in her response to the Sibelius cult of the 1930s. Seeing that the current vogue for Sibelius's music offered her the chance to publicise her own version of their friendship, she began work on a memoir (itself based on a short account of their friendship that was published in the programme booklet for Wood's Sibelius concert on 9 September 1937, and republished on 20 September the following year). As she wrote to Sibelius on 21 February 1939:

> I have discovered that in England people were always asking me for a long biography, in the tradition of the legends that the English always want to preserve about you: that's to say the portrait of a man as solemn as the Finnish forests;

---

[92] Wood, *My Life of Music*, p. 206.
[93] Newmarch, *Jean Sibelius*, p. 87/p. 61.
[94] Wood to Sibelius, 15 and 26 February and 1 March 1937, NAF SFP Box 32.
[95] 'South Coast Festivals', *Musical Times* 78 (1937), 270. See too Wood to Sibelius, 13, 15, 17, 25 and 26 February, 1 March 1937, NAF SFP Box 32, and Sibelius to Wood, 2 March 1937, BL Add Ms 56421, fol. 191.

> neglected in his youth and only discovered these last years by the critics of today! Whereas I wanted to show in miniature quite a different Sibelius: something more true – the composer who was so appreciated before the war, the comrade of Bantock, of Ernest Newman, of Henry Wood, and of myself.

With its documentary detail and intimate literary style, *Jean Sibelius: A Short Story of a Long Friendship* is an implicit riposte to those, such as Gray, Lambert, Legge and Beecham, who would claim that the 'Sibelius cult' was a new phenomenon and the result of their labours alone.

Newmarch's memoir can also be interpreted as a commentary on obsessive interest in the elusive Eighth Symphony. British musicians were certainly not the only ones pressing for the work (there was considerable interest in it in America too, not to mention in the composer's homeland and elsewhere in Europe too), and Sibelius did not help matters by his ambiguous and non-committal answers to speculation about its fate. Nonetheless, Sibelius's British admirers could be surprisingly tactless when dealing with his notoriously sensitive disposition, sometimes giving the impression that they were primarily interested in how the right to perform the Eighth Symphony could serve their own careers. Basil Cameron, who had heard from Gray that Sibelius was at work on a new symphony, regularly requested the right to give its first performance.[96] The Royal Philharmonic Society likewise wrote regularly during the 1930s to state its claim to the work's European première,[97] and Legge emphasised Beecham's interest in the work.[98] By contrast, Newmarch's long friendship with Sibelius meant that she seemed to have a greater understanding of his artistic needs. Writing of her visit to Finland in 1910, she observed:

---

[96] Cameron to Sibelius, 30 June, 12 and 30 July, 15 and 29 September 1931, NAF SFP Box 17.
[97] Royal Philharmonic Society to Sibelius, 20 November 1934, NAF SFP Box 26, Edward Dent to Sibelius, 24 February 1932, Keith Douglas to Sibelius, 25 February and 23 November 1932, 9 and 27 May 1933, 14 February 1935, 4 November 1938, 19 January and 13 March 1940, NLF Coll.206.48.
[98] Legge to Sibelius, 19 January 1934, 10 April 1935, 27 June 1936, 21 December 1937, NAF SFP Box 23. Legge's correspondence with Sibelius has been published in *Walter Legge: Words and Music*, ed. Alan Sanders (London, 1998), pp. 68–84.

> I believe his thoughts at that time were often centred on his Fourth Symphony ... but I never asked him. He hated talking above his unfinished compositions. It amounted almost to a superstition with him that a work discussed too soon came to nothing, and I have heard him give some mischievous answers to tactless questions as to 'what he was writing now.'[99]

Newmarch seems to be implying that if British musicians coveted the right to give the first performance of the long-awaited Eighth Symphony, then they should treat Sibelius with the same degree of delicacy as she had done during the composition of the Fourth and accept her view that 'we may be sure that if he had the least suspicion that inspiration or workmanship might fail him, he would *not* make the attempt'.[100]

THE LETTERS

Newmarch herself remarked that 'Sibelius was never a great letter writer, and one of our little jokes together was that there would be no ponderous tomes of Sibelius letters for anyone to edit after his departure'.[101] To be sure, there is a striking imbalance in the overall number and length of the letters that they exchanged between January 1906 and October 1939. In total, Newmarch's ninety or so surviving letters, notes and telegrams to Sibelius amount to nearly thirty thousand words; Sibelius's forty letters to Newmarch account for little more than four and a half thousand words, and in them he frequently comes across, as he so often does even when writing to close friends and collaborators, as guarded, telegrammatic and formal. But his letters to Newmarch are not always so reserved, and he vouchsafed to her some of his frankest statements about his own works and about his attitude to contemporary music. It is, for instance, in a letter to Newmarch that he made his widely quoted statement about the Fourth Symphony: 'My new symphony stands out as a complete protest against the

---

[99] Newmarch, *Jean Sibelius*, p. 29/p. 20.
[100] Ibid., p. 84/p. 59.
[101] Ibid., pp. 68–9/p. 47.

Introduction

compositions of today. Nothing – absolutely nothing of the circus about it' (2 May 1911). Sibelius's antipathy towards aspects of contemporary music was yet more forcefully expressed in a letter of 10 March 1930, in which he writes: 'I still go on composing but I feel very much alone. There is so much in the music of the present day that I cannot accept.' For all its brevity, this letter seems so revealing of Sibelius's situation at the time that it was included in an anthology of composers' letters, quite a distinction for someone frequently deemed to be unforthcoming and uncommunicative, at least on paper.[102]

Sibelius's letters to Newmarch have long been known to scholars and have been mined for what they reveal about his trips to Britain and his artistic personality. Newmarch cited two dozen of them in her memoir (either in extracts, or in their entirety), and from this source, many of them have passed directly into the secondary literature. Newmarch's letters are, unsurprisingly, less familiar. Their importance, however, can be seen from the fact that Erik Tawaststjerna, who had access to all of Sibelius's unpublished papers, frequently cited or paraphrased them in his biography of the composer. Tawaststjerna's emphasis is, naturally enough, on Sibelius, although much of Newmarch's personality comes through in his account of their relationship. The present edition, taking advantage of renewed interest in Newmarch as an important figure in British cultural and intellectual history, seeks to restore her letters to their rightful place, whether as documents chronicling Sibelius's reception in Britain, or as a private commentary on her own busy contribution to British musical life.[103]

---

[102] Gertrude Norman and Mirian Lubell Shrifte, eds, *Letters of Composers: An Anthology, 1603–1945* (New York, 1945), p. 325. This edition also includes another of Sibelius's letters, described as being to an unknown correspondent and dated 20 May 1918 (p. 324).

[103] On Newmarch's advocacy of Russian culture, see: Philip Ross Bullock, *Rosa Newmarch and Russian Music in Late Nineteenth and Early Twentieth-Century England*, Royal Musical Association Monographs 18 (Farnham, 2009); and Alfred Boynton Stevenson, 'Chaikovskii and Mrs Rosa Newmarch Revisited: A Contribution to the Composer's Centennial Commemoration', *Inter-American Music Review* 14 (1995), 63–78. On the role played by her programme notes in twentieth-century music appreciation, see: Charlotte Purkis, '"Leader of Fashion in Musical Thought"; The Importance of Rosa Newmarch in the Context of Turn-of-the-Century British Music Appreciation', in *Nineteenth-Century British Music Studies*, vol. 3, ed. Peter Horton and

Yet Newmarch's letters are not merely records of her own strongly expressed views, affections and antipathies; they potentially also give some impression of the long and detailed discussions that took place between her and Sibelius whenever they were able to spend time together. As Newmarch noted, Sibelius treasured such occasions:

> In many of the letters Sibelius refers to our talks and discussions. I never kept any record or notes of these, nor were any of them the outcome of my curiosity or importunity. I believe the 'interviewing' spirit is absolutely non-existent in me. Our discussions occurred in strange and casual places; in trains, on long journeys, in my study in Campden Hill Square, in gardens by the Finnish sea, in woodland walks, at various tables in Pagani's Restaurant, in hotels in Paris, London and Helsinki, and many in Sir Granville Bantock's music-rooms at Hazelwood and Broadmeadow, where a fine and placid Buddha presided over the destiny of the household.[104]

If Sibelius was economical and even reticent as a correspondent, he could clearly be a lively and engaging interlocutor in person; to judge Sibelius solely on the basis of his letters is to fail to take account of just how much he evidently valued personal communication. Santeri Levas, for instance, who served as Sibelius's

---

Bennett Zon (Aldershot, 2003), pp. 3–19; and Philip Ross Bullock, '"Lessons in Sensibility": Rosa Newmarch, Music Appreciation and the Aesthetic Cultivation of the Self', *Yearbook of English Studies* 40 (2010), 295–318. On Newmarch's poetry, see: Lee Anna Maynard, 'Rosa Harriet Newmarch', in *Late Nineteenth- and Early Twentieth-Century British Women Poets*, ed. William B. Thesing, Dictionary of Literary Biography 240 (Detroit and London, 2001), pp. 164–71; Florence S. Boos, 'Dante Gabriel Rossetti's Poetic Daughters: *Fin de siècle* Women Poets and the Sonnet', in *Outsiders Looking In: The Rossettis Then and Now*, ed. David Clifford and Laurence Roussillon (London, 2004), pp. 253–81; John Holmes, *Dante Gabriel Rossetti and the Late Victorian Sonnet-Sequence: Sexuality, Belief and the Self* (Aldershot, 2005), pp. 112–19; and Natasha Distiller, *Desire and Gender in the Sonnet Tradition* (Basingstoke and New York, 2008), pp. 135–52. For a critical edition of Newmarch's poetry, see John Holmes and Natasha Distiller, eds, *Horae Amoris: The Collected Poems of Rosa Newmarch* (High Wycombe, 2010).

[104] Newmarch, *Jean Sibelius*, p. 72/pp. 51–2.

secretary and recorded many of the conversations they had from the late 1930s onwards, recalls the composer's manner:

> Sibelius had an unusually lively – I might almost say restless – temperament. His movements were quick and his ideas were continually changing. He would rarely sit for long in the same chair. Suddenly he would jump up and quickly get a cigar before anyone had time to help him. Exhaustive discussion of one question was not for him, for his imagination continually made associations which took his thoughts in new directions. In the middle of a conversation something would come into his mind, and at once he would change the subject. Humour was a fundamental trait in his character, and he could see the funny side of most things. His speech was spiced with humorous turns of phrase and flashes of wit.[105]

Levas first visited Sibelius at Ainola in July 1938, at a time when the composer had embarked on the long silence of his final decades (the so-called 'Silence of Järvenpää') and become a dignified national and international symbol. Aware that the world was awaiting the long-promised Eighth Symphony, 'Sibelius had to weigh practically every word so as not to start rumours.'[106] How much more lively, sociable and engaging, then, must he have been at the time of his friendship with Newmarch. If, in her letters, she felt confident enough to express her opinions about modern music in general, and Sibelius's artistic path in particular, then this was not just because she herself was always forthright in her views, but because she believed Sibelius to be in sympathy with what she had to say. Moreover, in her garrulous and even unguarded reports about family life, mutual acquaintances and contemporary developments in European music, we can perhaps discern her attempt at transcribing some of Sibelius's own thoughts during his years of his greatest productivity and inspiration, at least as she remembered and interpreted them.

The overwhelming majority of the letters that Sibelius and Newmarch exchanged between 1906 and 1939 are to be found

---

[105] Santeri Levas, *Sibelius: A Personal Portrait*, trans. Percy M. Young (London, 1972), p. 19.
[106] Ibid., p. 97.

in the Sibelius Family Papers held in the National Archives of Finland;[107] a few other items are located in the National Library of Finland, and at least one more is known to be in private hands. A large part of the significance of this correspondence derives from the fact that, along with Sibelius's correspondence with his wife and with his friend Axel Carpelan, it constitutes one of the rare instances in the archives of an exchange of letters that is almost entirely complete on both sides. Given that Sibelius carefully preserved the enormous number of letters he received from a variety of correspondents, it is easy enough to understand how Newmarch's letters have come to survive. As to how Sibelius's letters to Newmarch found their way back to Finland, then a letter dated 31 August 1956 from Newmarch's daughter, Elsie, to Sibelius's daughter, Eva Paloheimo, provides the answer:

> Your letter gave me great pleasure and re-assurance that I had done right in sending your father's manuscript letters to you for safe custody till they shall ultimately find a permanent home in the Sibelius Academy. As you no doubt realize most of these letters were quoted, with your father's permission, in my mother's book 'Jean Sibelius – Short Story of a Long Friendship'. It does indeed give, as you say, a characteristic impression of Jean Sibelius as man & musician. What a sympathetic friendship & mutual understanding that was during those many years![108]

The establishment of a vast archive of manuscripts, letters and other documents was a key phase in Sibelius studies in the second half of the twentieth century and led directly to Tawaststjerna's monumental biography of the composer. Many of these sources were long known only through Tawaststjerna's use of them, but one of the most notable recent developments in contemporary Sibelius scholarship – alongside the ongoing critical edition of his complete works published by Breitkopf & Härtel – has been their publication in complete and reliable critical editions. Fabian Dahlström has produced extensively annotated editions both of the diary that Sibelius

---

[107] Newmarch's letters to Sibelius are at NAF SFP Box 24; his to her are at NAF SFP Box 121.
[108] Elsie Newmarch to Eva Paloheimo, 31 August 1956, NAF SFP Box 107.

kept from 1909 to 1944, and of his correspondence with his friend and champion Axel Carpelan.[109] SuviSirkku Talas has produced three volumes of Sibelius's correspondence with his wife, Aino.[110] Glenda Dawn Goss has published Sibelius's early letters to his family, as well as his correspondence with the American critic Olin Downes.[111]

In all these cases, language is a major consideration. Although he attended Finland's first Finnish-language grammar school (the *Normaalilyseo* in Hämeenlinna), Sibelius was, like many educated Finns in the nineteenth century, a native speaker of Swedish and tended to use this language in correspondence (often in combination with Finnish, even in the same sentence). Goss's edition of Sibelius's early letters to his family gives the texts both in the original Swedish and in Margareta Örtenblad Thompson's English translation (the correspondence with Downes was conducted in English). Dahlström's edition of Sibelius's correspondence with his friend and champion Axel Carpelan likewise presents their letters in the original Swedish. Dahlström's edition of Sibelius's diary preserves the various languages in which it was written: primarily Swedish, but also Finnish, with occasional comments in other languages. By contrast, a rather different policy has been adopted with respect to the letters exchanged between Sibelius and his wife. In the case of the first two volumes, dealing with the periods 1890–92 and 1892–1904 respectively, these letters are presented solely in Oili Suominen's Finnish versions, even where Sibelius himself originally wrote in his native Swedish. As these volumes are published by the Finnish Literature Society (Suomalaisen

---

[109] Fabian Dahlström, ed., *Jean Sibelius: Dagbok 1909–1944* (Helsinki and Stockholm, 2005), and *Högtärade Maestro! Högtärade Herr Baron! Korrespondensen mellan Axel Carpelan och Jean Sibelius 1900–1919* (Helsinki and Stockholm, 2010). Mention should also be made of Dahlström's invaluable and extremely detailed catalogue of Sibelius's compositions: *Jean Sibelius: Thematisch-bibliographisches Verzeichnis seiner Werke* (Wiesbaden, 2003).

[110] SuviSirkku Talas, ed., *Sydämen aamu: Aino Järnefeltin ja Jean Sibeliuksen kihlausajan kirjeitä*, trans. Oili Souminen (Helsinki, 2001); *Tulen synty: Aino ja Jean Sibeliuksen kirjeenvaihtoa, 1892–1904*, trans. Oili Suominen (Helsinki, 2003); *Syysilta: Aino ja Jean Sibeliuksen kirjeenvaihtoa, 1905–1931*, trans. Oili Suominen (Helsinki, 2007).

[111] Glenda Dawn Goss, ed., *Jean Sibelius: The Hämeenlinna Letters: Scenes from a Musical Life, 1874–1895* (Esbo, 1997), and Glenda Dawn Goss, *Jean Sibelius and Olin Downes: Music, Friendship, Criticism* (Boston, 1995), pp. 179–234.

Kirjallisuuden Seura), this policy is understandable enough; it is also one that Aino Sibelius, as a member of one of Finland's most prominent Fennoman families, would most probably have endorsed.[112] However, in the case of the third volume – which covers the period 1905–31, and is therefore of most relevance to Sibelius's friendship with Newmarch – Sibelius's original Swedish is retained, supplemented where relevant by Suominen's Finnish translations.

In the case of the present edition, the issues are rather different. Newmarch wrote in fluent and idiomatic French (Marc Vignal has characterised it as being 'en général des plus corrects').[113] She learnt the language as a child from her mother, and it was the language in which, as she claimed to Aino Sibelius, 'I find it easier to express myself intimately' (letter of 22 March 1909). As Newmarch herself admitted, her command of the language was not perfect. She rarely uses the subjunctive where required after certain constructions, neglects the agreement of past passive participles with preceding direct objects, is inconsistent in her use of accents and hyphens and makes frequent minor spelling errors (usually under the influence of English). Nonetheless, her command of the language was such that it allowed her to convey the full force and subtlety of her ideas, and gives a vivid impression of her own personality. Sibelius, on the other hand, was obliged to conduct his correspondence with Newmarch in languages that were not his own. He began by writing in French, but as his friendship with Newmarch developed, he rapidly shifted into the German that he had learnt whilst studying in Berlin and Vienna, and which he regularly used when writing to friends and colleagues abroad (especially his publishers, Breitkopf & Härtel in Leipzig). Although his spelling and word order can be idiosyncratic, and his grasp of grammatical endings is occasionally impressionistic (although his often barely legible handwriting makes it hard to be entirely sure), Sibelius's German is expressive and idiomatic. After the Great War, however, he shifted back to French out of respect for Newmarch's antipathy to German culture. Sibelius was clearly

---

[112] Talas has also edited a volume of Aino Sibelius's letters to her family as well as a selection of letters of Aino's mother, Elisabeth Järnefelt: *Aino Sibeliuksen kirjeitä Järnefelt-suvun jäsenille* (Helsinki, 1999); and *Elisabeth Järnefeltin kirjeitä, 1881–1929* (Helsinki, 1996).

[113] Marc Vignal, *Jean Sibelius* (Paris, 2004), p. 406.

less comfortable when writing in French than in German, and his letters become stiffer and more conventional in their expression (although there is no mistaking the sincerity of their sentiment). The formality of these later letters is in part due to the nature of his relationship with Newmarch in the 1920s and 1930s, which never regained its earlier intimacy. At the same time, drafts of letters written in French to Newmarch reveal that Sibelius would often rely on his wife, either to correct his own French, or to translate letters originally composed in Swedish, which he would then copy out in accurate French.[114]

Because of the bilingual nature of this correspondence (and also because the primary readership of this book is assumed to be one interested in Sibelius's reception in Britain and in his closest friendship with a member of British musical circles), all of the letters exchanged by Newmarch and Sibelius are given in English (a parallel online publication will make them available in the original languages). Newmarch was herself an experienced and accomplished translator from a wide range of European languages, and a fine prose-stylist in English; where she included Sibelius's letters in her memoir, they have generally been given in her own rendering (where minor inaccuracies have been corrected, these are recorded in the notes). The handling of Newmarch's own letters raises a rather different set of questions, not least because it involves translating her words back into her own native language. In fact, a number of Newmarch's letters were included in Robert Layton's English translation of Tawaststjerna's biography (itself originally written in Swedish, but first published in Finnish). Unfailingly felicitous, Layton's versions can be rather free in terms of both tone and syntax, and a careful inspection of the English edition suggests that Layton appears to have worked from Tawaststjerna's Swedish translations of Newmarch's original French. Confirmation of this supposition can be found by looking at a letter written by Newmarch to Aino Sibelius on 6 March 1921. In Layton's version, it reads as follows:

> I grumble at him at times for smoking and for not taking care of his health, but for the most part I think he has been very

---

[114] See, for instance, drafts of letters, 24 March 1908, 13 January 1909, 9 May 1910, 5 January 1921, 14 December 1935, 1 March 1939, plus various undated telegrams, NAF SFP Box 35.

> sensible during his trip . . . I hope that your husband does not go to America. I cannot imagine him as a professor or giving lessons. I do not believe that his nerves would survive such a life for as long as a year. Of course, there is always the question of money, but what is the point of money if the consequence is *un homme fini*. I have seen so many artists ruined by America: Dvořák, Safonov and others. Life there is far too hectic and inartistic. Sibelius is a creative artist, possibly the greatest who remains in our world. I am horrified at the thought of him squandering those years he has left to him on teaching. A concert tour is another matter. I am certain that he will be re-engaged here for the next season. He is fifty-five now, a critical age in a man's life, and he would have no one to look after him in America.[115]

But Newmarch's letter was one of the rare ones she wrote in English, and reads rather differently:

> I scold him sometimes about smoking, and not taking care of his health; but I think on the whole he has been very reasonable here . . . I hope your husband will not go to America. I do not see him giving lectures and teaching. I do not think his nervous system would endure the life for a year. Of course there is the money question, but what is the use of money if it means un homme fini! I have seen so many artists fail after America: Dvořák, Safonoff, and others. The life is too strenuous and inartistic. Sibelius is a creative artist, probably the greatest now left in the world. I think we grudge his years being given to teaching. A concert tour is different. I feel sure that he will be engaged here again next season, and perhaps for more concerts than this time. I cannot think he would be happy or well in America for a whole year. He is now 55; rather a critical time in a man's life, and he would have nobody to look after him in America.

For this reason, as well as for the sake of consistency, all of Newmarch's letters have been newly translated into English. Other documentary material cited by Tawaststjerna (such as Sibelius's

---

[115] Tawaststjerna, *Sibelius*, vol. 3, p. 203.

diary, or his letters to and from Aino and Carpelan) has, however, been quoted in Layton's English version, especially where it has been translated directly from the original Swedish. Given the large amount of previously unfamiliar material that has recently been made available, the opportunity has also been taken to amplify the commentaries with extensive quotations from archival material not cited by Tawaststjerna. Also included are the letters exchanged between Newmarch and Sibelius's wife, Aino, as well as a small number of letters sent by Newmarch's two children, John and Elsie, to Sibelius and members of his family.[116]

The letters and documents presented in this edition amply demonstrate why the friendship between Rosa Newmarch and Jean Sibelius proved to be as close and as enduring as it was. In Newmarch, Sibelius discovered a loyal advocate with an unwavering belief in his status as Europe's leading composer and an intuitive feeling for his development as an artist. Well established in British musical and social circles (although not quite the aristocrat that Sibelius imagined her to be), she was worldly – and forceful – enough to exploit her connections with conductors and publishers, and could offer Sibelius invaluable advice about how best to promote himself as widely and effectively as possible. As a well-respected and prolific author, she could advance the cause of his music in the press, especially when other critics failed to appreciate its importance. This professional commitment was mirrored by a strong personal attachment too. After treatment for a throat tumour in 1908, Sibelius had given up both alcohol and tobacco, and when he visited London the following year, Newmarch took an almost motherly pride in supporting his enforced moderation (even reporting back to his wife about his state of health), as well as arranging matters so that he could compose without being disturbed. Looking back on that particular trip from the perspective of the 1930s, Sibelius gave the following account of its importance to him, as both a human being and an artist:

> I received much kindness from my English friends and was invited to a great number of dinners which I enjoyed very

---

[116] Newmarch's letters to Aino Sibelius are at NAF SFP Box 101; Aino Sibelius's to Newmarch are at NAF SFP Box 121. Details of all other archival documents are given in the notes.

much, although I was not allowed to touch either wine or cigars. I found that the new régime benefited my composing. It was only when I dispensed with all narcotics that I found I could think and feel with real intensity. I heard a lot of new music: Elgar's new symphony, Bantock's 'Omar Khayam,' Debussy's new songs and his orchestral suite 'Nocturnes' – very interesting music. All I heard confirmed my idea of the road I had travelled and had to travel.[117]

Although Newmarch does not figure explicitly here, the combination of personal kindness and artistic understanding that Sibelius encountered in early twentieth-century Britain can be traced directly to her influence (tellingly, she even included the above passage in her memoir).[118] Harold Johnson reports the following anecdote about Sibelius's affection for the way his music had been received in Britain: '"Which foreign country has shown the greatest sympathy for your art?" Sibelius was once asked. "England," came the answer, "the country without chauvinism."'[119] Although early twentieth-century Britain cannot always be said to have been free of chauvinism, the sympathy and open-mindedness that Sibelius perceived there were entirely characteristic of Newmarch's friendship with him and are there to be read in every one of the letters that follow.

---

[117] Ekman, *Jean Sibelius*, p. 183.
[118] Newmarch, *Jean Sibelius*, pp. 24–5/pp. 14–15.
[119] Harold E. Johnson, *Sibelius* (London, 1960), p. 107.

THE CORRESPONDENCE

THE CORRESPONDENCE

1 ROSA NEWMARCH TO JEAN SIBELIUS
[ORIGINAL IN FRENCH]

52, Campden Hill Square,
W.
London. 15. January [1906].

Most honoured Maestro,

Are you still in Paris?[1] In which case I should beg you to come to my assistance. I have been invited to give a lecture at the 'Concert Goer's Club' at the end of next month.[2] With great temerity I have chosen 'The Music of Jean Sibelius' as my subject. Breitkopf & Härtel (via Mr Kling) have provided me with your compositions.[3] I confess to you, in all frankness, that my abilities in the <u>technical analysis</u> of music are not very strong. As far as possible I shall try to avoid saying anything stupid in this respect and shall treat your works from a literary, poetic and national perspective. I shall be on firmer ground there. I have dipped into all the books about the life and literature of Finland that I can find in London.[4] But if there exists a fairly detailed study <u>about you yourself</u> (in whatever language), I should ask you to let me know. Also, if you have anything to impart to me yourself about your ideals and your artistic views, and which you would be happy to discuss with me, I shall use it with discretion. The public that attends the soirées of the 'Concert Goer's Club' are relatively intelligent amateurs.

As for the music I want to have performed, I have arranged for an admirable pianist, Mr Richard Epstein, to be at the piano.[5] A friend, a singer of much experience with a beautiful contralto voice, will sing some of your songs,[6] and I shall also try to have the Violin Concerto.[7]

As Mr Epstein is in Paris at the moment, will you allow me to send him to visit you? You can let him know the music by which you would prefer to be represented. Unfortunately there can be no question of an orchestra. I am sending you a programme which may be of interest to you. I myself don't find it a very suitable occasion to perform one of your compositions for the first time! All the same, it will be a great honour for this young lady, and will attract all the intelligent critics to her concert. There is also this consideration: Mr Wood will probably try out the Suite with his orchestra (by way of rehearsal), before including it in a symphony concert later.[8] Accept, I beg you, my sincere friendship and the expression of my great devotion,

<u>Rosa Newmarch</u>.

---

[1] Sibelius had arrived in Britain on 29 November, conducting his First Symphony and *Finlandia* in Liverpool on 2 December. After leaving London on 4 December, Sibelius headed for Paris, where he spent the next month.

[2] Newmarch's lecture was given on 22 February 1906.

[3] Otto Kling (1866–1924), director of the London branch of Sibelius's German publisher, Breitkopf & Härtel.

[4] Studies available at this time and in languages with which Newmarch was then familiar include: Anna Cox Stephens, 'Music in Finland', *Musical Standard*, 18 September 1897, 184–5; A. E. Keeton, 'The Music of Finland', *Leisure Hour* 48 (1900), 1079–80; Karl Flodin, *Die Musik in Finnland* (Helsinki, 1900), trans. H. Biaudet as *La Musique en Finlande* (Paris, 1900), 'Die Entwicklung der Musik in Finnland', *Die Musik* 2 (1902–03), 355–62, and 'Die Erweckung des nationalen Tones in der finnischen Musik', *Die Musik* 3 (1903–04), 287–9; Ilmari Krohn, 'La Chanson populaire en Finlande', in *The International Folk-Lore Congress 1891: Papers and Transactions*, ed. Joseph Jacobs and Alfred Nutt (London, 1892), pp. 135–9, and 'De la mesure à 5 temps dans la musique populaire finnoise', *Sammelbände der Internationalen Musikgesellschaft* 2 (1900), 142–6; Heinrich Pudor, 'Zur Geschichte der Musik in Finnland', *Sammelbände der Internationalen Musikgesellschaft* 2 (1900), 147–57; Walter Niemann, 'Jean Sibelius und die finnische Musik', *Signale für die musikalische Welt* 62 (1904), 185–91; May de Rudder, 'Mélodies de Jean Sibelius', *Le guide musical*, 7 January 1906, 9–11. More wide-ranging English-language sources of information on Finnish history and culture include: *The Kalevala, the Epic Poem of Finland*, trans. John Martin Crawford, 2 vols (New York, 1888); John Croumbie Brown, ed., *People of Finland in Archaic Terms, Being Sketches of Them Given in the Kalevala and in Other National Works* (London, 1892); Bernard Fredrik Godonhjelm, *Handbook of the History of Finnish Literature*, trans. E. D. Butler, 2nd edn (London, 1896); Domenico Pietro Antonio Comparetti, *The Traditional Poetry of the Finns*, trans. Isabella M. Anderton (London, 1898); and Joseph R. Fisher, *Finland and the Tsars, 1809–1899*, 2nd edn (London, 1901). In her lecture, Newmarch explicitly cites works by Comparetti and Flodin, as well as Crawford's translation of the *Kalevala*.

5 Richard Epstein (1869–1919), pianist and son of Julius Epstein (1832–1926), professor of piano at the Vienna Conservatoire.

6 The contralto Mary Elizabeth Grainger Kerr (b. 1864). Grainger Kerr became a regular exponent of Sibelius's songs (a letter, written on 24 February 1908 during Sibelius's second visit to England and requesting a meeting so that Sibelius could hear her sing some of his songs in person, is preserved in NLF Coll.206.19). An article from 1909 reports that 'Jean Sibelius, who takes a keen interest in the work of the young British school, recently expressed his delight at Miss Grainger-Kerr's rendering of his songs, qualifying his opinion by saying that her interpretations left no room for criticism' ('Miss Grainger-Kerr, Contralto', *Musical Standard*, 22 May 1909, 327), an assessment corroborated in a letter to Carpelan, where he describes her performance of a dozen of his songs as 'excellent' (Sibelius to Carpelan, 27 March 1909, in *Högtärade Maestro! Högtärade Herr Baron! Korrespondensen mellan Axel Carpelan och Jean Sibelius 1900–1919*, ed. Fabian Dahlström (Helsinki and Stockholm, 2010), p. 234).

7 The concerto was eventually given its first performance in Britain on 1 October 1907 by the Belgian violinist Henri Verbrugghen (1873–1934), principal violinist of the Queen's Hall Orchestra (H. H., 'Sibelius's Violin Concerto', *Musical Standard*, 5 October 1907, 209).

8 Henry Wood (1869–1944), conductor of the Queen's Hall Orchestra. Newmarch was a close friend of Wood, and wrote an early and enthusiastic biography of him: *Henry J. Wood* (London, 1904). Sibelius's suite from *Pelléas et Mélisande* received its first British performance at Queen's Hall on 3 April. A brief notice in *The Musical Times* observed that it was 'distinguished by poetic delicacy and refined feeling' ('London Concerts', *Musical Times* 47 (1906), 334–5 (335)). The identity of the 'young lady' referred to by Newmarch is unknown, but it may be the violinist Katie Parker, who made her debut in London at Queen's Hall on 20 February 1906 playing Wieniawski's Second Violin Concerto. A copy of an advertisement in the National Archives of Finland (SFP Box 88) suggests that the first performance of Sibelius's music for *Pelléas et Mélisande* was initially scheduled for this occasion too.

2 ROSA NEWMARCH TO JEAN SIBELIUS
[ORIGINAL IN FRENCH]

52, Campden Hill Square,
W.
18 January 1906.

Most honoured Maestro,

Several days ago I wrote to you in Paris. But I hear from a musician friend that you have left,[1] and that my letter will probably never reach you.

As I have been invited to give a musical lecture next month at the 'Concert Goer's Club', I have had the temerity to choose 'Jean Sibelius and His Music' as my subject. I shall try not to say anything stupid. I am not very strong in the technical analysis of music, but I shall more likely discuss your compositions from a literary, poetic and national perspective. For some time now, I have been dipping into all the books about Finnish writers that I can find in London. I lack a lot about music. Therefore I ask you to come to my assistance by directing me towards a study – fairly detailed – of your compositions. It doesn't matter in which language, and if it is in Finnish, I shall have it translated. Also if you have anything to communicate to me about your opinions and artistic ideals, I shall use it with discretion.

I was thinking of having the musical illustrations in my lecture provided by an excellent pianist, Mr Richard Epstein, and the songs by a very intelligent friend with a beautiful contralto voice, Miss Grainger-Kerr. If it is possible, I shall also try to have the Violin Concerto performed – but, alas, there can be no question of an orchestra.

Mr Kling (Breitkopf & Härtel) has provided me with all your compositions and scores. How noble, sincere and original all this music is! Yes, the art of music is always advancing, and your music is one of the most recent signs of this progress. It belongs to that of the great masters – of that there is no doubt. So, if this letter does reach you, send me your blessing!

Believe always in my sincere friendship, and in the expression of my great esteem,

<u>Rosa Newmarch</u>.

Does any one of your symphonies have a programme? People talk of your 'Kullervo' symphony – is that a separate symphony, or did you suppress the title when it was published? Because neither the first nor the second has any such indication.

---

[1] Sibelius had arrived in Berlin on 10 January 1906.

3 JEAN SIBELIUS TO ROSA NEWMARCH
   [ORIGINAL IN FRENCH][1]

Järvenpää, Finland 8/II/1906

Chère Madame,

Sincerely touched by your interest for my music, I thank you for your letter, which I received upon my return from my travels. Now I want to answer you as fully as I can.

'Kullervo' is a symphony for soloists, chorus and orchestra; the text taken from the 'Kalevala'. It is an independent symphony which I wrote in 1892.

As regards my other two symphonies, they have no programmes; and the same may be said of all my compositions, except where a programme is indicated.

'The Swan of Tuonela' and 'Lemminkäinen's Home-faring' belong to a series of symphonic poems called 'Lemminkäinen', op. 22. The other poems of this series remain unpublished.

'En Saga' is a separate work. A Ballad, which has been dramatised as an Opera in one act, entitled 'The Maiden in the Tower', dates from my youth.

I should be glad, Madame, if you would correct a common error. Often I find that my themes are described as folk tunes in the foreign press; so far I have never made use of any themes but those which are absolutely my own. Therefore the thematic material employed in 'Finlandia' and 'En Saga' is my own invention.[2]

Accept my thanks and my best compliments,

   Yours
   Jean Sibelius.

---

[1] Translation cited in Rosa Newmarch, *Jean Sibelius: A Short History of a Long Friendship* (Boston, 1939), pp. 19–20, reprinted as *Jean Sibelius* (London, 1944), pp. 10–11 (hereafter referred to as *Jean Sibelius*, with page numbers given to both American and British editions, separated by a slash).

[2] Newmarch incorporated Sibelius's claim directly into her lecture:

> On first hearing it [*Finlandia*], I shared the general impression that it was a fantasia upon genuine national airs. The composer, however, assured me that the themes were entirely his own. Like Glinka, Sibelius avoids the crude material of the folksong; but like this great national poet, he is so penetrated by the spirit of his race that he can evolve a national melody calculated to deceive the elect. On this point the composer is emphatic. 'There is a mistaken assumption among the press abroad', he has assured

me, 'that my themes are often folk-melodies. So far I have never used a theme that was not of my own invention. Thus the thematic material of "Finlandia" and "En Saga" is entirely my own.' (Rosa Newmarch, *Jean Sibelius: A Finnish Composer* (Leipzig, 1906) p. 15)

Sibelius's statement was, in fact, distinctly disingenuous. As Erik Tawaststjerna argues with respect to *Kullervo*, Sibelius persistently downplayed his debt to folkloric sources in favour of his own originality:

> Sibelius's unwillingness to have it performed sprang from psychological origins. He was at pains to appear as a unique and independent phenomenon, uninfluenced by other composers or by folk music. He emphasized to his first Finnish biographer, Erik Furuhjelm, in 1915, that he had first learnt to know runic song in the autumn of 1892, *after* having completed *Kullervo*. He wanted to forget – and succeeded in doing so – that *before* writing *Kullervo* he had gone to Borgå expressly to listen to Larin Paraske. (Erik Tawaststjerna, *Sibelius*, trans. Robert Layton, 3 vols (London, 1976–97), vol. 1, p. 121)

For further detail on Sibelius's debt to folk sources, see Veijo Murtomäki, 'Sibelius and Finnish-Karelian Folk Music', *Finnish Music Quarterly* 3 (2005), 32–7.

4 ROSA NEWMARCH TO JEAN SIBELIUS [ORIGINAL IN FRENCH]

27 February 1906
HAZELWOOD,
COPPICE ROAD,
MOSELEY.

Most honoured Maestro,

You will recognise this address, surely? I am visiting the Bantocks for a few days.[1]

Thank you very much for your letter which helped me with several difficulties. My lecture took place last week in front of quite a large audience made up of amateurs and critics. I think it stirred up a lot of interest in the musical world.[2]

I am sending you the programme. Miss Grainger Kerr sang very well, she has a broad and simple style. Miss Münsterhjelm [*sic*], by contrast, has studied a lot in Paris, and invests her art with much finesse and intelligence.[3] Everybody was interested to hear some songs sung in Finnish. I think Finnish music will be very fashionable now. It is a terrible thing to say, but this is the way one must begin before winning for oneself a real and solid audience.

As I have had the honour and the pleasure of writing about your works, it is the view of Mr Bantock that I should do well to have it published in America (The Musician), since it would spread thereafter to all the musical journals.[4] At the same time, I should very much like to publish the new photograph which you told us about in Liverpool. Did you have it taken in Paris? We are very impatient to have it.

I left London the day after my lecture, but if on my return I find some reviews of any value at all I shall send you them.

Mr Bantock greets you. He will soon send you a programme.

Accept, I beg you, the expression of my friendship and my respect.

Rosa Newmarch.

---

[1] Granville Bantock (1868–1946) and his wife, Helena (1868–1961). Bantock was Principal of Music at the Birmingham and Midland Institute from 1900, becoming Peyton Professor of Music at the University of Birmingham in 1908. Helena was, like Newmarch, an accomplished poet; in addition to providing many of the texts for Bantock's vocal works, she also published two collections of poetry – *The Love-Philtre, and Other Poems* (London, 1897) and *A Woman's Love, and Other Poems* (London, 1911). On the literary and musical collaboration of the Bantocks, see Yopie Prins, 'Sappho Recomposed: A Song Cycle by Granville and Helen Bantock', in *The Figure of Music in Nineteenth-Century British Poetry*, ed. Phyllis Weliver (Aldershot, 2005), pp. 230–58.

[2] The following account of the evening is taken from Newmarch's much later memoir of Sibelius:

> The gods should have punished me for my temerity, but it was the first lecture ever given on the subject in London; I was an enthusiastic if inadequate pioneer, and I was supported by the famous Russian conductor, Vassily Safonov, who offered to take the chair. As this time Sibelius's songs were the only examples of his style which one could offer at a lecture, there being of course no gramophone records at my disposal; and I owe a lasting gratitude to my friend, Miss Grainger Kerr, who was always ready to tackle new work unselfishly, without counting the cost. (*Jean Sibelius*, p. 17/p. 9)

[3] Ester Munsterhjelm (1876–1966), Finnish soprano. Munsterhjelm was the daughter of the Finnish painter Hjalmar Munsterhjelm (1840–1905) and sister of the sculptor John Munsterhjelm (1879–1925), who produced a bronze bust of Sibelius in 1909. Ester Munsterhjelm performed some of Sibelius's songs at her debut recital at Aeolian Hall on 13 March 1906 (as noted in 'Music in London', *Musical Standard*, 24 March 1906, 187–8 (188), and 'London Concerts and Recitals', *Musical Times* 47 (1906), 261–2 (262)).

[4] *The Musician* was a monthly journal published in Boston by Oliver Diston. Newmarch's lecture was in fact published by Breitkopf & Härtel later that year as *Jean Sibelius: A Finnish Composer* (Leipzig, 1906), and in a simultaneous German translation by Ludmille Kirschbaum as *Jean Sibelius: ein finnländi-*

scher Komponist (Leipzig, 1906). Breitkopf & Härtel made extensive use of both versions of Newmarch's booklet to promote Sibelius's music throughout Europe, sending copies to Sibelius himself for publicity purposes (Breitkopf & Härtel to Sibelius, 16 October 1906 and 24 November 1909, NAF SFP Box 42). In late 1909, Carpelan asked Sibelius for the original English version to send to the American consul in Helsinki (Carpelan to Sibelius, 17 November and 2 December 1909, cited in *Högtärade Maestro! Högtärade Herr Baron!*, ed. Dahlström, pp. 256 and 258).

5 ROSA NEWMARCH TO JEAN SIBELIUS [ORIGINAL IN FRENCH]

HOTEL DE L'UNIVERS & DU PORTUGAL REUNIS[1]
10, RUE CROIX-DES-PETITS-CHAMPS
PARIS, 13 November 1906

Most honoured Maestro,

My husband wrote to me two or three days ago to say that you have sent one of your new photographs to me in London.[2] I thank you very sincerely for this fine reminder of the pleasant days we spent together with our excellent friend, Granville Bantock. I hear with the greatest of pleasure that you are going to visit us in London in April.[3] I hope I will be back, and that I shall have the great satisfaction of seeing you there. I am staying here until Christmas, after which I shall probably take a short trip to Italy.[4] At the moment I am working on two things which are very dear to my heart: a book which I want to dedicate to the memory of my dear old friend, Vladimir Stassoff;[5] and the translation of the texts of your new songs, and of those which do not yet have English words.[6] As a result, I am beginning to get to know them very intimately. Before long I hope to see the score of your new symphonic work; it's a very interesting and colourful page from the 'Kalevala', isn't it?[7]

Our friend Granville Bantock has just performed his magnum opus (so far): the first part of 'Omar Khayyam'.[8] Naturally all the pedants, scholars and 'grand and reverend seniors', as Shakespeare calls them, are against him.[9] No matter! It is still a work full of warmth and originality – above all in its instrumentation. He also achieves an admirable musical interpretation of this Eastern philosophy – sad and epicurean at the same time.

Don't forget me for too long, dear Maestro. I follow you from afar with the keenest interest and the greatest of hopes.

Believe always in my friendship and my great esteem,

Rosa Newmarch.

---

1. The Hôtel de l'Univers et du Portugal is described as 'well spoken of' in Karl Baedeker, *Paris and its Environs*, 17th edn (Leipzig, 1910), p. 9, where it is included in the section devoted to 'Other Hotels (First and Second Class)', after 'Hotels of the Highest Class' and 'Hotels of the First Class'. Newmarch is more evocative, describing it as 'an old-fashioned hotel ... the universe being thrown in as a small dependency of the kingdom of Portugal, as it then was. The Hotel du Portugal was rather dark, comfortable, and very little changed since its foundation, which may have dated back to the days of the first empire' (*Jean Sibelius*, p. 39/p. 26).
2. Sibelius was evidently cultivating his British contacts, as he also sent photographs to Bantock and Kling (acknowledged in Bantock to Sibelius, 22 November 1906, NAF SFP Box 16, and in Kling to Sibelius, 8 November 1906, NAF SFP Box 42).
3. In autumn 1906, Sibelius had been approached by Francesco Berger, Honorary Secretary of the Philharmonic Society, to conduct 'at one of the Philharmonic Concerts your new Symphony upon which we understand you are now engaged' (Berger to Sibelius, 16 October 1906, NAF SFP Box 26). Sibelius cabled his acceptance on 29 October 1906 (BL RPS Ms 363, fol. 143). Initially, the date proposed was either 17 April or 6 May 1907, with Sibelius due to conduct either the new symphony (the Third) or *Pohjola's Daughter* (Berger to Sibelius, 31 October 1906, NAF SFP Box 26; Berger to Sibelius, 30 October and 19 November 1906, NLF Coll.206.3 and Coll.206.47, Sibelius to Berger, 14 November 1906, BL RPS Ms 363, fol. 148). The trip was enthusiastically supported by Breitkopf & Härtel in London (Kling to Berger, 8, 15 and 20 October 1906, BL RPS Ms 337, fols 36–8, Kling to Sibelius, 8 November 1906, NAF SFP Box 26), and Bantock offered to arrange further concerts that spring in Liverpool, Hanley and Birmingham (Bantock to Sibelius, 22 November 1906, 1 and 16 January 1907, 6 and 19 February 1907, NAF SFP Box 16). The Philharmonic Society wrote to Sibelius at the end of March 1907 to remind him of the concert, now scheduled for 2 May (Berger to Sibelius, 29 March 1907, NLF Coll.206.3). Although Sibelius telegrammed to confirm his arrival (Sibelius to Berger, 10 April 1907, BL RPS Ms 363, fol. 151), the symphony was not ready and the trip was suddenly cancelled (Sibelius to Berger, 24 April 1907, BL RPS Ms 363, fol. 152), much to the concern of Breitkopf & Härtel, both in London and Leipzig (2 May 1907, NAF SFP Box 42). Nonetheless, the Philharmonic Society quickly moved to engage Sibelius for the following year (Berger to Sibelius, 21 June 1907 and 9 July 1907, NLF Coll.206.47, Sibelius to Berger, 4 July 1907, BL RPS Ms 363, fol. 153).
4. Newmarch did indeed spend the winter in Paris, leaving for Italy on

16 January 1907. However, her diary reveals that her visit was far longer than the 'short trip' mentioned here, and she did not return home until the summer, travelling via Austria and Germany, and arriving back in London on 7 September.

5   Vladimir Stasov (1824–1906), Russian art historian, critic and librarian of the Imperial Public Library in St Petersburg. Newmarch corresponded extensively with Stasov, and studied with him during her first trip to Russia in 1897. An ardent supporter of nationalism in all the arts (he was particularly associated with the group of Russian composers known as the 'Mighty Handful', i.e. Balakirev, Borodin, Cui, Musorgsky and Rimsky-Korsakov), Stasov did much to influence Newmarch's view of Russian culture. Newmarch's memoirs of her friend and mentor were published as 'Stassov as Musical Critic', *Monthly Musical Record* 38 (1908), 31–2 and 51–2, and (in Russian) as 'Vospominaniya priyatel'nitsy-anglichanki', in *Nezabvennomu Vladimiru Vasil'evichu Stasovu: Sbornik vospominanii*, ed. S. Vengerov (St Petersburg, 1910), pp. 77–81. She dedicated her book *Poetry and Progress in Russia* (London, 1907) to his memory (it is datelined 'FLORENCE, April, 1907').

6   Sibelius's 'new songs' are his *6 Songs*, Op. 50 (1906); Newmarch's translations were published in 1907 by Robert Lienau's Schlesinger'sche Buch- & Musikhandlung in Berlin, and by Frederick Harris in London. Her version of *The Captive Queen*, Op. 48 (1906) was published by Lienau in Berlin in 1908 (and by Jurgenson in Moscow). Around this time, Newmarch also provided English words for new editions of three of the *7 Songs of J. L. Runeberg*, Op. 13 (1891–2), three of the *7 Songs*, Op. 17 (1891–1904), three of the *6 Partsongs for Male Chorus*, Op. 18 (1893–1904) (incorrectly numbered as 7, 8 and 9, rather than as 1, 2 and 3), and the *5 Songs*, Op. 38 (1903–4), published by Breitkopf & Härtel in Leipzig in 1907 and 1908.

7   *Pohjola's Daughter* (*Pohjolan tytär*), Op. 49, premiered in St Petersburg in December 1906.

8   The first part of Bantock's *Omar Khayyam* was premiered at the Birmingham Musical Festival on 4 October 1906, with *The Musical Times* commenting: 'The brilliance, the resourcefulness, the originality of the music are quite undeniable, and were it pruned of what on a first hearing seems redundant, its many good qualities would be far more apparent' ('The Birmingham Musical Festival', *Musical Times* 47 (1906), 757–9 (758)).

9   Newmarch misquotes Shakespeare's original 'most potent, grave, and reverend signiors' (*Othello*, Act 1, Scene 3).

6   ROSA NEWMARCH TO JEAN SIBELIUS
   [ORIGINAL IN FRENCH]

[London, winter 1907/8][1]

Here I am back in London, after a year travelling in France and Italy. I am delighted at the idea of seeing you next month, and I hope that nothing will prevent you from coming to reap the great success which awaits you in London.[2] Everywhere nowadays,

people are interested in your works, only it is the nature of the public that it is always keen to know the personality of an artist; the revelation of his music is not enough for it. These conditions are quite tedious for true artists, and yet naturally enough, one must spoil the great child of the public from time to time! Please do remember me, and I hope that I shall see you here too, perhaps at the same time as the Woods and Granville Bantock. Accept the expression of my sincere feelings and my friendship,
Rosa Newmarch.

1 Although this fragment is tentatively dated 'Autumn 1907' in the National Archives of Finland, the allusion to Sibelius's visit 'next month' suggests a slightly later date.
2 Sibelius had completed his Third Symphony, dedicated to Bantock (Bantock to Sibelius, 9 October and 16 December 1907, NAF SFP Box 16), in the autumn of 1907. He travelled briefly to London in order to conduct the deferred performance of the work with the Philharmonic Society on 27 February 1908 (a postcard to Aino Sibelius signed by Newmarch, Sibelius, Kling and Bantock is at NAF SFP Box 96 and is reproduced as illustration 1 in the present edition). Bantock attended the performance (Bantock to Sibelius, 28 February 1908, NAF SFP Box 16), but Wood telegrammed with apologies for his absence (Wood to Sibelius, 27 February 1908, NAF SFP Box 32). The symphony was reviewed well, at least by the critic of *The Musical Standard*:

> Jean Sibelius, the celebrated Finnish composer, conducted the first performance of his Symphony in C, at the concert of Feb. 27. A good deal of his music has been heard recently, and it is likely that this Symphony will soon grow in popular favour, for it is conceived on liberal and coherent lines, and its general style, engaging thematic material and clarity of treatment engaged the attention throughout the work. There is a satisfactory air of finality about the composition, and it is exceptionally clear in outline. The first movement is reminiscent of 'Finlandia,' and in fact the whole work appears to be strongly national in sentiment. The second movement is of striking beauty and simplicity, while the final movement (there are only three) is well contrasted to the other two. The whole Symphony practically consists of dance rhythms alternated with plaintive folk-song-like melodies, and one is impressed by the prevalence of national colour. Sibelius conducted his work with confidence, and was awarded a splendid ovation at the close. (H. H., 'The Philharmonic Concert: A Sibelius Symphony', *Musical Standard*, 7 March 1908, 149).

Newmarch was, initially at least, more equivocal: 'This work being in three movements only, laid itself open to reproach from the more straight-laced critics as lacking in form and balance; a view I was inclined to endorse. But I completely reversed my opinion when I came to study this fine work more closely' (*Jean Sibelius*, pp. 20–21/pp. 11–12)). She also reports that 'one difficult passage which appeared in the programme notes was cut out in actual performance' (ibid., p. 21/p. 12). Although no notes or letters seem to have survived from this period, Newmarch claims to have seen Sibelius 'almost daily' during his visit to England in 1908 (*Jean Sibelius*, p. 21/p. 12). Whilst in London, Sibelius also met his wife's nephew, Konstantin Saranchov (Sibelius to Aino, 27 February 1908, cited in *Syysilta: Aino ja Jean Sibeliuksen kirjeenvaihtoa, 1905–1931*, ed. SuviSirkku Talas, trans. Oili Suominen (Helsinki, 2007), pp. 93–4, hereafter *Syysilta*). Saranchov, who was born in 1869, was the son of Elena Clodt von Jürgensburg and Dmitry Saranchov. An ardent Tolstoyan (like Sibelius's mother-in-law, Elisabeth Järnefelt, and his brother-in-law, Arvid Järnefelt), Saranchov emigrated to England, where he was part of the Tolstoyan community at Tuckton House (he may also have been involved in the activities of the revolutionary émigré community). The 1911 census records him as being an artist and landscape painter, another vocation common in the von Clodt/Järnefelt family. He was also close to Edward Carpenter (1844–1929), the radical socialist and pioneer gay rights' activist. Saranchov committed suicide on 31 May 1923, possibly as a result of an unhappy love affair with Edward Earle (as recorded in Chushichi Tsuzuki, *Edward Carpenter, 1844–1929: Prophet of Human Fellowship* (Cambridge, 1980), pp. 90–91, where the year of Saranchov's suicide is given as 1924). Saranchov followed Sibelius's visits to England keenly, as recorded in several letters to the composer (22 March 1906, 14 January 1910, 7 and 25 November 1913, 16 and 21 February 1921, NAF SFP Box 26), and Sibelius notes that he wrote to Saranchov (or 'Coitia Szarantoff' as he spells him) on 16 December 1913 (cited in *Jean Sibelius: Dagbok 1909–1944*, ed. Fabian Dahlström (Helsinki and Stockholm, 2005) p. 179 – hereafter *Dagbok*), although neither this nor any other letters have been traced. Writing to his wife on 13 February 1921, Sibelius mentions meeting Saranchov again during his visit to London (*Syysilta*, p. 293).

1. Postcard to Aino Sibelius signed by Rosa Newmarch, Jean Sibelius, Otto Kling and Granville Bantock, London, 27 February 1908. (courtesy of the National Archives of Finland) The musical motif in the top left-hand corner is taken from the final movement of the Third Symphony.

7 JEAN SIBELIUS TO ROSA NEWMARCH
[ORIGINAL IN FRENCH]

Järvenpää, Finland 24/III/1908

Chère Madame,

A thousand thanks for the very friendly letter that you have written to me.[1] I know that in you, I have a true friend.

I will accept Mr Wood's offer and by way of fee I should like £40 – do you think that is too much?

My wife sends you her most sincere thanks for remembering her so kindly.

Your most devoted
Jean Sibelius

[1] Newmarch's letter has not been traced.

8 ROSA NEWMARCH TO JEAN SIBELIUS
[ORIGINAL IN FRENCH]

52, Campden Hill Square,
W.
6 May [1908]

Dear Maestro,

I was waiting for a definitive reply from the directors of the Queen's Hall Orchestra before writing to you about your visit to London. At last I have been requested to ask you whether you will accept the sum of £30 (thirty pounds) as your fee.[1] I know it is not a princely reward, but you should understand that symphony concerts are very expensive in London because of the salaries of the musicians, which are quite different here from what they are in Germany or even in Russia. It is also necessary to engage a performer – a pianist or a singer – of high quality for the same concert. If you will permit me to advise you, I should accept the directors' offer if I were in your position. A definitive success in London is well worth the effort of a second visit, since it is exactly the moment to make a great impression. We need something strong and new.

Send me a brief line so that your name can appear on the programmes for next season.

I have just come back from the Westmorland Festival where I spent several days in the company of Mr and Mrs Wood.[2] They send you their warmest wishes.

Friendly greetings to Madame Sibelius, and believe always in my sincere and devoted feelings.

<u>Rosa Newmarch.</u>

[1] The day before, Robert Newman, manager of the Queen's Hall, had written to Sibelius, offering him a choice of 30 January or 13 February 1909 (Newman to Sibelius, 5 May 1908, NAF SFP Box 24).

[2] The 1908 Westmorland Festival took place between 29 April and 2 May ('Music Competition Festivals', *Musical Times* 49 (1908), 397–400 (397)). Founded in Kendal in 1885 by Newmarch's close friend Mary Wakefield (1853–1910), the festival consisted mainly of competitive performances of choral works by local amateur musicians. However, from 1904, as Newmarch notes:

> it was considered advisable to engage the services of Sir Henry J. (then Mr.) Wood and the Queen's Hall Orchestra; for, from that time forward, the dwellers in the rural districts of Westmorland have had the advantage of hearing one or two symphonic works performed in first-rate style during their Festival-week. (Rosa Newmarch, *Mary Wakefield: A Memoir* (Kendal, 1912), pp. 95–6)

Newmarch introduced Sibelius and Wakefield to each other during his trip to London in 1908:

> In February of this year I introduced to her the Finnish composer, Jean Sibelius. They met several times, and although neither of them spoke more than a few words of any language known to the other, they managed to understand something of their mutual artistic tastes and convictions. Sibelius's songs, with their lofty idealism and subtle reflection of nature of a landscape and atmosphere not unlike those of her own native district spoke very eloquently to Mary Wakefield. How she would have sung them twenty years earlier! (ibid., p. 116)

Newmarch also encouraged Wakefield to include Sibelius's part-songs in the repertoire of the Westmorland Festival, and provided a programme note for a performance of *The Captive Queen* for the 1912 festival. Sibelius's own recollections of his meeting with Wakefield accord so closely with those of Newmarch that it seems likely that he drew on her published memoir (a copy of which was in his library):

> Among others I met Miss Mary Wakefield, who had been a close friend of Ruskin's and Grieg's and was an outstanding personality in the musical life of England.
>
> A good singer in her youth, she had devoted her wealth and interest to far-reaching musical plans. In various English towns she had established

choral societies, which met annually in order to perform works for choir and orchestra from Bach to present-day composers in accordance with her guiding principle: 'to bring the greatest music within reach of the greatest numbers.' My 'The Captive Queen,' too, was included in the programme of these musical festivals. She was close on sixty when we became acquainted, and had already retired from the active management of her musical festivals, but still exercised a great influence. A very unusual woman, lively and interesting. An acquaintance certainly worth making. (Karl Ekman, *Jean Sibelius: His Life and Personality*, trans. Edward Birse (London, 1936), pp. 177–8)

9 JEAN SIBELIUS TO ROSA NEWMARCH
   [ORIGINAL IN FRENCH]

Järvenpää, Finland.
13/V/1908.

Chère Madame,

Thank you for your most kind letter. As far as the fee is concerned I declare myself happy with your proposal. I hope that I might count on other concerts in England at the same time.

Warmest wishes from my wife

Your most devoted

Jean Sibelius

10 ROSA NEWMARCH TO JEAN SIBELIUS
    [ORIGINAL IN FRENCH]

52, CAMPDEN HILL SQUARE,
W.
6 January. 1909

Dear Maestro,

Time is passing and the moment of your visit is nearly here. I am writing to today on behalf of the Committee of the London Concert Goers' Club – of which I am a member – to invite you to be the guest of the Club at a soirée organised especially in your honour. The Concert at Queen's Hall will take place on 13th February, and I have been told that you are going to Cheltenham, but I don't know on which day.[1] Therefore I should ask you to let me know as soon as possible if this idea is agreeable to you, and which evening you would be free in the week beginning 15th February.

We shall invite many musical people, and we shall play your own compositions.

How are you? Send me a brief line. All your friends are expecting you, dear maestro, and you can rely on me to help you, if you should have need of anything.

I wish you a happy new year. My warmest wishes to Madame Sibelius,
>   your devoted
>   Rosa Newmarch.

---

[1] Sibelius had been approached by C. E. Rainger, the Honorary Secretary of the Cheltenham Philharmonic Society, in autumn 1908, enquiring whether he would be willing to conduct *Finlandia* at a concert on 17 February 1909 (Rainger to Sibelius, 23 September and 11 November 1908, NAF SFP Box 17). Sibelius cabled his agreement to the second of these invitations (Rainger to Sibelius, 15 November 1908, NAF SFP Box 17), and *Valse triste* was added to the programme in the New Year (Rainger to Sibelius, 9 January 1909, NAF SFP Box 17).

---

11 JEAN SIBELIUS TO ROSA NEWMARCH
[ORIGINAL IN FRENCH]

>   Järvenpää, Finland,
>   13 January 1909.

Chère Madame,

Thank you for your kind letter. On 11th January I shall come to London, Langham Hotel.[1] On the 13th I shall conduct at Queen's Hall, and the 17th at Cheltenham. I shall therefore be at your disposal between these two dates. It will be a great honour to be present at the soirée of your venerable club.[2]

I am very well at the moment and I hope that this letter will find you in equally good health.

Best wishes from my wife and your very grateful
>   Jean Sibelius.

---

[1] Sibelius presumably means February.
[2] The president of the Concert-Goers' Club, Alfred Kalisch, subsequently wrote to Sibelius (NAF SFP Box 21, original in German) with further details of the proposed soirée:

THE CONCERT-GOERS' CLUB
4, TENTERDEN STREET,
HANOVER SQUARE, W
LONDON, 5.II.09.

Honoured Sir and Maestro!
    As chairman of the committee of the Concert Goers Club permit me in the name of the club to thank you most warmly for the honour you have shown us by your most kind promise. We learn from Mrs Newmarch that you have mentioned the evening of the 16th as one which you might be able to devote to us; and since that is the only evening when no other important concert is taking place in London, and in London Tuesday is generally a more favourable day for a soirée than Monday, we have chosen this day. The reception should, if it is convenient for you, take place at 9 o'clock, and I hope you will be satisfied with all the arrangements we shall make. We shall do everything possible so that the course of the evening should be worthy. A program will be arranged, consisting partly of your compositions in performances which will hopefully please you, and partly of English works which will hopefully interest you.
    After the reception, we take the liberty of asking you to do us the honour of coming to a small supper in the German Club. The Club is very near to my rooms, and hopefully you will spend a pleasant hour amongst friends and artists.
    With thanks again, I remain yours most sincerely
    A. Kalisch

The programme for the reception, held at the Royal Academy of Music, Hannover Square at 9pm on Tuesday 16 February 1909 (NLF Coll.206.68), reveals the evening to have consisted of the following pieces by Sibelius, as well as a number of British composers:

The following Music of M. Jean Sibelius will be performed.

> Songs – 'But my bird is long in homing', 'A maiden yonder sings', 'The song of roses', 'Black roses' (sung in English, in translations by William Wallace and Rosa Newmarch, by Miss Grainger Kerr)
>
> Songs – 'Berceuse', 'Rêve', 'Lever de Soleil', sung in French by Mr Maurice d'Oisly
>
> Piano solos – Romance, Op. 24, No. 9, Impromptu, Op. 5, No. 5, and Caprice, Op. 23, No. 3, performed by Miss Myra Hess
>
> Second movement from Violin Concerto, played by Philip Cathie, accompanied by Harold Brooke
>
> Songs – 'Ingalil', 'The Tryst', and 'The First Kiss', sung in Swedish by Miss Ellen Beck and accompanied by Arnold Bax

The following Music by British Composers will be performed.

> Songs – 'A Winter Night' (Joseph Holbrooke), 'A Shepherd's Love-Song' (Ernest Austin), 'Lullaby' (Cyril Scott), and 'Evoë' (Hubert Bath), performed by Miss Grainger Kerr
>
> Romance from Suite, B. J. Dale, played by Lionel Tertis and York Bowen

Songs – 'Heart o' Beauty' and 'Now' by Hubert Bath, sung by Mr Maurice d'Oisly

Pianoforte solos – Two Preludes (Paul Corder), Love Phases – 1. Doubts 2. Response (Tobias Matthay), performed by Miss Myra Hess

Songs – 'A Mother's Grief', 'Ragnhild', and 'A Dream' (Grieg), sung by Ellen Beck and Arnold Bax

At the piano – Hubert Bath

In his memoirs, the composer Arnold Bax (1883–1952) describes the members of the Club in unflattering detail:

> The Club members were mostly elderly, and notable for wealth, paunchiness, and stertorous breathing. Bulging pinkish bosoms straining at expensive decolletages, redundant dewlaps, and mountainous backs were generously displayed by the ladies, whilst among the men ruddy double-chins, overflowing their collars at the back of the neck, and boiled eyes were rife.

Bax then argues that 'this lamentable affair was a serious setback to the acceptance in England of Sibelius's best work, and delayed the recognition of the grandeur of the later symphonies for several years' (*Farewell, My Youth* (London, 1943), pp. 56–7 and 61).

12 ROSA NEWMARCH TO JEAN SIBELIUS [ORIGINAL IN FRENCH]

52, Campden Hill Square,
W.
10 February, 1909

Dear Maestro,

I am writing to you from the countryside, but I shall be back tomorrow. Mr Wood has asked me to tell you that the main rehearsal for 'En Saga' and 'Finlandia' will take place at Queen's Hall on Saturday at 10 o'clock in the morning.[1] On Friday there will be a rehearsal for the strings, but it is not necessary for you to be there. Therefore if I do not see you on Friday, I shall see you on Saturday morning at the rehearsal, and I should like to ask you to join Mr and Mrs Wood and myself for lunch at Pagani's at half past one.[2] We can also arrange things for the 16th, the soirée of the Concert Goers' Club. Granville Bantock will come especially for this soirée, and I expect that we can dine together in peace. Looking forward to the pleasure of seeing you again, à vous de cœur,

Rosa Newmarch.

1 On 13 February, Sibelius conducted *En Saga* and *Finlandia* at Queen's Hall. A notice in *The Musical Times* described *En Saga* as 'a long work' that 'displays the composer in a serious mood':

> The thematic material is not striking, but the colour and unexpectedness of the orchestration and the eerie treatment fascinate the attention and send the mind romancing. The strings are much divided, and the *timpani* are not employed – a reticence not usual with modern composers. We are not told what story the poem translates into music, but anyone with a poetic temperament can weave one for himself. ('Queen's Hall Orchestra', *Musical Times* 50 (1909), 178)

Sibelius was immensely pleased with his performance, as he wrote to his wife:

> It is all over now. Everything went well . . . Everyone has been very complimentary. After the *Saga* I was called back to the podium seven times, and after *Finlandia* many more times. The orchestra is altogether perfect. They all stood up as I made my entrance, which is the greatest honour I have ever been paid! The hall was sold out . . . It was so pleasant to be sober for once when I conducted. All my nervousness has gone. I conducted really well, people said. The *Saga* even prompted tears here and there among my admirers. (*Syysilta*, p. 99, translated in Tawaststjerna, *Sibelius*, vol. 2, p. 105)

2 Pagani's was an Italian restaurant on Great Portland Street, frequented by musicians and artists because of its proximity to the Queen's Hall. A guide to Victorian London contains the following evocative description of its ambience:

> One gentleman, with long hair and a close-clipped beard, she recognised as a well-known violinist; and a gentleman with a black moustache and a great bush of rebellious hair, she identified as a celebrated baritone, though he looked strange, she thought, without a frock-coat, lavender kid gloves, and a roll of music in his hands.
>   In the blue room on the first floor the tables were mostly occupied by couples, and Mrs. Tota wished to know if this was where the married musicians came. The gentleman with the clean-shaven face at the next table to ours, deep in conversation with a very pretty lady in a fur toque, was certainly a doctor, and the gentleman with a white moustache, who had secured the table in the little bow-window, was evidently a soldier; the two ladies dining *tête-à-tête* did not look musical, but on the first floor, as on the ground floor, the majority of the guests were evidently of the artistic temperament. (Nathaniel Newnham-Davis, *Dinners and Diners: Where and How to Dine in London*, 2nd edn (London, 1901), p. 224)

The same guide notes how the restaurant's famous diners were invited to sign the walls:

> The name of Julia Neilson, written in bold characters, catches the eye as soon as any other inscription on these sections of a wall of days gone by; but it is well worth while to take the panels one by one, and to go over these sections of brown plaster inch by inch. Mascagni has written the first bars of one of the airs from 'Cavalleria Rusticana,' Denza has scribbled the

opening bars of 'Funiculi, Funicula,' Lamoureux has written a tiny hymn of praise to the cook, Ysaye has lamented that he is always tied to 'notes,' which, with a waiter and a bill at his elbow, might have a double meaning . . . Paderewski, Pucchini [sic], Chaminade, Calvé, Piatti, Plançon, De Lucia, Melba, Menpes, Tosti, are some of the signatures; and as little Mrs. Tota read the names she became as serious as if she were in church, for this little chamber is in its way a temple dedicated to the artistic great who have dined. (ibid., p. 226)

Five of the panels have been preserved at the Museum of London, although it is not known whether Sibelius's signature appears on them (see Robert Payton, 'The Pagani Panels: The Conservation and Display of Painted Wall-Mounted Linoleum', *Conservator* 23 (1999), 3–10). The following undated note confirms that Newmarch was always assiduous in making sure that Sibelius was properly entertained during his trips to London:

A line to let you know that we have gone to the Restaurant Gourmand to dine before the concert. If you don't come and find us there, we will be back as soon as possible.
R. N.

13 ROSA NEWMARCH TO JEAN SIBELIUS [VISITING CARD, ORIGINAL IN FRENCH]

Mrs Henry Newmarch.
52, Campden Hill Square. W.
[February 1909][1]

I welcome you to London, and if you are not too busy I shall return in the hope that I shall be lucky enough to give you all my sincere congratulations.
R. N.

[1] This undated visiting card was presumably left at Sibelius's hotel by Newmarch upon her return from the countryside.

14 ROSA NEWMARCH TO JEAN SIBELIUS [ORIGINAL IN FRENCH]

52, Campden Hill Square,
W.
Monday [15 February 1909].

Dearest and respected friend,

I believe I have found just the thing for you. Two furnished rooms ten minutes from this house.[1] The price is 35 shillings a week including everything apart from the fire – which depends, of course, on the quantity of coal you burn. That's for the Wohnung.² As for the food, the good lady will give you breakfast and whatever you order thereafter. She will clean for you if you wish and will give you the bill at the end of the week, and she has promised me that she will be very economical. The house is in a quiet street and the rooms are quite gemüthlich.³ There is only one old lady aged 84 who lives upstairs. The rooms are unoccupied. Go and settle in early tomorrow morning, or even this evening if you wish.

 à vous de cœur,
  Rosa Newmarch.

One more thing, as you are not there for me to tell you in person. If you are going to Cheltenham on Wednesday, would it be better to stay at the Langham until then, but to send your baggage on to 15 Gloucester Walk. That way your week would not begin until the day you come back. Let me know what you decide.

---

[1] Sibelius had found his accommodation at the Langham Hotel too expensive for an extended stay, and had therefore asked Newmarch to find him something both more affordable, and more conducive to composition. The rooms that Newmarch found for Sibelius were at 15 Gloucester Walk, Kensington.
[2] 'Accommodation, apartment, flat' (Ger.).
[3] 'Cozy' (Ger.).

15 ROSA NEWMARCH TO JEAN SIBELIUS
[ORIGINAL IN FRENCH]

52, CAMPDEN HILL SQUARE,
W.
Monday evening [15 February 1909].

Most honoured friend,

I shall come and fetch you at the Langham a little before 1 o'clock tomorrow and we shall go to the Woods' together. I have let Mrs Dodd know that you will be coming to take the rooms.

 See you soon
  Rosa Newmarch.

16 ROSA NEWMARCH TO JEAN SIBELIUS
[ORIGINAL IN FRENCH]

52, Campden Hill Square,
W.
Wednesday [17 February 1909].

Dear and most honoured friend,

I hope you will find your small lodgings not too modest, and that your days there will be pleasant and profitable for your work.[1] I shall come to see whether you have settled in properly tomorrow at one o'clock. After that I shall leave you in peace. You know full well that should you need anything, I am here, and you must use this house as a second pied-à-terre. Come and go as you please. If I have work to do, I shall tell you 'the whole truth'. Lunch is at half-past one, tea between 4 and 5, and dinner at half-past 7. Such is the routine 'of the Working Classes'! Arbeiten Sie nicht <u>zu streng</u>, und vergessen Sie nicht die 'gesegnete Mahlzeit'.[2] That way, you will be strong and wise like Vaïnamoïnen and Goethe,[3] and your maturity will be as a blessing for all those who love and respect you. However, if you are ever afflicted by a moment of anxiety, do not despair. Life is made of new starts, even for the wisest and most virile.

your devoted,
<u>Rosa Newmarch.</u>

[1] Newmarch's hope was not entirely realised, as she later recalled:

> Madame Sibelius wrote asking me to find some rooms in London where he could stay and work undisturbed. He himself added the condition that there should be no music in the house. I found promising apartments in one of the quaint old 'Walks' that still survive in Kensington and Campden Hill. They were kept by three elderly ladies whom Sibelius, thinking of 'Macbeth', instantly named 'the Three Witches' (Die Hexen). I questioned them sternly as to their having no piano in the house, and left the composer to settle down (as I hoped) to the writing of his string quartet, 'Voces Intimae'. But the promise of peace was soon broken. I called one morning and found my friend terribly agitated. 'There *is* music', he said, 'and *such* music! I must leave at once!' It was soon found that a very old lady in the room below had a boudoir piano more or less her own age, and hearing that a composer lodged above her, could not resist making furtive attempts at the 'Moonlight' Sonata to express her sympathy with his art! I interviewed the 'witches' and prevailed upon them to silence the offender. Sibelius stayed on, and I believe finished the Quartet in that London drawing-room. (*Jean Sibelius*, p. 22/pp. 12–13)

Sibelius's immediate reaction was not quite so dramatic. Writing to his wife on 18 February, he claimed: 'I have now settled into my new quarters . . . In the neighbouring house there are sounds of someone practising. I can hear it faintly!!! We'll have to wait and see how long the damned Englishwoman carries on. In any event, I must confess that it does not bother me so much as before' (*Syysilta*, p. 103, partially translated in Tawaststjerna, *Sibelius*, vol. 2, p. 112).

2   'Do not work <u>too hard</u>, and do not forget the "blessed meal"' (*Ger.*).
3   Newmarch described Väinämöinen (not Vaïnamoïnen, as she spells his name here), one of the main characters in the *Kalevala*, as 'the Finnish Orpheus' and 'the ideal hero of the race. Profound wisdom and the power of magic song are his special attributes' (*Jean Sibelius: A Finnish Composer*, pp. 5–6).

17   ROSA NEWMARCH TO AINO SIBELIUS
     [ORIGINAL IN ENGLISH]

52, Campden Hill Square,
W.
London.
Feb. 18. 1909

Dear Madame Sibelius,

Your husband has spoken of you to me so often that I feel quite friendly. I think you will like to have some news of him from me, as women tell each other the things men always forget to speak of in their letters. First, let me say how happy it makes me to see him look <u>a new man</u> as compared with last year. He looks ten years younger. Now we have the true, fine nature of Sibelius <u>himself</u>. Last year I was very unhappy about him; he was allowing his life to pass out of the control of his own mind and soul, giving it away to foolish self-indulgence, and was becoming apparent that he could not go on another two of three years without spoiling his whole existence. But your husband, dear Madame, has a really great and loveable nature. An inferior man would have gone under, but he has risen above this weakness. What he has done during this year is <u>simply heroic</u>, for he has won one of the hardest of victories. But now if we can keep him in good health, and contented, I am sure that he will write some beautiful, mature works. I watch him very carefully and I see that his nerves are not yet quite calm. He does not smoke or drink anything but coffee. I have found him a very quiet little lodging (sitting-room and bedroom) about a quarter of an hour's walk from our house. He likes it very much, and I think the complete rest, among new surroundings, will be very beneficial for his health and work. It seemed to me much wiser than going to Paris. Here, he has a few sympathetic friends: the Woods, Mr Kling and the Bantocks. He can come to this house whenever he wants a little family life. We are all devoted to him. My husband only speaks English; my son is a young doctor 24 years old, and my daughter 20.[1] I can assure you that I will do all I can to help your husband and make his visit to London happy and restful. He seems well at present. A little nervous sometimes, but, with the quiet life, that will pass. If I was uneasy about him at any time I would persuade him to see a good doctor, and I promise you I would give him all possible care and attention if he were ill – just as I would for a younger brother. But I do not think there is any danger of his being ill so long as he leads this wise, moderate life. I tell him he must now cease to live like a student who wastes his days, and live like the great and noble man he really is! He takes the sermons of his 'grandmother' in very good part! I wish you could be here with him too, dear Madame Sibelius. You must pay us a visit someday. But perhaps for a little time it is good for your husband to lead a new kind of life with new friends. He would soon become very popular in society, but at present he wants to work, and that is better for him. With many kind greetings, believe me,

    your sincere friend,

    Rosa Newmarch.

I told your husband I should write to you.[2]

---

[1] In 1883, Newmarch (then Rosa Jeaffreson) had married Henry ('Harry') Charles Newmarch (1855–1927), who worked as a surveyor and estate agent; Sibelius refers to him as an architect (letter to Aino Sibelius, 15 February 1909, *Syysilta*, p. 101). Of the relationship between Sibelius and her husband, Newmarch wrote: 'though he and my husband had no language in common – each discovered in the other the true sportsman' (*Jean Sibelius*, p. 25/p. 15). Rosa and Harry's two children were John Henry Newmarch (1885–1947) and Elizabeth ('Elsie') Virginia Newmarch (1888–1970).

[2] On 19 February, Sibelius wrote to his wife: 'She writes to you today. Reply to her!' (*Syysilta*, pp. 105–6).

18 ROSA NEWMARCH TO JEAN SIBELIUS
[ORIGINAL IN FRENCH]

52, Campden Hill Square,
W.
Monday [22 February 1909?].

Dear and most honoured friend,

I have replied to the letter which you received from the music school in Manchester, saying that you were in Cheltenham and sending my little brochure about your works. Now you will see that Mr Cross asks you to send a short word of encouragement which he can read to his 400 students on the day when they give your Karelia Suite etc.[1] You can write in French, or in German (unfortunately there are lots of them in Manchester!!). What a real Stimmung we are having here in London today.[2] I am staying at home and working.

Your devoted,
Rosa Newmarch.

[1] Unidentified.
[2] 'Mood, atmosphere' (*Ger.*), possibly also a reference to the fog mentioned in the next letter.

19 ROSA NEWMARCH TO JEAN SIBELIUS
[ORIGINAL IN FRENCH]

52, Campden Hill Square,
W.
Tuesday, 23 February [1909]

Dear and most honoured friend,

Do you feel like working this evening? All my family are going 'bummeln',[1] so I shall be all alone by the fire, and if the night is not too bad, I shall be very pleased to see you at 8 o'clock to drink your coffee and to chat about musical matters. But do not think that this is a <u>duty</u> which you must fulfil. If you are working, and it is too hard for you to leave your own house, do not come. I shall understand perfectly, and since in any case I am staying at home, you do not need to reply to me. There are several things which we must chat about sooner or later. That's to say the acquaintances that you

must make during your stay in London and which we can arrange without wasting your time and your freedom.² Believe always in my sincere friendship,
 Rosa Newmarch.
Do not come should the fog become thicker.

[1] 'Strolling' (*Ger.*).
[2] In a letter to his wife written on 19 February (*Syysilta*, pp. 105–6, translated in Tawaststjerna, *Sibelius*, vol. 2, p. 105), Sibelius reports attending a society event designed to promote his reputation in Britain: 'I was invited to dinner with Lady Wakefield, Lady Burton (formerly Princess of Anhalt) together will Rosa N., all in full gala dress studded with jewellery. Rosa N., who is an aristocrat of the purest water, was similarly clad and bore a large diamond on her breast.' In another, undated letter to his wife, Sibelius gives further impressions of what he took to be Newmarch's social milieu: 'She is very keen to introduce me to the aristocracy at the moment. She moves in just such circles' (*Syysilta*, pp. 108–9).

20 JEAN SIBELIUS TO ROSA NEWMARCH
[ORIGINAL IN GERMAN]

Tuesday [23 February 1909?].

Chère et très honorée Madame,
 It would be very nice for me to come, but unfortunately I cannot on account of various matters, which I should like to take the liberty of discussing with you, chère ami [*sic*].
 Yours [*sic*] grateful[1]
 Jean Sibelius

[1] English in the original.

21 ROSA NEWMARCH TO JEAN SIBELIUS
[ORIGINAL IN FRENCH]

52, CAMPDEN HILL SQUARE,
W.
26 February [1909].

Dear and most honoured friend,
 I won't come to see you today, but I hope you are feeling better. Do not think too much about tragic things. Fortunately for us poor creatures, doctors are not always infallible. I cannot understand

why they suggested such a dire thought to you.¹ I think that they have exaggerated matters a little, perhaps to make you live with more moderation and good sense. If it were true, they would not have said it to you. For example, in the case of my dear friend whose photograph I showed you, the doctors <u>forbade</u> me from saying a word to her. Thus I alone carry the secret of her illness and I can see how much better that is. She is keeping well, and this will probably last for years. I have cared for her at various stages in her illness, whose symptoms I know very well, and I see nothing in you which makes me believe that you are threatened in the same way. And then, if one must not <u>hope</u> for too much from life, neither must one <u>fear anything</u>.² Here again is the sort of grandmotherly advice of which I believe you have no need! You will continue to live and will write your 'heroic symphony', in entirely your own way. This symphony is dear to all our hearts. Tomorrow I shall come and fetch you at <u>half past midday</u>, and we shall go together to Pagani's and then afterwards to the concert.³ Your sincere and devoted friend

<u>Rosa Newmarch.</u>

---

[1] In May 1908, Sibelius had undergone an operation in Berlin to remove a tumour from his throat, although he continued to be anxious thereafter. On 23 February 1909, he complained to Aino about the state of his heath: 'But if only I could be sure about my throat. Specialists here charge £10 for every consultation' (*Syysilta*, pp. 107–8, translated in Tawaststjerna, *Sibelius*, vol, 2, p. 111). Newmarch's attempt to reassure Sibelius extended to having her son examine him: 'People are taking good care of me. Rosa N's boy is a doctor and examined me yesterday. By the time you get this letter I'll probably be well again' (letter to Aino Sibelius, 25 February 1909, *Syysilta*, pp. 111–12). Newmarch herself recalled that 'my son did not find Sibelius's throat so seriously affected as to warrant our calling in a specialist' (*Jean Sibelius*, p. 24/p. 14).

[2] Newmarch's influence on Sibelius at this time can be seen from the fact that this same phrase – 's'il ne faut pas trop espérer de la vie, il ne faut rien craindre' – is cited verbatim (but unacknowledged) in a long and intimate letter Sibelius wrote to his wife on 1 March (*Syysilta*, pp. 113–14). Two days later, Sibelius wrote to Aino with the following assessment of Newmarch's character: 'Rosa Newmarch has a strange power and ability to weigh things and see them clearly. She has indeed done a great service to my art' (ibid., pp. 116–17).

[3] On 27 February, Claude Debussy (1862–1918) conducted the first British performance of his *Nocturnes* (along with the *Prélude à l'après-midi d'un faune*) at the Queen's Hall ('M. Claude Debussy', *Musical Times* 50 (1909), 258). Sibelius wrote to his wife on 25 February that 'On Saturday I am having lunch

with Debussy at Wood's' (*Syysilta*, p. 111), and his diary entry for 27 February records his impressions of the encounter: 'meeting with Debussy. Interesting. Compliments' (*Dagbok*, p. 34). Debussy also appeared at a meeting of the Concert-Goers' Club, as, did Vincent d'Indy (both events are recorded in characteristically sardonic style by Bax in *Farewell, My Youth*, pp. 58–60). Newmarch shared Sibelius's interest in Debussy's music. She had included Louise Liebich's study of the composer in her series of popular books ('Living Masters of Music') for John Lane the year before (Mrs Franz Liebich, *Claude-Achille Debussy* (London, 1908)), and wrote an appreciative eulogy of his music shortly after his death ('Debussy', *Contemporary Review* 113 (1918), 538–41).

22 ROSA NEWMARCH TO JEAN SIBELIUS
[ORIGINAL IN FRENCH]

52, Campden Hill Square,
W.
Thursday [4 March 1909]

Dearest and most honoured friend,

I have given much thought to your idea of leaving for Paris on the 9th, and for various reasons I am very sorry about your decision. Apart from the personal aspect – since your departure will be a great loss for me – I have in mind various events which you will be unable to enjoy. Firstly, you will hear neither Bantock's 'Omar Khayyám', nor Elgar's Symphony.[1] Secondly, Mrs Wood telephoned me today to invite us to dinner at their place on Tuesday the 9th. Thirdly, you will perhaps miss the opportunity of seeing the Speyers again – a connection which could be useful later.[2] But, after all, perhaps it is necessary for you to follow your fantasy. In a true friendship, one can advise, suggest, but one must not insist. I do not know what is going on in your thoughts – you probably have good reason to take this decision. Only it seems to me that having completed your quartet,[3] you might have enjoyed several days of laziness and built up your connections here. There's the voice of a woman of the world whispering in your ear![4]

I am convinced that you will see your life more and more clearly, and that you will eventually find the form and subject of your masterpiece. Life is never truly tranquil for those who think and struggle with their creativity. Only one must never miss the rare opportunities to rest one's spirit, and to take a step back before going into battle again. It is never an easy matter to draw spirit from stone, as Michelangelo said.

    à vous de cœur,

        <u>Rosa Newmarch</u>.

If I do not see you, send me a brief line, so that I can reply to Madame Wood.[5]

1 These works were due to be performed at the Queen's Hall on 24 March.
2 That same day, Sibelius wrote to his wife: 'Rosa N has just written and pointed out many things which I would lose if I left now. Included was a letter of introduction to Sir Speyer – he has 300 million francs and is interested in me – une connaissance qui pourrait être utile plus tard' (*Syysilta*, pp. 118–19). The phrase in French is an exact citation of Newmarch's own words in this letter. Sir Edgar Speyer (1862–1932) was an American-born financier of German extraction who had taken British citizenship in 1892. From 1902 to 1914, he was the principal financial backer of the Queen's Hall concerts, until anti-German sentiment forced him to leave Britain for the United States in 1915. He was married to the American violinist (and later, poet) Leonora von Stosch (1872–1956).
3 Sibelius was working on his String Quartet at the time, although he had not actually completed it, as Newmarch suggests. He began the second movement on 18 February, and sketched the third movement by 25 February, and his diary records that he was still at work on it on 15 March (*Dagbok*, p. 34).
4 A short note sold at Sotheby's in 2003 reveals that Sibelius immediately agreed to Newmarch's suggestion that he should spend a little more time in London.
5 Wood's first wife was the Russian-born singer Olga Mikhailov (1869–1909), whom he married in 1898 (he had been her singing teacher since 1891). She often provided the musical illustrations for Newmarch's lecture recitals.

23 AINO SIBELIUS TO ROSA NEWMARCH [ORIGINAL IN ENGLISH][1]

Järvenpää
March.5.1909

My dear Mrs Newmarch,

So many hearty thanks for yours [*sic*] most charming letter.[2] I was so pleased when reading what you wrote about my husband. How glad, how thankful I am in seeing what a real good friend he has won in you. Receive my sincere thanks for taking such good care about him.

I wish too to thank you for the volume of poetry, which you sent me with my husband.[3] My knowledge in English is not great, because I have studied it only a short time, but still I understand it enough to be able read them. There are many among your beautiful poems which have found in my soul a deep understanding, especially the one about Schumann.[4] I always have the same feeling you in your little song describe. You are fond of music and nature. I think that is the reason why you understand my husband so well. I am so glad you are in London by this time. He is badly in need of such friends as you. And now it is still more necessary for him, when his life is going to take another course. This last year has indeed been of great importance for him, and I hope as you do, that it would show influences in his art too. –

He writes me having caught cold and that your son has been to see him. Do you think London climate might be bad to his throat? I feel a little uneasy about it. In that case I am afraid he ought to change his present residence, which he seems greatly to enjoy.[5] I trust you will kindly advice [sic] him what to do.

With my best love and thanks.
    Yours
        Aino Sibelius.

[1] Cited (with minor changes) in *Jean Sibelius*, pp. 23–4/pp. 13–14.
[2] On 24 February, Aino had written to Sibelius, saying that 'I have received a sweet letter from Rosa Newmarch' (*Syysilta*, pp. 109–11). On 2 March, she wrote again: 'I have drafted a letter to Rosa Newmarch, but I still need to tinker with it. It is a very humble letter, but as you took all the dictionaries with you, all I have left is the English to Finnish one, so I cannot find the words other than by guessing . . . R. N. wrote so nicely about you, you can read it when you come. Learn English now, whilst you are there' (ibid., p. 116).
[3] *Horæ Amoris: Songs and Sonnets* (London, 1903). On 23 February, Sibelius wrote to Aino: 'write something to Rosa N. about her poems. It is absolutely essential. They are particularly atmospheric' (*Syysilta*, p. 107). Previously, Newmarch had sent a copy of *Horæ Amoris* to Edward Elgar:

> The book is so short that even in your busy life you may find a moment to spare for it. But I do beg of you not to feel obliged to answer this letter. I know what the frittering away of time in correspondence means. Mrs Elgar may, if she will be so kind, send me a line to acknowledge the book's safe arrival, and someday, if I have the pleasure of meeting you again, you may tell me if anything interests you in 'Horæ Amoris'. A friend of mine says my sonnets are as cryptic as your Variations. I am afraid that is all they have in common. (Newmarch to Elgar, 2 December 1902, Elgar Birthplace Museum, L2309)

Eventually, Elgar was to set three of her translations from the Russian – 'Death on the Hills' (Maikov), 'Serenade' (Minsky) and 'A Modern Greek Song'

(Maikov) – as his part songs (Opp. 72 and 73, published by Novello in 1914). Newmarch's translations from *Horæ Amoris* were also set by Norman O'Neill as his *Two Songs*, Op. 16 (1904).

4   A reference to Newmarch's poem, 'At the Piano' (from *Horæ Amoris*, p. 8):

> At the Piano
>
> *'Sweet airs that give delight and hurt not.'*
>
> Play me some sober tune of long ago:
> A minuet of Lulli, stately sweet,
> Or march of Handel, strong in rhythmic beat,
> Wherein no tides of passion come and go.
>
> For, dearest, if you plunge my soul again
> In those dark waters, turbulent and deep,
> Of Schumann's anguish, I must surely weep
> Fresh tears into that bitter sea of pain.

The poem entitled 'Modulation' contains a further allusion to 'Schumann's sorrow' (*Horæ Amoris*, p. 9).

5   On 10 March, Sibelius wrote to Aino with details of his new residence – 15 Gordon Place, Campden Hill (*Syysilta*, p. 122).

24 ROSA NEWMARCH TO JEAN SIBELIUS [ORIGINAL IN FRENCH]

52, CAMPDEN HILL SQUARE,
W.
Sunday [7 March 1909].

Dearest and most honoured friend,

I shall come and fetch you a little after half past 5, if you fancy hearing Bantock's 'The Pierrot of a Minute'.[1] We shall be very happy to see you at half past one if you are inclined, but it all depends on your Stimmung.

A vous de cœur,

Rosa Newmarch.

---

1   Sibelius's programme for this concert is preserved in NLF Coll.206.68. In a letter to his wife (8 March 1909, *Syysilta*, pp. 119–20), Sibelius mentions dining after the concert with Newmarch, Kling and Oskar von Hase, head of Breitkopf & Härtel. In his memoirs, Wood gives the following description of *The Pierrot of the Minute*: 'An intensely beautiful though difficult work, it ought to have become more widely-known than it has. Had Ravel or Debussy written it, there would have been no question: it would have been played the world over' (*My Life of Music* (London, 1938), pp. 308–9).

25 ROSA NEWMARCH TO AINO SIBELIUS
[ORIGINAL IN FRENCH]

52, Campden Hill Square,
W.
22 March [1909].

Dearest Madame Sibelius,

Your letter gave me much pleasure, and I am astonished to see how well you write in English. Of course, there are some small things, but the choice of words is absolutely right. I do not really know why I write to you today in French, – perhaps it is 'nur Stimmung',[1] as your husband says. Moreover, although I make many spelling errors when writing in French, I find it easier to express myself intimately in this language, which I spoke with my mother from the age of three or four.

I think that I can give you good news about Mr Sibelius. His life in London has been a period of tranquillity. Doubtless he could really have thrown himself into society if he had wanted, and perhaps from a worldly perspective, I ought to have pushed him a little more to make some acquaintances. But he always looks so happy, working on his quartet etc in his little apartment, that I have left him in peace; since, after all, composition is the main thing, after his health. As for that, I have observed him well – much more than he guesses! It seems to me that he has put on a little weight since arriving in London. Twice he has complained a little about his throat, but that was only a small illness, <u>very ordinary</u>, which passed quickly upon treatment. He has told me everything about his sad experiences in Berlin. How I should like to talk with you about that! Since I believe, dear Madame, that they made a terrible mistake in mentioning a word to him that could alarm him about the future. Certainly at the moment there is not <u>a single symptom</u> of a serious illness. I am attempting to make him forget this terrible word. Sometimes he strikes one as being a little nervous (in his movements), but that will become less with time. When I think how sad and aging he looked a year ago, I praise the good Lord – however unorthodox – each time I see him now. He has his 'Stimmungen',[2] his moments of sadness and despondency – he will always have them on account of his artistic temperament. But each day he sees in life beautiful things of which he has been unaware until now. I think that from now until the age of fifty, we shall see him developing enormously. And what great talent! There is in his music a power and an austere and almost sculptural beauty, unlike <u>any other</u> of the composers of today. You will forgive me, won't you, if I write to you too frankly of what is happening in my spirit? But I am sure that you understand me. I have great confidence in your husband's genius, and equal confidence in the true nobility of his character. He has his faults perhaps, but these are little faults that will never be cured. If I dare to say it, I think that in the future you will find beautiful consolations for your anxieties, and rewards for your devotion. You have most likely already found some. One cannot speak of those matters that pertain to the soul.

I am going to send you my second volume of verses, since you were kind enough to tell me that you found something to interest you in 'Horae Amoris'. I much prefer these songs ('Songs to a Singer'), they are more mature, and they have more fervour than the sonnets, and infinitely more art.[3]

If only it were not so far from London to Helsingfors, or from Helsingfors to London! I think we should be good friends. And I also want to get to know your Eva and Catherine, and the younger two.[4] Since I am Mr Sibelius's grandmother, these are all my great-granddaughters! But I do not despair. Perhaps one of these days I shall come in summer to see the country that has become so interesting to me, thanks to my friendship for you and your husband.

He is going to Paris on the 30th of this month. I regret this very much, but perhaps the change of life will not be bad for him. I leave for a fortnight on the 1st of April. It is a moment of respite between concerts and I am going to spend this vacation with a friend in Belgium. I shall be very happy to go there, since it will be a little sad after your husband's departure. He enjoys a great place in my heart and in my life, since we have many interests in common, and I much enjoy our conversations about music and about life in general.

You cannot imagine how much I wish to promote his music. He is very well known for one or two works, but his best compositions still remain too little played. It is not a good time for music here because there is <u>too much going on</u>. Each day a new orchestra is formed in London, with the result that the increase in number of concerts results in great losses, and people are scared to risk their

money by performing novelties. And the difficulty is that your husband is now too great an artist to require <u>small</u> efforts to make him better known. If he gives a concert of his own works, it must be a <u>great success</u>. I will not lose sight of this idea. But for the moment, it is wisest not to risk anything. In the meantime, I hope that he has made some friends like Wood and Landon Ronald,[5] who will play his music more and more. Sometimes one wishes to be rich in order to help ones friends! And yet I have seen so much that ends in nothing. In truth, I am convinced that there is only one way to make a reputation – that is to write with all our conviction and all our personality – and then to wait. But it is a severe test of our patience, and perhaps it is even worse for those who wait without doing anything than for the artist himself. Forgive me this long dissertation, since the topic should interest you, shouldn't it? Believe in my devoted friendship
    <u>Rosa Newmarch</u>.

[1] 'Just a mood' (*Ger.*).
[2] 'Moods' (*Ger.*). Although Sibelius's time in London was a productive one (from the point of view of work on the String Quartet) and a profitable one (from the point of view of his growing British reputation), he was nonetheless prone to moments of considerable doubt; Newmarch recalled that 'he was rarely morose or irritable, but there were days when he felt ill and depressed' (*Jean Sibelius*, p. 25/p. 15). Sibelius's moods were partly the result of continued anxieties about his health, but he also seems to have been tortured by doubts about his British friends and colleagues, and his diary records a number of elusive hints about his condition. On 27 February, for instance, he alludes to 'The dark shadowy "business"', and by 25 March, the tone has become yet bleaker: 'that snake Delius. My heart bleeds about Bantock; I never imagined that I would lose him of all people. Destiny gradually catches up on me: alone, penniless, disgraced and miserable' (*Dagbok*, p. 34, translated in Tawaststjerna, *Sibelius*, vol. 2, p. 112). In a letter to Aino of 25 March, Sibelius again refers to his disappointment in Bantock: 'Bantock himself is probably the same, but with me, he is not the same as before, it seems to me. It may well be that my enemies fight with him. In any event, he invited me to conduct a concert in Birmingham' (*Syysilta*, pp. 126–7). The details of Delius's and Bantock's supposed dereliction have yet to be discovered. Delius's subsequent response to the first British performance of the Fourth Symphony in 1912 is recorded by Newmarch:

> At the final rehearsal of the Fourth symphony I sat next to Delius. I do not think that he was able to enter into the true Sibelian frame of mind – the two men were so absolutely unlike and had few points of contact; but he was fully appreciative of the Finnish composer's forcible originality. 'Damn it, this is not conventional music,' he drawled at intervals in his

soft, rather nasal voice. He sincerely admired what was so different, and what one might have expected to be almost repellent, to his own nature. (*Jean Sibelius*, pp. 46–7/p. 32)

Newmarch's account is corroborated by a letter Delius wrote to his wife, Jelka, on 2 October 1912:

Last night I heard the 'Musik Makers' Elgar & the Symphony of Sibelius – Elgars work is not very interesting – & very noisy – The chorus treated in the old way & very heavily orchestrated – It did not interest me – Sibelius interested me much more – He is trying to do something new & had a fine feeling for nature & he is also unconventional – Sometimes a bit sketchy & ragged. But I should like to hear the work again – He is a very nice fellow & we were together with Bantock before & after the Concert – Today I tried to hear the Matthew Passion but could not stand more than 40 minutes of it – I see now definitely that I have done forever with this old music. It says nothing whatever to me – Beautiful bits – Endless recitations & Chorale. My goodness! how slow! (cited in Lionel Carley, *Delius: A Life in Letters*, 2 vols (Aldershot, 1983–88), vol. 2, p. 93)

3   *Songs to a Singer and Other Verses* (London, 1906). The copy in Sibelius's library is inscribed 'à madame Sibelius, amie invisible mais pas inconnue. Rosa Newmarch. March 1909' (cited in *Catalogue of the Library of Jean Sibelius* (Helsinki, 1973), p. 92).
4   Sibelius's daughters, Eva (1893–1978) and Katarina (1903–84). At the time of writing, Sibelius had two other daughters (although only one was younger than Eva and Katarina) – Ruth (1894–1976) and Margareta (1908–88) – and one more, Heidi (1911–82) would follow shortly thereafter. Another daughter, Kirsti (1898–1900), died in childhood.
5   Landon Ronald (1873–1938), conductor of the New Symphony Orchestra from 1908.

26 ROSA NEWMARCH TO JEAN SIBELIUS [ORIGINAL IN FRENCH]

52, Campden Hill Square,
W.
March 24 [1909]

Dearest and honoured friend,

I shall go to Queen's Hall this afternoon just in time to hear the Symphony and then I shall return directly home to dress and I shall head quickly to Pagani's a little before 7 o'clock. I shall need to leave the house (here) at a quarter past 6. But if I do not see you at the Landon Ronald concert, I shall wait for you at Pagani's.[1]

What a wonderful and happy evening yesterday, wasn't it?[2]

And my head and my heart are all full of your music – and in spite of that, I must write 10 lines about 'Die lustigen Weiber von Windsor'!!!³ Truly the ironies of everyday life are too funny. But perhaps all that is good for me, it prevents me from becoming too difficult. You know that your music has qualities which spoil for me the pleasure of hearing any other which is less distinguished. I do not much care for t-his word 'distinguished' – but after all, it is a very striking quality of your art – which resembles only itself.

Once again, 'Credo in Sibelius' – not only as a composer, but also as a man, which should be one and indivisible.

à vous de cœur,

Grandmother.

---

[1] That afternoon, Ronald conducted the New Symphony Orchestra in a performance of Elgar's First Symphony (as well as Hamilton Harty's Violin Concerto, performed by Joska Szigeti) ('New Symphony Orchestra', *Musical Times* 50 (1909), 320). In the evening, the second part of Bantock's *Omar Khayyam* was performed by the London Choral Society and the London Symphony Orchestra (conducted by Arthur Fagge) ('London Choral Society', *Musical Times* 50 (1909), 320). Sibelius's letter to his wife of 25 March shows that he accompanied Newmarch to both concerts: 'And yesterday, two concerts. At 3 o'clock I heard Elgar's new symphony, which I very much liked, and at 8, I heard Bantock's new second part of Omar Khayyam. It is very dramatic' (*Syysilta*, pp. 126–7).

[2] Writing to his wife on 25 March, Sibelius gives his impression of a society dinner to which he had been invited: 'The day before I visited Lady B. She is now about 64 years old, but she was the most beautiful woman in England 40 years ago, and had a relationship with Napoleon III. Now she occupies a grandiose apartment and held a soirée for me, where Madame Wood sang my songs, and a tenor also performed two of them. Then we dined, when I sat next to Lady B., and even accompanied her into dinner. I received many compliments. It was swarming with aristocrats, you can just imagine' (*Syysilta*, pp. 126–7). Sibelius's impression of the dinner were relayed to Carpelan in similarly enthusiastic detail (Sibelius to Carpelan, 27 March 1909, in *Högtärade Maestro! Högtärade Herr Baron!*, ed. Dahlström, pp. 234–5). Lady B. is Alice Maria, Countess of Bective (1842–1928). Newmarch would have known Lady Bective through Mary Wakefield's Westmorland circle (indeed, she is acknowledged in Newmarch's preface to *Mary Wakefield*, p. 7), as her husband – Thomas, Earl of Bective – was Member of Parliament for the area.

[3] Otto Nicolai's overture *The Merry Wives of Windsor* was given at a Queen's Hall Sunday Afternoon Concert on 28 March 1909 (as advertised on the first page of *The Times* for that day).

27 ROSA NEWMARCH TO JEAN SIBELIUS
    [ORIGINAL IN FRENCH]

52, Campden Hill Square,
W.
Thursday [25 March 1909].

Dear and honoured friend,

I have not had a moment today to allow myself the pleasure of chatting a little with you. But perhaps you have worked better, for the good reason that I have not come to distract you in D major when you were thinking in C minor, which is the key of hypochondria! Although I am very happy to see you managing your life with so much wisdom, I should be infinitely saddened to hear you keys lining up in the same way. But no! you will never become a second César Franck, who has been so able to depict angels, but had no idea as to how to suggest the tail and forked feet of the poor Devil by means of a beautiful dissonance![1]

What nonsense I am writing to you here!

I shall come tomorrow a little before 1 o'clock to go together to Pagani's.[2] I hope you are feeling well, since the weather makes me a little worried about you. Believe always in my affectionate friendship,

Rosa Newmarch.

[1] César Franck (1822–90), Belgian composer and organist. Newmarch's translation of Vincent d'Indy's study of him was published by John Lane in 1910.
[2] Writing to his wife on 25 March (*Syysilta*, pp. 126–7), Sibelius refers to 'an unsuccessful lunch organised for me by Dr von Hase' (the meeting had been proposed in a letter from Breitkopf & Härtel (23 March 1909, NAF SFP Box 42) for Thursday or Friday of that week).

28 ROSA NEWMARCH TO JEAN SIBELIUS
    [ORIGINAL IN FRENCH]

[London, late March 1909]

Dearest friend,

On returning home, I found the photographs. I now see that I ordered only the two poses which you preferred. If you would be so kind as to write on one for Madame Wood, I shall make sure it is sent to her tomorrow. I think that you should not forget dear, kind Kling either.

As for me, just put <u>your name</u> on one of these sad and intimate portraits.[1] I do not want any inscriptions, whether of gratitude or of friendship. We have no need of all that. I will miss you much in my life, and I like to believe that you will come back to me one of these days. I feel for you a tenderness which is neither banal nor without dignity. In all situations in life you can count on me – whether you write great and beautiful works (which you will), or whether you write nothing else; whether you are always as wise and noble as now, or whether you suffer moments of weakness – none of this will have any effect on our friendship, and I think that you know it.

Farewell, look after yourself, and do not waste your precious life.

John will bring you the photographs.[2] They did not send a bill, but if you really feel like paying me, give him £1 – if it is any more, we can sort it out in 1910.

à vous de cœur,

<u>Rosa Newmarch</u>

1 A signed photograph ('To Madame Rosa Newmarch with gratitude Jean Sibelius') was sold at Sotheby's in 2003. It has proved impossible to trace the current owner of this image (which, according to the sale catalogue, is annotated 'about 1908'). An unsigned copy is reproduced as illustration 2 in the present edition.

2 The National Archives of Finland (SFP Box 24) contain the following note and prescription (in English) for Sibelius by Newmarch's son, John, which may well have been delivered at the same time as her letter:

<u>March 29th 09.</u>
Dear Mr Sibelius,
    here is the prescription for sore throat.
    Bon voyage,
    yours sincerely
      <u>J. H. Newmarch.</u>

Rp.
Formalin   4%
Eucaine (or Cocaine)   2%
Glycerine   ad 100%
    as pigmentum (2 hourly)

On his return to Finland, Sibelius clearly wrote and thanked John Newmarch, sending him a book about the Finnish landscape, to which John Newmarch replied (again, in English) as follows:

2. Photograph of Jean Sibelius (Atelier Nyblin, Helsinki, 1912). (courtesy of the Sibelius Museum, Turku/Åbo)

52 Campden Hill Square
London W

September 5th 09
Dear Mr Sibelius,

I write to thank you for the very interesting book which you so kindly sent me; – the landscape views are most fascinating and make one long to go and see the actual country, which indeed I hope to do one day.

I should have written to thank you before but just after receiving the book I went off for a holiday with some friends and spent a pleasant time yachting on the 'east coast.'

I have now returned to work at the hospital, where I hope to gain some more knowledge for the benefit of my patients past & future!

yours sincerely,
John H. Newmarch

29 JEAN SIBELIUS TO ROSA NEWMARCH [ORIGINAL IN FRENCH][1]

Paris, 31/III/1909

I am staying at:

Hotel du Quai Voltaire,

19 Quai Voltaire.

A little ill – migraine.[2]

I am sending you some flowers and 'one pound'.[3]

Your true friend

J. S.

[1] Cited in Newmarch, *Jean Sibelius*, p. 26/p. 15.
[2] Newmarch's own translation of the original French ('Un peu malade – migraine') reads: 'Rather seedy with a touch of "flu".'
[3] In her memoir, Newmarch attributes Sibelius's debt to the need 'to pay for two lost latchkeys which he afterwards found in his pockets' (*Jean Sibelius*, p. 26/p. 15) rather than the photographs referred to in the previous letter.

30 ROSA NEWMARCH TO JEAN SIBELIUS [ORIGINAL IN FRENCH]

52, Campden Hill Square
W.
1 April 1909

Dearest and most honoured friend,

How happy I was to receive your address today! I have not left for Brussels yet. Alas, here I am in my bed with what the doctor says is real 'influenza'. I am a little worried that your migraine might perhaps be the same thing? Be sure to look after yourself for a few days, because it is so wearisome and so bad for you who must not drink any cognac. Therefore, if you continue to feel unwell, see a good doctor. Do you know Landowski in Paris? Although he's a Pole, he's a good doctor who has looked after my son and several of my friends very well. Perhaps you need some sort of tonic.

The Hexen have sent me your Légion d'honneur cross.[1] I shall send it to you today now that I have your address.

I don't know when I'll be able to leave. My poor Elisabeth is very aggrieved at this naughty trick that fate has played on us.[2] But today I no longer have a fever, so we must be hopeful.

Forgive these lines which I write with difficulty, but I am not allowed any ink![3]

Your devoted
Grandmother.

[1] The 'Hexen' (witches) were Sibelius's landladies at 15 Gloucester Walk. Sibelius received the *Légion d'honneur* in recognition of his contribution to the 1900 World Exhibition in Paris.
[2] Most probably Newmarch's close friend Elisabeth Johnson. Newmarch and Johnson met in Florence in 1907, and Johnson soon began to accompany Newmarch on her various journeys, taking the place of Newmarch's intimate friend Elizabeth ('Bella') Simpson, who had accompanied her to Russia in 1897.
[3] This note is indeed written in pencil, and not on Newmarch's customary headed paper.

31 ROSA NEWMARCH TO JEAN SIBELIUS [POSTCARD, ORIGINAL IN FRENCH]

Friday [postmarked 9 April 1909].
52, Campden Hill Square
W.

Thank you, I am feeling better, although really a little weakened by this terrible 'influenza'. I am planning to leave tomorrow directly for Bruges (Hôtel du Commerce) where we shall spend several days. Then we shall go to Antwerp, and afterwards I have no idea. When will you leave Paris? I hope you are feeling well. We have forgotten a photo that was promised to Landon Ronald. A vous de cœur

R. N.

32 ROSA NEWMARCH TO JEAN SIBELIUS
[POSTCARD, ORIGINAL IN FRENCH]

[Bruges, postmarked 15 April 1909]

We are leaving on Friday for Brussels. – Hôtel de la Poste. Then next week for Antwerp. How are you? We are well here, and so quiet! your friend,
R. N.

33 JEAN SIBELIUS TO ROSA NEWMARCH
[ORIGINAL IN FRENCH]

[Berlin, April 1909][1]

<u>Awfully</u>. In Berlin! My throat! Have seen Dr Fränkel! Better today! Without illusions but hard at work. Your grateful friend J. S.

[1] Sibelius's diary records that he visited Fränkel on 10 April, 'who dispelled the fears and clouds' (*Dagbok*, p. 35). Fränkel was the leading Berlin specialist who had treated Sibelius's throat condition in May 1908.

34 ROSA NEWMARCH TO JEAN SIBELIUS
[ORIGINAL IN FRENCH]

52, Campden Hill Square,
W.
19 May 1909

Dearest and most honoured friend,

Where are you and what are you doing at the moment? I think that you have now given up the idea of returning via Hull. Probably you are already in Jarvenpää, and that the countryside is beautiful at the moment![1] I should like you to see our gardens in Campden Hill now. The greenery is so fresh, and the lilacs, with their various delicate hues, flutter in the wind like the feathers on the helmets of a proud cavalry regiment. And then there are the crimson fleurs-de-lis which exude Florentine scents, and then also the laburnums which are beginning to cast down their golden tresses – I assure you it is ravishing.

If only you knew how much I wanted to know whether the quartet is finished;[2] whether you are keeping well; whether you are still our true and wise Sibelius; whether you have begun anything

3. Signed photograph of Rosa Newmarch, inscribed to Jean Sibelius (Klary, Brussels [April–May 1909]). (courtesy of the Sibelius Museum, Turku/Åbo)

new; whether Madame Sibelius and the children are keeping well (I could continue up to op. 150) – you might satisfy my curiosity by the Marconi system.

Speaking of opp. 1,500, Max Reger has just visited London.[3] Of course, he was grandly received by the Germans – the clique of the German Athenæum. Er ist ein famoser Kerl!⁴ I saw him swallow four litres of beer with my own eyes. Dearest friend, if you really fancy drinking anything, let it not be Pilsner beer, because in the first place it would prevent you, like Max Reger, from seeing your own feet ever again, even with a telescope, but also because it spills over into the music. When he's not writing 16-part fugues on themes borrowed from the late Herr J. S. Bach, he has moments of simplicity – but of that sentimental simplicity produced by a surfeit of Löwenbrau. As I am almost the almost person I know who does not speak of his music in a tone of religious apprehension, perhaps I lack good taste. But what is to be done? I do not understand chamber music manufactured without themes; and find that the music of M. R. seems more like an anthology than a new development in his art. Whether all of this comes from a colossal knowledge of, or a very cynical ignorance of his predecessors, I have no idea. But so far, I cannot fall on my knees before the new 'Germanic' god. He has one good quality: that of being an admirable pianist, and that helps a lot when you want to hawk your wares across Europe.

At last I am sending you my photographs which are not too bad, especially the one where I am busy letting my inspired thoughts run free at an improvised writing table, all the while observing Klary with an uneasy look.⁵ They are thought to be a good likeness, so I suppose I am, after all, this very bourgeois, very well-rested person, this unflappable representative of custom and propriety! I know you are very lazy when it comes to your correspondence, so I don't ask you to write to me. But as women are always victims of the weaknesses of men, would you ask Madame Sibelius to send me a brief note to reassure me that all is well with you and your family. You shouldn't leave your grandmother without news for too long. Life is so miserable and so miserably short that one must not loose sight of true and great friendships; and although it is not at all in your nature to forget – I should never think this, even after ten years of silence – sometimes I need to know some details of your life. I should also be very obliged if later Madame Sibelius would be so good as to let me have some details about the history of 'Svanevhit', since during the summer I am planning to write something about it for the Promenade Concerts.⁶

I send you my blessing, very sincere but not at all orthodox, and I am as ever,

> Your devoted friend
> Rosa Newmarch.

That I send my greetings to your wife, to Ruth, to Katarina, to your little runo singer, and the baby – goes without saying.

1. Sibelius had arrived home on 23 May 1909 (*Dagbok*, p. 35).
2. Sibelius completed the Quartet in Berlin on 15 April 1909 (*Dagbok*, p. 35).
3. Max Reger (1873–1916) made his first visit to London in May 1909, performing two concerts of his chamber, vocal and piano works at the Bechstein Hall (10 and 14 May). As a member of the Concert-Goers' Club, Newmarch may well have attended a reception in Reger's honour held at the Royal Academy of Music on 11 May, at which Wood's wife performed some of his songs (as she had on 14 May). See 'Herr Max Reger', *Musical Times* 50 (1909), 387.
4. 'He is a splendid fellow' (*Ger.*).
5. Newmarch had evidently had her portrait taken whilst in Belgium that spring. Her signed photograph ('à mon bien cher et honoré ami Jean Sibelius') is in the possession of the Sibelius Museum in Turku/Åbo and is reproduced as illustration 3 in the present edition.
6. *Svanevit* (*Swanwhite*), a play by August Strindberg (1849–1912). Sibelius wrote the incidental music for a production at the Swedish Theatre in Helsinki in 1908, and a seven-movement suite based on this music was published as his opus 54. It was eventually performed at a Promenade Concert on 29 September 1909 (not 28 September, as Newmarch suggests in her letter of 8 September) ('Musical Gossip', *Athenaeum*, 2 October 1909, 403; 'By the Way', *Musical Standard*, 2 October 1909, 220–21 (220)).

35 JEAN SIBELIUS TO ROSA NEWMARCH [ORIGINAL IN GERMAN][1]

> Järvenpää, Finland
> 26/VI/1909

Chère Madame,

You should not think ill of me because I haven't written at all. I thank you with all my heart for your friendly letter, from which I see that you have not forgotten me. Hopefully you are well.

I think so often of you and am very grateful for everything that you have given me.

I have many new compositions. They will be sent to you.

Finland is very beautiful at the moment and awaits you.

My wife greets you warmly, as does your true and grateful friend,
> Jean Sibelius

[1] Translation partially cited in Newmarch, *Jean Sibelius*, p. 26/pp. 15–16 ('I often think about you and all you have done for me. I have many new compositions which shall all be sent to you. Finland is now very beautiful and awaits your coming.')

36 ROSA NEWMARCH TO JEAN SIBELIUS
[ORIGINAL IN FRENCH]

8 September 1909.

Dearest and most honoured friend,

For two months now I have been working for the Promenade concerts without catching breath! For six weeks I have been in the country, apart from several trips to London to hear the novelties. But tomorrow – or the day after tomorrow – I am returning to Campden Hill Square, which I won't leave any more apart from to go to the Birmingham Festival for the third part of Bantock's 'Omar Khayyam'.[1] I shall send you the season prospectus, which will give you an idea of what I have had to do of late. I am happy to be able to let you know that they have been <u>very successful</u>, the last year having been rather poor for music. I received from Schlesinger 'Swanehvit' and 'Nächtlicher Ritt & Sonnenaufgang'.[2] As far as the former is concerned, you will see the date that Mr Wood will give it – the 28th of this month. I think I have written rather a good note, having done it with all my heart.[3] And then I found a Swedish lady in London who helped me to read and translate Strindberg's play.[4] I find the music has much charm, but does not join the ranks of your great works. 'Nächtlicher-Ritt' interests me much more. It seems to me that it is of an astonishing originality. True Sibelius – as well as something that I don't entirely recognise yet. I am so curious to hear it![5] I have also just received 'Theodora', and I shall busy myself with the translation as soon as I am back.[6] Once I have finished with these programmes which proliferate, I shall have a little leisure for my own interests.

I was very happy to receive your little letter assuring me that you are still at work, and there will soon be more – not <u>opuses</u> – but works. I am very often near you in my thoughts. Do you know Safonoff?[7] To tell the truth, I don't find him very sympathetic, either as man or conductor, but as Richter grows older and frailer,[8]

Safonoff will try to replace him in England, so it would be useful to cultivate him to perform novelties. There's a woman of the world speaking to you! And also your sincere and affectionate friend who always wishes for you to occupy the place you deserve in the world. Greet dear Madame Sibelius and the children on my behalf, and believe always in my affection and loyalty,

<u>Rosa Newmarch</u>.

I hope you have received the photographs.

1   The third part of Bantock's *Omar Khayyam* was performed on 7 October ('Birmingham Musical Festival', *Musical Times* 50 (1909), 735–7 (737)).
2   The Suite from *Swanwhite*, Op. 54, and the symphonic poem *Night Ride and Sunrise*, Op. 55, were published by Robert Lienau in Berlin by March and July respectively.
3   Newmarch's note for *Swanwhite* is republished in *The Concert-goer's Library of Descriptive Notes*, 6 vols (London, 1928–48), vol. 5, pp. 85–8.
4   Later identified in a letter from Newmarch to Sibelius (8 January 1911) as Mrs Sillem.
5   *Night Ride and Sunrise* was not in fact performed in Britain until 1930, when Basil Cameron programmed it as part of the Hastings Festival.
6   Newmarch's translations of Sibelius's *2 Songs*, Op. 35 (1908) – No. 1, 'Jubal', and No. 2, 'Theodora', were published in Leipzig by Breitkopf & Härtel in 1910.
7   Vasily Safonov (1852–1918), Russian conductor, who had chaired Newmarch's 1906 lecture-recital on Sibelius. In her 1916 profile of the conductor, Newmarch claimed that 'Since the death of the French veterans, Lamoureux and Colonne, and the retirement of Hans Richter, he is undeniably the most notable of the "guest" conductors who regularly visit our shores' ('Wassily Safonoff', *Musical Times* 57 (1916), 9–12 (12)).
8   Hans Richter (1843–1916), Austrian conductor. Richter had given the first British performance of Sibelius's Second Symphony at a Hallé Society Concert in Manchester on 2 March 1905, 'without creating any pronounced impression' ('Music in Manchester', *Musical Times* 46 (1905), 266–7 (266)). However, a review in *The Musical Standard* was more enthusiastic about the symphony, arguing that the work's cool reception was more the result of unfortunate programming than of any deficiencies in the work itself:

> It was a little unfortunate that works by Strauss [*Till Eulenspiegel*] and Dvořák [*Carnival*] preceded a work of such length by a man entirely unknown at these concerts, and from that point of view the programme was not arranged considerately. It was not surprising, therefore, amid an atmosphere kindled by such imaginative writers that the work should have been received somewhat coldly. On a first hearing I was impressed by its marked individuality. It rarely betrays any influences of the more 'advanced' writers. There is a sombre hue in its thematic material, and the extent of its working out produces a sense of monotony, emphasized, further, by an absence of tonal colouring; and this makes the composition

appear rather academic. The gloomy forebodings of the second movement, *Andante*, is not very appreciably relieved by Section 3, *Vivacissimo*, and the *Finale*; and I am inclined to surmise that the composer's endeavour has been to reflect in this work some of the characteristics of his country and its people. (W. H. C., 'Manchester', *Musical Standard*, 11 March 1905, 156).

37 ROSA NEWMARCH TO JEAN SIBELIUS
[ORIGINAL IN FRENCH]

52, CAMPDEN HILL SQUARE,
W.
8 November 1909

Dearest and most honoured friend,

Here, at last, is a moment of relative rest! The Promenade concerts are finished, and my translation, with a foreword, of Vincent d'Indy's book about César Franck is in the hands of the publishers,[1] and I can take advantage of the relative calm to write a reasonably long letter you to. Recently I have been thinking much of you and of your affairs. A number of your compositions have reached me. The song 'Theodora', which I have just translated into English; the short 'Romance' for strings,[2] which arrived just in time to include in the autumn programmes; and last of all, the Quartet.[3] About this last piece, what can I say to you? I think that of all musical forms, the most difficult to grasp <u>without having heard it</u> is the string quartet. Unfortunately the Brussels Quartet didn't perform it during their only concert in London this season.[4] The Petersburg Quartet (Kranz etc) and several English organisations are left.[5] Although I have not yet had chance to hear the work played, there are several movements which are already 'intimate voices' to me. For instance, the first Andante, the Adagio and the Allegretto. It seems to me that there is something very strong and very personal there; at times a little severe, because of the type of 'simplicity' that you put into your music from time to time; but a simplicity that is not at all naïve! On the contrary, it's the sign of your very refined individuality, which is always somewhat ahead of others. But it is what prevents your music from becoming popular, for the time being, because the world is still obsessed with everything that is noisy and which seems very complicated. Your art, my friend, does not correspond to the era of automobiles, but will correspond well to the more elevated and gracious epoch of aviation. Because there will be a reaction against this terrible phase of commercialism and cheap effects; if not, music will cease to be an art, and will simply become a form of financial speculation. Perhaps I am a little pessimistic today. I have just been assured that £2000 worth of tickets has been sold for a concert at which Paderewski is to play a concerto and Richter will conduct his symphony.[6] Imagine £2000 to hear a symphony by Paderewski! And as a result all the other concerts which will take place this month, however good they might be, with excellent artists such as Sapellnikov,[7] Thibaud,[8] Bauer,[9] etc., must suffer by being deprived of an audience. And our sycophantic press assures us that we are a musical nation! We are nothing but a nation <u>of snobs</u>! There, I feel better! Let's talk about astronomy![10]

Where will your star lead you this winter? Do you have any engagements to conduct in Sweden or in Germany? And what about spring? Heavens, how I should like to know all of this without making you write! As well as all your other news, domestic, artistic, and medical. As for me, I have to stay in London during the winter and work wisely. But all the same, if there were any possibility of seeing you, or of hearing one of your symphonies somewhere, it would not be impossible for me to take a little trip. In spring I shall be freer, and sometimes I make plans! <u>Let me know yours in a few words</u>. Here, in what seems to be a terrible situation that never changes, we have too much music and too many concerts, with the result that they kill each other off and no one dares risk a novelty unless it's something 'sensational'. Everything is decided by money. It is all very depressing. Today I have seen that because of the enormous success of the Paderewski Concert they are going to repeat the whole stupid thing.[11] That's another £2000 of tickets sold! However, according to the press, even the symphony is said to be a poor affair, without ideas and without form.[12] It's the halo of golden hair that does all of that. And for the next Symphony concert it's almost impossible to find an audience for a new Suite by Bantock and for a great artist like Thibaud.[13] If you want success, buy yourself immediately some sort of halo and write a symphony for 50 sarrusophones accompanied by a machine to imitate earthquakes.[14]

We speak of you very often. Very often I play over your dear and beautiful music, which brings me consolation in the midst of all this mischief. And then there are few days when I don't think of you, of your life and your family, here in the little room that you know, with Michelangelo's 'Il Penseroso',[15] your photograph, and that of Saint Elisabeth always in my gaze.[16] As far as the latter is concerned, she has been here with me for 9 months. She is well, and was due to leave for Florence this week, but an accident to her foot which happened to her as she was getting off an omnibus will prevent her from leaving for some time. All the better for me! All my greetings to Madame Sibelius and the children, and to you, dear and excellent friend, all my best wishes and many sincere and affectionate thoughts,

Rosa Newmarch.

[1] Vincent d'Indy, *César Franck: A Study* (London, 1910).
[2] The Romance in C, Op. 42 (1904) was published by Breitkopf & Härtel in October 1909. Of a performance at Queen's Hall in early 1910, *The Times* described it as 'pretty and unpretentious with the kind of prettiness that should make it into an attractive piece for young ladies to strum over in a pianoforte arrangement' ('Queen's Hall Symphony Concert', *The Times*, 14 February 1910, 11).
[3] The String Quartet, Op. 56, was published by Robert Lienau in Berlin in September 1909.
[4] The Brussels Quartet appeared at Bechstein Hall on 21 October 1909, performing works by Mozart, Beethoven and Dvořák (F. M., 'Bechstein Hall', *Violin and String World* 23 (1909), 44).
[5] The Petersburg Quartet (in which Naum Kranz played second violin) was, according to a contemporary review, 'the private quartet to H. H. The Duke George Alexander zu Mecklenburg Strelitz' (F. M., 'The St. Petersburg Quartet', *Violin and String World* 12 (1908), 49). The ensemble had performed three concerts at Bechstein Hall in London in late 1907, including the three Tchaikovsky quartets on 4 December ('London Concerts', *Musical Times* 49 (1908), 39–41 (40)). The players returned to perform quartets by Glazunov, Taneev and Tchaikovsky on 21 November 1908, again at Bechstein Hall ('London Concerts', *Musical Times* 49 (1908), 800). Five days after Newmarch's letter (on 13 November), the Petersburg Quartet included an unspecified quartet by Glazunov in a concert at Bechstein Hall ('London and Suburban Concerts', *Musical Times* 59 (1909), 796–7 (796)). A later review describes the quartet as 'one of the finest in Europe', and 'pre-eminent in the interpretation of Russian works, whilst their performances of the classics are scarcely equalled by any other existing quartet' ('St. Petersburg Quartet', *Violin and String World* 24 (1912), 22). For a survey of British quartets at that time, see W. S. Meadmore, 'British Performing Organizations: (2) Present-Day Organizations', in *Cobbett's Cyclopedic Survey of Chamber Music*, ed. Walter Willson Cobbett, 2 vols (London, 1929–30), vol. 1, pp. 203–12. The first performance of Sibelius's Quartet seems to have been given

by the Leeds Bohemian Quartet on 4 March 1913 ('Music in the Provinces', *Musical Times* 55 (1914), 260–7 (266)).

6   Ignacy Jan Paderewski (1860–1941), Polish pianist and composer (and later Polish Prime Minister). Paderewski's B minor Symphony, Op. 24, was given its first English performance by the London Symphony Orchestra, conducted by Richter, on 8 November 1909.

7   Vasily Sapelnikov (1867–1941), Russian pianist, who performed Tchaikovsky's First Piano Concerto under the direction of the composer on 11 April 1889 ('Philharmonic Society', *Musical Times* 30 (1889), 278), as well as giving the first British performance of Rachmaninov's Second Piano Concerto on 29 May 1902 ('London Concerts', *Musical Times* 43 (1902), 481–2 (482)). Sapelnikov had given a solo recital at Steinway Hall on 21 October 1909 ('Mr. Sapellnikoff's Recital', *Musical Standard*, 30 October 1909, 283), and was due to perform Tchaikovsky's First Concerto at Queen's Hall on 11 November. Newmarch's anxiety that the performance of Paderewski's Symphony would lead to a reduced audience for other concerts was not borne out in this case; as *The Musical Times* reported, 'The audience was a large one. It may be hoped that the success of the concert is a good augury for the season's operations' ('Philharmonic Society', *Musical Times* 50 (1909), 794).

8   Jacques Thibaud (1880–1953), French violinist. Thibaud appeared at Queen's Hall on 13 November 1909, performing concertos by Mozart and Lalo ('Queen's Hall Symphony Concerts', *Musical Times* 50 (1909), 794–5 (795)).

9   Harold Bauer (1873–1951), British pianist (and pupil of Paderewski). He was the soloist at a Philharmonic Society Concert on 25 November 1909 under the direction of Bruno Walter ('Philharmonic Society', *Musical Times* 51 (1910), 24).

10 In her memoir of Sibelius, Newmarch recalled that in the wake of Sibelius's throat problems in 1908, 'nothing seemed comforting enough except very strong coffee, and no subject big enough to relieve the gloom but astronomy' (*Jean Sibelius*, p. 25/p. 15).

11 *The Musical Times* noted: 'The demand for seats was so great that, as in the case of the Elgar Symphony, the directors of the concerts arranged to give an extra performance at a special concert to be held on December 18' ('M. Paderewski's New Symphony', *Musical Times* 50 (1909), 794).

12 A review in *The Musical Times* suggested that 'Although public interest in the work was evidently not exhausted at its first hearing, there was some reserve noticeable in its reception on the second hearing' ('London Symphony Orchestra', *Musical Times* 51 (1910), 24).

13 Bantock conducted the first London performance of his *Old English Suite* at Queen's Hall on 13 November 1909 ('Queen's Hall Symphony Concerts', *Musical Times* 50 (1909), 794–5 (795)).

14 Newmarch's comments echo the review in *The Musical Times*: 'The introduction of the sarrusophone and a special instrument, the tonitruone, "to imitate the sound of distant thunder," does not provide the necessary high lights' ('M. Paderewski's New Symphony', 794).

15 Michelangelo's statue of Lorenzo de' Medici was dubbed 'Il Penseroso' (Newmarch would have seen it in the Medici Chapel in Florence, and it was also the inspiration for the second movement in the second set of Liszt's *Années de pèlerinage*).

16 Newmarch's friend and travelling companion, Elisabeth Johnson.

38 ROSA NEWMARCH TO JEAN SIBELIUS
[ORIGINAL IN FRENCH]

52, Campden Hill Square,
W.
27 February 1910.

Dearest and honoured friend,

I have just received a letter which concerns you. It is an invitation to come and conduct some of your works at one of the new Symphony concerts at Birmingham. The secretary has requested me to approach you about this matter and to ask, if you accepted, what your fee will be? Although they have contacted me, I am sure that this invitation <u>comes from Bantock</u>. He will probably write to you too. Doubtless he believes that it will be a great pleasure for me to be the first person to discuss this matter with you – which is true. He is very busy at present, but although he is very successful everywhere, I think that he must be having difficulties and problems in Birmingham. At least I can assure you that he always speaks to me of you most affectionately, and that he said several months ago – 'I so much want to arrange a "Sibelius Concert" in Birmingham.' The dates of the concerts are:

<u>1910.</u>	<u>1911</u>
19th October	1st and 15th February
2nd and 16th November	1st and 15th March.
14th December.	

I think you would do well – should you accept – to offer a choice of two dates. As for the fee, I would suggest that it should not exceed £50. We shall do our best to make sure that your visit is not too expensive,* and perhaps we can organise something else. In Birmingham there is always the possibility of performing one of your works at the 'Festival' of 1912. Reply to me soon, won't you?

Let's move onto something else. I don't know if you have read in the newspapers that a little before Christmas we had the great sadness of losing dear, kind Olga Wood? Although she seemed a strong and beautiful woman, she suffered much from time to time. She had a hard life in her youth, with this devil of a man who was her first husband. All the same, we were not expecting the sad outcome of an operation of which she herself suspected no danger.[1]

For me it is a loss which I feel <u>very much, very much</u>. But for <u>him</u>, poor man, it must be simply torture. To begin with he didn't realise this. He is very courageous, even rather jolly, as she would have demanded, with her 'Christian Science' principles. But those who know him well know how much he is suffering, above all when he is at home. Fortunately he has a lot to do. Work is the great consolation of this earthly life, isn't it?

<u>One more question which absolutely requires an answer.</u> Are you going to be at home during April and May? Mr Kling is thinking of making a sort of tour of Russia. B. & H. is sending him to Berlin, Warsaw, Moscow, Petersburg, and then he will also pass through Helsingfors. We have discussed a plan which might perhaps come off. Which is that I should take advantage of the chance to have a travelling companion, and that I should come with him, at least for part of the time. I cannot say for certain whether I can abandon my jobs for such a long time; but what is absolutely certain is that I would not make the journey to Finland if you weren't there. But if you are in the countryside, and Madame Sibelius could find me some sort of cottage (very simple) near you and your family, I should contemplate it seriously. Is it usually <u>really</u> spring there at the start of May? Find someone to reply to all these questions if you are busy yourself!

Kling has told me that you are resolved to reject Miss Maud Allen's [sic] offer.[2] I am happy, because there is only one Sibelius in the world and he must work according to his inspiration. The short romance for strings has much charm. I saw the score of 'In Memoriam' for a moment – it might be performed in the autumn.[3]

Forgive me for writing in haste. All my friendly greetings to Madame and the family – and believe me to be always your devoted
    <u>Rosa Newmarch</u>.
*You see that I am still very good at saving money

---

[1] Olga Wood died on 20 December, having been 'intermittently ill through most of 1909' (Reginald Pound, *Sir Henry Wood* (London, 1969), p. 107). She had married George Edward Hillman in 1888, but left him in 1896. According to Reginald Pound, 'There was gossip among her friends in London about his mental health and their money differences', and the couple divorced in 1898 (ibid., pp. 62 and 65).

[2] Maud Allan (1873–1956), Canadian-born dancer. Allan had approached Sibelius in spring 1909 with a view to commissioning a score for a ballet

entitled *The Sacrifice* that was to be performed at the Palace Theatre, London, in February 1910 (Allan to Sibelius, 6 April and 15 September, 1909, NLF Coll.206.1). Negotiations about the commission continued late into that year (Kling to Sibelius, 25 November 1909, Breitkopf & Härtel to Sibelius, 21 and 31 December 1909, NAF SFP Box 42), by which time Sibelius's initial enthusiasm for the project had waned, not least because he felt that the proposed fee was insufficient. Allan's original scenario was eventually taken up by Debussy as *Khamma*. This was not, however, the end of Allan's interest in Sibelius's music, as she added a dance based on his *Dryad* to her repertoire ('Miss Maud Allan's Matinée', *The Times*, 11 February 1911, 10, noted by Sibelius himself in *Dagbok*, p. 69).

3 *In memoriam*, Op. 59 (1909, revised 1910) was published by Breitkopf & Härtel in Leipzig in August 1910. It was inspired by Eugen Schauman, who, in June 1904, shot Nikolay Bobrikov, the Russian Governor-General of Finland, before taking his own life.

39 JEAN SIBELIUS TO ROSA NEWMARCH [ORIGINAL IN FRENCH][1]

Järvenpää, Finland
10/III/1910

Très honorée et chère Madame,

I thank you with all my heart for your letter. You are still the same and very dear friend. Mr Bantock's invitation made me very happy, and of the dates you have been so good to offer me, the 14th December suits me best. As far as the fee is concerned, I should naturally be happy with £50 if you find that possible.

And last of all, welcome a thousand times to Finland!

I cannot say how delighted my wife and I are at this great piece of news.

Because the weather has been most extraordinary this year, I think it would be best for you to come at the beginning of June or at the end of May. April is always rather cold and grey here.

In any case my wife and I will be at home all through the spring. Welcome!!

Warmest wishes from my wife and from your grateful friend
    Jean Sibelius

[1] Translation partially cited in Newmarch, *Jean Sibelius*, pp. 26–7/p. 16.

40 ROSA NEWMARCH TO JEAN SIBELIUS
[ORIGINAL IN FRENCH]

52, Campden Hill Square,
W.
7 April [1910].

Dearest and honoured friend,

At last I think it's all decided. If my health permits it, I hope to arrive in Petersburg at the start of May. I shall spend quite a long time there seeing my old friends, and then I shall come to your country, and I shall finally return home via Stockholm and Copenhagen. Since my family is worried by the idea of my making this long trip alone, I have persuaded dear, good Miss Johnson (the Elisabeth of the photograph above my writing desk) to leave Florence a little earlier this year and to join me in Cologne. I really think it's a good idea. I cannot leave with Mr Kling the week before, since I still have a lot to do. Moreover, I could never stand the idea of making this journey at speed, so we shall linger in all the cities of Russia. I shall never make a good tourist, still less a good commercial traveller! This time it is Finland I want to see above all. Therefore, travelling with a friend, I shall be more independent. Kling likes cities, business and, fine man that he is, restaurants. I am myself not entirely indifferent to restaurants, but I prefer the countryside and the simple life. Therefore my ideal, if it can be achieved, would be an inn fairly near to you and your family so that I can see you often, where Elisabeth and I might spend some time. To see you, and to get to know Madame Sibelius and the children better, without disturbing you in any way – that's what I have in mind, dear and good friend, during my stay.

Everything will be arranged in Birmingham, and we can discuss the details of the concert when I see you.[1]

If it's possible, I'll leave London on the 24th of this month and arrive in Petersburg for Easter.[2] From there I'll send you my address. Friendly greetings to all the family. A vous de cœur,

Rosa Newmarch.

---

[1] The proposed concert did not take place, and Sibelius next visited Britain in autumn 1912.
[2] Newmarch's diary suggests that she eventually left on 20 April, travelling to Moscow with Elisabeth Johnson via Berlin and Warsaw.

41 ROSA NEWMARCH TO JEAN SIBELIUS
   [ORIGINAL IN FRENCH]

Hôtel Continental
Moscow.
20 April/3 May [1910].[1]

Dearest and honoured friend,

We've been here in Moscow for a few days now. We shall leave on Friday (the 6th) for Petersburg where my address will be
   Grand Hôtel
   'Ville de Paris'
   Morskaïa, 16.
I don't yet know how long I shall spend in Petersburg – probably 8 to 10 days. Then, if all goes well, and I receive your news, we shall come to Viborg or to Helsingfors,[2] как Вам угодно![3] You'll advise me well, won't you?

Mr Kling is staying at the hotel Metropole, opposite us. He has been enjoying himself a lot during the Easter holidays, and doesn't come home until 3 o'clock in the morning. I shall have some pretty tales to tell…! He has probably already written to you that Kussevitsky has invited him to accompany him during his tour (with orchestra) along the Volga, as far as Astrakhan![4] In which case I don't know when he will arrive in Finland, or whether he won't be obliged to abandon the idea of returning to the north.

I received your 'telegram' the day before my departure; it was the thought of a real friend.[5] I am now impatient to turn my steps towards Petersburg, en route for Finland.

I'll keep my news until we meet. Greet Madame Sibelius on my behalf, and believe always in my loyal friendship
   Rosa Newmarch.

---

[1] Newmarch gives the date according to both the Julian calendar (the so-called 'old style', in use in Russia until 1918) and the Gregorian calendar (in use in Western Europe, including Finland, and usually referred to as 'new style'). Newmarch's other letters to Sibelius from Russia are dated according to the new style only.

[2] Viborg is the Swedish name for Viipuri, then a town on the Finnish side of the border, but ceded to the Soviet Union in 1944 (and known as Vyborg in Russian).

[3] 'As you wish' (*Russ.*).

[4] Serge Koussevitzky (1874–1951), Russian-born conductor.

[5] 'Telegram' in English in the original. The item in question has not been traced.

42 JEAN SIBELIUS TO ROSA NEWMARCH
[ORIGINAL IN FRENCH]

Järvenpää, Finland
9/V/1910

Chère Madame,

We are very happy to learn that your trip has worked out so well. Now I should like to propose first of all a journey through Finland to see our great waterfall at 'Imatra' and if it were to suit you, also the 'Punkaharju', where the nature is very characteristic and 'Finnish'.[1] This trip would start at Viborg where my wife and I will come to meet you.[2] Be so kind as to write to me a few days before you leave Petersburg. I am daring to propose all of this to you even though it is still a little cold and spring has barely arrived here. But let us hope that the weather will be good and that everything will work out as well as possible – naturally, conditions are very primitive.

Farewell and welcome to Finland.

Your most devoted
    Jean Sibelius.

---

[1] The rapids at Imatra were a popular tourist destination before they were damned in 1929. The following description is taken from a contemporary travel guide:

> The actual fall of the river is not great compared with that of many other waterfalls. The Imatra rapids extend over half a mile, in the course of which the fall is about 61 feet. It is the volume of water, the narrowness of the gorge, and the ruggedness of the channel which give the scene its grandeur. This flood is the overflow of a thousand lakes, the tribute of the North. The noise is like a storm among trees, with a deep bass undertone as if thousands of great boulders were rolling down the gorge, beating the rocks to fragments. Or one might describe the race of the waters as like a troop of wild horses galloping madly down the pass, rearing and leaping on each other's backs. (A. MacCallum Scott, *Through Finland to St. Petersburg* (London, 1908), p. 121)

Newmarch's own account of her visit to the rapids closely matches this description, and makes a striking parallel between the sounds of nature and the sources of Sibelius's musical inspiration:

> Next day we walked through forests wrapped in peace profound, and reached the sombre boundaries of the Falls, where the water boiled up in white foam, and the threat of engulfment in the rush of it, are very trying to the nerves. This is indeed a 'strait place'; the whole of the waters of Lake Saïma [*sic*] press to get through this bottleneck, and the roar of protest given out by Imatra is terrible. Sibelius had at that time a passion for trying to catch the pedal notes of natural forces. The pedal note of Imatra no man

has guaged, but he often seemed satisfied with the results of his rapt listening, when he caught the basic sounds of the forests or of the wind whistling over lakes and moorlands. To share Nature with him is a wonderful but silent experience. (*Jean Sibelius*, p. 28/p. 19)

Like Imatra, the ridge at Punkaharju became (and remains) a popular tourist destination:

> A peculiar feature of the Finnish lakes is the number of long narrow ridges of land which stretch out into the water. They consist not of rock but of rubble. Sometimes they stretch for miles, undulating, now a hundred feet in height, and now almost level with the surface of the water. Often they have the appearance of an artificial embankment, so narrow, and regular, and steep are they . . . Punkaharju, near Nyslott, one of the most beautiful spots in Finland, is just such a ridge. Sometimes a long, low tongue of land, a few feet wide and almost level with the water, shoots out from an island across the channel till it almost meets a similar tongue jetting out from the other side. They are continued under water, and a couple of poles indicate where they dip sufficiently to allow the steamer to pass. (Scott, *Through Finland to St. Petersburg*, pp. 130–31)

2   In the event, Aino Sibelius did not join them at Viborg (Newmarch describes her as 'never a good traveller and fully occupied with her young daughters at home' (*Jean Sibelius*, p. 25/p. 16)).

43 ROSA NEWMARCH TO JEAN SIBELIUS [ORIGINAL IN FRENCH]

10 May 1910.
Hôtel 'Ville de Paris'
Морская 16.
St Petersburg.

Dear and most honoured friend,

I thank you warmly for your letter, received yesterday. We arrived in Petersburg on Sunday, but for the time being, we are poor creatures. In Moscow there was an almost tropical heat, whereas here we have encountered a cold rain. The contrast has given us a terrible cold, and I have had to spend the entire day in bed. I don't dare go out today either. Miss Johnson has been affected in her eyes. But I think all of this will be over by the end of the week, and perhaps then we will be used to the change in climate. In any case, even if the conditions are, as you say, 'primitive', I think that life in Finland is cleaner and healthier than in Russia. Although I like Moscow and the Muscovites very much. We shall quietly stay here for a few days because we don't want to arrive in Finland ill and tired.

What you propose seems very interesting to me, and I cannot express to you how happy and grateful I am for this generous welcome. Only I am terribly afraid of wasting your time. You, who know me so well now, will you tell Madame Sibelius that I am a very straightforward person, and that we are both of us very easy to know and without affectation?

You will have plenty of time to tell me about everything you have done since last year, and we can talk about the future, and about the Birmingham concert. At the moment, I no longer have any voice, but it is coming back a little today. So I shall write to you on Saturday, and I hope that next week we can meet in Viborg. See you soon, and believe always in my sincere friendship

    Rosa Newmarch.

If a registered letter arrives for me at Jarvenpää, I would ask you to keep it for me until I see you in Viborg. I gave this address to my daughter, not knowing when I would be leaving Petersburg.[1]

---

[1] At this time, Newmarch was at work on a translation of the libretto of Musorgsky's *Boris Godunov* (to be published by Breitkopf & Härtel in Germany, and W. Bessel & Co. in Russia) and was dealing with the proofs of this during her journey.

44 ROSA NEWMARCH TO JEAN SIBELIUS
[ORIGINAL IN FRENCH]

                              Ville de Paris
                              Morskaïa 16.
                              [St Petersburg]
                          Saturday [14 May 1910].

Dear and most honoured friend,

I think we would do well to take advantage of this good weather. Therefore we will leave Petersburg next Wednesday for Viborg. We can wait for you there until Thursday, if that suits you. Only, send me a wire to let me know which hotel you are staying at? Forgive me for writing in such haste, I have so much to do today. Best wishes,

    à vous de cœur
    Rosa Newmarch.

45 ROSA NEWMARCH TO JEAN SIBELIUS [TELEGRAM, ORIGINAL IN FRENCH]¹

Petersburg
16/5/1910

I have been asked to stay until Friday. Ньюмарчъ

---

¹ This telegram is at NLF Coll.206.53. Sibelius travelled to Viborg on 19 May, meeting Newmarch and Elisabeth Johnson there the following day. They travelled first to the rapids at Imatra, and then to Lake Saimaa, before heading to Helsinki and Järvenpää (Newmarch's extensive impressions of her stay are recorded in *Jean Sibelius*, pp. 27–35/pp. 16–24). Sibelius was pleased to see Newmarch and enjoyed being away from Helsinki, but his impressions of her travelling companion were more ambivalent, as illustrated by this letter to his wife:

> It's strange how different Rosa seems here. So very easygoing. She has also found somewhere a certain Miss Johnson – a real old-fashioned maid dressed in ermine. A far from beautiful sight. But it is better to keep a straight face. They are quite pretentious. But Rosa always shows what a wonderful person she is. Full of imagination and understanding. (21 May 1910, in *Syysilta*, p. 161)

According to Newmarch's memoirs (as prepared by Elsie after her death), Newmarch and Johnson also took a steamboat trip through the archipelago to Porvoo (Swedish: Borgå), and visited Sibelius's birthplace of Hämeenlinna (Swedish: Tavastehus), as well as Tampere (Swedish: Tammerfors).

46 ROSA NEWMARCH TO JEAN SIBELIUS [ORIGINAL IN FRENCH]

Hôtel Phoenix
Abo.¹
Thursday [9 June 1910]

Dearest and honoured friend,

We arrived yesterday at around 4 o'clock. The town is very smiling and pretty in this good weather, the lighthouses and the gardens all in flower and delicious. We climbed the Värdbergen [*sic*] where we spent a quiet hour.² Today we shall go to Runsala;³ and tomorrow at 5 o'clock we take the boat to Stockholm. I feel this it is what I ought to do now, although the thought of leaving Finland makes me sadder than I can say. I should so much have preferred to settle somewhere for the rest of the summer. But it's better not to let oneself be tempted, as I must not neglect my work and family obligations any longer. I have learnt two things that are very important to me: that it is not really very difficult to visit Finland, so I am not as cut off from the life of my dear and good friend as I had previous thought I was; and secondly that Finland works a true poetic and restful charm on me. Certainly have I learned many other things besides, and above all to know your wife a little, which counts for much, since now I understand that there is a source of strength and true tenderness in your life. Truly you have much to rejoice in, because with her and the charming and kind young creatures who surround you, you have no reason to fear being alone and without purpose in this world. Even if you were never to write another note of music again, you have there something that would occupy you for the rest of your life with dignity. But you will write many things, stronger and more beautiful than the works of your youth, precisely because your existence now teaches you new experiences every day. I think that even the most gifted people only begin to understand the great truths in ways that in our youth we are stupid enough to believe <u>too ordinary</u>. I mean, the simple things in life, which are in the end the most important. I am not advising you to write a 'Sinfonia Domestica'![4] It is not necessary to render <u>in realistic sounds</u> Margarita's cries when she does not want to go to bed! It is just that I believe that in the life you are currently leading you are perhaps approaching humanity and matters of the soul more closely than when you imagine yourself to be freer and more impassioned. You see, I am trying to joke, but nonetheless I am not at all in a mocking mood. I am very sad to be leaving, it's part of the sorrow of life! But I feel that we are even better friends now that I know your 'home' and your family.[5] I shall write to you later. My best wishes to Madame Sibelius, I hope this is only the beginning of our acquaintance. And for you, dear friend, I wish you all that is good for you and your work – but most of all for <u>you</u>. You think that I am putting the man and his character before his art? Not entirely. But I admit that for me it's very difficult to see them individually, separately.

    à vous de cœur
        <u>Rosa Newmarch</u>.

My address in Stockholm
   Hôtel Anglais
   Stureplan.
Miss Johnson sends tanti saluti.[6]

[1] The Finnish name for Åbo is Turku.
[2] 'Observatory Hill', from where a panorama of Turku is visible.
[3] 'Numerous small steamers play on the river between the town and the islands, of which Runsalo, a large island six miles long lying just as the mouth of the river, is the favourite resort . . . This beautiful island, now the property of the town, was formerly a royal domain. It has some bold and picturesque cliffs, and the climate is so mild in this sheltered spot that trees grow luxuriantly which are seldom to be found in other parts of Finland. . . . On a hot summer day this leafy island, redolent with the scent of the pines, is a very paradise' (Scott, *Through Finland to St. Petersburg*, p. 92).
[4] Newmarch's reference suggests something of her mild antipathy towards the music of Richard Strauss, although this did not prevent her from writing a long and appreciative programme note on the *Sinfonia Domestica* for a Promenade Concert on 25 August 1908:

> The programme of the Sinfonia Domestica (The Home Symphony) has been a great stumbling block to a certain class of people who believe that no beautiful poetry or music can be woven around any subject which is not of the heaviest epic of dramatic calibre. It is perhaps unnecessary to point out that these objections usually proceed from those who are deficient in imagination and poetic vision. A day in the life of three human beings may be packed full of poetry and emotional experience, strangely and fascinatingly interwoven with the commonplaces of daily existence; the beauty and interest of the inner life being actually enhanced by incongruous and contrasting surroundings. Poets have long since dealt fearlessly with similar subjects, and where a Victor Hugo, a Wordsworth, or a Tennyson has led the way, a modern musician is, happily, free to follow. The love of a husband and wife, and their mutual love for their child is a subject of sufficient dignity. It neither stands in need of apology nor of a symbolical interpretation. We may accept it simply as it is presented to us.

At the same time, Newmarch's comments were astutely pitched to appeal to Sibelius's own ambivalence about Strauss's music and confirm (as well as flatter) him in his own musical direction. Although *Don Juan* had appealed to him enormously upon hearing it in Berlin in 1890, by 1910, Sibelius had begun to distance himself from the rhetorical and orchestral opulence of Strauss's music, especially as he began work on the Fourth Symphony.

[5] 'Home' in English in the original.
[6] 'all good wishes' (*It.*).

47 ROSA NEWMARCH TO JEAN SIBELIUS
[ORIGINAL IN FRENCH]

52, Campden Hill Square,
W.
13 July, 1910.[1]

Dearest and honoured friend,

How difficult it is to write, once one has returned to work and daily life! I've been back here since the 25th of June, and although you are very often in my thoughts, I have not been able to find a moment to send you a brief line. We had such beautiful weather for our journey. From Abo to Stockholm it was a long poem of light waxing and falling on waters of utter tranquility, like the crystal sea in the Revelation of St John.[2] And from Stockholm to Jönköping the same thing. Only, as I travelled ever further from Finland and Russia, I began to feel sad. Because you know that both countries are dear to me because of the good friends who live there, and who knows whether it will ever be possible to make such a long journey again, a journey that already seems a little like a dream? I immediately dived into the affairs and troubles of life; but what does that matter. I have begun the translation of this terrible libretto of 'The Queen of Spades'![3] Is it possible that one can bother setting such trifles to music! No, I cannot really bear this opera in my mature years. And here is London wrapped in a very thick atmosphere of opera. People speak of Beecham and opera, opera and Beecham without end. London is like a dog which can only eat one bone at a time. If only it would swallow the operatic bone quickly![4]

I am sending you the photographs. What a shame that I took you against the light, or I should have had a quite charming photograph of Madame Sibelius. Something can be seen through the shadows.[5]

Mr Kling returned several weeks ago, and then left immediately for Geneva, where his mother died several days ago. How strange it seems to me, this good fortune of still having a mother until one is more than 50! It seems that poor Kling was still rather ill during his trip on the Volga, and that several times he regretted not having come with us to a cooler climate and in healthier conditions.

That's all I can write to you for the moment. Miss Johnson leaves for Ireland tomorrow. I expected Granville Bantock on Saturday, but he wired to say that is was impossible to leave Birmingham. He wrote to me of his great regret for the fiasco with the concert, but for the time being, the Jewish element is very dominant in Birmingham.[6]

I don't ask you to write me long letters, only let me know what you are doing during the autumn, because I would make a long journey to hear one of your symphonies or orchestral poems.

My affectionate greetings to Madame Sibelius and the children. It's good in this world of pretensions and banal and undistinguished enthusiasms to know that somewhere in the world, buried in the granite rocks of Finland, there are real diamonds – hearts and spirits that are as sincere and strong as yours. I think that all true great souls were thus. It is a consolation when one must live in a social circle which resembles a drop of water under a microscope in which very elementary creatures are devouring each other. We'll soon make a good meal ourselves, I hope!

May the Lord protect you. A vous de cœur,
　　Rosa Newmarch.

---

[1] Possibly also 18 July – the handwriting is obscured here by overwriting.

[2] 'And before the throne there was a sea of glass like unto crystal' (Revelation 4:6).

[3] Newmarch had been commissioned to translate the libretto of Tchaikovsky's *Queen of Spades* by the publisher Jurgenson whilst in Russia earlier that year. Her critical comments about the quality of the libretto are in distinct contrast to her earlier judgments: 'The libretto of this opera, one of the best ever set by the composer, was originally prepared by M. Modeste Tchaikovsky . . . It is difficult in a few words to do justice to a subject which is really intensely dramatic, and the thrill of which is enhanced by the introduction of a supernatural element' ('The Development of National Opera in Russia (Fourth Paper): Tchaikovsky', *Proceedings of the Musical Association* 30 (1903–04), 57–73 (66–7)).

[4] Thomas Beecham (1879–1961), British conductor. In 1910, Beecham used his family's wealth to stage a series of three opera seasons at Covent Garden and His Majesty's Theatre, thereby transforming musical life in London in a way that mirrored Wood's commitment to symphonic music at Queen's Hall. Beecham's first, month-long season opened at Covent Garden on 19 February 1910 and included the first British performances of Strauss's *Elektra* ('Music: The Beecham Opera Season', *The Times*, 19 February 1910, 8), as well as Sullivan's *Ivanhoe*, Wagner's *Tristan und Isolde*, Delius's *A Village Romeo and Juliet*, Smyth's *The Wreckers*, Debussy's *L'Enfant prodigue*, Humperdinck's *Hänsel und Gretel* and Bizet's *Carmen* ('Opera at Covent Garden', *Musical Times* 51 (1910), 227–8). Between May and July, Beecham staged a season

4a. 'Sibelius at Lake Saïma', in Rosa Newmarch, *Jean Sibelius: A Short Story of a Long Friendship* (Boston, 1939)

4b. 'Mr. and Mrs. Jean Sibelius in their Garden at Jarvenpää', in Rosa Newmarch, *Jean Sibelius: A Short Story of a Long Friendship* (Boston, 1939)

of comic operas at His Majesty's Theatre, including Offenbach's *Les Contes d'Hoffman*, Humperdinck's *Hänsel und Gretel*, Missa's *Muguette*, Stanford's *Shamus O'Brien*, Massenet's *Werther*, Mozart's *Die Entführung aus dem Serail*, *Le Nozze di Figaro* and *Così fan tutte*, Johann Strauss's *Die Fledermaus* and Richard Strauss's *Feuersnot* ('The Beecham Opera Comique Season', *Musical Times* 51 (1910), 378; 'The Beecham Opera Season', *Musical Times* 51 (1910), 443–4; 'The Beecham Opera Season', *Musical Times* 51 (1910), 525–6). The year closed with an extensive run of operas at Covent Garden, including d'Albert's *Tiefland*, Thomas's *Hamlet*, Leroux's *Le Chemineau*, Gounod's

Faust, Verdi's *Rigoletto*, Beethoven's *Fidelio*, Strauss's *Elektra* and *Salome*, Mozart's *Don Giovanni* and *Le Nozze di Figaro*, Wagner's *Tannhäuser*, *Tristan und Isolde* and *Der fliegende Holländer*, Rossini's *Il Barbiere di Siviglia*, Offenbach's *Les Contes d'Hoffman*, Humperdinck's *Hänsel und Gretel*, Clutsam's *A Summer Night*, Bizet's *Carmen* and Debussy's *Pelléas et Mélisande* ('Beecham Opera at Covent Garden', Musical Times 51 (1910), 732; 'Beecham Opera Season', Musical Times 51 (1910), 789–90; 'Beecham Opera Season', Musical Times 52 (1911), 28). Although Newmarch seems to have been rather sceptical about Beecham's 1910 opera seasons, she took a greater and more sympathetic interest in his work thereafter, not least because he collaborated with Diaghilev's Ballets Russes on a series of performances of Russian operas and ballets in 1911, 1912 and 1913. For Beecham's own account of the 1910 seasons, see *A Mingled Chime: Leaves from an Autobiography* (London, 1944), pp. 87–105.

5 The first edition of Newmarch's memoir of Sibelius (published in the United States) contains, alongside some more official portraits, two photographs that were evidently taken by Newmarch during her trip to Finland in 1910: 'Sibelius at Lake Saïma' (opposite p. 29) and 'Mr and Mrs Jean Sibelius at their garden at Jarvenpää' (opposite p. 43, and possibly the photograph referred to in this letter, as it is clearly shot against the sun). Despite their poor quality, they are reproduced as illustrations 4a and 4b in the present edition.

6 It has not been confirmed to whom Newmarch is referring here.

48 ROSA NEWMARCH TO JEAN SIBELIUS [ORIGINAL IN FRENCH]

52, Campden Hill Square,
London. W.
5 November, 1910.

Dearest and honoured friend,

I have long owed you a letter with an explanation of the telegram I sent from Winchelsea.[1] It was the very moment when Mr Wood was preparing his programmes for the Symphony Concerts. They were very interesting, with several novelties, and he thought that if your symphony were ready,[2] it would add prestige to the programmes. You replied that you did not think you could guarantee that it would be finished in time.[3] Then, several weeks later, after a meeting of the Queen's Hall Orchestra Concert committee, they completely changed Mr Wood's programmes for commercial reasons, removing the novelties and replacing them with Beethoven symphonies! This timid and backwards policy distressed me, and I think that Mr Wood was also offended. But in the end, what can one do? Even millionaires don't like taking risks!

They are poor people who have the courage of their convictions. In the meantime we must have patience.

I very often wonder: what is he doing, what is he going to do? Will you travel to Stockholm, to Berlin to conduct? I see that 'In Memoriam' will be performed in several cities; in Antwerp, which isn't very far from London. I am charmed by your 'Impromptu' for women's voices. There's a text absolutely made for you. The music is very fresh and characteristic too. The only thing I don't like is the title. Why Impromptu?[4]

For many months now I have been working very much; even too much. But at present I am well, despite everything. I have had plenty of unpleasant stories since my return, principally because of my husband's affairs. I had long suspected that he was making a mess of them, and I have tried for several years to persuade him to sell this house and to face up to his affairs honestly. Seeing that, like many people whose judgment is rather weak, he was very obstinate, I ended up by not discussing it any more. However, as you have seen, I set about working and making myself independent of anything that might happen. At last, during the summer, several things occurred which forced him to tell me the whole truth, and this was most disagreeable! Poor man, it's not that he's not honest, or even hardworking. Rather, he lacks judgment about the way life works. If he has to choose between two paths, it's always the worse and the most roundabout that he prefers. But let's not speak of this any more! I am not wasting any energy on trying to change the way he sees things; I shall just have to take control of matters myself and try to prevent him from making too many blunders. Fortunately John is going into the hospital in December, and for two years, at least, he will earn his crust without much help. As for me, as long as I am well, I make enough money to lead a tolerably decent life, and I am even putting something aside. Who knows? Perhaps I'll end up being a wealthy woman!

And you – and dear Madame Sibelius – and the girls? Is life going well? Do you have snow already? I can picture the pretty little house surrounded by Weinachtsbäumer,[5] and Madame Sibelius's labours in the garden completely covered in snow. But perhaps it's still too early for winter. It's been cold here for three days now. Miss Johnson is getting ready to flee to Florence. I think next year we must absolutely travel a little, don't you think? It could be good for your art, since Helsingfors is a little far from the great centres of music. The other day, I saw that Madame Akté [sic] had just sung at a Sunday concert, under the direction of Landon Ronald. I am so sorry that I didn't hear her. I can't see her name any more, and I don't know what she is doing here.[6]

In December I lost my dear friend, Mary Wakefield.[7] What a great heart and strong spirit! All of northern England was saddened. But it is better for her. I spent a week with her at the start of July. She was feeling better, and we took long drives across her wild and beautiful country. She never tired of hearing about your music and about the country that inspires you. But she felt that her life's work was almost completed; and it seemed that the doctors feared for a cerebral lesion. She was very happy the day she died, which she spent with several friends who had come to see her. During the night, she suddenly lost consciousness and several hours later she was dead. This was lucky, since she would never have regained the ability to speak and to work. But she was only 55, and a rare soul, and so courageous!

This is a sad latter I am sending you, yet I am not really sad at heart at the moment. Life always interests me, and death yet more so.

It's pointless to say 'write to me'! Only, should you find yourself anywhere near London, in Antwerp, in Paris, send me a telegram!

Bantock is at work on a symphonic poem on a theme of Dante.[8] Elgar has just completed a Violin Concerto, which people talk about in a very eulogistic manner.[9] Dr Walford Davies has written a very modern overture in a very ancient style.[10] There is much talk of _English_ music, and he is the only really _English_ composer, in the sense that Wordsworth and Tennyson are English. Although his talent is perhaps rather limited, he interests me for this reason. I fear that Elgar's music resembles those little chicks which one raises in an 'incubator'.[11] One must always pamper it; it lacks the strength to withstand a poor performance. Yet truly great music can survive many atrocities. Write music that does not suffer too much when it is mistreated. During his visit to England I met Rachmaninov.[12] I have never been keen on his music, apart from his songs. But it seems to me that he is a very singular character and made to be respected. He is so reserved – almost as much as you; and the courage to defend his opinions when attacked, which is becoming rather rare in our all too compliant and servile world.

All my greetings to your dear wife and the children. We speak of them often. And for you, dear friend, my affection which never changes, and all my best wishes for the health of your soul and body. A vous de cœur

<u>Rosa Newmarch</u>.

---

1. This telegram has not been traced, but it is referred to in an entry in Sibelius's diary (4 September 1910, *Dagbok*, p. 53).
2. Sibelius had been at work on his Fourth Symphony at the time of Newmarch's visit, and she had evidently told Wood of the new work.
3. Sibelius's response has yet to be traced.
4. Newmarch's translation of Sibelius's *Impromptu*, Op. 19 (1902, revised 1910) was published in Leipzig that year by Breitkopf & Härtel.
5. 'Christmas trees' (*Ger.*).
6. Aino Ackté (1876–1944), Finnish soprano. Ackté was in London in late 1910 in order to perform the title role in the first British performance of Strauss's *Salome*, at Covent Garden on 8 December (conducted by Beecham). The production of the opera aroused considerable discussion in the musical press, not least because Wilde's original play was still banned by the Lord Chamberlain, so it seems surprising that Newmarch was unaware of the reason for Ackté's presence in London. Ackté was famed not just for her vocal interpretation of the lead role in the opera (she would regularly programme the final scene in orchestral concerts), but also for the fact that she danced 'The Dance of the Seven Veils' herself. The concert referred to by Newmarch has not been identified, although the programme for Ronald's Sunday concert at the Royal Albert Hall (as advertised in *The Times*, 28 October 1910, 8) included Senta's Ballad from Wagner's *Der fliegende Holländer*.
7. Wakefield in fact died on 16 September 1910.
8. *Dante and Beatrice* (1910), a revised version of *Dante* (1901).
9. Elgar's Violin Concerto, Op. 61, was premiered by Fritz Kreisler at Queen's Hall on 10 November 1910. Even before the first performance, Ernest Newman had written a detailed and appreciative account of the work ('Elgar's Violin Concerto', *Musical Times* 51 (1910), 631–4), to which Newmarch may be alluding here.
10. Henry Walford Davies (1869–1941), English composer and organist. His *Festal Overture* was given at Queen's Hall on 20 September ('The Promenade Concerts', *Musical Times* 51 (1910), 657–8 (658)) and again on 1 October and 5 November ('Promenade Concerts', *Musical Times* 51 (1910), 731–2 (731)). The two composers were introduced by Newmarch during Sibelius's trip to Britain in 1912, as related here by Henry Colles:

> The Birmingham Festival, at which the *Song of St. Francis* was given its first performance, was otherwise memorable for the visit of Jean Sibelius to this country to conduct the first performance of his Symphony No. 4 in A minor. Mrs. Rosa Newmarch brought the two composers together, carrying them off to tea in an interval of the London rehearsals. Something was said about the popularity of Walford's 'Solemn Melody'. 'What is this

Solemn Melody?' asked Sibelius innocently. 'It is Dr. Walford Davies's Valse Triste,' was their hostess's apt rejoinder.

Sibelius and Walford, though without much language in common, found each other congenial. Mrs. Newmarch brought Sibelius out to dine and spend a quiet evening at West Heath Drive, and the two retired to Walford's study after dinner to browse over music. Walford played on the piano some Haydn which Sibelius evidently enjoyed. 'But,' he said, 'Haydn builds up his harmony from the bass with the melody as its crown. Now I think of my melody first and of the harmony as depending from it.' The remark seemed to go some way towards explaining what it is that separates Sibelius's Fourth Symphony decisively from the classical prototype. (H. C. Colles, *Walford Davies: A Biography* (London, 1942), pp. 102–3)

Colles's description of Sibelius's compositional style was first given (without reference to Walford Davies) in 'Jean Sibelius', in *Great Contemporaries: Essays by Various Hands* (London, 1935), pp. 396–407 (p. 403).

[11] English in the original.
[12] Rachmaninov performed his Second Piano Concerto and conducted his Second Symphony at the Leeds Festival on 12 and 13 October 1910 ('Leeds Musical Festival', *The Times*, 13 October 1910, 12, 'Leeds Musical Festival', *The Times*, 14 October 1910, 10, 'The Leeds Festival', *Musical Times* 51 (1910), 719–20 and 729). Newmarch translated several of Rachmaninov's songs, as well as the libretto of his opera *Aleko*, all for Chester.

49 ROSA NEWMARCH TO JEAN SIBELIUS [ORIGINAL IN FRENCH]

52, Campden Hill Square,
W.
22 December, 1910

Dearest and most honoured friend,

I saw Madame Acté [*sic*] yesterday and we spoke together for a long time.[1] I find her very likeable, and for a prima donna at the height of a brilliant success, she seems very straightforward and unspoiled. She is a true artist and I think she is also a superior woman. For all these reasons I was sad to find her very bothered and unhappy about the collapse of the tour which you were planning to undertake together, and abort which people were beginning to talk a lot in Germany and even here. She wondered – 'why has he changed his mind so suddenly about this tour?'[2] And in truth, my dear friend, if everything she told me about the detailed arrangements is true – and I don't think she is a woman to exaggerate – you ought to have some very strong reason for going back on your intentions now that the preparations have been made. I know you are a little Stimmungsvoll[3] when it comes to the small things in life, but very certain in great matters. Thus you ought to have a good explanation. I can well imagine several reasons for not embarking on such a tour <u>at the outset</u>. I know that you don't much like the role of composer-conductor; that perhaps you don't want to interrupt your pleasant life in Jarvenpää; that you detest advertising, etc. But as it was organised – ? But I have neither the right to scold you, nor the intention of doing so! I can only tell you that I was expecting much of these concerts, because it is time that the world knew better the beauty and powerful originality of your music. And then to travel like that with a singer who really understands your songs (because she speaks of them with much intelligence) is such a rare chance in this world of so few ideals. I think that I am almost as distressed as poor Acté [*sic*]. And then I worry a little, and wonder – is it because of your health? Have you really acted wisely? At least write to this excellent singer. She suffers because of her amour propre – and <u>you</u> of all people should know what that means. But all the same she speaks of you and of your music most touchingly.

 à vous de cœur
  Rosa Newmarch

---

[1] Since her letter to Sibelius of 5 November 1910, Newmarch had made contact with Ackté, as the following letter (one of four, all written in French, NLF Coll.4.12)) demonstrates:

           52, Campden Hill Square,
                W.
            12 December 1910.

 Dear Madame,
  I barely dare write to you, since you are doubtless very busy, and I would not like to trouble you for anything in the world. Only I think that we have a mutual interest – our admiration, and our friendship, for Jean Sibelius. He has spoken so often of you to me; and, in talking about his songs, he has said a hundred times, 'Ah, you should hear Madame Ackté sing them, she understands my music so well!' In June I spent several weeks in Helsingfors, and we saw each other almost every day then. But you know how poor he is at writing letters! I would be so pleased to hear his news.
  I am delighted that you are thinking of giving some concerts together. We must certainly organise something for London. I am always working to make his music appreciated, but appreciation is slow, because his art is of an originality that is quite out of the ordinary. It yields itself slowly, and

with reserve. I think that it is for a simpler, more distinguished, and yet more refined generation than the present one.

But I am running away with myself! Forgive me, Madame, and if you have a few moments at your disposal, please allow me to come and see you?

Accept the expression of my respectful consideration and my most enthusiastic admiration,
<u>Rosa Newmarch.</u>

2   Sibelius had abandoned a planned tour of Germany in early 1911, during which a new work – a setting of Edgar Allen Poe's 'The Raven' – would be performed (the tour was to be organised by Emil Gutmann, the impresario who gave Mahler's Eighth Symphony its nickname of 'The Symphony of a Thousand'). When Ackté heard of his decision, she wrote to Sibelius:

> Herr Sibelius, I am not accustomed to being treated in this fashion and being made a laughing stock. It would have been more honest if you had said right at the outset that the idea of Sibelius concerts abroad do not appeal to you. You would have saved me a great deal of trouble . . . and I would have been spared this ridiculous and embarrassing position *vis-à-vis* Gutmann and others, with whom you have ruined my prospects for the future. (letter of 13 December 1910, translation in Tawaststjerna, *Sibelius*, vol. 2, p. 162)

Sibelius's letter to Newmarch accords with his reactions elsewhere. To Carpelan (12 December 1910), he stated: 'I leave the diva Ackté to drown in her own publicity . . . When I give a concert no diva or prima donna should be the centre of interest – it's my symphonic music that will triumph', and was particularly offended to read an interview with Ackté in which she was said to have declared: 'I am taking Sibelius with me' (cited in ibid., p. 163). Sibelius's attitude towards the proposed tour may also have been complicated by his slow progress on *The Raven* (as well as premature reports about its progress in the German press), his need to find time to work on the Fourth Symphony, and the ill health of his wife. Relations between composer and singer were soon mended, however, and plans for a vocal *scena* for Ackté eventually came to fruition in the form of *Luonnotar*.

3   'Prone to introspection' (*Ger.*).

50   JEAN SIBELIUS TO ROSA NEWMARCH
[ORIGINAL IN GERMAN][1]

Järvenpää, Finland 1/I/1911

Chère Madame,

Je vous remercie de vos deux lettres.[2] – The first found me in a thoroughly bad humour. I had just come back from Berlin, where I had been staying for two months. As usual I acquired an unconquerable distaste for the 'modern tendency'.[3] And out of this grew a sense of solitude.

I received your second friendly letter concerning Madame Ackté, whom I admire, and I must confess that there is no other way I could have acted.

The affair took a direction quite unlike what had been presented to me at the outset. Above all the publicity.

As the publicity described precisely and in detail what sort of composition it is, which direction it takes etc., all without the piece being finished – the whole composition became impossible for me.

Furthermore they wanted to present me as a completely unknown composer – in Munich! Etc!

The children thank you with all their heart for your great kindness. My wife has been in bed for eight weeks with rheumatoid arthritis; a wretched life for her!

I am busy on new works. In Christiania I conducted,[4] and in February I shall be giving concerts in Gothenburg, Riga and Helsingfors. – It seems as though my Symphony IV will be ready in February.

To my astonishment I see that my works are being performed a good deal on the continent, although they have no 'Modernity' in them.

I am very curious about Bantock's new work.

Forgive my writing <u>to you</u> in German. Mais que faire!*[5]

My wife and I send you best wishes and greetings with all our heart.

    Your most devoted
    Jean Sibelius

*I have no time to write French at the moment.

---

[1] Letter partly cited in Newmarch, *Jean Sibelius*, pp. 35–6/p. 24.
[2] 'Thank you for your two letters.' (*Fr.*).
[3] Sibelius's diary records that whilst in Berlin, he heard works by Rachmaninov ('there is a feeling for sonority and culture but a certain tameness'), Arensky ('good, naïve'), and Reger ('National, German, a little too ornate and occasional *longeurs*, but just because of its German quality, good') as well as Debussy's String Quartet ('A "small-scale" composer! Refined, but in my view, small-scale') (*Dagbok*, pp. 57–8, translated in Tawaststjerna, *Sibelius*, vol. 2, pp. 109 and 146).
[4] Since 1925, the modern name of Christiania has been Oslo. Sibelius arrived there on 2 October, conducting a concert of his works (including the Second Symphony, *Night Ride and Sunrise*, the Suite from *Swanwhite*, *The Dryad* and *In memoriam*) on 8 October, before heading to Berlin (*Dagbok*, pp. 55–9)
[5] 'What is to be done!' (*Fr.*).

51 ROSA NEWMARCH TO JEAN SIBELIUS
[ORIGINAL IN FRENCH]

52, Campden Hill Square,
W.
8 January 1911.

Dearest and honoured friend,

How happy I am to receive your fine long letter! I have long suspected that you dislike publicity; but how to make that clear to a <u>prima donna</u>, even one as likeable and intelligent as Madame Ackté? That is their life, isn't it? Now it would appear that it is the life of great creative artists too. The recent publicity for Elgar's new concerto is a little repulsive; and as for Strauss………? But is it really worse than in the past? It seems to me that Wagner was not the first to understand the art of selling himself! It's the growth in the number of papers and the public that makes this all more and more inevitable. Personally I have seen nothing in the papers apart from a short notice in a German musical journal, and more or less the same thing in an English newspaper. But let's not talk of this any more. If your actions are not good from the worldly and commercial point of view, at least I understand them well enough! You are a singular man, thank heavens! I love you dearly, and I respect you with all my heart; but because I am something of a woman of the world, and very ambitious when it comes to my friends, there are moments when I would be so weak as to say to you – 'let others take care of things for you'! But probably you're the one who is right.

I am sorry to learn that Madame Sibelius has been so ill. Give her <u>all my sympathy</u> and best wishes for a rapid recovery. But when your snows begin to melt, should she not go away for the start of spring? This illness must not take hold of her. Are there any spas nearer to you than Germany? I know you don't like it when people discuss your health, but when you tell me that you have just spent two months in Berlin – a city you don't like – I cannot prevent myself from anxiously wondering – 'what was he doing there, if not seeing doctors?' Do not hide you misfortunes from me should you have any – that is not true friendship. But perhaps I am worrying about nothing.

As for what you say about modern tendencies, I entirely share your opinion, that is to say, about modern German culture. There is no longer anything idealistic either in the art or the literature of this country. The books I read are extremely crude.[1] The music is equally coarse, noisy, and at the same time, not really original. But is all of that really modern? Is it not the case that for thinking, selective people, these recent emanations of the German school give off the odour of putrefaction rather than that of the freshness of morning? In France things are better, because they put more taste into things, and if their ideas are not so grandiose, at least they are not vulgar. In France they have long given up wanting to épater les bourgeois! The truth is simple: these days, people talk a lot about making art accessible to the public; but the works that are concocted with this aim in mind are no longer art. I wrote many stupid things on this subject in my youth, but now I am convinced that – apart from Volkslieder[2] and dance – there can be no such thing as music that is both democratic and artistic.[3] It is a contradiction in terms. But in Germany, and even here, we have – with this idea in mind of making music popular – created abominations by letting tradesmen get their hands on art, by promoting all kinds of small people as so-called 'artists', by creating a race of entrepreneurs and 'concert agents' who are worse than bandits! This might be modernity, but it isn't really progress, which always exists, but in very small quantities, throughout the centuries. Therefore I am not surprised that when you find yourself right in the midst of this whirlwind which goes nowhere, you feel 'alleingefühl'.[4] You should feel your isolation, because you are really not part of all that. I will say – and I don't care if I am the only person in the world to hold this opinion – that the most modern composer at the moment is neither Strauss, nor Debussy, nor any of their imitators, but – Sibelius. With your music I always expect something that will make me search and think, but which is at the same time not 'willed' – in short, inspiration – that most abused word. But since it is quite rare for people to like to search and think, and we have almost lost the gift of imagination (what, for example, do the most recent works of Strauss leave to the intuition or the imagination?), we must wait and see. An élite public, or even people who have not, for the moment at least, lost the sound sense of hearing, that's something that is slow to take shape. You will laugh, since I am much more impatient than you.[5]

I note of all the concerts that you are giving in the north of Europe with great interest. Unfortunately all of those cities are a little too far away to visit in winter! If you were to come closer – . But perhaps later, with the Fourth Symphony. At home at the moment I have the manuscripts of your four new songs. Tavaststjerna's words are pretty difficult to translate![6] But my Swedish friend, Mrs Sillem, has read them in English for me.

Farewell for today, since I have written too much. I am happy to receive a letter in German, as long as I don't have to reply in that language! Take care of yourselves, both of you, and try to cure poor, dear Madame as soon as possible. My affectionate greetings to the 'children'.

à vous de cœur,

<u>Rosa Newmarch.</u>

Henry Wood has just been made a knight! He is now Sir Henry Wood. It is the only honour that we give to both artists and grocers with great impartiality. Still, the intention is a good one, and it has pleased the public enormously.

---

[1] Newmarch's correspondence with John Lane reveals that she was regularly reading contemporary French and German fiction with a view to acquiring the translation rights for the Bodley Head. Reviewing a proposal to translate Anatole France's *Histoire comique*, she observed: 'Almost all the German contemporary novels touch upon these nasty, unnatural sides of life, but I am very much in favour of keeping them out of English editions, both from the moral and commercial points of view.' Clara Viebig's *Our Daily Bread* led her to remark that 'German realism always seems to me rather bald, and lacking in the subtlety of observation that saves Dostoievsky and Flaubert from becoming tiresome and commonplace', and the same author's *Absolvo te* was 'scarcely less sordid' (Undated letters from Newmarch to John Lane, Harry Ransom Humanities Research Center, University of Texas at Austin, John Lane Company Papers, Box 34, Folder 5).

[2] 'Folksongs' (*Ger.*).

[3] Contrast this with the following statement Newmarch made about Wood in 1904: 'Henry J. Wood is the democratic force in music. His greatest service to his art and his country lies undoubtedly in the fact that he has liberated music from its exclusive spirit and offered it to the people' (*Henry J. Wood*, p. 80).

[4] 'Sense of isolation, loneliness' (*Ger.*). This was a word used frequently by Sibelius to describe his moods.

[5] In his diary (16 January 1911), Sibelius noted: 'Rosa Newmarch has written with great understanding' (*Dagbok*, p. 67).

[6] Sibelius's *8 Songs*, Op. 61 (1910) also include, alongside five songs to texts by Karl August Tavaststjerna, settings of Bertel Gripenberg, Johan Ludvig Runeberg and Viktor Rydberg.

52 ROSA NEWMARCH TO JEAN SIBELIUS
[ORIGINAL IN FRENCH]

52, Campden Hill Square
W. 20 April 1911.

Dearest and honoured friend,

I don't know whether you are at home at the moment?[1] Here is the main reason for my letter. I have read in the papers that several of your country's musicians will come as representatives to the International Congress of Music at the end of May. Although I detest this Congress, with all its chauvinism, snobbery and vulgarity, I shall be very happy to greet your friends and compatriots on their arrival, and to do all I can to add to the pleasure of their visit to London.[2]

And you? And dear Madame Sibelius? And the children? And the 4th Symphony? It seems our friendship can be easily summed up in a series of ???

How beautiful your latest songs are – and how difficult to put into English! Above all the one called 'the enchantment of spring'![3]

I think that our house is sold.[4] We shall move soon, and neither you nor I shall ever see again my dear little room with my Michelangelos and my pictures of Mother Moscow, where you came several times, and where in years gone by I argued determinedly with Stasoff.[5] But since it is both necessary and good to do this, I won't spend too much time regretting and 'sentimentalising'. What does it matter where we spend the little time that is left for us on this earth provided we work and we remain worthy?

à vous de cœur,

Rosa Newmarch.

---

[1] Sibelius was at home in Finland in April 1911.
[2] The congress was to be held in London from 29 May to 3 June. A report on the conference lists Otto Andersson, Dr and Mrs Armas Launis, and Ilmari Krohn as the Finnish delegates and paper-givers ('The International Musical Congress, London, May 29 to June 3', *Musical Times* 52 (1911), 441–54). Newmarch's disdain for the congress's 'chauvinism, snobbery and vulgarity' may have been triggered by the kind of sentiments expressed in an article in the March issue of *The Musical Times*, which included statements such as 'the only rational course for the committee to adopt ... was to make it a great and memorable festival of British music', and quoted Lord Redesdale as saying: 'We desire foreigners to come here, and hear the best music that modern England can provide, and that they should become familiar with such names

as Elgar, Parry, Cowen, Mackenzie, and other names' ('The International Musical Congress, London, May 29 to June 3', *Musical Times* 52 (1911), 160–64 (160 and 162 respectively). The proceedings were published the next year as *Report of the Fourth Congress of the International Musical Society, London, 29th May–3rd June 1911* (London, 1912).

3 'Vårtagen', Op. 61, No. 8, with words by Gripenberg, translated by Newmarch as 'The Spell of Springtide'. Her translations of Sibelius's *8 Songs*, Op. 61 (1910) were published by Breitkopf & Härtel in 1911, along with her version of *Ukko the Fire-Maker*, Op. 32 (1902, revised 1910, also known as *The Origin of Fire*).

4 For all her stoicism, Newmarch was clearly devastated by the loss of the family home, and several rather ostentatious references to the move – although not the reasons for it – are made in her published memoir of Sibelius: 'In the spring of 1911 circumstances made it necessary to sell our house in Campden Hill Square, to which I was very much attached' (*Jean Sibelius*, p. 37/p. 25); 'The loss of my home to which I was very much attached, the wearisome search for another dwelling-place and the need for carrying on a considerable volume of work in the meanwhile . . . left me very tired at the close of the autumn season' (ibid., p. 38/p. 26); and 'I was . . . rather depressed about the loss of my old home in Campden Hill Square' (ibid., p. 45/p. 31).

5 Stasov had visited Newmarch regularly during his visit to London in 1901.

53 JEAN SIBELIUS TO ROSA NEWMARCH
[ORIGINAL IN GERMAN][1]

Järvenpää, Finland
2/V/1911

Chère Madame,

Thank you so much for your fine letter. From it I see that you are well. My family and I are healthy. We often think of you, chère Madame.

My Symphony IV is finished. It has twice been heard in concerts in Helsingfors.[2] Although the work is by no means a 'concert item', it has brought me many friends.

I have performed in Norway, Sweden and the Baltic provinces this year.[3]

It made me very sad that the familiar little room where I so often used to visit you, has passed into other hands.

But – your personality is so strong that it will not be difficult for you to found a new, warm home. –

I am glad you find my new songs attractive. My new symphony stands out as a complete protest against the compositions of today. Nothing – absolutely nothing of the circus about it.[4]

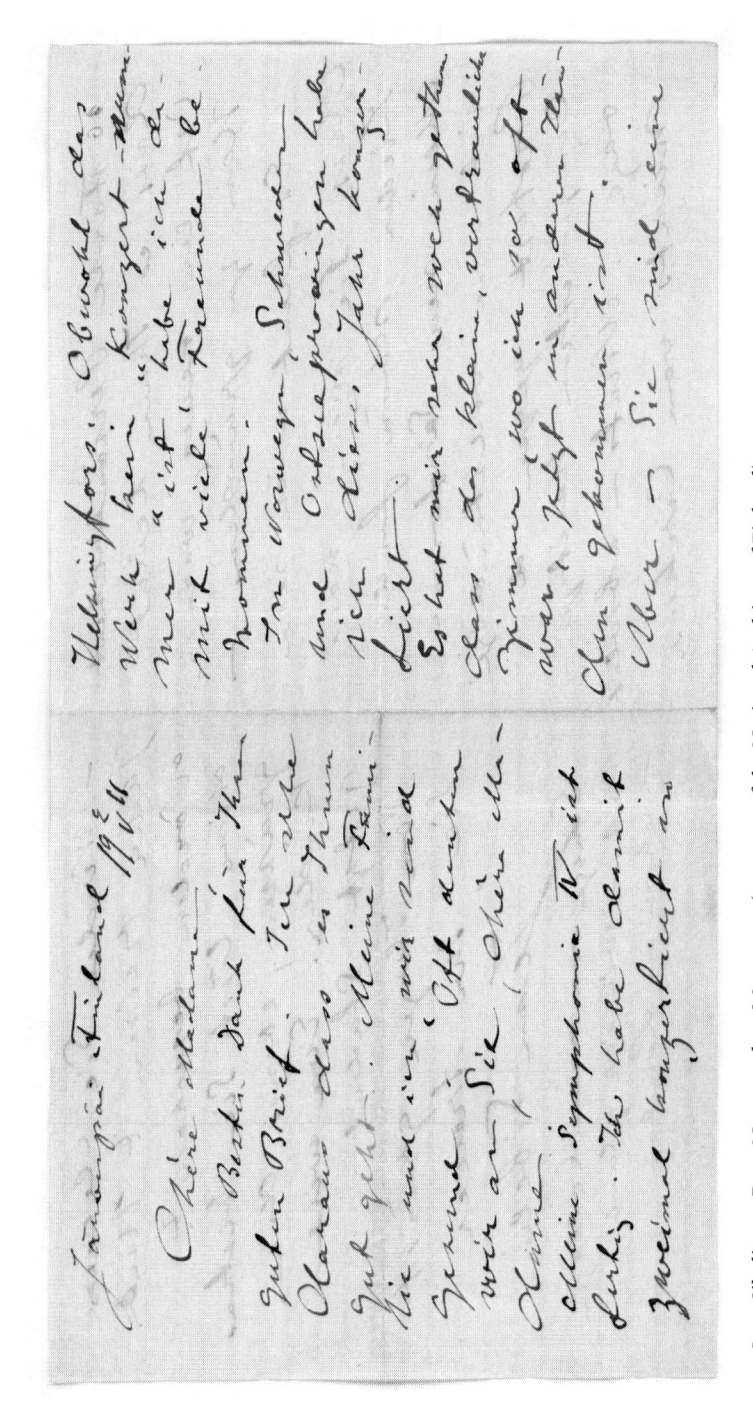

5. Jean Sibelius to Rosa Newmarch, 2 May 1911. (courtesy of the National Archives of Finland)

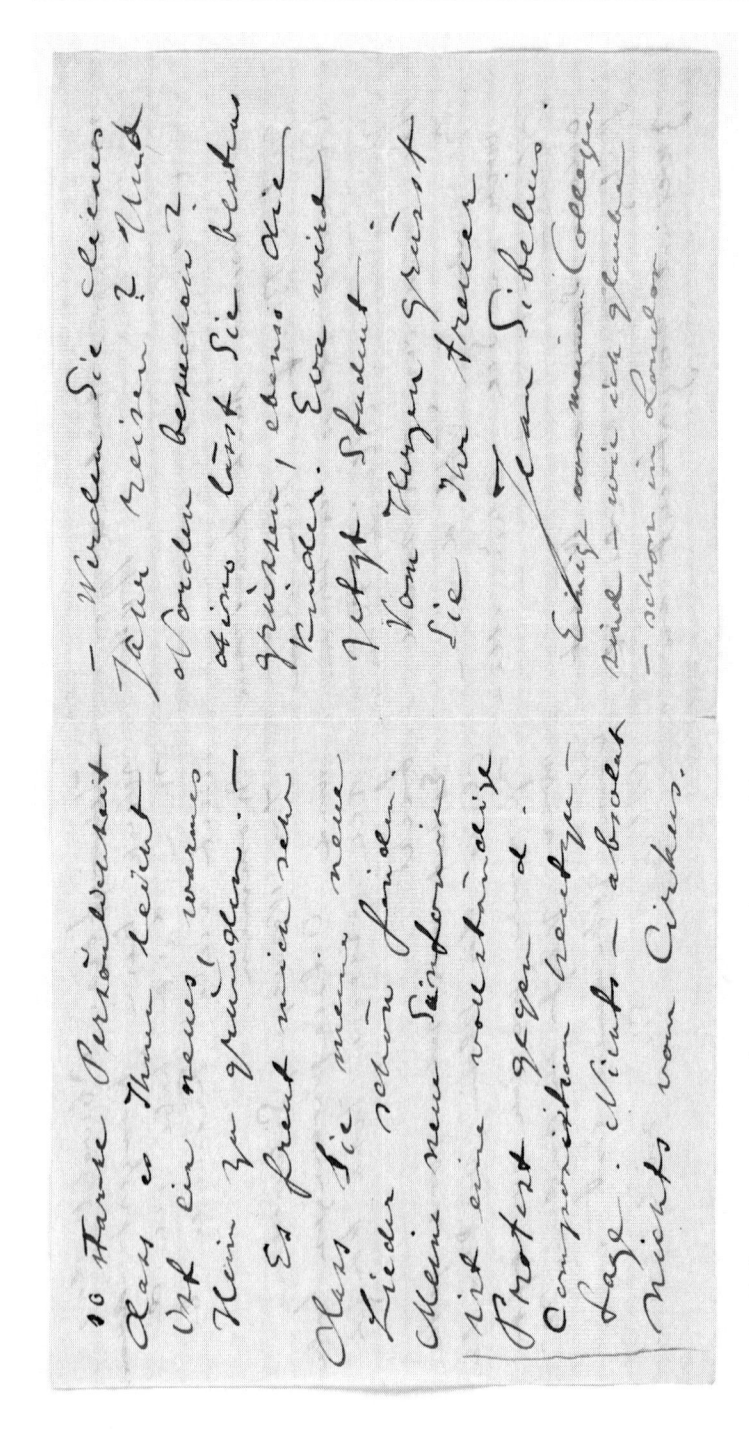

5. Jean Sibelius to Rosa Newmarch, 2 May 1911. (courtesy of the National Archives of Finland)

– Will you travel this year? And visit the North?

Aino sends her best wishes, and the children too! Eva is now to become a student.

With warmest wishes from your faithful

    Jean Sibelius.

Several of my colleagues are – I believe – already in London.

---

1. Letter partly cited in Newmarch, *Jean Sibelius*, pp. 36–7/ pp. 24–5.
2. Sibelius had completed the Fourth Symphony on 2 April, writing in his diary 'Jacta alea est!' ('the die is cast!') (*Dagbok*, p. 74), although revisions were subsequently made after its first performances in Helsinki on 3 and 5 April 1911.
3. Sibelius had conducted concerts of his own works in Gothenburg (Sweden) on 6 and 8 February 1911. Thereafter, he travelled to Latvia, where he gave concerts in Riga on 13, 15 and 16 February, and in Jelgava (Mitau) on 17 February (*Dagbok*, pp. 69–71). His trip to Norway had, in fact, taken place the previous year, when he appeared in Oslo on 8 October, before heading to Berlin.
4. Although usually reticent about his works, Sibelius seems to have been particularly keen to broadcast some kind of commentary on the Fourth Symphony. His comments to Newmarch echo statements made about the symphony in articles by both Carpelan ('As a whole the symphony can be regarded as a protest against prevalent musical tendencies') and Katila ('a sharp protest against the general trend in modern music') (cited in Tawaststjerna, *Sibelius*, vol. 2, p. 172).

54 ROSA NEWMARCH TO JEAN SIBELIUS [ORIGINAL IN FRENCH]

18 August. 1911.

                                  Heathfield
                              Chesham Bois.
                                        Bucks

Dearest and honoured friend,

Here we are for the time being in the country. We sold the old house in June, and at the last minute I found that it was more prudent not to take on another house for the time being at my own expense. Therefore I have rented this little 'cottage' with a garden, one hour from London.[1] I have done well, since life in the city is really unbearable this summer, because of the abnormal heat. I am writing to you in the garden, where I spend almost all my life, and I can assure you that I am relieving my woes by growing cabbages and green beans!

I have just received the cards letting me know (is that right?) that Eva is engaged?[2] But not yet married? You always used to tell me that Eva ought to marry to be happy! May she be as happy as possible! She is a dear and charming girl. I noted that she was already something of a young woman a year ago. She had much <u>savoir faire</u>, much tenderness. I think that her future husband is lucky to have found such a companion. Only she is very young to set out in life – this life which requires so much courage and devotion if it is to be truly lived. Are you happy, you and dear Madame Sibelius?

I go up to London only when it is absolutely necessary. But in October I must go back and live nearer to my occupations. We live in a state of social disorder very much to be regretted. It is the end of the false radicalism and hypocritical socialism at which the middle classes here have been playing. Gladstone's liberalism – Lloyd George – Kier Hardie ... The end?[3]

I have heard, and sometimes read, of your success. Do you think you will come to Paris later? Perhaps Eva's engagement will change your plans. You talked of letting her study there for a few months. As for myself, I am resolved not to have a 'home' for at least a year.[4] I shall rent a furnished house or flat, whilst I see if my husband's affairs improve, or whether they go from bad to worse. I shall try to make economies and then in several months – 12 to 18 – I shall take on a pied-à-terre so that John can begin to build up a clientele for himself. Not having any money, it's the only way I can establish his career. How distasteful and yet how good money is! I should truly like to have a great fortune at my disposal!

I am a little unsure of our address, but a letter to our excellent Kling – Breitkopf – 54 Great Marlborough Street. W. will always reach me. My congratulations to Eva, and many affectionate greetings to your wife,

à vous de cœur,

<u>Rosa Newmarch</u>.[5]

---

[1] 'Cottage' in English in the original.
[2] These cards have not been traced. Eva's fiancé was Arvi Paloheimo (1888–1940).
[3] Here, Newmarch alludes to a series of events that had taken place in 1910 and 1911. Two parliamentary elections in January and December 1910 had reduced the Liberal Party's previous landslide majority and produced a hung parliament. On the one hand, the two elections – the first fought over the issue

of the so-called 'People's Budget' of 1909, the second designed to undo the power of a House of Lords dominated by the Conservatives – constituted a victory for progressive politics (notwithstanding the reduction of the overall Liberal majority). On the other hand, in a hung parliament, the Liberal Party was now dependent on the votes of smaller parties – both the Irish Nationalists and the nascent Labour Party – in order to pass legislation. The Liberal Party – already committed to greater social reform as a result of its 1906 parliamentary victory – was increasingly perceived by many middle-class voters as having moved yet further to the left. In addition to increased importance in parliament, the Labour movement made itself felt in a series of industrial disputes, particularly the Liverpool general transport strike of summer 1911, as well as a strike at the London Docks in early August that same year. The three figures mentioned by Newmarch – William Gladstone (1809–98), David Lloyd George (1863–1945) and James Kier Hardie (1856–1915) – trace the development of British politics from Victorian liberalism via early twentieth-century liberal reforms to socialism. For a highly readable account of the era, see George Dangerfield, *The Strange Death of Liberal England* (London, 1936).

4 'Home' in English in the original.
5 In his diary (22 August 1911), Sibelius wrote: 'Rosa Newmarch, my good friend, has written a beautiful letter' (*Dagbok*, p. 87).

55 JEAN SIBELIUS TO ROSA NEWMARCH [ORIGINAL IN GERMAN][1]

Gd Hotel de Malte
63, Rue de Richelieu
Paris, 8 Nov 1911
Addr: Paris, poste restante

Chère Madame,

I thank you with all my heart for the friendly lines.[2]

I have come here – to Paris – for a while. Voilà la solitude![3] Give me either the loneliness of the Finnish forests or of a big city – Tertium non datur![4]

I marvelled that the English critics understood 'Herbstabend'!*[5] I shall come with the greatest pleasure if I am invited, especially for the sake of seeing and talking with you, Madame.

Eva is engaged to a lawyer, Arvi Paloheimo. He is handsome and rich. I think that Eva – between ourselves – will have a very serious life.

I am here until Noël. But after Christmas I hope to be back again. Perhaps Aino will also come.

Once again thank you for your great friendship!
Jean Sibelius
*I am getting highly respected!

1. Letter partly cited in Newmarch, *Jean Sibelius*, pp. 37–8/pp. 25–6.
2. Unless Sibelius was more than usually dilatory in maintaining his correspondence, the letter referred to here has not been traced.
3. 'Here indeed is solitude!' (*Fr*).
4. 'There is no alternative' (*Lat*.). Sibelius travelled to Paris at the end of October, stopping briefly in Berlin – which he found 'unbearable' (*Dagbok*, p. 100) – on the way.
5. Newmarch records that on 21 October 1911, 'Aino Ackté gave the first performance of the Song with Orchestra "Autumn Night" ("Hostqvall") at a Queen's Hall Symphony Concert, conducted by Sir Henry Wood' (*Jean Sibelius*, pp. 37–8/pp. 25–6). In a review in *The Musical Times*, 'Autumn Night' is described as 'an "atmospheric" song of great freedom of design and expression, which nevertheless owed most of the effect it made to Madame Ackté's interpretation' ('London Concerts', *Musical Times* 52 (1911), 730 and 735 (730)). A review in *The Times* characterised the song 'as a clever piece of landscape' in which:

> the suggestions of the words are faithfully carried out in the orchestration, and its vocal declamation is sufficiently large in outline to appeal to an artist of Mme. Ackté's powers, so that, although there is no great distinction in the music, the whole effect is imaginative and picturesque.' ('The Queen's Hall Orchestra', *The Times*, 23 October 1911, 12)

56 ROSA NEWMARCH TO JEAN SIBELIUS [ORIGINAL IN FRENCH]

155, GOLDHURST TERRACE,
HAMPSTEAD, N.W.
9 November [1911].

Dearest and most honoured friend,

Your letter quite astonished me! I don't really know why, but I had no idea that you were so near to us. I should so like to see you. Tell me <u>the real truth</u> – would you like me to interrupt your solitude? If it suits you, I would come to Paris for <u>two or three days</u> before winter has set in? I can only pay a flying visit between two concerts. I shall stay at my old Hôtel de l'Univers et du Portugal. If you thought of coming to visit us later, I should wait. But if you are going to remain in Paris all the time, I should like to see you there lest you should fly away without letting me know! It will be very easy. I know that you will tell me frankly what you prefer: – either a line saying 'come and see me', or three words 'Leave me be'. And I shall understand.[1]

à vous de cœur,

Rosa Newmarch.

[1] A letter in Newmarch's papers to her sister, Caroline, gives further details about her motivation for visiting Sibelius in Paris (and the financial implications of doing so):

> Sibelius is in Paris and writes daily asking me to go! Today Breitkopf & Härtel said they <u>wanted</u> me to go, so that somebody might see about his new works getting corrected and printed – the new symphony for the Birmingham Festival, and something historical which wants an explanation written. If they are going to give me something to do that will pay my expenses, perhaps I <u>will</u> go next week. He is so erratic about business and so helpless in all languages but Swedish and Finnish. It would be very nice to see him again and also the Robinsons. But I can't afford to go unless there is a prospect of earning something.

The Robinsons were Newmarch's childhood friends from Leamington Spa, A. Mary F. Robinson (1857–1944) and Frances Mabel Robinson (1858–1956). Mary – a well-known poet – first married the French orientalist James Darmesteter (1849–1894) and then the biologist Emile Duclaux (1840– 1904); Mabel, a novelist, was also engaged in politics and women's education. They settled in France in 1888 and 1897 respectively.

57 ROSA NEWMARCH TO JEAN SIBELIUS [ORIGINAL IN FRENCH]

155, GOLDHURST TERRACE,
HAMPSTEAD, N.W.
11 November [1911].

Dearest and honoured friend,

Many thanks for your wire.[1] I think that I could not leave <u>before</u> next Sunday, because of my engagements – but then I hope to enjoy several days of leisure, and if nothing prevents me I shall come and see you that day.[2] What an unexpected pleasure, and yet so long desired!

If you change address in the meantime, send me a wire, since I shall send you a brief line to inform you of my arrival and the hotel where I'll be staying.

A vous de cœur,

Rosa Newmarch.

1   This telegram has not been traced.
2   Newmarch indeed arrived in Paris on Sunday 19 November, leaving again on Thursday 30 November. On 19 November, Sibelius wrote to his wife: 'I am looking forward to Rosa's arrival. I am glad that I shall be able to talk about music with her' (*Syysilta*, p. 203). Sibelius's diary contains a number of references to the time they spent together (for instance, 'Rosa Newmarch here in Paris. She is a good old friend. But sensitive to criticism of musical life in England', *Dagbok*, p. 106). Newmarch's impressions were later detailed in *Jean Sibelius*, pp. 38–41/pp. 26–8, where she records seeing Sibelius 'almost daily in much the same way as when he used to come to London' (pp. 39–40/p. 26).

58   ROSA NEWMARCH TO JEAN SIBELIUS
[ORIGINAL IN FRENCH]

155, Goldhurst Terrace,
Hampstead, N.W.
Thursday evening [30 November 1911].

Good and dear friend,

Here I am again! I am not very tired and the crossing was splendid. A grey sea, if a little fresh, and I like the sea in <u>all</u> its phases; even when it resembles, as it did today, a piece of grey and dirty flannel.

I have given much thought to the idea of this concert, and in the end I remembered Minnie Tracy [*sic*]?[1] Isn't she an American? Are you quite sure she is an artist of your calibre? I seem to remember having heard her sing in London and that she wasn't at all of the highest quality.[2] But then you'll see her yourself. It's better not to associate with anyone but artists of the highest rank. This is not a proper letter, only a brief word of warning.

I shall write at greater length in a few days. In the meantime, I thank you for the wonderful hours we had in Paris, and I am always your devoted friend
<u>Rosa Newmarch.</u>

1   Minnie Tracey (1870–1929), American singer. In a letter from Sibelius to his wife written on 30 November, Sibelius mentioned having been invited to tea by Tracey, who was then resident in Paris (*Syysilta*, p. 211), and his diary suggests that she was planning a concert of his works (*Dagbok*, p. 109). On 5 December, he wrote that Minnie had held a reception for him at which she had performed three of his songs 'very sentimentally' (*Syysilta*, p. 218). By 19 December, Sibelius was confiding in his diary – somewhat mysteriously –

that 'Miss Tracey will soon become my enemy' (*Dagbok*, p. 112); as Tracey was a keen exponent of the songs of the Swedish composer Emil Sjögren (1853–1918), a degree of personal and professional jealousy on Sibelius's part cannot be ruled out.

2   Before moving to Paris, Tracey had performed widely in Britain. Of an early performance as Donna Anna in Mozart's *Don Giovanni* at Covent Garden in 1892, the *Athenaeum* suggested: 'She will certainly not prove the long anticipated dramatic soprano, but she was fairly efficient vocally and dramatically, and may be termed a useful artist' ('Music', *Athenaeum*, 25 June 1892, 832–3 (832)). A review of a vocal recital at Aeolian Hall on 22 April 1904 confirmed her ambiguous reputation in Britain: 'The voice is a well trained mezzo-soprano; the "head" notes of good quality and pure, but some of the higher notes harsh and unpleasant. Dramatic power is displayed, but the vocal organ sounds devoid of sympathy' ('Music in London', *Musical Standard*, 30 April 1904, 281).

59 ROSA NEWMARCH TO JEAN SIBELIUS [ORIGINAL IN FRENCH]

155 Goldhurst Terrace
Hampstead N.W.
[8 December 1911]

Dear and good friend,

How can I not shake you by the hand on this, your birthday, and loudly give you my best wishes and blessings! I wish you many years to bring to completion all that is noble and beautiful within you; but not a life that is too long; that can become terrible. I also wish you the calm and strength necessary for your work – and ardour too. I don't entirely wish you success, as it is understood by the musicians of today. And yet it pains me to think that the recognition of the world might be a long time in coming for you; because I am feminine in this regard: how impatient I am, how much I suffer, thinking that even <u>one</u> of your great works might be neglected.

As for my blessings, they are truly sincere, since although I neither believe nor practice in the conventional sense of the words, I believe in something which is beyond us. I am convinced that we carry within us a part of that divine and indefinable life which we recognise everywhere, and without which the whole world would be cold and barren, like those lunar landscapes described by astronomers. This little ray of spiritualised light is the best thing we possess, and we owe it neither to science nor to perfected instinct. But to what, then? I am only just beginning to recognise this wisp of divine life in myself. Very weak perhaps, but it's a phenomenon that I can attribute neither to my physique nor to my intelligence. I have caught a glimpse of it in your inner life too. Go my friend! It is no good telling me: 'I am utterly without morality'! I am not too worried about your morality! When you are faced with a new crisis in your life, you will soon see whether or not you are without this morality, and of the highest kind. In the meantime, live your life as you see fit. What seems fit to you is probably truly good for you – at this point in your evolution. As long as passion is truly sincere and it can feed the forces of life, there is probably nothing unnatural about it. But when the only thing left of passion is nothing more than a habit, a reflection of the beauty and the ardour of youth, then it's high time to be done with it. Poor Don Juan! I think he remained an idealist until the end of his days! I am sure that he was always searching for something he could not have found in a dissolute life. But he didn't live too long. Aged sixty or seventy he would have lost all of poetry. There's a nice essay on the eternal problem of Tannhäuser!

On Saturday your two bagatelles 'Canzonetta' and 'Valse Romantique' were performed at Queen's Hall, after a fashion.[1] That day, Wood had a vast rehearsal, and he didn't have enough time to work on these two small pieces properly. Now, if you perform little things like that the execution must be perfect. I see that with more polish, the Canzonetta would become a little jewel. As for the Valse – ? As I always tell you the truth, I would tell you that I can never be interested in those things, which you could consign to oblivion without doing any harm to your renown. What a good thing for Mr Jean Sibelius that Madame Rosa Newmarch is not a critic.*

At Dover, Madame Renée Chemet got in my carriage – she was coming to perform at a Sunday Concert.[2] We talked about new violin concertos, and in fact she told me that she had – the day before – just bought yours, with the intention of studying it. I heard her at the concert on Sunday. She has made enormous progress. I would say that she is now an artist of the highest rank, and I am convinced that she has a future, since she is only 25, I believe.

You could quite happily entrust her with the performance of your concerto.

What have you been doing of late? I think of you very often. To tell you the truth I miss you very much. We get on so well together, and after we have spent a week together like that, seeing each other and chatting intimately every day, I feel a great emptiness and darkness when I leave you; because life is so uncertain, and sometimes so cruel to friendship. In short, I love you dearly. Not like the lady from Moscow,[3] but in my own way.

I have a lot to do, and must work very seriously this winter. It is decided that John will study for several months in Germany and in Paris. He has been promised a position as an <u>anaesthetic intern</u> (?) at the hospital in June 1912. In the meantime, I must help him as much as I can. There is no one apart from me who can, or who will, look after the future of these young creatures, John and Elsie.

All my affectionate wishes for you, for your art, and for your family. When one has, as you do, a true genius, life is simpler, since that is your duty above everything else. Do not stifle it, whether for pleasure or for money – in short, for anything in the world. Imagination – what a gift! And how sad and dispiriting it is to realise that one has lost the power of poetic imagination! Farewell, and may that never happen to you,

à vous de cœur,

<u>Rosa Newmarch</u>.

*Contrary to what I expected, the press was almost entirely favourable.

---

[1] Sibelius's diary (4 December 1911) contains a passing reference to the 'fiasco' of this performance (*Dagbok*, p. 110). A review in *The Musical Times* next month described the works by Sibelius as 'delicately scored and mildly fanciful, but not otherwise interesting' ('Queen's Hall Orchestra', *Musical Times*, 53 (1912), 41).

[2] French violinist (b. 1888).

[3] Sibelius had made his only visit to Moscow in November 1907 to conduct, amongst other works, his Third Symphony. It is possible, although far from certain, that 'the lady from Moscow' refers to the following encounter, as described in an undated letter from Sibelius to his wife: 'Just now there was a lady here, a Russian, who will play my pieces at a concert. She played *Pelléas et Mélisande*, the Romance in D flat, 'Minun kultani' (my arrangement of a Finnish folk song) and the third movement of *Kyllikki* excellently' (Sibelius to Aino Sibelius, 15 November 1907, in *Syysilta*, p. 86, translated in Tawaststjerna, *Sibelius*, vol. 1, p. 81).

60 JEAN SIBELIUS TO ROSA NEWMARCH [ORIGINAL IN GERMAN][1]

Järvenpää, Finland
13/XII/1911

Chère Madame,

Many thanks for your very kind letter, and above all for the happy hours in Paris![2]

Here I am back again in the forests with new plans and new ideas.

I will soon write to you further.

With friendly compliments,

Your grateful

Jean Sibelius

[1] Letter cited in Newmarch, *Jean Sibelius*, p. 42/p. 28.
[2] Newmarch mistranslates Sibelius's original ('die schönen Stunde') as 'happy days'.

61 ROSA NEWMARCH TO JEAN SIBELIUS [ORIGINAL IN FRENCH]

155, GOLDHURST TERRACE,
HAMPSTEAD, N.W.
26. December [1911]

Dear and honoured friend,

Today I am sending you a letter which has been sent to me to address to you. Since the letter was open and I knew from whom it came, I took the great liberty of reading it. It's very probable that you have entirely forgotten about the existence of this young man, who was, at the time of your visit, first viola in Beecham's orchestra.[1] He was present at the soirée, given in your honour, at the 'Concert Goers' Club', and which he played something by Dale, I think.[2] He's a talented young man (and very vain too), and if you were minded to write some piece for viola, he will play it with intelligence. But perhaps I don't need to advise you that you shouldn't accept a commission from <u>him</u> to compose whatever it might be –

for him alone. I don't think he is a great enough artist for Jean Sibelius to sell him one of his works! It's quite simply a small matter of his ignorance. <u>If you</u> do write for his instrument, make all the necessary arrangements <u>with your publishers</u>, and let him play your composition afterwards. I concede you might compose something especially for Ysaÿe or Cazals [*sic*]– but not for Lionel Tertis.[3] That is, not for a fee he would give you. Don't you think I'm right? Don't offend him either – simply make an excuse that you don't intend to do what he asks of you. But if you like the idea of composing for viola, don't let him have your composition for any fee whatsoever. Forgive me, dear friend, for meddling in your affairs like this, but you know that they are always dear to my heart.

Many thanks for your letter. I write to you today in haste.

I wish you all that is good for the next year,

à vous de cœur,

<u>Rosa Newmarch</u>

---

[1] Lionel Tertis (1876–1975), English violist.
[2] Tertis had played the 'Romance' from the *Suite for Viola* (1906) by Benjamin Dale (1885–1943).
[3] Eugène Ysaÿe (1858–1931), Belgian violinist, and Pablo Casals (1876–1973), Spanish cellist. Tertis's letter to Sibelius is located at NLF Coll.206.38:

Smalldown,
Belmont,
Surrey
England
Dec: 12th '11

Dear Mr Sibelius

You will no doubt remember hearing me play on your last visit to England and the reason I am writing to you is to beg of you to write a short work for Viola and Orchestra. (I remembered that you said you might do this one day). I want to treat this from a business point of view, and would like to know what would be your lowest fee for doing this. I would also bear the expense of copying the Orchestral parts. I should be extremely grateful if you would think seriously about this. As you well know, the Viola is most fearfully neglected, and a work from your pen would be a tremendous help towards getting the Viola recognized as a solo instrument. I await most anxiously your reply.

Yours truly
Lionel Tertis

62 ROSA NEWMARCH TO JEAN SIBELIUS
[ORIGINAL IN FRENCH]

155, Goldhurst Terrace,
Hampstead N.W.
London.
23 January [1912]

Dearest and most honoured friend,

Several days ago, the editor of our 'Edinburgh Review' invited me to write an article for the April edition about 'Nationality in Music'.[1] It's a great compliment that he has paid me, since this review is the most important one we possess in England, and so far musical articles have rarely appeared there. I have agreed, but on condition that the 'star turn' would be <u>Finnish music. Now, for the love of God, you must help me!</u> Apart from your music, I know only a little, and nothing at all, relatively speaking, about national music. And yet I am probably less ignorant about this subject – thanks to you – than the majority of my compatriots. I know you are always very busy, but do you know someone in Helsingfors who would like to take on the task of helping me a little? Is there a journal in Swedish or in Finnish devoted to music? <u>Who writes on this subject – can one find Flodin's articles anywhere – or can one contact Flodin himself?????</u>[2]

I don't ask you to do all of this yourself. Just find an enthusiast who is not also a great composer. You shouldn't waste your time on this matter. Only I think I could say many artistic truths in this article under the pretext of nationalism.

It doesn't matter what language the books or articles are written in. Whatever I don't understand, I could have translated here.

How are you? I have been rather poorly since the new year. I spent 10 days in bed with a terrible cold. But now I am better. On Thursday I hope to go to Manchester to hear Bantock's new Choral Symphony ('Atalanta in Calydon').[3] This letter reminds me of dear old Stassov, who was in the habit of underlining in blue, red or green, depending on the importance of his questions![4]

Why is Helsingfors so far from London? But find me a friend who would be interested in this project.

I won't write any more today. Many affectionate thoughts to you, to Madame Sibelius and the family,

your devoted friend,
<u>Rosa Newmarch.</u>

1. *The Edinburgh Review* was founded in 1802 and rapidly became an established venue for lengthy, serious and intellectual reviews on a variety of social, political and cultural topics. It closed in 1929.
2. Karl Flodin (1858–1925) was music critic for a series of Swedish-language papers in Finland (*Nya pressen* and *Aftonposten*), edited the *Helsingfors posten*, and founded the avant-garde periodical *Euterpe*. His 1900 volume *Die Musik in Finnland* (also translated into French as *La Musique en Finlande*) was timed to coincide with the opening of the Finnish pavilion at the 1900 World Fair in Paris, and one of the few works on Finnish music available to non-Swedish and non-Finnish speakers. A volume of his reviews was published as *Musikliv och reseminnen* (Helsinki, 1931).
3. *Atalanta in Calydon* was a setting of words by Algernon Charles Swinburne. Bantock's setting for large unaccompanied chorus was first performed in Manchester on 25 January 1912.
4. A number of lines in this letter were underlined in red pencil by Newmarch herself, and she also added, after her address, the injunction: 'Read this! <u>Very important</u>.'

63 JEAN SIBELIUS TO ROSA NEWMARCH [ORIGINAL IN GERMAN][1]

Järvenpää, Finland 27/I/1912

Chère Madame,

Gratuliere! (Quel mot affreux!)[2]

I will send you everything concerning the essay. – Flodin lives in – Buenos Ayres.[3] He is not the man best qualified however to help, but rather Katila,[4] with whom I have been talking today. He will send me the most important articles so far published on 'Nationalité dans la Musique en Finlande',[5] and will write something for you himself. All this I will send to you. Shall I get it translated?

All of us (including myself) are <u>very</u> glad that you are going to write about Finnish music. It will really be a famous bit of work

My family and I send you, chère Madame, our best greetings.

Your grateful friend,

Jean Sibelius

1. Letter cited in Newmarch, *Jean Sibelius*, p. 42/p. 29.
2. 'Congratulations' (*Ger.*) and 'What an awful word!' (*Fr.*).
3. Flodin lived in Buenos Aires between 1908 to 1921, where he worked as music editor for *La Plata* (whilst continuing to write for *Nya pressen*).
4. Evert Katila (1872–1945) was music critic for a number of notable Finnish-language newspapers and journals.
5. Newmarch translates this phrase as 'the national feeling in Finnish music'.

64 ROSA NEWMARCH TO JEAN SIBELIUS
[ORIGINAL IN FRENCH]

155, Goldhurst Terrace,
Hampstead, N.W.
London
2 February
1912

Dearest and most honoured friend,

On coming home last night I found your letter. I went to Manchester to hear Bantock's choral symphony, and I came back with him to spend two or three days at his house at Broad Meadow.

Many, many thanks for your promptness. I am looking forward to everything that Mr Katila can send me. I would ask you to thank him for me. Everything written in Swedish I can have translated easily, since I have a friend, a very intelligent Swedish lady, who helped me with the translation of your songs. With Finnish it will be perhaps more difficult, but I think Mr Hagberg Wright might be able to find me someone.[1]

Bantock has had a great success with 'Atalanta in Calydon'; there are some beautiful moments, but the choir in Manchester is not up to singing something so new and so difficult well.[2]

We have had a very cold week. At Bantock's the weather was so beautiful! The whole countryside was covered with snow under a bright blue sky, with a brilliant sun! It was like being in Switzerland. But here in London it is cold without being beautiful. For five weeks I have had a terrible cold. But not ill enough to take to my bed, even though I'm still tired and full of cold.

I will do my best – I have always waited for the right moment to write more about your music. In haste,

à vous de cœur,

    Rosa Newmarch

---

[1] Sir Charles Theodore Hagberg Wright (1862–1940), librarian of the London Library from 1893 until his death. An accomplished linguist (his mother was Swedish), he was a committed Tolstoyan, translating two volumes of Tolstoy's stories (*Father Sergius and other Stories and Plays* and *The Forged Coupon and other Stories and Dramas*, both in 1911).

[2] In his review, Ernest Newman noted that 'The Hallé choir did well on the

whole in the first performance of the work, but lapses of intonation obscured the musical logic of several passages, and the phrasing was throughout not sufficiently elastic' ('Mr Granville Bantock's "Atalanta in Calydon"', *Musical Times* 53 (1912), 166–7 (167)).

65 ROSA NEWMARCH TO JEAN SIBELIUS
[ORIGINAL IN FRENCH]

13 March, 1912.

Dearest and most honoured friend,

I am writing to you from the country where I am spending several days near my sisters.[1]

I never received a letter from your good Mr Kartila [*sic*],[2] but in the end I've gathered quite a lot of details. What I need most is to know something about your <u>younger</u> composers – those who are in some way your pupils.

Is it true that you have been offered a Professorship in Vienna?[3] I can't see you in this job! Have you thought any more about the idea of an opera? Two or three weeks ago I dined (in London) with Madame Ackté who mentioned to me the idea of a 'musical Festival' (in Nyslott, I think).[4] That could be enormously interesting, if it were organised in a really representative manner. I think that in London the season will not be a good one because of the great losses that industry will make because of the strikes.[5]

Until 20 April I shall remain in London, then I am a little unsure. I shall rest, and during this time, I shall write my article on national music. But I shall always send you my address. My son is in Munich at the moment, but I won't join him in Munich. I shall go, I think, <u>to a convent</u> in Brittany! Who knows? Perhaps I'll become the mother superior of this establishment. No! I cannot bear women <u>en bloc</u>! I'll perhaps spend 4 or 5 weeks there to be completely rested and to work. I should so much like to speak with you. At the moment I am completely drowned in your violin concerto. There are moments of poetry – of such a moving intimacy – in this music. Why are the virtuosi not arguing over who will be the first to perform this work? Is it laziness, is it the spirit of commerce which makes them play the same things all the time? In fifteen years it will be a 'classic' like the concertos of Beethoven, Brahms and Tchaikovsky; but I am keen to hear it <u>now</u>. If only Vecsey would to play it the next time he comes to London.[6] This boy has great talent.

Here spring has already begun. The earth smells good, and all sorts of little things are growing there, things wrapped in mystery and which one can't quite make out. I love the start of our spring, which is so long in coming; which advances and withdraws like a timid girl. This is my land of my birth, right in the middle of England, not far from the little town where Shakespeare first saw day.[7] It is a dense, calm, sylvan landscape, very grey and very green, with fields that look like cultivated lawns, and ancient and solemn oaks and elms.

Until 20 April I shall be at: 155 Goldhurst Terrace
S. Hampstead
N.W.

Later I shall let you know my address.

My regards to Madame Sibelius and the children,
à vous de cœur
Rosa Newmarch.

---

[1] Newmarch was the youngest of eight children; her three sisters were Louisa Sophia (1845–1919), Marie Thérèse (1848–1913) and Caroline Georgiana (1850–1939). According to an interview given by Newmarch to *The Musical Times* in 1913, 'her eldest sister was an excellent pianist who had studied under Kullak in Berlin'. According to the same interview, another sister (Marie Thérèse, also known as Lily), 'studied singing with Bussine in Paris' before taking a diploma at the Royal Academy of Music (M. 'Mrs. Rosa Newmarch', *Musical Times* 52 (1911), 225–9 (225)). The family history of the Jeaffresons reveals that Louisa Sophia married Fred Williams, and that Marie Thérèse 'established herself, on the death of her father, as a teacher of music and singing in the town of Leamington' (M. T. Jeaffreson, *Pedigree of the Jeaffreson Family with Notes and Memoirs* (London, 1922), p. 16).

[2] In her memoir of Sibelius, Newmarch writes that 'I can find no trace among my papers of any correspondence with Katila, but I did receive a number of articles, mostly in Swedish, and much of the information contained in them went into my analytical notes for the Fourth Symphony, and into various other short notices' (*Jean Sibelius*, p. 43/p. 29).

[3] On 17 January, Sibelius had been offered the chair in composition at the Academy for Music and Performing Arts in Vienna after the retirement of his former teacher, Robert Fuchs. He declined the position on 1 March.

[4] Nyslott is the Swedish name for Savonlinna. Ackté had sung there in 1905 and become convinced of the potential of its castle as a venue for the performance of operas on nationalist themes. Between 1912 and 1916, Ackté herself directed five annual summer festivals, before the events of 1917–18 put an end the enterprise. The Savonlinna Opera Festival was refounded in 1967.

5   A national coal strike had been called in February 1912, which was resolved with the passing of the Minimum Wage Act, one of the so-called 'liberal reforms', although this did not prevent the dock strikes of that summer.
6   Franz von Vecsey (1893–1935), Hungarian violinist and dedicatee of the revised version (1905) of Sibelius's Violin Concerto. Vecsey had made his British debut with a series of concerts in May 1904 ('Franz von Vecsey', *Musical Times* 45 (1904), 379), and later performed Bruch's Violin Concerto on 26 February 1912 ('London Concerts', *Musical Times* 53 (1912), 258–60 (258)). Newmarch's wish to hear Vecsey perform the Sibelius concerto in London was realised more quickly than she might have imagined, as he gave 'an exhilarating interpretation' of the work (accompanied by Richard Epstein) at Bechstein Hall on 21 March ('London Concerts', *Musical Times* 53 (1912), 319–20 (320)).
7   Newmarch was born in Leamington Spa.

66 ROSA NEWMARCH TO JEAN SIBELIUS
[ORIGINAL IN FRENCH]

> Chez Les Sœurs de la Croix
> Merdrignac. Côtes-du-Nord
> France.
> [June 1912]

Dear and honoured friend,

I've been here in the convent for five weeks now! It's the 'simple life' in full swing! I am perfectly happy here and have grown younger by at least ten years. The weather at present is splendid. I am writing to you outdoors, my chaise longue under an old apple tree, and between the intertwined branches, I can see a sky as blue as an Italian sky. I have worked much since my arrival. My article for the 'Edinburgh Review' is finished. It's not at all what I had intended to make of it at the outset.[1] I shall write a 'continuation' later, and perhaps at last I shall know more about Finnish music.[2] This country is smiling and charming. I wouldn't say exactly beautiful, but everything is green and fresh. The Convent is on a little hill, and from my room – with its three windows – I can see far, far into the distance, as far as the mountains in another part of Brittany. Life is very calm, but not sad. The good sisters work from morning until evening and seem to be always jolly. The Breton character interests me, because there is much poetry and mysticism in this Celtic people. Men are excluded from this paradise! But there is one exception. There's a young priest of 26 who fell ill in Rome and who has been sent here for his health. I fear he has tuberculosis, and to distract him a little, I have him read to me in English, and in return he hums a great number of Breton folk-tunes, which he learnt from the people. There are several which are charming.

I often wonder what you are doing? My daughter will join me here at the end of this week for a fortnight. After that, I shall stay here until 20 July, and then I must return to England to be nearer to the Queen's Hall before the Promenade Concerts begin. Send me a postcard. At least I shall know whether you are still in Jarvenpää, or whether you are travelling.[3]

Don't imagine that I am leading a religious life! I get up at 7 o'clock; from 9 until 11 I work; from 11 until midday I stroll in the garden, where I give my English lesson to the 'boy-priest'; after lunch I read, or I work until 3; then I take tea, and then Miss Johnson joins me for a long walk through the fields. We dine at 6.30 and in the evening I stroll again in the garden, or I amuse myself at the piano (what a piano!). At 9 o'clock everything shuts up, but in my large room, as neat and severe as a prison, I light my lamp and write until half past 10. The food is simple, but not bad, and for <u>all of this</u> I pay 78 francs per month, laundry included! I speak French from morning to evening, I am almost back in my childhood. I think I was much in need of this life for a few months, because I was so extremely tired as a result of the winter which I spent without a 'home'.[4] I am as always your devoted friend
<u>Rosa Newmarch</u>

[1] Newmarch's finished article was indeed quite different from what she had intended. Ostensibly a review of Parry's *Style in Musical Art* (1911), Cecil Forsyth's *Music and Nationalism* (1911), Edward MacDowell's *Critical and Historical Essays* (1912) and Guido Adler's *Der Stil in der Musik* (1911), it was published under the title of 'Chauvinism in Music' in the July edition of *The Edinburgh Review* 216 (1912), 95–116. Newmarch began by suggesting that contemporary British interest in establishing a 'national' school of music was, in fact, a more complicated and ambiguous phenomenon:

> The passionate desire to advocate the claims of British music is in itself legitimate and laudable; but some who love the art in all its manifestations, and have not lost all critical discrimination in frenzied Chauvinism, may object to many of the methods used to forward the ends in view. (95)

In particular, Newmarch mocked attempts to found a national school on folksong:

> it is so long since any section of our society has been nourished on the folk-song diet that out of an average of concert-going public in this country it

may safely be predicted that hardly one person in every fifty could sing, or recognise if heard, more than about ten of those once popular songs. (97)

By contrast, she praised the catholic and cosmopolitan tastes of modern audiences:

> For good or ill, the elder people who frequent concerts in England have been brought up on Handel, the German classics, and a proportion of Italian opera music; while the younger generation have imbibed Wagner, Tchaikovsky, Richard Strauss and Debussy. The child that has tasted meat will refuse to pap. (97)

Newmarch then went on to to declare that: 'The aim of this article is to protest against the exaggerated reaction against that foreign element which is still in some measure necessary to our musical life' (98). After surveying the contents of the five books under review, Newmarch concluded her article with a brief consideration of Sibelius:

> Only in the Finnish school, the latest comer in the world of music, which is in some measure a link between Scandinavian and Slavonic music, can we discern a musical star of greater magnitude. The Danes, the Swedes and the Norwegians express themselves chiefly in their respective dialects; but the Finns already show in the change of style noticeable in the music of their leader, Jean Sibelius, a tendency to a less exclusive and naïve reiteration of national sentiments. Comparing the later with the earlier works of this complex and interesting composer, we note a tendency to increased subjectivity; to the substitution of personal utterance – and always delicately restrained – for the more epic and pictorial art of his early symphonic works, which were based on episodes from the Finnish 'Kalevala' and kindred subjects. His disciples, too, are following on the same lines with an even stronger bent towards abstract music.
>
> The concluding paragraphs of an article are hardly a suitable place in which to give, even in outline, a history of this, the youngest among the legitimate folk-idioms of Europe. 'It sometimes happens,' says Sir Hubert Parry, 'that a race numerically inferior takes the lead in such a speciality as musical taste.' A long and careful study of the music of Sibelius points to the conclusion that the Finns may possibly lead the way to a more chastened and sober taste in the art of music. Already we are accustomed to hear Sibelius described by the full-bodied realists of the day as reactionary. But reaction is often progress in disguise. Sibelius has reserved to himself the right of using the older classical forms as well as those of the symphonic poem. He has ideas which could not always be suitably adapted to the latter, and a sense of form such as one would expect to find in a man to whom sculpture makes a greater appeal than painting. Noting his tendency to shed much of the extravagant luxury of means employed by contemporary composers; his omission of much that is superfluous, or merely reiterative; his restraint in the matter of temperamental explosions, and his dislike of violent and noisy orchestration; his choice of themes which are not merely flashlights but sufficiently sustained and luminous to be the guiding stars of his movements; and his susceptibility to the undertones of nature – we are justified in feeling that Sibelius is no reactionary, but that perhaps on the contrary he has stepped ahead out of the dust and din of

the blatant and motley pageantry which at the present moment occupies the high-road of musical progress. But this is a fresh subject, and worthy of separate treatment, although it touches very closely on the legitimate and natural uses of native idiom in music. (115–16)

'Chauvinism in Music' is one of Newmarch's most programmatic and confessional pieces of writing, and illustrates her commitment to promoting music that was at once national and modern (or, to use her preferred terminology, progressive). The tone and content of one particular paragraph provoked criticism from Charles MacLean, general secretary of the International Musical Society, who objected to Newmarch's description of the society's recent congress in her article and her opposition to what she saw as

the strange retaliatory policy of the British branch of the International Musical Society, who during the festival week held in London last season saw fit to produce nothing but the music of our own countrymen; a proceeding so at variance with English traditions of courteous hospitality that it can only be compared to asking guests to dinner, setting before them nothing but local dishes, and boring them with an endless conversation about the merits of our own cooks. It is not by such methods that we shall help to establish, or preserve, in our midst a school of national music; for, to be worthy of the name, such a school must reflect all our noblest and sincerest qualities rather than our pettiest and most insular defects. (106)

MacLean attempted to refute her account in a letter to *The Musical Times* ('Chauvinism in British Music', *Musical Times* 53 (1912), 520), and Newmarch replied the next month ('Chauvinism in Music', *Musical Times* 53 (1912), 594–5), reiterating and even amplifying her criticisms.

2 Newmarch does not appear to have written a continuation of this article, nor did she ever write anything substantial about any Finnish musician other than Sibelius. The only other manifestation of her interest in Finnish music appears to be her translation of Oskar Merikanto's 'Finnish Cradle Song' (London, 1917).
3 Sibelius was in Finland that summer, working on various compositions, including the three *Sonatinas* for solo piano, Op. 67 (*Dagbok*, pp. 141–2).
4 English in the original.

67 ROSA NEWMARCH TO JEAN SIBELIUS [ORIGINAL IN FRENCH]

15, Crossfield Road
S. Hampstead
London. N.W.

23 August [1912].

Dearest and most honoured friend,

I was very happy to receive from Henry Wood the news that you have accepted the invitation to come and conduct your IV Symphony in Birmingham.[1] I fear, from what I hear, that the fee is meagre – because of the losses from the last Festival, they have made some rather silly economies. But you will have a warm reception from your friends. As for me, I have no need to tell you that it is a real joy to think that we shall soon be reunited. You'll come for the rehearsals, won't you? It is <u>so important</u>, because you know that you speak a musical language that is not easy to grasp, and the authority of your presence is to be desired. Write to me if I can arrange a room for you. As far as Birmingham is concerned, we can sort that out later. I think that perhaps rather than staying in Birmingham, I shall settle in my home town half an hour from Birmingham. Perhaps you would prefer that? – but we have plenty of time.

I came from France almost three weeks ago. I am looking for a house in London.

Today, the Birmingham Committee asked me to write an analysis of your Symphony. For several reasons, I should have much preferred Ernest Newman to do this.[2] But if not, I shall do my best. If you have any suggestions to give me you'll write soonest, won't you? Time is pressing.

Henry Wood is happy. He now has a charming little daughter who is one month old.[3]

Bantock, Scriabine, Elgar and Walford Davies will have novelties performed at the Festival.[4]

For six weeks now we haven't seen the sun at all, although the weather is said to be beautiful in the north. I shan't write any more this evening. I am horribly tired and the only thing that comforts me is the thought of seeing you soon, dear and very taciturn friend.

My best wishes to your wife and all the family,

    à vous de cœur,

        <u>Rosa Newmarch</u>.

---

[1] The initial invitation does not appear to have been preserved in the Sibelius Family Papers, but a letter from Wood to Sibelius of 11 June 1912 (NAF SFP Box 52) gives details of the proposed rehearsal schedule and the concert itself.

[2] Ernest Newman (1868–1959) was an important early advocate of Sibelius's music and wrote a number of important reviews of the Fourth Symphony (he also produced the programme note for the performance of Elgar's *The Music Makers* at the Birmingham Festival in 1912). Previously, Newmarch had written rather tartly of Newman, who appears to have rejected an appeal to write something for her series *Living Masters of Music*, published by John Lane:

> like so many writers on musical subjects, he entirely overlooks the fact that such a series is planned for *the public* and not for a few specialists. His

remark that he would not write or read a book on the subject of Paderewski contains the whole reason why musical books have become traditional failures: – because most of our writers have indulged this priggish spirit to the full, and who says 'musical literature', says 'ponderous specialism', 'boredom' and total disregard of the requirements of an intelligent, but amateur, public. (Rosa Newmarch to John Lane, 11 January 1904, Harry Ransom Humanities Research Center, University of Texas at Austin, John Lane Company Papers, Box 34, Folder 5)

However, Newman's book on Richard Strauss was eventually published in Newmarch's series in 1908, and his interest in contemporary European orchestral music and commitment to writing for a wide, educated public echoed Newmarch's own practice as a critic.

3 Wood's first daughter, Tania, was born in June 1912.
4 These new works were Bantock's *Fifine at the Fair*, Elgar's *The Music Makers* and Walford Davies's *The Song of St Francis*. Scriabin's *Prometheus* was announced, but not in fact performed, apparently because of insufficient rehearsal time; it was eventually given its first British performance on 1 February 1913 at a Queen's Hall Symphony Concert.

68 JEAN SIBELIUS TO ROSA NEWMARCH [ORIGINAL IN GERMAN][1]

Järvenpää, Finland
29/VIII/1912

Chère Madame,

I am very happy to receive your worthy letter.

I am coming to London (Langham Hotel) on the 24th or 25th of Sept.[2] On Thursday 26th Sept I have a rehearsal at Queen's Hall from 11–1. My second rehearsal is in Birmingham Town Hall in the evening 7.30–10.30.

Mr Bantock has invited me to his place 'in the country during your visit.'[3] Chère Madame, you can imagine that I have accepted the invitation with joy, and am glad to have Bantock as a friend again.

I'll send you a wire when I get to London. It will be a great joy to see you again. Is it necessary to write about the symphony? I am not really for this at all. In any case, it would be better to omit this. But – this is a mattter about which I have nothing to say.[4]

I spent the whole summer with my family on a sporting holiday to Päijänne, a large lake in the middle of Finland. We spoke of you very often, and my wife sends warm greetings.

Your trip to France must have been very interesting. I have always had a great affection for Normandy and Brittany.

Until our imminent and friendly reunion,

Your grateful friend

Jean Sibelius

1. Letter cited (in the original German) in Newmarch, *Jean Sibelius*, pp. 43–4/ p. 30.
2. The National Archives of Finland (Sibelius Family Papers Box 52) contain Sibelius's hotel and restaurant bill (for £1 5s 2d) from the Hotel Richelieu, Oxford Street (24–8 September 1912), rather than for his customary Langham Hotel.
3. English in the original. Sibelius's diary entry for 26 August records that 'Bantock has invited me to stay with him' (*Dagbok*, p. 149). His letter accepting Bantock's invitation (29 August 1912) can be found at BL Add Ms 64961, fol. 3.
4. Newmarch herself observed that 'Sibelius, like many composers, fought justifiably shy of analytical notes. It was useless to consult him on this question in the hope of sucking information' (*Jean Sibelius*, p. 46/pp. 31–2).

69 ROSA NEWMARCH TO JEAN SIBELIUS [ORIGINAL IN FRENCH]

15, Crossfield Road.
S. Hampstead.
N.W.

7 September [1912].

Dear and most honoured friend,

So it's all agreed! You'll send me a wire before arriving, and I shall perhaps come and meet you, or in any case, I shall see you the next day at Queen's Hall. I am very happy you're going to stay with Bantock during the Festival.[1]

As far as your Symphony is concerned, don't worry. I won't write too many stupid things, and thank heavens, you won't have to read it all! It's a custom that does neither good nor ill – that's all. What is important is that you yourself should come – that's much, much more important for the success of your work. Until we meet soon.

All best wishes to Madame Sibelius,

à vous de cœur,

Rosa Newmarch.

1. Newmarch devotes considerable space in her memoir to describing Sibelius's stay at Bantock's house:

6. Rosa Newmarch to Jean Sibelius, 7 September [1912]. (courtesy of the National Archives of Finland)

The Bantocks were then living at Broad Meadow, a charming house with a large garden well away from the din and murk of the Midland city. Our days and evenings were mostly spent at rehearsals or performances in the Town Hall at Birmingham, but we seem to have had time for other interests, because I distinctly remember that Granville Bantock was then orchestrating *Omar Khayyam*. He had a selection of instruments lying about his music room, and one wet morning we each seized upon one, and promenaded up and down the hall making hideous cacophony, for of course we chose the ones we knew least about, and invented our own themes spontaneously. The household in general thought that Bedlam was let loose. Another day was memorable in quite a different fashion. I had slipped into the library to look up a Chinese poem which had pleased me very much by its subtle reflection of the disillusionment following on first sight impressions. I was sitting in a darkish corner of the room with the volume in my hands when the door opened and Sibelius slipped in and went to the writing table. I saw at once that he had neither eyes nor thoughts for anything but some bit of creative work. I dare not leave the room for fear of breaking in on his thoughts, so I went on sitting breathless and learning what creative transport really meant. After a time I felt so sure that nothing material existed for him, that I slipped out of the room without him observing it. Something of depth and beauty was assuredly engendered in those moments; but I never ventured to ask about it or to reveal the fact of my presence. (*Jean Sibelius*, pp. 45–6/pp. 30–31)

Sibelius's brief diary entries for his trip to Birmingham reveal that he also visited Stratford-upon-Avon (*Dagbok*, p. 153), something confirmed in an undated letter to his wife possibly written on 26 September 1912, as well as an undated postcard sent from the Shakespeare Hotel (*Syysilta*, p. 223). In her memoir, however, Newmarch misremembered the year of their trip to Stratford, which she claimed took place on 16 February 1921:

We made an early start for my native town of Leamington, where I had ordered a carriage and a pair of sound horses, which we mutually agreed would be a more comfortable way of seeing the land than going in one of those 'uncertain stinks' as a busdriver once described to me the somewhat primitive motor cars of the day. Sibelius's delight at this, probably his first glimpse of rural England, is still fresh in my memory. I had once been invited in Finland to go a considerable distance to see a clump of oak-trees, a rare sight in that country. The musician's pleasure at the beauty and rich foliage of the individual trees, descendants of those which flourished in the Forest of Arden, made me feel proud of my Warwickshire home. I had taken many tourists to Stratford-upon-Avon, but none whose realisation of its atmosphere made the trip so enjoyable. (*Jean Sibelius*, pp. 60–61/ p. 42).

There are, however, no references to a visit to Stratford in Sibelius's letters to his wife of February 1921; indeed, a letter of 16 February, suggests that he was in fact in London on that day (*Syysilta*, p. 295). The confusion is also noted in Tawaststjerna, *Sibelius*, vol. 2, p. 219.

70 ROSA NEWMARCH TO JEAN SIBELIUS [POSTCARD, ORIGINAL IN FRENCH]

[London, postmarked 27 September 1912]

In case you lose the piece of paper I gave you –
Paddington Station
 Depart. 9.10
Leave the hotel – 8.30
Ask for the train for Birmingham.
 R. N.

71 ROSA NEWMARCH TO JEAN SIBELIUS
[ORIGINAL IN FRENCH]

write now to
4, Crossfield Road
South Hampstead
N.W.
Sunday [6 October 1912].

Dearest and most honoured friend,

Enclosed are two notices about the Symphony which are not bad. There was a rather intelligent one in the Yorkshire Post which I have not yet been able to get hold of, but I think that Kling has all of them.[1] In light of the great ignorance which reigns in our musical press at the moment, and the bias for everything national, as well as the prejudice against everything that comes from outside, I think we could not have expected more than 5 or 6 tolerably favourable reviews. It is clear enough that most of these gentlemen regard your work as a problem too difficult to solve! But all the same, the Symphony has awoken a <u>very great</u> interest. The more I think about it, the more I am sure and proud of my friend, Jean Sibelius. It is, I think, the beginning of a series of great and beautiful fruits of your maturity. Now you have to write your 'fifth', like Beethoven. How to tell you all the inward joy I felt during your visit, seeing the man and the artist walking together towards a supreme goal. I was – I admit – a little afraid that your life, so much changed, might ruin that state of extreme sensitivity which seems to be necessary for the creative life. And how I observe, to my great relief, that you have picked yourself up and are even stronger than before. Do you know how you are at the moment? I am not flattering you when I tell you that you spread 'a beautiful atmosphere' wherever you go now, just as Elgar spreads an ugly one.[2] I am not, as you know, orthodox in my religious beliefs, but quite simply and sincerely I have thanked everything that represents for me 'the good Lord' for having seen you as you have become. You are always 'yourself' now; <u>one</u> soul and <u>one</u> will concentrated on one ideal – whereas before you were in danger of squandering your moral and creative energies. So I say again: 'God be praised for one who has found his way'.[3]

I am writing you these lines very late at night, because I am so busy during the day with the new house, and I don't want to leave you too long without a letter.

After your departure, I found several envelopes containing 'postcards' at the Town Hall,[4] with requests for your autograph. No need to trouble yourself with all that. Just sign the cards I am sending you and return them to me – I shall have them sent on to your admirers. Without this, you will forget to post them, and all these good people (I think I should be using the feminine gender here!) will be horribly upset. Thank you so much for everything. How much they lose, those who have been unable to understand your music. Poor devils! I shall write soon to Madame Sibelius.

à vous de cœur,
    Rosa Newmarch

---

[1] The symphony was extensively reviewed in the press, with most critics recognising that it was a significant work, but one that was difficult to understand on first hearing. The first review in *The Times* was typical:

> M. Sibelius's symphony . . . was received rather with courtesy towards a distinguished visitor than with any enthusiasm for the music itself. The hearers, indeed, could hardly be blamed if they failed to trace the logical sequence of its development, the way in which ideas dimly suggested at first blossom into greater fullness in the later movements. The music stands aloof, suggests where most composers would command, and seems to dream of old half-forgotten memories and new unrealized visions of the future. Its harmony and orchestral colour are alike strange, and yet really so simple that time must make their beauty clearer. For a modern work, quite a small orchestra is used, and every instrument in the score tells. It was not perfectly played. Some of the details which ought to come out were lost, and one often wanted greater distinction and delicacy of phrasing. ('Birmingham Musical Festival: Mr Elgar's New Cantata', *The Times*, 2 October 1912, 10)

Subsequent reviews in *The Times* returned to the question of the work's perplexing originality. The next day it was described as 'music which stands far apart from the common expression of the time' ('Birmingham Musical Festival: Four New Works', *The Times*, 3 October 1912, 9), and by the end of the festival, it was felt that 'Sibelius's Symphony has shown us that we shall have to consider him as a far more important factor in modern music than such compositions as *Finlandia* and *En Saga* gave any warrant for supposing' ('Birmingham Musical Festival: The Final Day', *The Times*, 5 October 1912, 8). This question of the work's relationship to modernism had already been alluded to in *The Standard*: 'The composer appears desirous of plumping in favour of ultra-modernity. It is as if he had boiled down all the nebulous phrases and antagonistic harmonies of Stravinsky, Ravel, and Schonberg [*sic*], and then stirred into the compound a spoonful of his sauce' ('The Birmingham Festival: New Sibelius Symphony', *Standard*, 3 October 1912, 11). Faced with this seemingly intractable score, some reviewers claimed that the symphony had some unspecified meaning. *The Standard* had observed that 'the music strikes one as being of the programme order', and *The Yorkshire Post* went even further in trying to intuit a specific programme (inspired, perhaps, by Newmarch's note):

> though the composer has not vouchsafed any explanation to the hearer, one suspects that the movements are in fact a series of impressionist landscapes. Without such a cue the hearer finds it difficult to follow the design which it may be assumed the composer has had in his mind ... One can well believe it represents the composer's own impressions perhaps of his native forests and fjords, but this is all conjecture, in which it is not wise to indulge. It is like a series of illustrations to a story which is withheld, so that their point is obscure if not indecipherable. ('Birmingham Festival: Sir Henry Wood's Birmingham Debut', *Yorkshire Post*, 2 October 1912, 6)

The Monthly Musical Record similarly lamented the lack of any commentary: 'The composer was apparently working to some picture in his mind; in that case any hint as to the subject would have proved helpful' ('The Birmingham Festival', *Monthly Musical Record* 42 (1912), 285–6 (286)). It was left to *The Musical Times* to attribute the difficulties attending the reception of the symphony not to the work itself, but to the inability of the audience to understand it:

> Sibelius's Symphony brought us into another world – one with which most of us are so unfamiliar that we stumbled in our endeavour to understand. The idiom of the music and its form – with ends that did not seem to finish – left one in bewilderment ... It is impossible here to discuss the new work, especially as we feel obliged to state frankly that we do not at present understand it sufficiently, which is a way of confessing that the limitations are our own. But we may say that, after hearing rehearsals as well as the performance, the work grew in interest, and we shall be prepared to rank ourselves with its admirers when we are more familiar with its peculiar mode of expressing temperament. ('The Birmingham Musical Festival', *Musical Times* 53 (1912), 722–7 (724).

Other reviews include: 'Music', *Illustrated London News*, 12 October 1912, 536; F. H. Bond, 'Birmingham Triennial Musical Festival', *Musical Standard*, 12 October 1912, 224–6; and 'The Puppet Show, by One of the Puppets', *Musical Opinion and Music Trade Review* 36 (1912), 108–9.

2   Newmarch's private attitude to Elgar here (and in her subsequent letter of 23 October) is in marked contrast to her earlier warm relations with him, as evinced by numerous letters to him around the time of the première of the First Symphony in 1908, and publications such as 'Edward Elgar: His Career and His Genius', *World's Work* 3 (1904), 547–9, and R. J. Buckley, *Sir Edward Elgar* (London, 1905), included in her series *Living Masters of Music*. Her preference for Sibelius over figures such as Elgar also echoes a general perception that for all its difficulty, the Fourth Symphony had been the highlight of the Birmingham Festival and had served to expose deficiencies in British music

(in his article in *The Nation*, for instance, Newman had written scathingly of Bantock's *Fifine at the Fair*).
3   Newmarch may be echoing Luke 15:7 here: 'I say unto you, that likewise joy shall be in heaven over one sinner that repenteth, more than over ninety and nine just persons, which need no repentance.'
4   'Postcards' in English in the original.

72 ROSA NEWMARCH TO JEAN SIBELIUS
   [ORIGINAL IN FRENCH]

4, Crossfield Road
South Hampstead
23 October [1912]. N.W.

Dearest and most honoured friend,

I have had an infernal fortnight, but at last it's over! Now I am in my little room which is not at all unpleasant. It is more peaceful than the one you remember in Campden Hill Square, and I think that if my health holds out, I shall be able to do some interesting things here; whilst growing old as philosophically as possible. But the move itself was awful. I spent 10 days here, like Goethe on his deathbed, always crying out 'light – more light!' – but without reply from the companies which provide electricity and gas. There were no curtains, no carpets and I ended up with a worrying cold; and all the while these awful programmes came everyday, as merciless and inescapable as the Fates! How happy I am that your visit was over before the start of these disturbances. For your visit was gentle and good; full, for me, of a deep and quiet joy, which I shall long remember. I am happy to know that you are still capable of writing things of such an elevated and noble expression as the symphony. As long as you write <u>works of a poet</u>, I shall not worry about you. 'If you have art and science you have religion. If you have neither art nor science – Then have religion'.[1]

I am sending you the postcards at last. Sign them, won't you, for those good ladies who requested me to ask you for them? One of them, Lady Winifred Elwes, is the wife of our tenor, Gervase Elwes, who might sing your songs well, since he has much intelligence and idealism.[2]

After your departure, we heard two Requiems at Birmingham: the protestant Requiem, so mystical and so German and tender, of

Brahms; and that of Verdi, so dazzling, so picturesque, so restless – and so Italian. Listening to them, I realised that there is still room for a Requiem <u>without a Credo</u>; a Requiem in which one could sum up the most serious and touching things that men had said about their future destiny; a sort of <u>Ultima Verba</u>. I would take the text from everywhere; from Eastern philosophers, Marcus Aurelius, Shakespeare, Goethe, St Francis of Assisi. The first part would be grave and philosophical; the second – a very short and very human expression of personal sadness and regret; the third – a consolation; the fourth – a triumph. But very condensed – not at all long. For all of this, grave, simple music would be needed, at once very austere and very tender. All the texts would be taken from books which are widely available, it would be possible to find good translations for all these ideas in different languages. Voilà. I shall busy myself with this during my hours of leisure. When it's finished, I shall send it to you to see if you might be keen on the idea. If not, I shall make a present of it to Mackenzie, Stanford – or perhaps Elgar![3]

Enclosed you'll find what Newman has already written about the symphony in the 'Nation'.[4] A few days ago I saw Dr von Hase.[5] From everything he said, I think that the house of Breitkopf & Härtel is very well disposed to you. In the meantime, have you heard anything else about a work for the Gloucester (? or Worcester) Festival?[6] I don't want to be impractical and pessimistic, but I have such a horror of these Festival commissions! This is how we always ruin so many of our best composers in England, by making them work at speed and a little 'to order'. They end up writing too much: Parry, Mackenzie suffered in their youth; Elgar is rapidly going downhill under the strain of more or less commercial projects; Bantock writes too much, with the result that half of what is performed of his is a little 'facile'; – is it any surprise that I do not want to see you become 'fashionable', like poor Dvořák twenty years ago?[7] For since the death of Brahms you are the only composer, it seems to me, who is <u>creating</u> in peace, with inspiration, allowing your spirit and your soul to speak, rather than throwing notes at the paper in order to be finished by the 20th or the 25th of such and such a month. But if you already have something ready, or almost ready – then that's quite a different matter.

Forgive me these sermons! You, and your art, are for me the two most dear and pressing interests at the end of my life. It is even a consolation 'for growing old',[8] that I can help you better with my accumulated years and experience.

Farewell, and all best wishes to Madame Sibelius. I shall write to her soon. As for you, all my blessings – you know that you are never absent from my thoughts for long,

Rosa Newmarch.

I am not sure that your baton isn't too long to post. In which case, I shall keep it for you until there is a convenient moment.

[1] English in the original. A phrase from Goethe's *Zahme Xenien IX* (the original reads: 'Wer Wissenschaft und Kunst besitzt, hat auch Religion; wer jene beiden nicht besitzt, der habe Religion').
[2] The English tenor Gervase Elwes (1866–1921) was closely associated with the part of Gerontius in Elgar's *The Dream of Gerontius*, and gave the first performance of Vaughan Williams's *On Wenlock Edge*. He took part in the performances of Bach's *St Matthew Passion*, Elgar's *The Apostles* and Handel's *Messiah* during the 1912 Birmingham Festival.
[3] Newmarch seems to have produced no such text. In the light of her interest in the idea of a requiem without a creed, her response to Janáček's *Glagolitic Mass* is significant:

> His Mass is something quite disassociated from the mystical emotion induced by the 'dim religious light' of church interiors. It is intended to be joyful and popular . . . It cannot be compared with any other Mass: its gaiety is quite a different thing from Haydn's cheerfulness – something more approaching to animal spirits; its pathos is not the pathos of Beethoven; there is none of Verdi's tone-painting; it is absolute music; and although the national impulse shows in both works, it does not pair with Kodaly's *Psalmus Hungaricus*, but contrasts with it; nor has it anything of the asceticism of the Eastern Church. (*The Music of Czechoslovakia* (London, 1942), p. 223)

During the Great War, Newmarch also wrote an article discussing Aleksandr Kastalsky's *Requiem for Allied Heroes*, a polyglot setting of the words of the requiem mass alongside other texts, with music to express the alliance between Britain, France, Russia and Serbia. See 'A Requiem for the Allied Heroes', *Musical Times* 58 1917), 496–7.
[4] Newman's long review of the Birmingham Festival included the following section on the Fourth Symphony:

> Sibelius's fourth symphony gave the audience the toughest of nuts to crack, and left them frankly puzzled. The work confuses, at a first hearing, not by reason of any elaboration of tissue, but by its drastic simplification of both idea and of expression. Sibelius has no need of the grossly swollen orchestral apparatus of the average modern composer. His scores are as simple in appearance as those of Beethoven. With his clean strength of thought he has no need to be dressing platitudes in sumptuous raiment. In this fourth symphony he has carried his normal simplicity and directness of speech to extraordinary lengths. Those who were confounded by it at the Festival

may be assured that its appeal grows greatly as one knows it better. It is still the Sibelius of old – dour and tender in turns, rarely smiling, but without Tchaikovski's tearfulness and self-pity – but the soul of the man has now obviously retired further into itself, and is brooding at a depth to which it is not easy to follow him without a guide. But even the Philistine, one imagines, must feel at once that here is a powerful brain seizing upon life in its own way. (Ernest Newman, 'The Birmingham Musical Festival', *Nation*, 12 October 1912, 100–01).

Other articles by Newman connected with the Birmingham performance of the Fourth Symphony include 'Final Rehearsals', *Birmingham Daily Post*, 30 September 1912, 12, and 'Birmingham Musical Festival', *Birmingham Daily Post*, 2 October 1912, 7.

5   Oskar von Hase (1846–1921), head of Breitkopf & Härtel.
6   Two days after Newmarch's letter, Bantock also enquired as to whether Sibelius would be able to fulfil this commission: 'Please let me know soon, if you can let them have a sacred choral work for the Gloucester Festival. Arrangements have to be made soon, & Mrs Newmarch & I will see to your interests, if you can send her a vocal score shortly' (Bantock to Sibelius, 25 October 1912, NAF SFP Box 16). Bantock wrote again in December to enquire whether Sibelius was minded to compose anything for the festival (Bantock to Sibelius, 5 and 30 December 1912, NAF SFP Box 16). In fact, Sibelius's involvement with the Gloucester Festival goes back somewhat earlier. In the autumn of 1909, Herbert Brewer (1865–1928), organist of Gloucester Cathedral, had written to Sibelius to suggest a performance of a suitable work during the 1910 Festival (NAF SFP Box 17):

Palace Yard,
Gloucester.
Nov: 12. 1909

Dear Mr Sibelius,

I do not know if you will remember me, but I had the pleasure of meeting you at Cheltenham early in this year.

We shall soon be making our arrangements now for the Gloucester Musical Festival, which take place in September next, and I have been wondering whether you have a new work, choral, or orchestral, which would be suitable for performance in the Cathedral, and if so, whether you would allow us to produce it in England. I might mention that the Festival is one of the oldest in existence, the first one took place in 1723! The orchestra is a London one, and the Chorus consists of nearly 300 singers.

With kind regards,
   Yours very truly
      A. Herbert Brewer (Conductor Gloucester Musical Festival)

7   Newmarch's warning about the fate of Dvořák (whose *Requiem* had been performed at the Birmingham Festival in 1891) was based on a particular distaste for the religious legacy of the oratorio tradition and its effects on the long-term reputations of foreign composers in Britain (see in particular her 'Anton Dvořák: A Plea for Remembrance', *Chesterian* n. s. no. 28 (January 1923), 97–100).
8   English in the original.

73 JEAN SIBELIUS TO ROSA NEWMARCH [ORIGINAL IN GERMAN][1]

Järvenpää, Finland 9/XI/1912

Chère Madame,

For the wonderful hours which I spent with you in England, thanks once again from the bottom of my heart.

Many artists – including Busoni[2] – have spoken enthusiastically about my Symphony IV. It gives me great joy that you too, chère Madame, think well of the work.

Inwardly I grow stronger and my ideas clearer day by day. I begin – like Beethoven (mais sans comparaison)[3] – to believe that strength is really human morality. I mean of course strength in its highest and widest sense. –

My family sends you hearty greetings and especially your grateful, sincerely grateful

Jean Sibelius.

[1] Cited in Newmarch, *Jean Sibelius*, p. 47/p. 32.
[2] Ferruccio Busoni (1866–1924), Italian composer and pianist. Busoni had spent a considerable amount of time in Finland from 1888, and was a profound influence on the young Sibelius.
[3] 'But without making any comparison' (*Fr.*).

74 ROSA NEWMARCH TO JEAN SIBELIUS [ORIGINAL IN FRENCH]

4, Crossfield Road,
N.W.
Dec. 3. 1912.

Dearest and honoured friend,

From the depths of my soul I wish you all that can be of assistance in your future life. Strength, and then development – and then yet more development – <u>until the end</u>. And when one loves someone, that is all one dare and should wish him. For although with ordinary people, one can very well wish them a pleasant and happy life, for those who, like you, should make their impression on the world, this is not the condition most to be wished for. But the strength to cope with all that happens to us and to overcome life and weakness – that is assuredly what I can most legitimately desire for you. Only as I am very human, I am tempted to desire for you all sorts of things which are not really good for anything: such as success, money, admiration, and all those trifles.

I am sending you a little book which I much like myself, although I hope I have moved on a little from the pessimism expressed therein. But all of us have hours of weakness and fear, and so my little breviary, which contains so many great and wise thoughts, has often given me some moments of restorative consolation. Put it in your pocket sometimes when you travel or when you take long walks.[1]

Well then! When you receive this letter, the great year (47!) will have struck, or will be about to strike. Where will it take you? But in any case if you are still thinking of undertaking a tour of America, do not leave without consulting business people about a good manager; and above all insist on being paid a portion of the promised money in advance. You might end up being abandoned without a penny, like Ysaÿe![2]

Since you left, I have visited Leamington, but for sad reasons: the illness of my sister. I shall go again this week because I am still worried about her health.[3]

Farewell, good and dear companion. I shall think of you on Sunday when I am in the country, and I shall raise a silent glass (of warm water) to your health. I embrace you most cordially. My best wishes to Madame Sibelius.

Rosa Newmarch.

---

[1] Sibelius's diary reveals that this book was Jean Lahor, *Le Bréviaire d'un panthéiste et le pessimisme* (Paris, 1906); the copy in his library is inscribed 'Jean Sibelius from Rosa Newmarch. Dec. 8. 1912' (*Catalogue of the Library of Jean Sibelius*, p. 74). Jean Lahor was one of the pseudonyms of the French symbolist poet Henri Cazalis (1840–1909). A friend of Stéphane Mallarmé, he is perhaps best known as the author of the 'Danse macabre', which inspired Saint-Saëns. Newmarch had clearly been reading the breviary before sending a copy to Sibelius, as the quotation from Goethe she cited in her letter of 23 October 1912 is included (in French translation) on p. 192. She also cited a poem by Cazalis in her description of Scriabin's *Prometheus* in her letter to Sibelius of [February] 1913.

[2] By 1913, according to Ekman, 'One organisation after another had approached him with a request that he should cross the Atlantic and give the American musical public an opportunity of hearing his own interpretation of works that

they had learnt to appreciate and love through others' (Ekman, *Jean Sibelius*, p. 195).

3   Marie Thérèse Jeaffreson.

75   JEAN SIBELIUS TO ROSA NEWMARCH
       [ORIGINAL IN GERMAN]¹

Järvenpää, Finland 30/XII/1912

Chère Madame,

For your Christmas present – the book – and your greetings, my warmest thanks!

The wonderful book will follow me everywhere.² –

My family and I, chère Madame, send you our best wishes for the New Year.

In friendship, your grateful

Jean Sibelius

I <u>cannot</u> go to Gloucester, because I have no new choral work to offer. So far I have no inspiration to write one, and cannot, and will not, force myself.

So your opinion has proved quite correct.

1   Cited in Newmarch, *Jean Sibelius*, p. 48/p. 33.
2   In her translation, Newmarch misconstrues Sibelius's original German ('Das wunderbare Buch wird mich immer folgen') as 'wonderful memoir', and confuses her gift of Lahor's *Bréviaire* with a copy of her own *Mary Wakefield: A Memoir*. Sibelius's copy of Newmarch's *Mary Wakefield* is inscribed 'To my friend Jean Sibelius, this memoir of another dear friend. Rosa Newmarch. Oct. 1. 1912' (*Catalogue of the Library of Jean Sibelius*, p. 92), and must therefore have been given to him in person during his visit to Birmingham earlier that year.

76   ROSA NEWMARCH TO JEAN SIBELIUS
       [ORIGINAL IN FRENCH]

4, Crossfield Road
S. Hampstead
N.W.
[February 1913]

Dearest and honoured friend,

It is terribly cold, with a wind that blows from the north-east and cuts off your nose like a knife at every street corner. And yet one can see, by the yellowish sun and luminous sky, that it is no longer winter; spring is already on the way, telling one very refreshing things in a severe manner, like a good friend with a brisk and forthright manner of address. For example, spring tells me that I have been very apathetic about my correspondence, and above all that I should have written to you long ago, since I promised myself that I should have the pleasure of writing to you every other month, and already the second month of the year is passing quickly. Doubtless Der Wilde Mann schläft noch immer in seinem gefrorenen Wald. Was macht er in seinen Träumen?[1] I should like to disguise myself as a deer (like Nijinsky in the ballet 'l'Après midi d'un Faune') and come and roam a little in your wood, in order to listen to what is going on in your head at the moment.[2]

Here we have had several novelties. The seventh Symphony of Mahler.[3] What a strange mixture of things already heard, moments of real nobility and moments of vulgarity that recall a café-chantant in Vienna! For all its faults, it is sometimes very interesting, if only it did not last so long. For example, in the three middle movements there is no imagination – but at least there is some fantasy there. Then Henry Wood gave Scriabine's 'Prometheus'.[4] Something else altogether! One cannot judge it as _music_ exactly, but as combinations of very new sounds, sometimes strangely and hypnotically moving. Wood performed it twice at the same concert, so that people might judge the work better.[5] But what a pianist he had found somewhere around Birmingham![6] Perhaps in a piano shop! It was naughty to ask this poor boy, unknown and respectable, to have these fits of voluptuousness and 'desires building nearly to delirium'![7] Despite the weakness of this important part of the work, it must be said that everybody was much impressed by it here, and it provoked a lively controversy. I have taken a lot of effort to grasp the governing idea of 'Prometheus'; I have thrown myself into theosophical literature and discussed all the details with several representatives of the Theosophical Society. Where it touches upon the philosophy and wisdom of the East, I find much that strikes my heart and my mind. But the 'spiritualist' side seems very dubious to me. In any case, I cannot doubt Scriabin's sincerity, and there are some moments in 'Prometheus' which are truly intoxicating, and when one has the impression that

'The sky, covered in a rich mantle,
Passionate and mad, dressed in blue,
The sky whirls like a Dervish,
Turns without end, made drunk by God.'[8]

But whether such dizziness is good or evil, I would not want to judge.

I have just corrected the final proofs of the article on your 4th Symphony which I have written for Breitkopf & Härtel.[9] You will probably never read a single word of what I have said about you and your work; that is even to be desired, since naturally we cannot always be in agreement and I see you in a light quite different from the one in which you see yourself. It may well be that you do not at all like what I have said; but my composure is supreme; I would only reply, like Pontius Pilate, 'What I have written, I have written'.[10] But if one day you happen to read this analysis of your art, you will read between the lines many things which I was careful not to say, being afraid of all exaggeration. These days, it is fashionable to say of each musician that he is 'the beginning of a new era'. I have already survived the eras of Strauss, of Debussy, of Elgar, of Ravel, of Percy Grainger, and now it's completely the era of Mr Rag-Time. So I do not give you an era all of your own! But what I refrained from mentioning as warmly as I could have done was my own love for your music. I prefer rather <u>too little</u> to rather <u>too much</u>, don't you?

The third novelty was the two overtures of Strauss, 'Le Bourgeois Gentilhomme' and 'Ariadne auf Naxos',[11] which the orchestra played in the large music room of the Speyers' new house.[12] The music is very nicely done in the style of the 17th and 18th centuries. The orchestration is clear and not very noisy – an entirely retrograde step. It may be fashionable, but will it last? But, to tell the truth, the outlook of the so-called musical world here disgusts me so much that if I did not need to earn a little money, I should go and live in Italy, where there isn't any music, and I should spend the rest of my life studying the <u>Upanishads</u> and the <u>Bhagavat Gita</u>.[13]

How is your family? I hope you have avoided illness this winter, and that Madame Sibelius is keeping well. I have not yet seen Madame Ackté, who is always so loyal, and who sometimes brings me news from Finland (mixed with some gossip too!).

Farewell, dear friend, you live much in my thoughts, and you are a part of what is most precious in my life,

Your devoted,

Rosa Newmarch.

We are very keen on the Sonatinas, which we play often. I like the one in D flat enormously, and I play it with startling virtuosity![14]

[1] 'The wild man is still asleep in his frozen forest. What is he doing in his dreams?' (Ger.).

[2] Vaslav Nijinsky (1890–1950), Russian ballet dancer. Nijinsky choreographed Debussy's *L'après-midi d'un faune* for Diaghilev's Ballets Russes, dancing it for the first time in Paris on 29 May 1912. He performed it in London for the first time on 17 February 1913 at Covent Garden ('The Russian Ballet: "L'Après-Midi d'un Faune"', *The Times*, 18 February 1913, 8), although Debussy's score had been performed regularly at Queen's Hall before that (and was the subject of one of Newmarch's most detailed and evocative annotations).

[3] The first British performance of Gustav Mahler's Seventh Symphony was given at Queen's Hall on 18 January 1909 in front of 'an overflowing audience' ('London Concerts', *Musical Times* 54 (1913), 115–16 (115)).

[4] The performance of Scriabin's *Prometheus* on 1 February 1913 at Queen's Hall left *The Musical Times* wondering:

> What to think of it all is bewildering. Is it a natural progressive evolution of art, or is it a freakish and sterile variation? For our part, we are content to record the general impression the work leaves of power, dim immensity, seriousness merging into ecstasy, and a consistency of idiom that made for form. ('London Concerts', *Musical Times* 54 (1913), 174–6 and 182 (174–5)).

Newmarch's extensive and detailed note was published the next year as '"Prometheus": The Poem of Fire', *Musical Times* 55 (1914), 227–31.

[5] Just before the first performance of *Prometheus*, Newmarch gave a lecture at the Halcyon Club on Scriabin, and especially *Prometheus*, which prompted one correspondent to write into *The Times* with the following suggestion:

> In view of the complexity of this work, the startling novelty of its harmonic texture, and its strange psychological basis, may I be allowed very respectfully to suggest to Sir Henry Wood and the directors of the Queen's Hall Orchestra that it would be a positive boon if they would break through custom and give the work twice on this occasion? (W. G. McNaught, 'Scriabine's "Prometheus": A Suggestion', *The Times*, 24 January 1913, 9)

The subsequent review in *The Musical Times* observed: 'The majority of the audience remained for the second performance, and applauded vigorously: perhaps more in recognition of Sir Henry's labours than in appreciation of the music' ('London Concerts', *Musical Times* 54 (1913), 175).

[6] The solo piano part was taken by Arthur Cooke, who, according to *The Musical Times*, 'battled ably with the pianoforte part' (ibid.). The work's part for a *tastiera per luce* ('keyboard of light' or 'colour organ') was not performed.

7 This appears to be a slightly misremembered quotation of two of Scriabin's consecutive markings in the score of the *Poem of Ecstasy* (at rehearsal numbers 7 and 8): 'avec une ivresse toujours croissante' and 'presque en délire'. Dahlström identifies the same quotation in Sibelius's diary entry for 15 August 1910: 'A wonderful day! Have forged a little but have dreamt of even more! The atmosphere this evening was wonderful. As always when stillness speaks: there are dreadful overtones of eternal stillness – life's *Angst*. Learn to live "avec une ivresse toujours croissante presque en délire"' (*Dagbok*, p. 51, translation in Tawaststjerna, *Sibelius*, vol. 2, p. 142). Copies of both the *Poem of Ecstasy* and *Prometheus* were among the few contemporary scores in Sibelius's library.

8 This is the opening quatrain of Jean Lahor's 'Fantasie orientale', one of the *Chants panthéistes* published in the second edition of his *L'Illusion* (Paris, 1888), p. 144.

9 Newmarch's original note for the Birmingham Festival performance of the symphony was revised and expanded as a brochure and published as *Jean Sibelius: Symphony No. 4 in A minor, Op. 63* (London, [1913]), and in Ludmille Kirschbaum's German translation as *Vierte Sinfonie von Jean Sibelius (A moll, op. 63): Kleiner Konzertführer* (Leipzig, [1913]).

10 John 19:22.

11 The overtures were subsequently given in public at Queen's Hall on 14 February 1914 ('London Concerts', *Musical Times* 55 (1914), 187–9 (188)), although Molière's play *Le bourgeois gentilhomme*, with Strauss's interpolated music for *Ariadne auf Naxos*, had already been staged in Somerset Maugham's English translation as *The Perfect Gentleman*, directed by Herbert Beerbohm Tree (and with music directed by Beecham) at His Majesty's Theatre on 27 May 1913 ('Ariadne in Naxos', *Musical Times*, 53 (1913), 456).

12 In 1910–11, Speyer had converted two properties at 44 and 46 Grosvenor Street in Mayfair into a single residence, including a large music room (details can be found in F. H. W. Sheppard, *The Grosvenor Estate in Mayfair, Part II (The Buildings)*, Survey of London 40 (London, 1980), pp. 45–7).

13 Both the *Upanishads* and the *Bhagavad Gita* are Hindu philosophical texts. Newmarch's interest is characteristic of her general interest in 'oriental' thought (alluded to several times in her letters to Sibelius), and her corresponding scepticism about institutional Christianity (itself typical of the age). As to the source of her interest, then Newmarch was clearly familiar with the writings of Jean Lahor, such as his *Histoire de la littérature hindoue* (Paris, 1888) or the *Bréviaire d'un panthéiste et le pessimisme* that she sent to Sibelius on 3 December 1912 and which contains a number of extracts from Hindu philosophical texts. She may also have been familiar with the work of the German-born philologist and orientalist Max Müller (1823–1900), whose two-volume English translation of the *Upanishads* was published in 1879 and 1884. In her 1906 brochure on Sibelius, Newmarch refers to Müller's description of the *Kalevala* as being 'on a level with greatest epics of the world' and possessing 'merits almost equal to those of The Iliad, of the Nibelung' (*Jean Sibelius: A Finnish Composer*, p. 5).

14 Newmarch presumably means the third sonatina in B flat.

77 JEAN SIBELIUS TO ROSA NEWMARCH
[ORIGINAL IN GERMAN][1]

Järvenpää, Finland 18/IV/1913

Chère Madame,

Time passes quickly and all my good intentions to become a better correspondent have come to nothing.

With my heart I thank you for your last, interesting letter. As regards Scriabin's art, I believe that the religious music of the future may proceed from such works combined with opera.

I am working diligently myself. This season I have conducted a lot, including in Copenhagen.[2]

Cordial greetings to you, Chère Madame, from my family and above all from your grateful

Jean Sibelius

[1] Translation partially cited in Newmarch, *Jean Sibelius*, pp. 48–9/p. 33.
[2] Sibelius had travelled to Copenhagen at the end of November 1912, conducting the Fourth Symphony, *Scènes historiques II*, *Night Ride and Sunrise* and a selection of songs on 3 December. The reviews – which reached Sibelius upon his return to Finland – were not altogether sympathetic, as his affronted reaction in his diary suggests (*Dagbok*, p. 158), although it is characteristic that he should mention nothing of this to Newmarch.

78 ROSA NEWMARCH TO JEAN SIBELIUS
[ORIGINAL IN FRENCH]

4, Crossfield Road,
N.W.
22, May [1913]

Dearest and honoured friend,

For several weeks I have been trying my best to write you a nice long letter in peace, but it is impossible. There are so many impediments at the moment. The very serious illness of my sister which interrupts me from time to time with the need to travel to Leamington, and then lots of work to complete – I am hastily translating the operas of Moussorgsky[1] – and then there is the old age which inevitably descends on my life and makes it slower for me to do the tasks of the day.

I see with much interest the announcement of the impending

visit of your famous Helsingfors choir.[2] If only I knew in advance what they were going to sing for us, I could perhaps be of use to them with our press. In your little letter – which I was very happy to receive, because I see from it that you were keeping well and very busy – you say nothing of Eva's wedding, and I should willingly have known whether it was fixed for June. Will you go travelling afterwards? I think that this year I ought to stay in England; I am afraid to go too far away from my sister; moreover, I need to save money for John, who will soon have to leave the hospital and establish himself in a modest apartment at the heart of the medical world. Still, if you were to find yourself as near as Paris, Brussels or the north of Germany, I should be very tempted to come and meet you. But I won't make any long voyages.

The Woods are now in the north of Italy. Sometimes I get very tired with all this work for Queen's Hall; it is rather drab, and it also seems to me that a lot of music is performed that (for me) lacks true artistic worth. It is probably the same everywhere. But there are moments when I truly feel like disassociating myself from all that belongs to the 'world of music' (concerts, programmes, performers and tutti quanti!) and to give myself entirely over to art, and to the study of aesthetics and psychology.[3] You are somewhat to be envied in your forest! You see that I am going through a misanthropic phase. Remember me affectionately to all the family, and believe always in my devoted friendship,

Rosa Newmarch.

A little mourning for my little sister-in-law, who had been ill and suffered much for 20 years.

---

[1] Newmarch's earlier translation of *Boris Godunov* was published in 1910 (followed by translations of *The Musicians' Peepshow, Songs and Dances of Death* and *Yeremoushka's Lullaby* in 1911). Her version of *Khovanshchina* (subtitled *The Princes Khovansky*) was published in 1913 by Bessel (in Russia) and Breitkopf & Härtel (in Western Europe) and may have been intended to coincide with the season of Russian operas staged at the Drury Lane Theatre in summer 1913. Her translation of Rimsky-Korsakov's *Pskovityanka* appeared in 1912 (with the subtitle *Ivan the Terrible*), and her version of the libretto of Borodin's *Prince Igor* for Beliaeff was published in 1914, again to coincide with the opera's British première on 8 June that year (reviewed in '"Prince Igor": Russian Opera at Drury Lane', *The Times*, 9 June 1914, 10). In 1913, Newmarch contributed an article on Musorgsky to *The Musical Times*, in which she wrote: 'In France they seem to have found permanent anchorage;

whether they will sail into the haven of our affections and remain there, is a question that the next few weeks will decide one way or the other' ('Moussorgsky's Operas', *Musical Times* 54 (1913), 433–9 (439). These early British performance of Russian operas were in fact given in Russian (alongside performances by Diaghilev's Ballets Russes), and it was not until 1917 that Newmarch's translation of *Boris Godunov* was heard in performance, adapted by Paul England ('"Boris Godunov": Its Performances', *The Times*, 2 June 1917, 9).

2   The Finnish choir Suomen Laulu (The Song of Finland) performed three concerts at Queen's Hall on 13, 18 and 20 June, as well as visiting Bournemouth and Eastbourne.

3   Newmarch's reference to aesthetics and psychology suggests an interest in the work of her near contemporary Vernon Lee (pseudonym of Violet Paget, 1856–1935). A prolific author of both fiction and non-fiction, Lee published extensively in the field of aesthetics, often drawing on emerging disciplines such as psychology. She was particularly interested in the aesthetics of music; the culmination of her work in this area was *Music and its Lovers: An Empirical Study of Emotion and Imaginative Responses to Music* (London, 1932). Newmarch and Lee were certainly acquainted, most probably through the Robinson sisters (Lee and Mary Robinson were intimate friends in the 1880s).

79 JEAN SIBELIUS TO ROSA NEWMARCH [ORIGINAL IN GERMAN]

Järvenpää, Finland
30 May 1913

Chère Madame,

I thank you with my heart for your amiable lines.

Our choir 'Suomen Laulu' is coming to London soon. I should like to ask you to be as helpful as possible, and above all to promote Maikki Järnefelt, a singer who is travelling with them.

This time the choir has not been singing so well as before, but I believe they have been practising too much.

Please ask Beecham and others to come to the concert and listen to Frau Järnefelt (Palmgren).

Most amicably, your grateful
    Jean Sibelius
I shall write in more detail soon.

---

1   Maria ('Maikki') Järnefelt (1871–1929), Finnish soprano. She had previously been married to Sibelius's brother-in-law, Armas Järnefelt, but became the wife of composer Selim Palmgren in 1910.

80 JEAN SIBELIUS TO ROSA NEWMARCH
   [ORIGINAL IN GERMAN][1]

Järvenpää, Finland
1/VII/1913

Chère Madame,

How can I thank you enough for all that you have done for us in Finland?

Your dear name is inscribed for ever in letters of gold in the history of our culture.

Eva's wedding went off very well, and your wire was greatly appreciated by us.[2]

I am working very hard and will shortly write to you about it.

Aino and the children greet you cordially. But most of all, chère Madame, greetings from your grateful, truly grateful

    Jean Sibelius

I received the baton safely; it is a message from you.[3]

---

[1] Translation partially cited in Newmarch, *Jean Sibelius*, p. 49/pp. 33–4.
[2] Eva married Arvi Paloheimo in June 1913. Newmarch's telegram does not appear to have been preserved.
[3] Newmarch took advantage of the visit of Suomen Laulu to England to return the baton that Sibelius had left behind in Birmingham the previous autumn (mentioned in Sibelius's diary, entry of 29 June, *Dagbok*, p. 172).

81 ROSA NEWMARCH TO JEAN SIBELIUS

13 August 1913.
Uplands
Alfriston.
Sussex.

Dearest and honoured friend,

I am very late in writing to you but I am – as always – very busy with the preparations for the 'Promenade' concerts. As far as <u>Suomen Laulu</u> is concerned, then I can only say that it was a true pleasure to do all I could to help your compatriots, several of whom were very nice. I got to know everybody a little. It is a shame that the choir was obliged to leave just as people were beginning to appreciate it. I would say that for a first trip the success was remarkable. Especially for London, where there is not such a warm reception for choral music as in the north of England.[1] Shortly after the choir left I was very unwell. It was the result, I think, of all the trouble and exhaustion I have had all this year because of my sister's illness. That goes on, and in circumstances which add unpleasantness to pain. She is cared for by a devoted but careless friend, who creates all sorts of difficulties between the poor patient and her family. In the end, the doctor sent me away to rest in the country, where I have been for three weeks now, and where I must remain until 1 September. I am well at the moment.

As for Madame Maikki, I did what I could, but I must tell you very frankly that she did not make a very good impression in London. One cannot argue that she is (or used to be) a performer of talent and temperament; but she is brazen in her way of dressing and presenting herself in public. A beautiful interpretation can sometimes make one forget her personality; but here, above all, personality counts for a lot! The poor young man is nice enough, and his compositions, although they lack vigour, are very interesting; but neither of them possesses the gift of tact. Perhaps she would have done better to come without Suomen Laulu, since the glory of the choir eclipsed her everywhere.[2]

After the Finnish choir, we have had the Russian opera.[3] What a great artist and man Chaliapin is![4] He came to see me, and I visited him several times, and we chatted and relived our memories of our mutual friend, Vladimir Stassoff. Chaliapin is a true pupil of Vladimir Vassilich! His spirit is direct and imposing. In my room he saw your photograph on the fireplace and asked me 'who is that?' We spoke of your music. As he is coming back next year we shall see each other often, I hope.[5] What are you going to do this autumn? Will you let me know if you come anywhere nearer us? I saw Bantock on several evenings at the Russian opera. I don't know what he is doing at the moment. I am working as much as I can on a new book; or rather, I should say, on a book which I began years ago, and which I put to one side until a more auspicious moment.[6] My thoughts are very often with you –
    your devoted
        Rosa Newmarch.

[1]   The concerts were reviewed in *The Times* ('Suomen Laulu', 19 June 1913, *The Times*, 10), *The Musical Times* ('"Suomen Laulu": The Finnish Choir', *Musical*

    Times 54 (1913), 465) and *The Musical Standard* ('Music in the Provinces', *Musical Standard*, 1 August 1914, 539).

2 In fact, *The Musical Times* wrote warmly of Järnefelt's performances, describing her as 'an artist of high rank, using a beautiful voice in displaying her alluring temperament'.

3 The season of Russian operas at Drury Lane consisted of the first British performances of Musorgsky's *Boris Godunov* (24 June, reviewed in 'Russian Opera Season Opened: "Boris Godunov" at Drury Lane', *The Times*, 25 June 1913, 9) and *Khovanshchina* (1 July, reviewed in '"Khovanstchina": Mousorrgsky's Opera at Drury Lane', *The Times*, 2 July 1913, 10), and Rimsky-Korsakov's *Pskovityanka* (8 July, reviewed in '"Ivan The Terrible": Rimsky-Korsakov's Opera at Drury Lane', *The Times*, 9 July 1913, 8).

4 Fyodor Chaliapin (1873–1938), Russian bass. Newmarch was first introduced to Chaliapin by Stasov during her first trip to Russia in 1897, and heard him perform in Diaghilev's 1908 season of Russian opera and ballet in Paris. They met frequently during his visit to London in 1913, and remained closed friends thereafter. Their relationship was chronicled in a number of articles by Newmarch: 'Russian Opera in Paris: Moussorgsky's "Boris Godunov"', *Monthly Musical Record* 38 (1908), 147–9; 'Feodor Ivanovich Shaliapin', *Musical Times* 55 (1914), 437–40; 'The Outlook in Russia', *Musical Times* 56 (1915), 521–3; 'In the Russian Hospitals', *Outlook*, 24 July 1915, 108–9; and 'Fedor Shalyapin', *Slavonic and East European Review* 17 (1938), 209–11.

5 Chaliapin did return in June 1914, performing in Musorgsky's *Boris Godunov* and Borodin's *Prince Igor* ('The Art of M. Chaliapin', *The Times*, 6 June 1914, 10).

6 *The Russian Opera* (London, 1914). This book was based on the five lectures that Newmarch had given to the Musical Association between 1900 and 1905, but the specific impetus to return to the topic seems to have been the Russian opera season at Drury Lane in the summer of 1913.

82 JEAN SIBELIUS TO ROSA NEWMARCH [ORIGINAL IN GERMAN][1]

Järvenpää, Finland 10/X/1913

Chère Madame,

Time – or rather, the times – slips away without bringing me the pleasure of meeting and talking with you. – It is to be hoped that in the course of this season I may come to London as a tourist. A month hence I shall be leaving here for abroad, where I intend chiefly to work and to 'listen'; I shall also do a little conducting.

It strikes me more particularly that musicians are still writing in the post-Wagnerian style – with the same laughable poses and the still more laughable would-be profundity. But that sort of thing does not easily die out.

Perhaps you may know that Madame Ackté sang a new work by me at the Gloucester Festival.[2] Now this work is written in 'my own' style for which, apart from my friends, I get so little recognition.

It is to be hoped that you are well – I know that you, chère Madame, are always working enormously hard. I am filled with curiosity about your new book – the book of which you have told me.

I know that you will soon write to me concerning it and that always makes me very happy.

Best wishes to you from your faithful

Jean Sibelius

---

[1] Translation cited in Newmarch, *Jean Sibelius*, p. 50/pp. 34–5.
[2] Having earlier failed to secure a new choral work for the 1913 Gloucester Festival, Brewer was nonetheless able to programme an important Sibelius première. Ackté had been engaged to sing the closing scene from Strauss's *Salome*, and that summer, she asked Sibelius to compose a companion piece for her – the vocal scene, *Luonnotar*, Op. 70. In August 1913 (not 1912, as his letter incorrectly states), Brewer wrote to Sibelius, inviting him to conduct the first performance of the new work on 10 September (NAF SFP Box 31, original in French):

THE THREE CHOIRS' MUSICAL FESTIVAL
GLOUCESTER
5.VIII.1912

Dear Sir,

You will probably remember that I had – with my friend Bantock – the pleasure of meeting you last year at the Birmingham Festival. I was delighted to hear from Madame Ackté that she will sing at our 'Festival' in September. She tells me that she will sing one of your new works, 'Luonnotar' for soprano and orchestra.

Will you be in England at that time? 10 September? If so, I would be delighted if you would do us the honour of conducting the orchestra. If you won't be here, I would like to ask if you would be so kind as to send me the full orchestral parts and the 'full score' as soon as possible so that I can study them.

Accept, Sir, my keen admiration and profound gratitude

A. Herbert Brewer

After several more requests (Brewer to Sibelius, 24 August 1913, NAF SFP Box 31, 29 August 1913, NLF Coll.206.5), the score and parts seem to have arrived with Ackté herself, just in time for rehearsals in London. After the concert (which also included a performance of Mozart's B flat major Piano Concerto (No. 27) with Saint-Saëns as soloist, Brewer's own choral ballad *Sir Patrick Spens*, Debussy's *Danse sacré et danse profane*, and W. H. Reed's *Will o' the Wisp*), Brewer wrote to Sibelius (13 September 1913, NLF Coll.206.5) to report that 'Madame Ackté sang your new work in her imitable manner', and sent him two reviews. Writing of the concert, *The Times* observed:

> Sibelius's tone-poem 'Luonnotar' is probably his very latest work; at any rate, when asked for the score and parts a fortnight ago he replied to the Festival authorities that it was 'still in his head.' It was specially written for Mme. Ackté, and so perfectly suits her range and extraordinary powers of vocal interpretation that it is likely to remain her special property. An English audience is naturally at a disadvantage because, with only a rough English version by which to follow the obscure Finnish legend of the daughter of the air who becomes the mother of the water and apparently of 'the lofty arch of heaven' and the stars as well, one could get only the vaguest idea of the poetic content. Still everyone could, or ought to have been able to, realize it is the musical conception of an intensely imaginative mind working on purely individual lines. The voice part is a free rhythmic chant, based no doubt upon folk-song style, but Sibelius's use of suggestions from folk-songs is different from that of many composers, who use it more consciously than he does. While they tend to fence it round with restrictions he unchains it from such restrictions as it originally has. Those who have admired the delicate orchestral suggestions of his Symphony in A minor will delight in the atmosphere with which the orchestra surrounds the voice in this poem. But it is a work to hear often before one dare to attempt to describe, much less to criticize it. ('The Gloucester Festival', *The Times*, 11 September 1913, 8).

The review in *The Morning Post* confined itself to suggesting that 'With its atmospheric and original effects the composition bears the mark of having been specially written for Mme. Ackté, and it will probably remain her special possession' ('Three Choirs Festival', *Morning Post*, 11 September 1913, 8). Ackté herself telegraphed Sibelius to let him know that she had taken six curtain calls after the performance (noted by Sibelius in his diary, 12 September 1913, *Dagbok*, p. 176). The score – with a piano reduction of the orchestral parts – was published by Breitkopf & Härtel in 1915, but to judge by a letter from Bantock, it seems that Sibelius may also have considered submitting the work to Novello, possibly in order to capitalise on his recent British success (Bantock to Sibelius, 9 September 1913, NAF SFP Box 16).

83 ROSA NEWMARCH TO JEAN SIBELIUS [ORIGINAL IN FRENCH][1]

[after 10 October 1913]

Dearest and honoured friend,

Here I am at last in my own home again! Home at last![2] And your letter arrived today too. I am very happy to hear your news. Since I wrote to you I have had many woes. I had arranged everything so that I could go to Gloucester to hear your 'Luonnotar' sung by Madame Ackté – but just eight days before, I was called to my poor sister's bedside.³ After an illness which lasted 11 months, she died on 2 September.⁴ Apart from the sadness of separation, many things and a huge correspondence have almost crushed me during these few weeks. I had to go to the seaside for a while with my other poor sister, who is not married, and who found herself, after 30 years living with the deceased, completely alone in the world.⁵ All that, and the upset it caused to my activities has horribly <...> during the summer. I lost weight so suddenly that the doctors were initially afraid that something was wrong with my kidneys. But after a very tedious and disagreeable dietary regime, I was declared out of danger. It's not that I was really incapacitated, neither was I confined to my bed; but this loss of weight, and a great sense of tiredness, made them suspect something serious. As for myself, I think that it was really just the vexations and sad responsibilities of these last 6 months.

You see, dear friend, that I was unable to hear your Scena, but the score, on its way from Henry Wood to you, was entrusted to me for an hour. I went through the work, which interested me greatly. It seems to me that it is <u>one of your best works</u>. It is such a shame that there is no chance of repeating this composition. Madame Ackté did her best to have it included in the programme for Manchester. To tell the truth, the concert there is too much in the popular vein to be favourable to your work.⁶

Let me know something of your travel plans. I hear that Balling is going to play your Scènes Historiques in Manchester.⁷ How good it would be to have you <...> But I <...> that you would not gain much – in the musical sense – from being in Paris. The novelties at the Wood concerts for this season are:

The Divine Poem – Scriabine (18 October)⁸
Concerto im Alten Stil – Reger (1 November)⁹
Five Characteristic Pieces – Arnold Schönberg (17 January)
People are already preparing oyster shells and rotten eggs for its reception.¹⁰
Symphony 'Das Lied von der Erde' – Mahler (31 January)¹¹
and then, later, a repetition of Scriabine's 'Prometheus', at which he himself will play the piano part.¹²

I have many things to tell you – things that are better said than written. I feel that one of our long chats about art would do me much good. As for my poor book, then the demands of the Queen's Hall programmes prevent me from working on anything more serious. I ought to finish it one of these days, before I become too old. And <...>

<...> likeable. She is a petty soul <...> and really dry; and rather stupid. I fear that all his old friends are beginning to feel rather cut off from him. She understands no more about art than a prim and proper 16-year-old schoolgirl; and yet she interferes in everything. Previously, much that was boring about my work went well, because I was always completely at ease with Wood. We would discuss projects, I would share my thoughts frankly, we would be excited by new ideas – but now that's all changed, and this is to be regretted.[13]

Well, that's enough of me! Let me know in good time what you are going to do. I shall be completely at your disposition. Remember me well to Madame Sibelius and the family,

your devoted friend
Rosa Newmarch.

---

[1] The top part of this letter has been torn off, and portions of the text are missing (marked <...>).
[2] English in the original.
[3] Compare the following letter (originally written in French) from Newmarch to Ackté (NLF Coll.4.12), which refers not only to the performance of *Luonnotar*, but also to the visit of Suomen Laulu early that year:

4, Crossfield Road,
N.W.
September 22 [1913]

Dear Madame,

Many, many thanks for your kind letter. I had made all my arrangements to come to Gloucester to hear you sing the new work that Sibelius has dedicated to you. But alas! My dear elder sister, who had suffered much since the start of the year, suddenly became more unwell. I arrived just in time to see her alive, to receive her final smile, and then she 'changed her world', as the Orientals say, and they are perhaps more wise than the rest of us. All of this happened in the first days of September, and naturally I had to abandon any idea of hearing you at Gloucester. I called the hotel when I got back to London, but you had already left.

What you say about 'Luonnotar' makes me very impatient to hear and to see this score. I think that most of our critics understand little of this music, but some of them – like Mr Colles of the 'Times', speak of it with great enthusiasm. I fear that Henry Wood is afraid of risking this scena in a concert as frankly popular at the Brand Lane one, but as I am for the time being by the sea, I have heard nothing definite. We must really find an opportunity to hear it in London.

When you come back to England I shall come and see you. I want to chat with you. People have told me of your triumph at Gloucester, and how you electrified the good 'clergy men' of this ancient town! Your personality, and your art, as vital and moving as they are, cannot but have a good influence on our Festivals, which are routine affairs and lack inspiration.

I have 'some gossip' to discuss with you! Do not believe all you might hear about the visit of Suomen Laulu to London. About the choir – yes! Their success was truly indisputable, but the place you have won here will never be filled by that woman who accompanied them!

Forgive such a short letter. The death of my sister leaves me with a vast correspondence. I look forward to your return. Believe always in my sincere and affectionate friendship,

Rosa Newmarch

4   The death of Newmarch's sister was noted in 'Obituary: Marie-Thérèse Holcroft Jeaffreson', *Musical Times* 54 (1913), 661.
5   Caroline Georgiana Jeaffreson.
6   Ackté had been engaged to sing the closing scene from *Salome* at the Brand Lane Concerts in Manchester, conducted by Wood ('Manchester and District', *Musical Times* 54 (1913), 676–7).
7   Michael Balling (1866–1925), German conductor who succeeded Richter as conductor of the Hallé Orchestra between 1912 and 1914 (S. Langford, 'Mr. Michael Balling', *Musical Times* 54 (1913), 9–10).
8   The first British performance of Scriabin's Third Symphony, Op. 43 (*The Divine Poem*) was given on 18 October at the opening concert of Queen's Hall Symphony Concerts for 1913–14, and was notable not just for the première of another new work by Scriabin (alongside a performance of the Dvořák Cello Concerto by Casals), but also for the fact that in the especially enlarged orchestra, 'six of the newcomers were ladies' ('London Concerts', *Musical Times* 54 (1913), 747–8 (747)). Wood later recalled that the decision to admit women was taken because many of the women presenting themselves for audition 'had equalled or even surpassed the men players' (*My Life of Music*, p. 371). However, Newmarch misremembered both the timing of and the reason for admitting women to the Queen's Hall Orchestra – an irony, given that she was President of the Society of Women Musicians at the time:

> I cannot say that I remember any first-class professional orchestras in London which opened their doors to our sex before 1914. During the war a small number of competent women players were admitted by Sir Henry Wood to the New Queen's Hall orchestra. Some of us shook our heads – I was among the number. The fact that nothing lamentable happened in consequence of their co-operation is perhaps the best justification of this open-door policy. The women naturally and simply 'made good'. They showed themselves as punctual, as musically alert, and as physically fit as the average, rather crude male instrumentalists who make up the padding in many orchestras. They helped through ten glorious educative years of Promenade Concerts; the years which popularised Bach, Haydn and Brahms. Suddenly, our musical *petits maîtres*, with their abnormally acute

ears and infallible *flair* for tone-quality, tell us that the weakness brought about by the participation of women was audible to them almost before they entered the concert room. 'Where,' they ask, 'have fled the full, rich tone, the steadiness, the passion, the exhilarating virile noise, of the old wholly masculine orchestra?' Vanished, gone for ever, extinguished by the presence of eight or ten women distributed among the strings! ('Women's Musical Activities', *Time and Tide*, 4 January 1929, 19–20 (20))

9   Reger's *Concerto in the Olden Style*, Op. 123 (1912) was performed on 1 November, with *The Musical Times* describing it as a work 'wherein the composer colours the idiomatic outlines of two hundred years ago with harmonies and other technical ways that were invented later', but that 'the interest evaporated as the work proceeded' ('London Concerts', *Musical Times* 54 (1913), 808 and 816–18 (816)).

10 Schoenberg's *Five Pieces for Orchestra*, Op. 16, had in fact received their world première on 3 September 1912 at Queen's Hall, conducted by Wood. This performance, infamously, 'was actually hissed by a section of the audience which, having begun by being amused, ended by being bored'. Schoenberg himself conducted the work on 17 January 1914, by which time 'it was listened to with considerable attention and even some satisfaction' (Robert Elkin, *Queen's Hall, 1893–1941* (London, 1944), p. 31). Wood suggested that the hostile reception of the first performance 'goes to refute the popular idea that the Promenaders accord acclamation to every work played, no matter what', and that the second performance 'drew a large and appreciative audience' that delighted the composer (*My Life of Music*, p. 355). Although Newmarch was clearly no fan of Schoenberg's music, her long and detailed descriptive note for the Queen's Hall performances of the *Five Pieces for Orchestra* was remarkably fair-minded and shows little sign of wanting to prejudice the audience against the work.

11 In the first British performance of *Das Lied von der Erde* at Queen's Hall on 31 January 1914, the solo parts were taken by Doris Woodall and Gervase Elwes ('Queen's Hall Orchestra: Mahler's Symphonic Song-Cycle', *The Times*, 2 February 1914, 11).

12 On 14 March 1914, Scriabin himself appeared at Queen's Hall to perform the solo piano part in his *Prometheus*, as well as his Piano Concerto in F sharp minor ('London Concerts', *Musical Times* 55 (1914), 256–9 (257)).

13 This would appear to be a disparaging reference to Wood's second wife, Muriel Ellen Greatrex (1882–1967), whom he married in June 1911. Relations between Newmarch and Muriel Wood seem to have been tense, and Elsie Newmarch – who was then working as Wood's secretary – later recalled that 'Muriel Wood was difficult and unsympathetic. She was interested in Sir Henry's work only in so far as it brought an income. It was obvious to me that she intended to keep everything firmly under her own control. So I did not continue after a year or so' (quoted in Pound, *Sir Henry Wood*, p. 115). The marriage was not, it seems, a happy one, and both Rosa and Elsie Newmarch were supportive of Wood's subsequent relationship with Jessie Linton (1882–1979), who, because Muriel Wood would not agree to a divorce, took the step of changing her name to Lady Jessie Wood (Pound, *Sir Henry Wood*, pp. 186–94).

84 ROSA NEWMARCH TO JEAN SIBELIUS
[TELEGRAM, ORIGINAL IN FRENCH]

London
8/12/1913

Blessings affectionate greetings.
Rosa.

85 ROSA NEWMARCH TO JEAN SIBELIUS
[ORIGINAL IN FRENCH]

4, Crossfield Road
London. N.W.

12 December [1913].

Dearest and honoured friend,

Thursday 18 December Godfrey will give your 4th Symphony with his municipal orchestra in Bournemouth.[1] As this will be the first public performance since Birmingham, and that Godfrey has gone to a great deal of trouble to study and understand the piece, I think that if you receive this letter in time, it would be very gracious of you to send him a wire – a small word of thanks?[2]

The concert will take place in the afternoon, so I plan on going there myself. Most conductors lack the courage to include your symphony in their programmes, or they are too lazy to work at it. For the time being – farewell – I shall write at greater length later – à vous de cœur

Rosa Newmarch.

Address
Dan Godfrey
Bournemouth.

---

[1] Dan Godfrey (1869–1939), British conductor. Godfrey founded the Bournemouth Municipal (later, Symphony) Orchestra in 1893, and was a noted advocate of a variety of new music, including that of Sibelius. The inclusion of the Fourth Symphony was a distinct departure from the kind of Sibelius works that had been previously performed in Bournemouth, when, predictably enough, *Valse triste* and *Finlandia* figured regularly on programmes (alongside the *Praeludium* by Sibelius's brother-in-law Armas Järnefelt). Godfrey had originally planned to perform the Fourth Symphony on 19 December 1912, after the work's first British performance in Birmingham, but withdrew it at the last moment on the grounds that it 'would be very uninteresting to the

general public' (Hamilton Law, 'Bournemouth', *Musical Standard*, 28 December 1912, 441). The situation had evidently improved by December 1913, although *The Musical Times*, whilst positive about both the symphony's merits and Godfrey's interpretation, remained sceptical about the work's potential appeal to British audiences:

> Beyond all else, the outstanding event of the month just past was the production at the eleventh Symphony Concert of Sibelius's Symphony No. 4, in A minor, a work which has not been heard in England since the initial performance, under the composer's direction, at a recent Birmingham Festival. Mr. Dan Godfrey had evidently bestowed an immense amount of care upon its preparation, and the orchestral playing was splendid; but although the audience applauded the performance in generous measure, it is not likely that the composition will benefit by many performances in this country. ('Music in the Provinces', *Musical Times* 55 (1914), 119–23 (119)).

A copy of a souvenir brochure giving details of the Bournemouth Orchestra's history and activities – Hadley Watkins, ed., *The Bournemouth Municipal Orchestra: Twenty-One Years of Municipal Music, 1893–1914* (Bournemouth, 1914) – is in Sibelius's library (*Catalogue of the Library of Jean Sibelius*, p. 18).

2   On 16 December, Sibelius noted in his diary: 'The day after tomorrow Dan Godfrey is performing my Fourth Symphony in Bournemouth. The brave man! I have sent him a telegram' (*Dagbok*, p. 179).

86 ROSA NEWMARCH TO JEAN SIBELIUS
[TELEGRAM, ORIGINAL IN FRENCH]

London
19/12/1913

Admirably well played and received.
Rosa

87 ROSA NEWMARCH TO JEAN SIBELIUS
[ORIGINAL IN FRENCH]

4, Crossfield Road
N.W. London
2 January 1914.

Dearest and honoured friend,

I wish you a happy new year, with all possible success, good health, tranquillity of spirit – in short, as much good fortune as is permitted to us poor mortals here below. I wonder – is he still at home? Has he ever embarked upon his pilgrimage to hear the music of which he told me in September?[1]

How happy I am to have heard the IV Symphony again, which has not ceased to haunt me since the first time at Birmingham! Things were really not at all bad at Bournemouth, given the difficulty of understanding this piece for the first time, and the fact that Godfrey, although very experienced, is far from being an <u>ideal</u> conductor. But he put heart and courage into his interpretation, and the public (not very large down there in Bournemouth) evidently found the symphony interesting, since he writes that he has received several requests for it to be repeated before long. He was very gratified by your telegram!

I am very busy, and I feel better than at the beginning of autumn; so I shall stay at home and write until April or May, and then will take a short holiday.

Send me few lines when you have a little spare time. Know that you are very dear to me, and that I am as always
 your devoted friend,
  <u>Rosa Newmarch</u>.

[1] Sibelius spent the second half of January and the first half of February 1914 in Berlin, where he worked on *The Oceanides* and heard a wide range of contemporary music, including Mahler's *Das klagende Lied* (1 February, 'a wonderful piece'), Fifth Symphony (4 February) and *Kindertotenlieder* (8 February), Schoenberg's *Chamber Symphony* (4 February, 'A result achieved by excessive cerebration') and Second Quartet (9 February, 'It gave me a lot to think about . . . He interests me very much'), and Strauss's *Elektra* (11 February, 'Strauss is a genius') (*Dagbok*, pp. 181–5, translated in Tawaststjerna, *Sibelius*, vol. 2, p. 262).

88 JEAN SIBELIUS TO ROSA NEWMARCH [ORIGINAL IN GERMAN][1]

Etablissement 'Trocadero'
Bremen, 18 May 1914

Chère Madame,

So I am actually on my way to America. (I shall be returning in a few weeks). I had a commission to write a new composition and now I am invited to conduct it there myself.[2]

I think of you very often, and often, very often, long to be able to exchange thoughts with you.

I hope that this letter will find you well and vigorous. So much of what you, chère Madame, foretold has proved to be true. So Miss Minnie Tracey has now become my declared enemy,[3] and has, amongst other things, written an article about me in the January edition of 'La nouvelle Revue'. I really roared with laughter over the criticism of my symphonies.[4] Next winter I must see you, chère Madame. I have been considering the giving of a concert of my own compositions in London. Do you think that I might realise the idea without running too great a risk?

I am looking forward to the journey and believe that the ocean will leave a very great impression on me.[5]

Your sincerely faithful and grateful

Jean Sibelius

The plans of a London concert must at present remain a secret between us.

---

[1] Translation cited in Newmarch, *Jean Sibelius*, pp. 51–2/pp. 35–6.

[2] *The Oceanides* (*Aallottaret*), Op. 73. In 1913, Sibelius had been approached to compose three songs for children by the American composer Horatio Parker (which were published as *Three Songs for American Schools*). Parker subsequently acted as intermediary for Carl Stoeckel and Ellen Battell-Stoeckel, who wished to commission a symphonic poem for performance at the 1914 Norfolk Music Festival. Sibelius sailed for America on 19 May, and conducted the first performance of *The Oceanides* at Norfolk on 4 June. Whilst in America, he also visited the Niagara Falls and received an honorary doctorate from Yale University, before returning to Europe on 18 June (*Dagbok*, pp. 189–91).

[3] Newmarch's published version of this letter substitutes 'A certain person' for the identity of Minnie Tracey. In his diary (entry for 16 May 1914), Sibelius wrote: 'My enemy, Miss Tracey, is really hurting me, but will this last long? What is important is not to let these writings spoil the time' (*Dagbok*, p. 189).

[4] Sibelius's account here appears to be somewhat confused. The article in the first volume of *La Nouvelle Revue* for 1914 was in fact written by Maurice Touchard ('Un Musician Finlandais: Sibelius', *La Nouvelle Revue*, 1 January 1914, 55–65). Touchard writes appreciatively of the tone poems and his songs, largely because he sees Sibelius primarily as a nationalist and a colourist. By contrast, his attitude to the symphonies is more dismissive:

> In his symphonies, one might think that a borrowed personality has been substituted for that of our composer. There, he finds himself both too confined, since he moves with nervous caution, and too much at liberty, since he is unable to fill the structure and repeats himself. The third, with its pleasing *Andantino*, is perhaps the most successful. Overall, these are the works of a diligent pupil rather than a master; their ideas are weak and the form – rhapsodic. The shoulders of the man from the countryside are decidedly cramped and lost in his detachable collar and urban attire. All of this suggests that Sibelius has embraced scholastic forms without

conviction, and only as a result of a crisis of stagnation, just as a man grabs at a branch when he slips. (p. 60)

Sibelius may have had Minnie Tracey in mind, as she published a short article in October 1912. In it, she discussed her personal impressions of both Emil Sjögren and – at greater length – Sibelius himself ('Music Masters of Scandinavia', *Musical America*, 26 October 1912, 5).

5   Sibelius's impressions of the sea during the Atlantic crossing are recorded by Ekman:

> The ocean was an unforgettable memory to me. The weather was fine and beautiful throughout the whole voyage except for one day of storm and thunder. I saw many glorious nights on the Atlantic. In particular I remember a sunset that was one of the most enchanting I have ever seen. I have never seen such a high sky arching itself over an almost wine-coloured sea – violet and blue clouds, a wonderful combination of colour. One morning the sea was quite silver-grey. Its colour merged imperceptibly into the faintly clouded sky that it was suddenly impossible to see where the horizon began. Suddenly there was a moving ripple of darker grey in the distance across the smooth, silver-grey field – and fifty porpoises that slowly approached the ship and passed it in a playful row. (Ekman, *Jean Sibelius*, pp. 198–9).

89 ROSA NEWMARCH TO JEAN SIBELIUS
   [ORIGINAL IN FRENCH]

London
4, CROSSFIELD ROAD,
N.W.
11. November 1914

Dearest and most honoured friend,

It is so long since I heard any news from you, although I think very often of you and your family! This letter will reach you sooner or later, and will probably find you at home. I won't write to you about this war which is so cruel and so necessary![1] I think that you and I have long had the same opinions about the so-called 'Kultur' of Berlin! I shall merely tell you that here we are very calm and very determined. We are building up our army day by day; little by little we are rediscovering our former instincts for battle – and do not believe anything you might hear to the contrary, since it seems to me that in the north of Europe, people are not at all well informed about the spirit that prevails here at present. Of course, everything to do with our dear art is suffering a little, although the first-rate societies are continuing to put on concerts. I am a little worried about your music <u>for the future</u>, since the house of Breitkopf & Haertel <u>in London</u> is said to be in a very precarious situation. Have you given this any thought? Mr Kling, being a Swiss subject, is not forbidden from trading here. Meanwhile, your 'Finlandia' and 'Valse Triste' are, as always, performed everywhere. In any case, I feel some responsibility, since I pushed you a little towards the house of B. & H., and, after all, it's hard to get on in the world of music without this ancient house. But in France, England and Russia, its agencies and offices will long be viewed with hostility. Perhaps you would do well to write to Mr Kling?[2]

My son has joined the navy as a surgeon. At the moment he is working in the large fleet hospital at Plymouth, where he is completely safe. But he wants to see war close up. As for me, I am resigned to the fact that he will help his country in any way he can, but naturally I should be horribly worried if he were on a warship. But I can well understand his feelings. If I were ten years younger, I should not be content to remain quietly here, knitting socks for soldiers! The most interesting thing I have to do is to teach a little practical French to the classes of 'Tommy Atkins'.[3] They are splendid, these young men. My son has been almost on his own in caring for wounded <u>Belgians</u>, since fortunately the number of wounded sailors has been almost negligible so far.

Send a brief line with news of you, and of your family. And believe always in my affection

<u>Rosa Newmarch</u>.

---

[1] War had broken out in the summer of 1914 (Britain declared war on Germany on 4 August). Finland's position in the Great War was distinctly ambiguous. As a Grand Duchy of the Russian Empire, Finland was technically on the side of the Allies (Britain, France and Russia) against Germany and the other Central Powers. However, conscription did not extend to Finland (a proposed policy of abolishing the Finnish army and enlisting Finns into Russian regiments had been suspended in 1905), and there was a strong strain of pro-German sentiment within Finnish society. Some Finns – members of the so-called Jäger movement – even received military training in Germany in an effort to overthrow Russian domination (Sibelius's 'Jäger March', Op. 91a, is a setting of patriotic words by the Finnish Jäger Heikki Nurmio and became an anthem of the White cause during the Finnish Civil War).

[2] Breitkopf & Härtel had been Sibelius's publisher since 1910 (and had acquired a number of his earlier works as well), and as a German firm, it was forbidden from trading with the Allied countries. Kling took over the publishing

business of J. & W. Chester in 1915 (as reported in 'Occasional Notes', *Musical Times* 56 (1915), 81). In summer 1915 (upon his return from a trip to Finland and Russia), Kling wrote to Sibelius (NAF SFP Box 47, original in French), giving details of his attempts to promote his works in England, despite the difficulties imposed by the war:

> J. & W. Chester
> 54 Great Marlborough Street
> London, W.
> July 19th 1915

My dear Maestro,

Here we are again in London after our most interesting journey. I am eager to let you have some sign of life and to say that we are well and that we have brought back with us charming memories of Helsingfors, thanks to you and Madame, to whom please express all our affectionate sympathy! What a charming walk we took, what a beautiful country! After leaving you, we were in Petrograd, then in Moscow, and the return journey was by the same route. At Riki Maki we would willingly have stopped and descended on Jarvenpáá to shake your hands warmly again, but we had to return as quickly as possible. – Madame Newmarch and her daughter remained in Moscow to spend a few days with Chaliapin. We have not had any news, but we think they are well. – Now here I am hard at work again and I really ought to stir myself. I will mainly be dealing with the music of Finland and Russia and I am pleased to have the support of Fazer, Westerlund and Apostol. Unfortunately I was not very lucky in my interview with Mr Blomstedt (Lindgren): he promised that he would write to me, but nothing has come, either to Russia or to London. – As your new works are published by him, I am very keen to have them for England, and I even believe that I have the moral right to it, since I have been interested in your works for a number of years. Couldn't you, when the occasion presents itself, talk to Mr Blomstedt about this matter and arrange for him to grant me the monopoly on his stock, or at least on <u>your works</u>. Would you be so kind and obliging as to send me all compositions published in Helsingfors, so that I can deal with this matter seriously! – I know well that these publishing questions are not part of your battlefield, but a word from you, dear Maestro, would do much. Thanks in advance! – In Russia I had a lot of good luck, and <u>all</u> the publishers granted me the monopoly for England, not just for music, but also for operas and mechanical copyrights. If only this dreadful war could finish so that we might work! But I am terribly afraid that it will be very long! However, we are very optimistic in England and we are certain of victory!

What season is it in Jarvenpáá and what are you doing? I can imagine the beautiful walks you can take there, now that I have seen it!

I hope that this letter finds you, and Madame Sibelius, happy and in good health. Thanking you warmly once again for your kind welcome, accept, dear Maestro, my most affectionate good wishes.

<u>Otto Kling</u>

3 'Tommy Atkins' (or simply 'Tommy') had been a term for a soldier in the British Army since the nineteenth century, and became particularly widespread during World War I.

90 JEAN SIBELIUS TO ROSA NEWMARCH
[ORIGINAL IN FRENCH][1]

Järvenpää, Finland
23/XI/1914

Chère Madame,

I thank you cordially for your welcome letter.[2] I wrote to you several times, even on my departure from Bremen for America, but always without reply.[3]

I think often, <u>very often</u>, of you, Madame, whose patriotic heart must be beating more warmly at this moment.

As far as my publishers are concerned I cannot yet be sure since I am dependent on my contracts.[4]

We are well and we are all very charmed by your letter.

With friendship your most devoted
    Jean Sibelius.

When I write in French, you know that I am nothing but a real Thommy [sic] Atkins.

[1] Translation partially cited in Newmarch, *Jean Sibelius*, p. 53/pp. 36–7.
[2] In his diary (entry for 20 November 1914), Sibelius wrote: 'a welcome letter from Rosa Newmarch' (*Dagbok*, p. 204).
[3] In her memoir, Newmarch writes:

> Although he mentions in a letter written later in the autumn that he had corresponded with me several times while in America, without response on my side, I can find no trace of any letter earlier than one dated November 23 of that memorable year . . . During the first year of the war our correspondence was practically at a standstill. Letters were censored; those in which he wrote chiefly in German were probably a little suspect seeing that he was a Russian subject. (*Jean Sibelius*, pp. 52–3/pp. 36–7)

The war also led to the loss of two of Sibelius's compositions in which Newmarch had an involvement. On 8 July 1914, Breitkopf & Härtel sent Newmarch manuscript copies of the first two of Sibelius's *6 Songs*, Op. 72 ('Farewell', and 'Orion's Belt') to be translated into English. Breitkopf & Härtel wrote to Newmarch in 1920 to enquire as to the whereabouts of the manuscripts, but by 1925, they reported to Sibelius that 'Mrs Newmarch was unable to recall these songs and could not find them' (Breitkopf & Härtel to Sibelius, 6 February 1925, cited in Fabian Dahlström, *Jean Sibelius: Thematisch-bibliographisches Verzeichnis seiner Werke* (Wiesbaden, 2003), p. 316).

[4] As Sibelius was technically a subject of the Russian Empire, the outbreak of war with Germany threatened to put a stop to direct contact with Breitkopf & Härtel, although the payment of royalties was sustained by the intervention of Skandinavisk Musikförlag in Denmark. In fact, relations with Breitkopf & Härtel were maintained for some time, although Sibelius did sign contracts

with two publishers in Helsinki (R. E. Westerlund and Axel E. Lindgren) and with Wilhelm Hansen in Copenhagen (Tawaststjerna, *Sibelius*, vol. 3, pp. 2 and 48–9, and Dahlström, *Jean Sibelius: Thematisch-bibliographisches Verzeichnis seiner Werke*, p. xxv).

91 ROSA NEWMARCH TO JEAN SIBELIUS [TELEGRAM, ORIGINAL IN FRENCH]

Torneå
6/6/1915

We arrive Helsingfors tomorrow five o'clock.[1]
Newmare [sic]

---

[1] Newmarch and her daughter travelled through Finland to Russia in summer 1915:

> partly to keep in personal touch with dear friends out there, partly to collect material for two books I had in hand – *The Russian Arts* and *The Devout Russian* – and partly to help my friend, Mr. Otto Kling, director of Messrs. J. & W. Chester, (who accompanied us on the journey) in finding a method whereby Russian music could be kept to the front during the war. (*Jean Sibelius*, pp. 53–4/p. 37)

They crossed the North Sea on a Norwegian steamer, first visiting Edvard Grieg's wife, Nina, in Bergen and then Sibelius's brother-in-law, Armas Järnefelt, in Stockholm. They then took the land route to Finland, travelling through the border-town of Tornio (from where this telegram was sent). Their visit to Finland was brief, yet Newmarch believed it to have been 'a happy interlude in a period when friends were so widely divided' (*Jean Sibelius*, p. 56/p. 38). Sibelius's feelings were more ambivalent, and Newmarch's conviction that she and Sibelius had 'long had the same opinions about the so-called "Kultur" of Berlin' was not shared by the composer, who noted in his diary (entry for 7/8 June 1915): 'In Helsinki. Rosa Newmarch, Else [sic], O. Kling and his wife. French all day. Their hatred of the Germans!' (*Dagbok*, p. 232). Otto Kling's account of their journey was published as 'A Voyage to Russia in War Time', *The Chesterian* no. 1 (November 1915), 3–8. During the war, Sibelius also had occasional news from his other British friends. Bantock wrote in March 1915, describing a student performance in Birmingham of the first two movements of the Third Symphony (Bantock to Sibelius, 23 March 1915, NAF SFP Box 16). A facsimile of Sibelius's reply to Bantock's letter of 8 May 1915 is reproduced in the British edition of Newmarch's memoir, in which he writes:

> During these times it often has entered my mind what a high mission have we, who sacrifice our lives for the ideals of the spirit. We ought to keep up the sacred fire so that the continuity does not break between a time, wich [sic] was and that, wich [sic] is sure to come. (*Jean Sibelius*, p. 95, original at BL Add Ms 64961, fol. 6)

Bantock wrote again at the end of 1917, this time with details of a performance of *En Saga* (Bantock to Sibelius, 27 December 1917, NAF SFP Box 16).

92 ROSA NEWMARCH TO JEAN SIBELIUS
[ORIGINAL IN FRENCH]

Hôtel Dagmar
Sadovaja, 9
Petrograd

11 July 1915

Dear and most honoured friend,

I am sorry to inform you that – given all the circumstances – I think I must return directly to London, without stopping in Helsingfors. The moment of the 'Promenade' concerts is at hand, and the management, fortunately being totally new, is keen for me to return. And then, I must admit that I have already spent a rather large sum, and I feel the need to make the return trip economically. We are leaving Petrograd on Wednesday, and travel directly to Bergen without stopping, except perhaps at Christiania.

We shall see each other again, I hope, before too long and in happier circumstances. My husband writes to me that of the six doctors sent to Plymouth at the start of the war, our son is now the only one left, all the others having been sent on active service. Who knows when his turn will come? And I should like to be there to bid him farewell in case this should happen.

We send our sincere greetings to Madame Sibelius and to all the family

à vous de cœur
Rosa Newmarch.

93 ROSA NEWMARCH TO JEAN SIBELIUS
[ORIGINAL IN FRENCH]

4, Crossfield Road
N.W.3

31 December, 1918.

Dearest and honoured friend,

I am taking advantage of the visit of Mr George Pawlo to send you this little letter, which he will probably place in your hands. I have very often thought of you and of your family since I left you in Helsingfors, in 1915. At the beginning of this long separation I wrote to you several times, but I do not know whether you received my letters, testimony of a friendship and an affection which does not change with the changes of history.[1] Of late it seemed pointless, perhaps even imprudent, to write to you. I have no idea whether you have suffered much during these terrible events.[2] Do you recall the long conversations which we had in the past about the great troubles of the world and their solutions? Well, the lightning struck quicker than we thought. But let us not talk politics or history! The future lies before us.

Fortunately, during the war I did not lose any of those close to me. My son, John, joined the navy on the first day. He saw almost two years of active service, in the Mediterranean and the Indies. Elsie is also well. She joined a firm to replace a young man; we also did some voluntary work, Elsie most of all, in the hospitals and during the famous 'air-raids'. But at my age I found it more convenient to stay quietly by the fireside during the nocturnal visits of the Zeppelins and the Gothas.

Music has never stopped in London, although there have been moments when concerts were not really in fashion, because of the lack of light in the streets and the possibility of an obbligato of barrage during the symphony.*[3] However, Henry Wood has continued to conduct the series of Promenade and Symphony Concerts. During the 'Promenades' we had some tense moments on more than one occasion. But the audience displayed a very British sense of calm! The few disgraceful scenes usually took place in other parts of the city, inhabited by a very varied population. Now I think we have a great thirst for music. I should like to see you here as soon as it is possible to undertake the journey. After all, you know that we English are not too bad, and are always prepared to give our old friends a warm welcome! It was a great pleasure to hear Mr Pawlo sing your songs, which I hadn't heard for so long. I think you would have been very happy with this interpretation, so well thought through, so delicate, and full of reserve.[4]

I am still working a lot. You can imagine how pained I am not to have had any news from Russia for such a long time – but let's not talk about all that!

We so need to know how life is with you, and dear Madame Sibelius, and the children, and above all, my friend Kattarina? Have I been forgotten amidst this cyclone that is existence these days? Don't be too long in writing to me, dearest friend. The memory of the good and bad days which we have spent together, in London, in Paris, in Birmingham, in Helsingfors, near Imatra – all of that comes back to me very often! And although my health is not bad, I am no longer young. One must not expect too much from the future. So we must begin to make arrangements for you to return here. Bantock will be nicely pleased, and Kling, and <u>me</u>.

All friendly best wishes to Madame Sibelius. I am as ever,
   your devoted friend,
     <u>Rosa Newmarch</u>.

Have you forgotten the ogresses and the <u>latch-keys</u> at Gloucester Walk?[5] And the cinema in Paris? How sad life would be were it not for these memories!

*Usually it was Wagner's music which drew the fire on us!

---

[1] No such letters have been preserved in the Sibelius Family Papers.

[2] In her memoir, Newmarch later wrote: 'It was only later that I learnt some of their sufferings during the early months of the revolution, and of Sibelius's narrow escape from being shot by the disaffected Russian soldiery' (*Jean Sibelius*, p. 57/p. 39).

[3] The repertoire at Queen's Hall had been something of an issue at the outset of the war, with the popular press calling for a boycott of German music altogether. As lessees of Queen's Hall, Chappell & Company were in a position to respond to this anti-German mood, as Elkin observes:

> Chappell brought pressure on Robert Newman to substitute a Franco-Russian programme for the Wagner programme which had come to be regarded as traditional on Monday nights at the Proms. Newman, however, issued a statement in which he announced his determination to adhere to the original scheme as nearly as possible, and declared, very properly, that 'the greatest examples of Music and Art are world possessions and unassailable even by the prejudices and passions of the hour.' (Elkin, *Queen's Hall*, pp. 31–2).

William Boosey later justified his actions by claiming that 'Sir Edgar Speyer's programmes were aggressively German – in fact, contained nothing but German music' (William Boosey, *Fifty Years of Music* (London, 1931), p. 106). However, despite her own occasional bias against aspects of German music (or at least the presumption that it was somehow superior to other national traditions), Newmarch refuted Boosey's claims in a long letter to the *Monthly Musical Record*, which had quoted Boosey's words in its January edition:

The absurdity and impossibility of cutting out the great classics – Bach, Beethoven, Brahms and others – was acknowledged from the beginning. Where else could material have been found from which to make up a series of sixty-one programmes? But in the scheme for 1914 there will be found side by side with these 'German' geniuses the names of Elgar, Bantock, Vaughan Williams, Rutland Boughton, Walford Davies, Goossens, O'Neill. Continental music was represented by César Franck, Bruneau, Saint-Saëns, Debussy, Dukas and Ravel, Dvořák, Sibelius, Moussorgsky and all the Russian school. ('Queen's Hall in 1914–15', *Monthly Musical Record*, 62 (1932), 36–7 (36)).

4 Pawlo gave an 'Anglo-Finnish Art Song Recital' consisting of works by Bantock and Sibelius at Aeolian Hall on 6 June 1918 ('A Week's Music in London in War-time', *Musical Times* 59 (1918), 324), and performed songs by Melartin, Palmgren and Sibelius (described as 'lugubrious vocal examples') in Liverpool on 9 December 1918 ('Music in the Provinces', *Musical Times* 60 (1919), 38–43 (40)).

5 'Latch-keys' in English in the original.

94 JEAN SIBELIUS TO ROSA NEWMARCH [ORIGINAL IN ENGLISH][1]

Järvenpää, Finland
3/V/1919[2]

Dear Madame,

Your warm, most kind letter gave me a great pleasure. Still more, when I found out that you and your family have not suffered of the war.

We are all here very well. Eva has a boy and a girl.[3] Ruth, who also is married, has a boy.[4] Katherina goes to school and both the youngest children are still at home. My wife takes a great interest in her garden and I have been composing several things among others a symphony.[5] However since year 1914 I have not been able to publish anything.

<u>My thoughts do often wander to you</u>. I wish I had very soon the pleasure and honour of pressing your hand.

With my most affectionate compliments, yours sincerely,

   Jean Sibelius

1 Cited in Newmarch, *Jean Sibelius*, pp. 56–7/p. 39, where Newmarch comments: 'The English is so fluent and took me so completely by surprise that I am afraid I suspected the guiding hand of Madame Aino Sibelius, who knew a good deal more English than her husband.'

2 In her memoir, Newmarch erroneously dates the letter 3 January, misconstruing the roman numeral V for a I (admittedly, Sibelius's handwriting can be difficult to read, but the letter is correctly dated in the catalogue of the National Archives of Finland). Pawlo did not, in fact, visit Finland until the spring (as reported in 'Jean Sibelius', *Musical Herald*, 1 April 1919, 107–8 (108)), and Sibelius's diary reveals that he wrote 'to my English friends', including Newmarch, on 6 May 1919 (*Dagbok*, p. 286).
3 Martti Paloheimo (1917–87) and Marjatta Paloheimo (b. 1915)
4 Ruth Sibelius married the actor Jussi Snellman (1879–1969) in 1916. Their son, Erkki Virkkunen, was born in 1917.

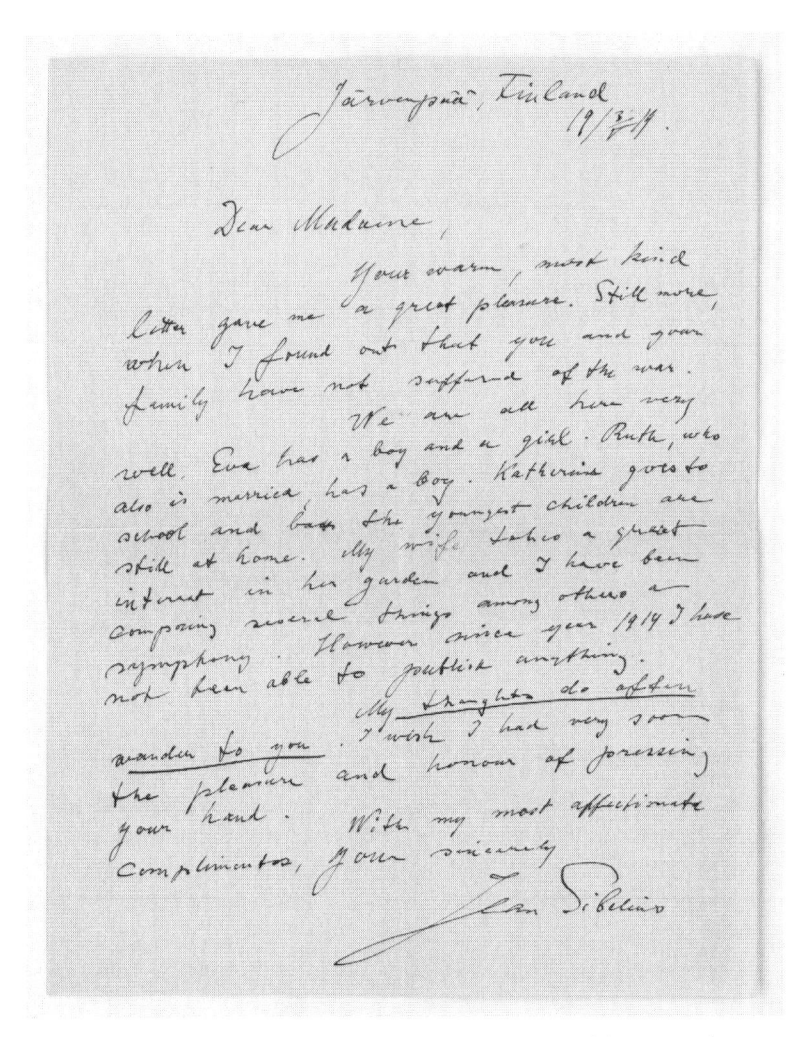

7. Jean Sibelius to Rosa Newmarch, 3 May 1919. (courtesy of the National Archives of Finland)

5 The final version of the Fifth Symphony, Op. 82, was completed by the beginning of May 1919 (*Dagbok*, pp. 285–6), and first performed on 24 November that year, although Sibelius had contemplated its revision as early as January 1917 (*Dagbok*, p. 256). Two earlier versions date from 1915 (performed 15 December, *Dagbok*, p. 240) and 1916 (completed 24 November and performed 8 December, *Dagbok*, p. 254).

95 ROSA NEWMARCH TO JEAN SIBELIUS
[ORIGINAL IN FRENCH]

Hotel Beau-Sejour
Champel.
Geneva

17 July, 1920.

Dearest and most honoured friend,

You will perhaps be surprised by my writing to you from here after such a long silence. I am here for 3 weeks' rest on my way back from Prague.[1]

First I must perform a task entrusted to me by Mr Robert Newman, manager of the Queen's Hall Orchestra,[2] who has asked me to approach you about a visit to England. In short, he asks whether you would be inclined to conduct one of your compositions (the new symphony?) on 12 February 1921, and what fee you would propose for such an occasion.

I would ask you to let me know <u>as soon as possible</u> if this invitation is convenient for you, and it would be best to reply to me in London:

4, Crossfield Road
   London. N.W.3

The concert on 12 February is one of the series of Symphony Concerts at Queen's Hall.

How are you keeping? At Chester's I have seen several piano pieces which bear witness to your activity and I have heard talk of a 5th Symphony?[3]

As for me, I continue to work, but not with quite the same zeal as before. I turned 62 some time ago, and from time to time I begin to feel the weariness of my age. But people say I have not changed much! I received the invitation from Suomen Lauulu [*sic*] with great pleasure, as well as the beautiful book containing the history of the society.⁴ I was rather indisposed at that time, but I should very much like to have taken part in the celebrations. Write me a brief line soon. My friendly wishes to all the family,

à vous de cœur,

    Rosa Newmarch.

---

1. After the October Revolution of 1917, Newmarch switched the focus of her attention to the music of the newly formed Czechoslovak Republic. Her first articles on Czechoslovak music were published in *The Musical Times* as early as the autumn of 1918 ('The Music of the Czecho-Slovak Races', *Musical Times* 59 (1918), 391–2, 441–3, 495–7 and 541–5), and she paid her first visit to the country in the summer of 1919 (as reported in 'The Music of the Czecho-Slovaks: National Opera in Prague', *Musical Times* 60 (1919), 592–5). Thereafter, she visited Czechoslovakia almost every year, and published extensively on its music and musicians (especially Leoš Janáček).
2. English in the original.
3. British publishers were particularly keen to obtain new pieces by Sibelius for their lists in the early 1920s. In 1921, Chester published *Twelve Selected Pieces for the Pianoforte by Jean Sibelius*, containing works from his Opp. 75, 76 and 85 (other pieces from these sets were published by Augener, details of which are given in Dahlström, *Jean Sibelius: Thematisch-bibliographisches Verzeichnis seiner Werke*, pp. 327–37, 368–70). Ralph Hawkes (of Hawkes & Son) approached Sibelius in early 1919 with a view to publishing some 'charming compositions' that would be 'full of melody and charm'. Hawkes & Son published the *Valse lyrique*, Op. 96b in 1920 (ibid., p. 408), although nothing further came of this relationship (Hawkes to Sibelius, 17 February and 22 May 1919, 9 January and 12 February 1920, 10 February 1921, NAF SFP Box 47).
4. Suomen Laulu celebrated its twentieth anniversary in 1920, and Newmarch may possibly have been invited to attend its anniversary concert on 4 April in Helsinki. The choir's history was published (in Finnish) as *Suomen laulu: juhlajulkaisu, 1900–1920* (Helsinki, 1920).

96 JEAN SIBELIUS TO ROSA NEWMARCH [ORIGINAL IN FRENCH]¹

                          Järvenpää, Finland, 2/VIII/1920.

Chère Madame,

I see from your letter, chère Madame, that you are working as well as before. And this makes me happy.

I would very much like to come to London to conduct my new symphony (or other new compositions that would occupy from 40 to 50 minutes) and I propose a fee of £150 on account of the enormous expenses that a journey at this time would cost me.

My family is well and sends you best wishes.

Your grateful

Jean Sibelius

[1] Translation partially cited in Newmarch, *Jean Sibelius*, p. 58/p. 40.

97 ROSA NEWMARCH TO JEAN SIBELIUS
[TELEGRAM, ORIGINAL IN ENGLISH]

Lowestoft
15/9/1920

CHAPPELL OFFERS ONE HUNDRED FIFTY POUNDS FOR THREE CONCERTS TWO SYMPHONIES ONE BALLAD CONCERT FEBRUARY 12 19 25 REPLY ACCOMPANY WESDO LONDON ROSA NEWMARCH

98 JEAN SIBELIUS TO ROSA NEWMARCH
[ORIGINAL IN FRENCH][1]

Järvenpää, Finland
28 Oct. 1920

Chère Madame,

I thank you for the cordial letter which I received a few weeks ago.[2] You know how idle I am! Here is a list of my recent compositions.[3] Later I shall let you know the symphonic works on which I am working at present. That is all I can say about my compositions and there is no expert on my music who I could employ in this case.

What are the programmes for the 3 February concerts like? Are they all <u>Sibelius</u> concerts?

Best wishes to you from my family and
your very grateful

Jean Sibelius

[1] Brief citation in Newmarch, *Jean Sibelius*, p. 58/p. 40.
[2] This letter does not appear to have been preserved.

3   The following list – in Sibelius's hand – is included in the file of letters from Eric Blom (NAF SFP Box 16):

> Op 73 = *Aallottaret* (*The Oceanides*) Symphonic poem for orchestra.
> Op 34, 40, 74, 75, 76, 94, 97 = 60 piano pieces
> Op 77 = Pieces for violin or cello and orchestra
> Op 78, 79, 81 = Pieces for violin (or cello) and piano
> Op 87, 89 = 6 Humoresques for violin and orchestra
> Op 72, 86, 88 = 18 Romances
> Op 80 = Sonatina for violin and piano
> Op 83 = Music for a medieval play (Morality)
> Op 92, 93, 95 = Symphonic works for chorus and orchestra
> Op 82 = Symphony (E flat major)

99 JEAN SIBELIUS TO ROSA NEWMARCH [ORIGINAL IN FRENCH]

[Autumn 1920][1]

Chère Madame

I should like to recommend to you my young compatriot, Mr Ilmari Hannikainen. He is a talented pianist & composer for his instrument. I should be happy if you could do something for him – perhaps with Sir Henry Wood. Last season Mr Hannikainen made a successful appearance in Paris (Salle Gaveau).[2]

My best wishes to you.

    Your most devoted

        Jean Sibelius

---

[1] Tawaststjerna's annotation in the National Archives suggests autumn 1920 and spring 1921 as possible dates for this letter. Given the content of Newmarch's letter of 15 November 1920, the former suggestion has been preferred here (confirmed by letters from Hannikainen to Sibelius, 12 October and 11 November 1920, NAF SFP Box 20).

[2] Ilmari Hannikainen (1892–1955), Finnish composer. Hannikainen performed Palmgren's Second Piano Concerto ('The River') in Paris on 13 May 1920 in a concert also including works by Toivo Kuula, Robert Kajanus, Erkki Melartin and Leevi Madetoja, as well as Sibelius's Third Symphony, *The Swan of Tuonela* and *Finlandia* (R. H. M., 'Musical Notes from Paris', *Athenaeum*, 28 May 1920, 711).

100 ROSA NEWMARCH TO JEAN SIBELIUS
[ORIGINAL IN FRENCH]

4, Crossfield Road
London. N.W.3

15 November, 1920.

Dearest and most honoured friend,

Thank you very much for your letter and for the list of your recent compositions. But, alas, this is not what I need; that's to say it's not enough; and I am like the Israelites (heaven forbid!) when they were asked to make bricks without straw.[1] How can I write an article about your works without knowing their contents? What I want, dearest friend, is your 5th Symphony! Is there a manuscript copy, or has it already been published?[2] Even Henry Wood has asked me to write to you about it, because you know that it is impossible to study your works in a hurry like a Haydn symphony!

I saw your young musician, Ilmari Hannikainen. He is a very nice and very intelligent boy, but just at present it is very difficult to get on here.

I hope that you will come to London a little before your first concert. As for the 4th Symphony, the orchestra has already studied it during the previous season and they are reasonably familiar with it.[3]

If you cannot send me the symphony, ask your publishers to let me know all possible details.[4]

Affectionate greetings to Madame Sibelius, and take care of your health, always

your devoted friend,
Rosa Newmarch.

---

[1] A reference to Exodus 5, in which Pharaoh orders the captive Israelites to make bricks without straw.

[2] The score was not published until April 1921 (by Wilhelm Hansen, in Copenhagen and Leipzig).

[3] The Fourth Symphony was given its first London performance on 20 March 1920 at Queen's Hall, and elicited a lack of comprehension similar to that at its British première in 1912. *The Athenaeum* felt that the work 'was curiously awkward and uncouth in style, but might perhaps improve on further acquaintance' ('Concerts', *Athenaeum*, 26 March 1920, 423), and Alfred Kalisch, writing in *The Musical Times*, was yet more sceptical about its merits:

> Another important orchestral event was the playing at the Queen's Hall Symphony Concert on March 20 of Sibelius's fourth Symphony, which

was originally produced at the last Birmingham Festival before the war, and had not been heard since, and it hardly proved more acceptable on this occasion, in spite of the care obviously lavished upon it by Sir Henry Wood. The admirers of Sibelius are much impressed by what they call his 'terseness,' that is to say, his avoidance of all superfluous steps in his musical argument. It is a doctrine that looks very well on paper; but in this case, when translated into practice, it seems to mean the omission of everything agreeable and pleasant, which makes one doubt its value as theory even in the eyes of those who are least disposed to owe allegiance to established rules of construction. How it would work out in a composition in which the themes in themselves were powerful or beautiful it is hard to say – in this instance they are neither. And the whole work seems to express a sullen and generally unpleasant view of life in general.

We were informed in the analytical programme that the *Scherzo* is merry and buoyant, which causes one to wonder what sort of music Sibelius would write if he were depicting melancholy discontent. ('London Concerts', *Musical Times* 61 (1920), 313–15 (314)).

The reviewer for *The Times*, however, placed the problem with audiences, not the work itself: 'It is this reserve, together with a sort of angularity of melody, which will keep the symphony from becoming popular, but it is partly that which makes us want to know it better' ('Return of Mme. Calvé: Queen's Hall Symphony Concert', *The Times*, 22 March 1920, 14).

4   Sibelius's diary entry of 27 November strikes a rare note of exasperation with Newmarch: 'From Rosa Newmarch . . . a letter pestering me for details of the symphony, etc.' (*Dagbok*, p. 304).

101 ROSA NEWMARCH TO JEAN SIBELIUS
[ORIGINAL IN FRENCH]

4, Crossfield Road
N.W.3

2 January. 1921

Dearest and most honoured friend,

Let me first wish you and all your family a happy new year, more peaceful and happier than recent years; and then good health, without which life loses its interest and value.

I have just received a letter from Bantock. Doubtless he will write to you himself, but I shall convey his ideas to you.

Firstly, the dates of your concerts. The 12th and the 26th February are your Symphony concerts at Queen's Hall. Friday the 11th you will have the entire morning for the rehearsal of your 5th Symphony. Can you arrive in London on the 9th? I propose to arrange on the 10th (Thursday) a small reception in your honour at Claridge's Hotel. It is so long since you were here that I think it would be a good thing for you to meet your old friends again, and to see something of the new generation. This will be from 4 until 6 o'clock in the afternoon, and you don't need to stay for long if you find it tedious! It is just to let people know <u>that you are in London</u>.[2]

Then Bantock proposes to come to London on the 19th, the day of the Ballad Concert, and you will return with him that evening to Birmingham. The next day (the 20th) there will be a concert of your pieces in Birmingham; the <u>21st</u> there is a Recital of Bantock's songs in Birmingham; the 22nd he suggests a soirée at the University with an impromptu (more or less!) concert of your music by his students. The <u>23rd</u> you will come back to London. Bantock invites you to stay with him. It is proposed to cover the costs of this visit by means of a fee of 20 guineas. It's very little, but as it is <u>almost a family</u> affair, I think you can accept it without loss of dignity. As for matters at the Queen's Hall, then you will hear all of that from Robert Newman.

I don't need to tell you that I am looking forward to the joy of seeing you again. I have studied the <u>5th</u>. It has not replaced the beautiful <u>4th</u> in my affections, but like everything (almost everything) that you compose, it interests me greatly. Also I think it will be less intimidating for the public!

I am a grandmother! Respect, please! John got married in the spring to a widow who already has 3 children.[1] She is kind and still young. Now there is a fourth bambino.[2] And you are a grandfather.[3] Youth must not – and will not – be forgotten.

à vous de cœur,

<u>Rosa Newmarch.</u>

Enclosed is Bantock's letter,[4] and the list of our suggestions.[5]

---

[1] John Newmarch's wife was Gwendoline Mary Stephens, who already had three children: John ('Jack'), Barbara and Joan.

[2] According to Newmarch's granddaughter, John and Gwendoline's first surviving child was Michael (1920–94), who was followed by Helen (1922–2002) and Renée (b. 1928). A first child (Paul) had died in infancy.

[3] In addition to the three grandchildren mentioned in Sibelius's letter to Newmarch of 3 May 1919, Sibelius now had another granddaughter (Laura Enckell, b. 1919), his daughter Ruth's second child.

4   Bantock's letter to Newmarch is at NAF SFP Box 16:

30 Elvetham Road,
Edgbaston
Birmingham.

30th Dec. 1920

My dear Mrs Newmarch,

I was very glad to have your letter and to hear about the dates when Sibelius is expected to conduct in London. I went into town this afternoon & saw Appleby Matthews, who welcomes the idea of Sibelius conducting a concert of his works with the City Orchestra. The date we think the best will be that of Sunday 20th Feb, & we suggest the programme should contain his Third Symphony, En Saga, Finlandia, & Valse Triste. There will also be a good singer for his songs with pfte accomp. Matthews also suggests an honorarium of twenty guineas. Sibelius would have a fine <u>welcome</u> here, & if he could arrange to return with me here from London on Saturday evening on Feb 19th after his Ballad Concert, I would be so glad if he would stay with us until the Wednesday following. He would have a band rehearsal on the Sunday morning, & the concert in the evening would be at the Theatre Royal, where we get larger & more enthusiastic audiences than at the Town Hall.

On Monday, there is a vocal recital of my works at the Town Hall with Mullings & Astra Desmond, at which Sibelius might like to be present. On Tuesday, I propose a social evening at the University or Institute, where the Lord Mayor & some interesting people would be invited to meet him, & the students would get up an impromptu concert of his music in his honour. We would at any rate be able to show him how great is our regard & affection for him. So I hope you will persuade him to come, & that you will confirm as soon as possible the Sunday date of Feb 20th in order that Matthews make [sic] get to work, with preliminary rehearsals & a stirring-up campaign in the Press. I shall anxiously await your reply. Our united love.

Yours affectionately,
<u>Granville</u>

A few days later, Bantock wrote directly to Sibelius (NAF SFP Box 16):

The University,
Edmund Street,
Birmingham.
1st Jan. 1921.

My dear Sibelius

I hear with great pleasure from our old friend Rosa Newmarch that you are coming to London in February to conduct your new Symphony & No 4 at Queens Hall on Feb 12th & 26th, and also another concert probably on Feb 19th. Now will it be possible for you to come back to Birmingham with me on the evening of Feb 19th, & to conduct a concert of your own works with our City Orchestra at a Sunday evening concert on Feb. 20th at the Theatre Royal, where we get large & appreciative audiences. The programme should include – En Saga, Symphony in C (No 3), Finlandia and

Valse Triste – (all for orchestra), and the music will be rehearsed well beforehand so that you will only need the rehearsal on the Sunday morning. The honorarium for you would be twenty Guineas. I would expect you to stay with us in our new home until the Wednesday of Feb 23rd, when you could return to London, as on the evening of Tuesday Feb 22nd, I would like to have a reception for you at the University or Institute, on which occasion the students would give an Impromptu Concert & Vocal Recital of your music – including Songs – Piano Solos – & some movements from Voces Intimæ.

I do hope you will be able & willing to come, & that I may hear from you as soon as possible in order that I may go ahead with the arrangements. It will enable us to show you something of the great esteem & affection that we all feel & share for you & your work. Moreover, it will be such a pleasure to see you again, & to talk over the old times, which were lost sight of during the War.

With united regards from us all, believe me
   always affectionately yours
      Granville Bantock

5 Although the annotation in the National Archives of Finland (SFP Box 24) suggests that the enclosed document dates from Sibelius's 1908 trip, it must in fact date from 1921:

<u>Suggestions for London.</u>

<u>February 10</u>, I invite you to a small reception – 4.30 until 6 o'clock.
<u>Friday 11</u> Rehearsal at Queen's Hall from 10 until 1 o'clock.
<u>Saturday</u> 12 Perhaps an additional rehearsal – I don't know for certain. Concert 3 o'clock.
<u>Saturday</u> 19 Ballad Concert, Queen's Hall 3 o'clock. The rehearsal will be arranged. Leave that evening with Bantock for Birmingham.
Sunday 20. Concert that evening in Birmingham.
Monday 21. Recital of works by Bantock.
Tuesday 22. Reception and soirée at the University.
Wednesday 23 – Return to London.
Saturday 26 – Concert at Queen's Hall 3 o'clock.

Further documents relating to this visit (NAF SFP Box 52) include an invitation to a dinner at the Finnish Legation on Saturday 12 February and a reception (to which Newmarch was also invited) at the Grafton Galleries on Sunday 13 February organised by the British Music Society. Although annotated as dating from 1912, the following itinerary for the week beginning 14 February (NAF SFP Box 24) also clearly relates to the 1921 visit, and is further evidence of Newmarch's involvement in organising Sibelius's life during his trip to Britain:

Itinerary for this week

| <u>Monday</u> | – Free |
| <u>Tuesday</u> | – We meet at Chester's 11, Great Marlborough Street <u>at midday</u>. We lunch with the director of the Royal College of Music at 1 o'clock. Informal reception for the students afterwards. |

Wednesday	trains for Bournemouth leave from Waterloo Station: 12.30 (restaurant car) – 3.30 (?) and better still 4.30 (tea) Spend the night
Thursday	Rehearsal at the Winter Garden in the morning Concert afternoon Return immediately after the concert – dinner on the train.
Friday	Morning Queen's Hall 10 o'clock Afternoon Royal College of Music. 4–4.45
Saturday	Rehearsal for the Ballad Concert Queen's Hall 10 o'clock. The name of the conductor: Mr Alec Maclean. Bantock will come to the concert. You will leave together for Birmingham.

102 JEAN SIBELIUS TO ROSA NEWMARCH
[ORIGINAL IN FRENCH]

Järvenpää, Finland 5/I/1921

Chère Madame,

I shall leave for Hull on the 22nd of January and shall probably arrive in London on the 28th. Would it be possible for Mr Kling to be so kind as to arrange for me a 'single bedroom'[1] in an inexpensive hotel, and if so, could you let me know the address of this hotel.

Forgive me for asking you to look after this. I hope that the orchestral parts of my fifth have reached Sir Wood.

Thinking of the great pleasure of seeing soon, I wish you, chère Madame, a very good new year, and all my family joins me in these wishes.

Your very grateful
Jean Sibelius

[1] English in the original.

103 JEAN SIBELIUS TO ROSA NEWMARCH
[TELEGRAM, ORIGINAL IN ENGLISH]

Helsingfors
13/1/1921

I AM IN LONDON PROBABLY FEBRUARY SIXTH
SIBELIUS

104 ROSA NEWMARCH TO JEAN SIBELIUS
[ORIGINAL IN FRENCH]

4, Crossfield Road
N.W.3

Wednesday [9 February 1921]

Dearest, most honoured friend,

Do not forget <u>tomorrow</u> Thursday at <u>Claridge's Hotel, Brook Street 4.15</u>, or it will be like the tragedy of Hamlet without the part of Hamlet! Take dear Mr Blom as your guide.[1] Bantock and Henry Wood will be there.[2] A vous de cœur cordial,

<u>Rosa Newmarch</u>

---

[1] Eric Walter Blom (1888–1959), Swiss-born British music critic, journalist and editor. Blom had joined Newmarch as annotator for the Queen's Hall Concerts in 1919, having worked for Breitkopf & Härtel and J. & W. Chester. Shortly after Sibelius left London after his 1921 visit, Blom wrote to remind him of a promise that was to remain unfulfilled: 'Please do not forget the piece you promised to write for me; that will be something that I shall value and treasure very much indeed' (Blom to Sibelius, 30 March 1921, NAF SFP Box 16). Blom wrote the entry on Sibelius for the third edition of *Grove's Dictionary of Music and Musicians* in 1928 (E. B., 'Sibelius, Jean', in *Grove's Dictionary of Music and Musicians*, ed. H. C. Colles, 5 vols (London, 1927–28), vol. 4, pp. 748–51), and also provided 'A Bibliography of Works by Jean Sibelius', *Dominant* 1 (1928), 33–5 (Blom to Sibelius, undated and 27 November 1927, NAF SFP Box 16).

[2] Newmarch also invited a number of other important British musicians. On 6 February 1921, she wrote to Elgar:

> I am having a small reception for Sibelius who has been bottled up in Finland through the war and revolution. I think, however, that you (wisely) eschew these kinds of gatherings. But I need not say how delighted we should be to see you. In any case if your daughter is free perhaps she will look in upon us. It will not be too dull, because I expect nearly all the young people from the Finnish and Czech Legations. (Elgar Birthplace Museum, L6118).

At Claridge's, Sibelius also met Vaughan Williams, as his widow recalled:

> It was at a party that he met Sibelius . . . Ralph had been leaving when Sibelius asked who he was. They had been introduced earlier but Sibelius was not familiar with the English pronunciation of the name. When he realized it was a fellow composer whose work he admired, he rushed down the stairs to waylay him in the hall. It was, however, rather a disappointing meeting for they failed, partly through shyness and partly because their only common language was inadequate French, to make real contact with

one another though they were both full of goodwill. (Ursula Vaughan Williams, *R. V. W.: A Biography of Ralph Vaughan Williams* (London, 1964), p. 139)

[1912]

4, Crossfield Road
N.W. 3

mercredi

Très cher, très honoré ami,

N'oubliez pas demain jeudi à Claridge's Hotel, Brook Street 4.15, on ça sera la tragédie de Hamlet sans le rôle de Hamlet! Prenez le bon M. Blom pour guide. Bantock et Henry Wood y seront. À vous de cœur cordial,

Rosa Newmarch

8. Rosa Newmarch to Jean Sibelius, Wednesday [9 February 1921, not 1912 as annotated]. (courtesy of the National Archives of Finland)

105 ROSA NEWMARCH TO AINO SIBELIUS
[ORIGINAL IN ENGLISH]

4, Crossfield Road
N.W.3 [London]

March 6. 1921.

Dear Mrs Sibelius,

   I have not had time to write you a long letter since your husband came, because I have been very busy. I want to tell you what a <u>great</u> reception he has had in England this time. He has conducted 5 times at Queen's Hall,[1] 1 at Bournemouth, 1 at Birmingham and 1 at Manchester.[2] At Birmingham there was a great public (2,300 people), and at Manchester more than 3,000. It is the big public that have shown him such a warm welcome this time. The third, fourth, and fifth symphonies have been played. The Fifth will have to be repeated several times before people understand it. They are now just beginning to get interested in the Fourth, <u>which is my favourite</u>.[3] Both are beautiful works, full of poetry and nobility, and most original. I am more and more impressed by his creative power. He has been very well here. I think at first the noise and excitement of London tired him and made him a little nervous, but he looks much better than when he first came, because we have had wonderful weather and he has been out of doors a good deal. I scold him sometimes about smoking, and not taking care of his health; but I think on the whole he has been very reasonable here. I am sure he enjoys the change to a new life, and that it has been good for him physically and intellectually. Wherever he goes he makes friends. We all love him very much, and it makes me very happy to see him almost every day.

   After he had stayed with the Bantocks in Birmingham, I went with him to Oxford at the invitation of Sir Hugh Allen, the Professor of Music at the University and Royal College of Music.[4] He was delighted with the beautiful old town, and the weather was like May.[5] Very often he wishes that you were here, and I am sorry to hear what he tells me – that you suffer so much from rheumatism. You must have gone through a great deal. The last few years have aged us all. We often talk of you and of the children, who are no longer children. My friend Katarina must be quite a grown up

woman now! And Eva and Ruth married women. I should like to come to Finland again and see you all. Perhaps I may, for I am very active in spite of my 63 years. I hope your husband will not go to America.[6] I do not see him giving lectures and teaching. I do not think his nervous system would endure the life for a year. Of course there is the money question, but what is the use of money if it means un homme fini![7] I have seen so many artists fail after America: Dvořák, Safonoff, and others. The life is too strenuous and inartistic. Sibelius is a creative artist, probably the greatest now left in the world. I think we grudge his years being given to teaching. A concert tour is different. I feel sure that he will be engaged here again next season, and perhaps for more concerts than this time. I cannot think he would be happy or well in America for a whole year. He is now 55; rather a critical time in a man's life, and he would have nobody to look after him in America.[8] He will tell you how strongly I feel about it. There are great risks in that hurried, excitable race for life, which is America, for a man of his temperament. I send you affectionate greetings, and am always
yours very sincerely
Rosa Newmarch

[1] *The Times* referred to Sibelius's visit as 'the outstanding event of this week's music' ('This Week's Music: M. Sibelius's Visit', *The Times*, 7 February 1921, 8), and later wrote at greater length about the tour:

> Sibelius's present visit to England affords us an excellent opportunity to know more of his works, for not only is he to conduct them to-day and on February 26 at Queen's Hall, but a whole programme of his music, including the third symphony, is to be given at Birmingham to-morrow week under his direction, and he is to conduct the fourth symphony at Bournemouth next Thursday. We should, then, be in a better position to discuss his music a fortnight hence, by which time it may be hoped that a fairly large public in England will have revised and intensified the rather scattered impressions which have been gleaned hitherto. ('Sibelius in England: Vision and Reserve: A New Symphony', *The Times*, 12 February 1921, 8)

Sibelius conducted the British première of his Fifth Symphony at Queen's Hall on Saturday 12 February ('New Symphony by Sibelius: Performance at Queen's Hall', *The Times*, 14 February 1921, 8), appearing there again to conduct the Fourth Symphony in a concert on 26 February, at which Busoni also performed both his own *Indian Fantasy* and Mozart's Piano Concerto No. 22 in E flat ('Sibelius and Busoni', *The Times*, 28 February 1921, 8). In addition to conducting performances of these major symphonic works, Sibelius also appeared at a Saturday afternoon Ballad Concert on 19 February (advertised in *The Times*, 17 February 1921, 8). The programme for this concert – the *Karelia Suite*, the Romance in C and *Valse triste* – was, according to a letter sent by Newman to Sibelius, proposed by Newmarch, although Sibelius noted (in English) that the 'pieces are well old' (Newman to Sibelius, 8 January 1921, NAF SFP Box 24). These three concerts had been arranged the previous autumn (Newman prepared contracts worth £50 for each concert on 18 September (NAF SFP Box 24)). Whilst in London, Sibelius agreed to appear at two Sunday Concerts (each given twice, at 3.30pm and 7pm respectively), conducting the first British performance of *The Oceanides*, as well as the *Elegy* from *King Christian II* and the *Valse lyrique* on 27 February (advertised in *The Times*, 26 February 1921, 8), and *The Swan of Tuonela*, the *Festivo* from *Scènes historiques* and *Finlandia* on 6 March (advertised in *The Times*, 4 March 1921, 10). The contracts for these (worth £50 for each pair of concerts) were issued on 9 and 24 February respectively (NAF SFP Box 52).

2   At Bournemouth, Sibelius conducted the Third Symphony, *Valse triste* and *Finlandia* on 17 February, and his popularity meant that, according to *The Musical Times*, 'the audience was the largest ever known at a Bournemouth Symphony Concert'. Unfortunately, the symphony continued to baffle reviewers as much as it had done at its first British performance in 1908: 'The preponderance of so much music of a coldly bleak and desiccated type chills as would the sight of brittle, sapless limbs in a dead forest' ('Music in the Provinces', *Musical Times* 62 (1921), 282–93 (283)). Shortly after, Sibelius directed a long programme consisting of his Third Symphony, *En Saga*, *Valse triste*, *Valse lyrique*, *Finlandia* and four songs with the Birmingham Symphony Orchestra on 20 February (the slow movement of the Violin Concerto with piano accompaniment was also given) (ibid., 282). Whilst in London, Sibelius had been engaged by Brand Lane to conduct *Finlandia* and *Valse triste* in Manchester on 5 March (Lane to Sibelius, 20 February 1921, NAF SFP Box 17).

3   After Sibelius's departure, Newmarch published a brief article on him in *The Chesterian*, in which she devoted particular attention to the Fourth Symphony ('Sibelius', *The Chesterian* n. s. no. 14 (April 1921), 417–21).

4   Hugh Allen (1869–1946), organist of New College, Oxford, from 1901, Heather Professor of Music at Oxford and Director of the Royal College of Music from 1918. In his letters to his wife, Sibelius alluded to the possibility of being awarded an honorary doctorate by the University of Oxford (21 and 22 February 1912, *Syysilta*, pp. 299–300), but nothing came of this. Allen later arranged for Sibelius to be appointed a Fellow of the Royal College of Music (Allen to Sibelius, 15 October 1936, NLF Coll.206.1), and even returned to the question of an honorary doctorate (Allen to Sibelius, 28 July 1937, NLF Coll.206.1). In 1934, Cambridge University also approached Sibelius with the offer of an honorary doctorate, although, as in the case of Oxford, nothing transpired of this plan (F. T. Cameron to Sibelius, 12 March 1934, NAF SFP Box 31).

5   Writing to his wife, Sibelius referred to Oxford as 'a wonderful place' (1 March 1921, *Syysilta*, p. 301). Newmarch later recalled Sibelius's trip to Oxford in greater detail:

> We met at Sir Hugh's rooms at New College and spent the afternoon among a small circle of representative musical people. I seem to remember

that Sibelius, who was not fluent in English, found a little difficulty in taking his full share in the conservation and discussion which surrounded him.

Sibelius was entirely fascinated by the architectural beauties of the Oxford buildings. It was a moonlight evening, and we went for a short walk with Sir Hugh Allen as our guide to catch a glimpse of the exterior of New College and Magdalen Tower in the lovely light. In the evening Sibelius dined in hall, an honour for which I was naturally not eligible, but a pleasant, though solitary meal was served to me in Sir Hugh's college rooms. (*Jean Sibelius*, p. 62/pp. 42–3).

Ekman's biography suggests that the visit to Oxford took place during Sibelius's second visit to England in 1908, but this would appear to be erroneous:

'During my second visit to England,' Sibelius continues, 'I also attended a reception in Oxford that had been organised by my friends in London. I arrived in the venerable university town on the previous evening in the most wonderful moonlight. In this magic light Oxford reminded me in a strange way of Venice. The ceremony itself made a profound impression of me. I have seldom felt so impressed.' (Ekman, *Jean Sibelius*, p. 178).

6   In early 1920, Sibelius had been offered the position of Professor of Composition at the newly established Eastman School of Music at the University of Rochester. Alf Klingenberg, the school's original founder, visited Sibelius at Ainola that summer, and on 3 January 1921, Sibelius had telegraphed his acceptance of the offer, although with considerable equivocation (*Dagbok*, p. 308).

7   'A finished man' (*Fr.*).

8   Tawaststjerna argues that Newmarch's comments here possibly stem from her jealousy at Sibelius's fascination with the pianist Harriet Cohen (1895–1967), who was first introduced to Sibelius during his trip to London in 1921 (Tawaststjerna, *Sibelius*, vol. 3 pp. 203–5). In fact, Newmarch and Cohen were close friends, and Cohen's description of a visit to Finland in 1932 elicited the following response from Newmarch:

Have the dissipations of Helsingfors been too much for you? Personally I always led a most regular and respectable life there, and loved the sea trips and outdoor meals; but I believe people do sit up all night there if so disposed! So that is the once poetical Sibelius! The first time I saw him he was thin and upright, with a good deal of hair the colour of ripe barley, and eyes terrifyingly blue and fiery. A typical Viking! But Vikings too, I suppose, grow portly and faded and dullish. A retired Viking might look like that. (BL Ms Mus 1641, fol. 68)

Cohen's recollections of her friendship with Sibelius can be found in *A Bundle of Time: The Memoirs of Harriet Cohen* (London, 1969), in which she also refers to Newmarch as 'my beloved friend' (p. 229) and cites the letter reproduced above (p. 209).

106 ROSA NEWMARCH TO JEAN SIBELIUS
  [ORIGINAL IN FRENCH]

4, CROSSFIELD ROAD,
N.W.

7 March [1921].

Dearest, most honoured friend,

If I come tomorrow (at 11.30), would you like to stop by at the Royal College with me for a few moments to hear the Queen's Hall Orchestra play two or three novelties by young English composers, and to leave a card to bid farewell to Sir Hugh Allen?[1] I shall also bring you two short letters in English for the Queen's Hall Orchestra and the Brand Lane Orchestra, and, if you approve, we shall ask for them to be copied at the Legation and sent with your signature.[2] You must forgive me for bothering you with all these details, but I should like to establish the surest of foundations for your return next season. You know that I have long awaited the day of your great success here, and now I am convinced that it is here. Only, I beg you don't go wasting your energy teaching young Americans to write harmony and orchestration in the style of Sibelius.[3] They can study all of that in your works. You are a composer, not a teacher; probably the greatest creative musician of our age – and certainly the most noble and most original. <u>That should be your mission</u>. The devil take the dollars! Go back to Jarvenpää for the summer; don't smoke too many Coronas (to save money!); don't drink too often (on the advice of your Leibarzt,[4] Madame Rosa Newmarch) and write your Sixth (on the orders of the Heavenly Father). That is the real meaning of life for you. You don't have the right to decide how to spend the years that are left to you; which certainly do not belong to the youth of America. And neither should you give up your manuscripts without being sure of your future royalties. Ponder on the words of this literal-minded and materialist woman philosopher who is always your affectionate and devoted friend

<u>Rosa Newmarch</u>[5]

---

[1] Tawaststjerna notes that works by Pratt, Wilson, Erlebach and von Someren-Godfrey were conducted either by the composers themselves or by Adrian Boult (*Sibelius*, vol. 3, p. 205).

2   Newmarch's handwritten drafts are in the Sibelius Family papers:

> 2, Moreton Gardens
> South Kensington
> S.W.5
> March 8th 1921

Dear Mr Brand Lane,
    Before I leave England, let me express the pleasure which it gave me to conduct at one of your Concerts before such an immense and enthusiastic audience. I felt that with a splendid orchestra at my disposal I should have liked Manchester to hear one of my larger works – a Symphonic Poem, or Symphony; but I hope that this may come to pass. Meanwhile please give a farewell message of thanks from me to Mr Catterall and all of the gentlemen of your Orchestra,
    Yours very truly

> 2, Moreton Gardens
> South Kensington
> S.W.5
> March 8th 1921

Dear Sir Henry,
    Before leaving England for my tour in Norway, I write to thank you and Lady Wood for your friendly hospitality. But above all I want to express to Mr. Maurice Sons, and the other gentlemen and ladies of the New Queen's Hall Orchestra, my appreciation of their cordial reception, and of the sympathy and insight they have shown in their performance of my works – especially my Fourth and Fifth Symphonies. Thanks to you all, I carry away very happy memories of this visit to London, and I hope to have the honour of conducting the New Queen's Hall Orchestra again before we have time to forget our good understanding.
    Yours sincerely

3   On the back of a letter from Dan Godfrey to Newmarch (5 February 1921, NAF SFP Box 34) is Sibelius's draft of a telegram, declining the position at Rochester ('Come to America only as conductor and not this year'), although his final refusal did not take place until May that year.
4   'Doctor, personal physician' (*Ger.*).
5   Sibelius's diary entries relating to his trip to England that spring are brief ('Have been to England and Norway. Have had a great success. Rosa Newmarch, Bantock and all my old friends are the same', 14 April 1921, *Dagbok*, p. 308). His letters to his wife are more detailed, and are extensively reproduced in Tawaststjerna, *Sibelius*, vol. 3, pp. 196–205, and are given in full in *Syysilta*, pp. 290–303.

107 ROSA NEWMARCH TO JEAN SIBELIUS
[ORIGINAL IN FRENCH]

4, Crossfield Road
N.W.3. London.

5 August, 1921.

Dearest and most honoured friend,

Two days before receiving your wire, I had already written to Chappell to find out what their decision was regarding your Suite so that I could settle matters before leaving London. On receiving your telegram,[1] I telephoned immediately. They replied that Mr William Boosey was on holiday in the north of Scotland, but that they had already sent him my letter, and that they would ask for a reply as soon as possible. When I sent the manuscript, Mr Boosey replied that he would look after this matter personally; he was very polite, but he told me nothing definitive. It is such a bore that he has left without writing to me or returning the manuscript to me. I also have to leave on Monday, but I have explained matters to dear Mr Blom and have asked him to be sure to forward you your composition as soon as he hears anything from Chappell.[2]

I had meant to write to you to say that I am utterly vexed to see that, in the announcements for the coming season, people have completely ignored your success last season. I don't understand this at all. I was almost certain and was absolutely counting on an invitation for you for the spring of 1922. Nothing at all for the time being. I have questioned Newman. He replied that so far it has only been a matter of booking the performers. So I am not giving up hope entirely. This last year, concerts have suffered from a lack of first-rate virtuosos, this year it seems that people are concerned only to book Cortot,[3] Rosenthal,[4] Casals, etc., etc.

What figure would it take, do you think, for it to be worth the effort of coming? That's to day, <u>apart</u> from the Queen's Hall Orchestra concerts? Perhaps you can tell me later when you know whether you will have to come to Norway.

Do forgive such a short letter. I am very busy since we are leaving for several weeks in the country. But tomorrow I shall telephone Chappell again. A vous de cœur, and my best regards to Madame Sibelius and all the family,

<u>Rosa Newmarch</u>

1. This telegram has not been traced.
2. Sibelius had sent his recently completed *Suite mignonne*, Op. 98a, to Chappell via Newmarch on 29 June 1921 (*Dagbok*, p. 309).
3. Alfred Cortot (1877–1962), Franco-Swiss pianist.
4. Moritz Rosenthal (1862–1946), Polish pianist.

108 ROSA NEWMARCH TO JEAN SIBELIUS [TELEGRAM, ORIGINAL IN ENGLISH][1]

Buntingford
10/8/1921

CHAPPELL ACCEPTS SUITE NEWMARCH

[1] NLF Coll.206.44.

109 ROSA NEWMARCH TO JEAN SIBELIUS [ORIGINAL IN FRENCH]

4, Crossfield Road
N.W.3.
London.

Aug. 19. 1921

Dear and most honoured friend,

Enclosed you will find the cheque from Chappell for £200 (two hundred pounds) with the receipt for your signature.[1] Please be so good as to return it <u>directly</u> to Chappell, 50 New Bond Street, since I am in the countryside at the moment. Forgive me for writing at a time when I am very busy with domestic matters. Believe always in my sincere friendship,

<u>Rosa Newmarch</u>

[1] Chappell had written to Newmarch on 16 August, requesting her to pass the cheque on to Sibelius.

110 ROSA NEWMARCH TO JEAN SIBELIUS
[ORIGINAL IN FRENCH]

4, Crossfield Road
London. N.W.3

19 November, 1921.

Dearest and most honoured friend,

Here is a letter from a music publisher.[1] It is a very respectable house, I think, but probably not as rich as the largest ones. Yesterday I saw the piano score of your Suite Mignonne, which appears to have been nicely edited.[2]

I can't write a long letter today since I am in the midst of domestic woes; Elsie in bed with a type of 'flu; a servant who is behaving like a madwoman; and myself full of cold! That is everyday life for you! All my sympathy and a thousand good wishes to Madame,

Your devoted friend,

Rosa Newmarch.

---

[1] Most probably Joseph Williams, who had tried – unsuccessfully – to arrange a meeting with Sibelius during his trip to London earlier that year (Williams to Sibelius, 10 March 1921, NLF Coll.206.46). Using Newmarch as a trusted intermediary, Williams approached Sibelius again that autumn (original letter in German, NAF SFP Box 47):

JOSEPH WILLIAMS LIMITED
32, GREAT PORTLAND STREET
LONDON, W.1.
16 November 1921

Dear Sir,
It would be a great pleasure for us if you could let us have some of your valuable manuscripts. For a long time we have wanted to have your name in our catalogue (circa 15,000 items), but the war prevented much. Since we have a large number of schools in our clientele, we require relatively easy piano pieces which are suitable for study.* In the hope that we might hear from you before long,
We remain, respectfully
Joseph Williams Limited
Florian Williams

*Or piano compositions that are not otherwise too difficult.

However, when Sibelius sent them some pianos pieces the following May, Williams declined to publish them in their present form:

We regret to say that the Pieces are not exactly what we had expected, having hoped for something more important. However, if you could see your way to write a short Waltz, and also a little March, to take the place of the 'Esquisse' and 'Etude', we should be willing to pay you Twenty Guineas (£21:0:0) for the British, American and French Rights, leaving you free to deal with the rights for all other countries. (Williams to Sibelius, 27 May 1922, NAF SFP Box 47, original in English)

Sibelius eventually asked for the manuscript to be returned (Williams to Sibelius, 16 November 1922, NLF Coll.206.46), and the pieces were published in Helsinki as *8 Short Pieces*, Op. 99 by Fazer.

[2] Chappell wrote to Sibelius a few days earlier, informing him that the proofs of his *Suite mignonne* were ready and requesting him to make any final corrections before approving them for publication (Chappell to Sibelius, 12 October 1921, NAF SFP Box 47). Sibelius's subsequent attempts to interest Chappell in more of his works were, however, unsuccessful, and they rejected both offer of the *Valse chevalresque*, Op. 96c for £500 (Buchanan to Sibelius, 2 January 1922, NAF SFP Box 47) and the *Suite champêtre*, Op. 98b (Buchanan to Sibelius, 16 February 1922, NAF SFP Box 47). Both works were eventually published in Copenhagen by Wilhelm Hansen.

111 ROSA NEWMARCH TO JEAN SIBELIUS [TELEGRAM, ORIGINAL IN ENGLISH]

Sidmouth
16/1/1922

Can you conduct entire concert of your works Manchester February Twenty fifth fee sixty five guineas one rehearsal wire Newmarch York Hotel Sidmouth

112 JEAN SIBELIUS TO ROSA NEWMARCH [ORIGINAL IN FRENCH][1]

Järvenpää 10 July 1922

Chère Madame,

It is with great sadness that I pick up my pen to write to you. I lost my only brother on the 2nd of July. He died of a very serious malady from which he suffered for many years.[2]

He was always very charmed by your interest for me and my work.

At the same time I send you a new work for chorus and orchestra and ask you kindly to translate the text into English for me, and if possible to find me an English publisher. I have had much success with this composition.[3]

How are things with Mr Eric Blom and what is his address?

I thank you with all my heart for all that you do and have done for me. I do not think that you will take it amiss that I turn to you, chère Madame, in this matter.

The original Finnish text is good, but the Swedish translation, as you see, is rather commonplace; I trust that you will be able to strike a more sublime tone.

> Accept the most cordial compliments of all my family and your grateful and sincere friend
> Jean Sibelius

[1] Translation partially cited in Newmarch, *Jean Sibelius*, pp. 64–5/pp. 44–5.
[2] Christian Sibelius (1869–1922), medic.
[3] Sibelius's *Maan virsi*, Op. 95 (in Swedish, *Hymn till jorden*, and known in English as *Hymn to the Earth*) is a setting for choir and orchestra of a text by Eino Leino, and was written for the twentieth anniversary celebrations of Suomen Laulu, who first performed the work in Helsinki on 4 April 1920 (Dahlström, *Jean Sibelius: Thematisch-bibliographisches Verzeichnis seiner Werke*, p. 406).

113 ROSA NEWMARCH TO JEAN SIBELIUS [ORIGINAL IN FRENCH]

18 July. 1922.

4, Crossfield Road
N.W.3

Dear and most honoured friend,

I am sorry with all my heart to hear that you have suffered such a great loss. I never had the opportunity of meeting your brother but I was always interested to hear what you told me about him from time to time.

I have safely received the manuscript of the 'Hymn till Jorden' – it is not an ideal time since I am leaving for the country tomorrow; but, for the time being, I have placed it safely with Newman and will look after it as soon as possible. We must first find a publisher – do you have any thoughts as to a fee? It will also help me very much if you can have the poem copied separately for me – so that I can take in the form of the verses at a single glance.

Yesterday at the Minister's I met a young man, Bengt de Törne;

he is said to have a gift for orchestration, but I was not very impressed by what he played for me on the piano.[1] I shall write to you as soon as possible, my dear friend. All my best wishes to the family,

à vous de cœur,
    Rosa Newmarch

[1] Bengt Axel von Törne (1891–1967), Finnish composer and one of Sibelius's few composition pupils. His memoir – *Sibelius: A Close-Up* (London, 1937) – was one of the most visible manifestations of British interest in Sibelius in the 1930s and remains a widely quoted source for a number of Sibelius's supposed comments on music and musicians, especially with regard to orchestration.

114 JEAN SIBELIUS TO ROSA NEWMARCH
[ORIGINAL IN FRENCH]

Järvenpää, Finland 26/VII/1922

Chère Madame,
    With all my heart I thank you for your letter.
    I enclose the Swedish text.
    By way of fee I think £60 for all rights.
    Best wishes to you, chère Madame,
    Gratefully yours
        Jean Sibelius

115 JEAN SIBELIUS TO ROSA NEWMARCH
[ORIGINAL IN FRENCH]

Järvenpää, Finland
18 Sept. 1922

Chère Madame,
    Hoping that your trip to the country was pleasant, I thank you for your letter of 18 July.
    If it is difficult for you to find an English publisher for 'Hymn till jorden', I would ask you to return the manuscript to me.[1]

Forgive me for asking you to look after this and please accept, chère Madame, the best wishes of my family and of your very grateful friend
    Jean Sibelius

[1] Despite Newmarch's attempts to persuade Chester to take the work on, the *Hymn till jorden* was not eventually published in Britain, and the manuscript was returned to Sibelius in early 1923 (Chester to Sibelius, 5 January 1923, NLF Coll.206.44).

116 ROSA NEWMARCH TO JEAN SIBELIUS [ORIGINAL IN FRENCH][1]

until 7 September
OSTEND HOUSE,
NEAR HAPPISBURGH,
NORWICH.

August 13. 1924

Dearest and most honoured friend,

At last, by the seaside, I have a little free time for my correspondence. It is such a long time since we exchanged a word, and I believe the fault to be mine, since I am growing lazy in my old age – at least, I find that my daily work is usually enough for my energy. Not that I am not well. Despite all the doctors tell me, there is, thank heavens, still plenty of life in me. Now and again I have heard news of you, that is to say, I know that you spend almost all the time working in the country, although I have not yet seen 'the Sixth'.[2] There is little of note that one can mention about musical life here during these two years. People complain a lot about the financial losses on concerts, and about a great amount of activity that is not of the highest quality, but which is damaging to <…> organisations.

Poor Busoni! Well might he <…>, I think, with his spirit at least, and might <…> not too much to complain. <…> He <…> a lot these two years, and for him <…> a long and senile end.[3]

Now I have something to ask of you. A new publication specially devoted to *Chamber Music* has asked me to write an article about your music in this genre.[4] In fact, I don't think you have published anything apart from the quartet 'Voces Intimæ'? Is there a good analysis of this work? I should very much like to see it.

Has Kuula written any chamber music?[5] Don't put yourself out if it's too much trouble; just ask someone in Helsingfors to send me what I need.

How are you and Madame, and all the family? I was in Prague in March since the 'Times' asked me for some articles on the centenary celebrations for Smetana.[6] I never see Bantock. We have lost poor Kling.[7] He had his problems, I fear. And yet he was a fine man: perhaps too fine for the awful job of being a publisher.

Farewell dear friend. If you have a spare moment, send me a reply. If not, find a good slave to do it for you.

Your affectionate friend

Rosa Newmarch

---

[1] In *Jean Sibelius* (p. 65/p. 45), Newmarch notes that 'between the summer of 1922 and 1924 one or two of Sibelius's letters to me seem to have gone astray, and the only one that I have come across is a little note accompanying an invitation to his daughter Katarina's wedding in August of the latter year.' However, the reference in this letter to a period of two years elapsing suggests that Sibelius and Newmarch may well not have corresponded at all during this time. The transcription of this letter is complicated by the fact that it is heavily ink-stained and a number of words are obscured. Illegible portions of the text are marked <...>.

[2] Sibelius completed his Sixth Symphony in early 1923, conducting the first performance in Helsinki on 19 February (*Dagbok*, p. 319).

[3] Busoni died in Berlin on 24 July 1924.

[4] Most probably *Cobbett's Cyclopedic Survey of Chamber Music*, published in 1929 and 1930. In the end, the entry on Sibelius's Quartet was written by Eric Blom (vol. 2, pp. 416–17), although Newmarch did write on 'Czechoslovakian Chamber Music', 'Czechoslovakian Performing Organizations' and 'Smetana, Bedřich' (vol. 1, pp. 306–8 and 308–9, and vol. 2, pp. 425–32), and is listed in the introduction as one of translators, presumably of material relating to the music of Czechoslovakia (as had been the case with the third edition of *Grove's Dictionary of Music and Musicians* published in 1927–28).

[5] Toivo Kuula (1883–1918), Finnish composer. Blom contributed an entry on him to *Cobbett's Cyclopedic Survey of Chamber Music* (vol. 2, pp. 83–4), in which brief entries were also included on Erik Furuhjelm (1883–1964) (vol. 1, p. 440) and Erkki Melartin (1875–1937) (vol. 2, p. 127).

[6] Newmarch's articles appeared as 'The Smetana Centenary: Celebrations at Prague', *The Times*, 9 February 1924, 8 and 'The Smetana Centenary: A National Festival', *The Times*, 8 March 1924, 8.

[7] Kling died on 6 May 1924. An obituary by Georges Jean-Aubry was published in *The Chesterian* n. s. no. 39 (May 1924), 209–10.

117 JEAN SIBELIUS TO ROSA NEWMARCH
[ORIGINAL IN FRENCH]

Järvenpää, Finland, 22/VIII/1924

Chère Madame,

I have received your friendly letter & I thank you for it with all my heart. I shall reply to your questions soon.

For the time being, I wish only to inform you of the wedding of our daughter Katarina, which will take place on 30th August. She is going to marry Mr Eero Ilves and they will honeymoon in Scotland.[1]

With te [*sic*] best compliments, sincerely yours
    Jean Sibelius and family[2]

[1] Eero Ilves (1887–1953).
[2] Sentences in English in the original.

118 ROSA NEWMARCH TO JEAN SIBELIUS
[ORIGINAL IN FRENCH]

4, Crossfield Road,
N.W.
London

9 March, 1925.

Dear and most honoured friend,

I was very happy to read several weeks ago (in a Czech journal!!) of the great success you had in Copenhagen.[1] I was yet <u>more delighted</u> to learn that you will come here in September for the <u>Three Choirs Festival</u>.[2] Seeing that, I should like to have written immediately, but I was then in bed, and quite unwell. I am better now. As far as the possibility of arranging a concert for you in London, it is still too early to say anything for certain.[3] To speak frankly, things are not going well for the Queen's Hall Orchestra under the direction of C & Co.[4] Before Christmas, symphony concerts were still drawing a large crowd. Since the new year, 'takings' have obviously fallen. The Sunday concerts no longer exist. It's a long story – too long to relate to you. It seems to me that the future is gloomy. In any case, the management will have to come to some decision in the course of the coming month. You know that I should so very much like to see you at Queen's Hall, if at all possible. At the moment, orchestral music in London is suffering from I know not what illness. Perhaps it is a reaction against real music in favour of jazz? Perhaps it's the expansion of 'broad-casting'?[5] A lack of conviction and purpose amongst the critics? It's hard to say.

I should very much like to get to know your new symphony. I am intrigued to know what direction you are headed in! Will I grow as fond of it as the 4th?

I am sorry that I cannot accept the invitation of 'Suomen Laulu'.[6] It is already rather too early to undertake a long voyage northwards. The doctors advise me to visit Vichy or Marienbad. From time to time I am diabetic, and it is my diabolical energy that prevents me from becoming an invalid!

Henry Wood and Robert Newman have both had the flu – they are both quite well now, but poor Newman's face has grown long with all of these woes at Queen's Hall. We must only hope that some deus ex machina comes to save us, even if it should be a Jew.

All my best wishes to your dear wife, to the children – who are children no longer – and to you, as always, the affection of your old (and ever older) friend,

Rosa Newmarch.

---

[1] In September and October 1924, Sibelius conducted a series of concerts in Copenhagen (the first, attended by the King and Queen of Denmark and broadcast on Danish radio, included *Finlandia, Valse triste* and both the First and the newly composed Seventh symphonies). His appearance was reported in the December issue of the music journal of the Czechoslovak Artists' Union (*Umělecká beseda*): 'Sibelius's success was without precedent; tickets sold out within an hour and the concert had to be repeated four times' ('Z hudebního života', *Listy hudební matice* 4 (1924), 121–33 (125)). In fact, Sibelius's success was such that a sixth concert was arranged at the last minute.

[2] Sibelius had sent a copy of his Sixth Symphony to Bantock in late 1924 (Bantock to Sibelius, 16 December 1924, NAF SFP Box 16). Bantock quickly showed the score to Herbert Brewer at Gloucester, who approached Sibelius about the possibility of conducting the work at the 1925 Festival (Brewer to Sibelius, undated, NLF Coll.206.52). Sibelius agreed to come (Sibelius to Bantock, 25 January and 20 February 1925, BL Add Ms 64961, fols 8–9), and Brewer wrote in July to confirm the arrangements for his trip (Brewer to Sibelius, 1 July 1925, NLF Coll.206.52), and details of his appearance were

published in *The Times* later that month ('The Three Choirs Festival: New Sibelius Symphony', *The Times*, 25 July 1925, 10). However, Sibelius withdrew, citing other engagements and the delay in publication of his Seventh Symphony (Sibelius to Bantock, 14 July 1925, BL Add Ms 64961, fol. 13, and Sibelius to Brewer, undated drafts, NLF Coll.206.52, reported in 'Three Choirs Festival', *The Times*, 18 August 1925, 14). Ultimately, only *Finlandia* and *Valse triste* were performed at that year's Festival (Herbert Thompson, 'The Gloucester Festival', *Musical Times* 66 (1925), 922–4).

3   Bantock spent much of the earlier part of the year trying to arrange further appearances for Sibelius in Britain that summer, including concerts in Birmingham, Bournemouth, Edinburgh, Liverpool, London and Manchester (Bantock to Sibelius, 3 and 7 February, 21 March 1925, and Godfrey to Bantock, 4 February 1925, NAF SFP Box 16). By the summer, however, the situation was looking more precarious, which may have contributed to Sibelius's reluctance to undertake an extensive tour. That June, Bantock wrote to Sibelius that: 'the arrangements for your visit are not going as well as I could have wished. Liverpool, Glasgow, and Manchester, after many delays, say they are unable to pay the required fees', although he was able to confirm that the BBC was prepared to engage Sibelius for a broadcast performance of a concert of his works (Bantock to Sibelius, 28 June 1925, NAF SFP Box 16).

4   Chappell & Co., who had leased Queen's Hall since 1902, stepped in to support the concerts there after Edgar Speyer left for America in 1915; Speyer's cousin, Edward, estimated that the cost of keeping the orchestra going during the war amounted to around £35,000. As he goes on to recall: 'during the next six or seven years the financial results declined so much that Mr. Boosey had to consider giving them up altogether' (Edward Speyer, *My Life and Friends* (London, 1937), p. 202). Despite such losses, however, concerts at Queen's Hall nonetheless constituted an attractive financial position for Chappell & Company, at least in the first instance, since 'they had a platform for their own publications in the lighter Part 2 of each programme, and Chappell pianos were mainly used at the concerts' (David Cox, *The Henry Wood Proms* (London, 1980), p. 82).

5   English in the original. The British Broadcasting Company (later Corporation) was established in 1922, and Newmarch was not the only person to fear that this would mean an end to public concerts, at least in their existing form. The director of Chappell & Company, William Boosey, for instance, wrote to the *Daily Telegraph* on 19 May 1923 to complain about the threat posed by the BBC to concert life:

> No one in the entertainment world is so foolish as to imagine that broadcasting can be opposed or wiped out. It has obviously come to stay. The objection of the entertainment world is against broadcasting under its present conditions. The first thing that the public should appreciate, and which they do not yet appreciate, is that the Broadcasting Company is a big commercial concern exploited by very able business men. In other words, the Broadcasting Company is a competitor of the entertainment industry, paying no entertainment tax, but being absolutely subsidized by the Government. (Cited in Cox, *The Henry Wood Proms*, p. 83)

6   Newmarch had presumably been invited to the twentieth-fifth anniversary celebrations of the Finnish choir.

119 ROSA NEWMARCH TO JEAN SIBELIUS
[ORIGINAL IN FRENCH]

4, Crossfield Road,
N.W.3
London

18 November [1926]

Dear and most honoured friend,

  Yesterday I attended the rehearsal of your 6th Symphony.[1] It was the first time it has been rehearsed. Blom, who had already seen it, told me that it was a little in the style of the 4th,[2] but I don't find that's the case at all. It certainly looks like you on paper! One might even say at first glance that it looked like the other symphonies; but what struck me most of all on hearing it is that it is something completely new in your music. It also gave me great pleasure to see that your invention and ideas have not ceased to flow. The musicians like it and made very good sense of it; but the first movement is hard, and needs so much clarity and delicacy. So, thank heavens for one more wealthy work, and so fresh, and strong, and short!

  I hear from Manchester that you are going there in February.[3] Here in London we are going through a terrible phase for music. Continuing financial losses and the threat to sell Queen's Hall as a cinema, a hotel, heaven knows what! And then, two weeks ago, dear devoted Robert Newman died, after an illness that lasted 2 or 3 months.[4] He had for you ('Maestro Seibelius', as he always pronounced your name) an unwavering admiration.[5] It will be hard to replace him. He always put his entire soul into his work. But none of us, even Henry Wood, knows whether the concerts will go on.[6]

  How are you? I see that your art does not grow old. I am becoming old, and sometimes I suffer a little, being diabetic, but a short stay in Carlsbad [sic] always puts me back together. And I am still working hard. Do you remember Miss Simpson? She has just turned 82, and three weeks ago she fell, but as there was nothing broken, we hope she will soon be able to go out. My son has quite a good clientele in South Kensington, and I am a grandmother twice over. You also have grandchildren, don't you? But perhaps you have no idea at all! I remember that I always had to answer when people asked: 'How many children does Mr Sibelius have?'

I am looking forward to your visit very much. I shall go to Manchester with you, if you feel like a travelling companion.

21 November.

Your sixth received a fine interpretation yesterday, and there was, on the whole <u>very marked</u> enthusiasm for it. I hope it will be possible to repeat the work before long. We no longer have the Sunday concerts; that's one less opportunity. Will your publisher not give us a miniature score of this work? The price of the full score – 60/s (£3) – prevents us from buying one to make a detailed study. I am sending you several reviews, the first to appear.[7] What I like, dear friend, about the symphony, is the energy and exuberance of this music; it is still young at heart, but marvellously well put together. It is music that restores and fortifies you.

I know that – like myself – you hate writing letters, but let me know when you leave for England. All my best wishes to Madame Sibelius, I am always your old friend,

<u>Rosa Newmarch</u>

[1] Wood conducted the first British performance of the Sixth Symphony on 20 November 1926 at Queen's Hall.

[2] In his subsequent review of the first British performance of the work, Eric Blom suggested: 'As in the preceding Symphonies, notably the remarkable No. 4, one was again struck by the force and lucidity Sibelius gains by his unvarnished manner of saying exactly what he means and no more' (E. B., 'Queen's Hall Symphony Concert', *Musical Times* 68 (1927), 66–7 (67)).

[3] Sibelius had been engaged – via the concert agents Ibbs & Tillett – to conduct two Brand Lane concerts in Manchester on 19 and 26 February 1927 (Ibbs &Tillett to Sibelius, 12 and 16 July, 3 August 1926, NAF SFP Box 21). By the middle of August, however, Sibelius had changed his mind, citing the lack of sufficient rehearsal time before the concerts (Ibbs & Tillett to Sibelius, 19 and 26 August 1926, NAF SFP Box 21). Nonetheless, the concerts were still being advertised in the autumn ('Music in the Provinces', *Musical Times*, 67 (1926), 939–40 (939)). Ibbs & Tillett had earlier approached Sibelius in 1925 with a view to arranging more concerts during his proposed visit to the Gloucester Festival (Ibbs & Tillett to Sibelius, 3 March 1925, NAF SFP Box 21). Sibelius sought advice from Bantock (16 March 1925, BL Add Ms 64961, fol. 10), who was equivocal about the idea:

> I very much doubt whether the agents 'Ibbs and Tillett' can do anything for you. Do <u>not</u> however give them the <u>sole</u> agency, but refer them to me as your representative in this country. If they can get you arrangements in this country in addition to those I have in hand, so much the better for

you, but you will have to pay them a commission; whereas in those engagements for which I am responsible you will receive your fee direct. (Bantock to Sibelius, 21 March 1925, NAF SFP Box 16)

It seems possible that Bantock's failure to organise a complete set of concerts in 1925 drove Sibelius to accept the offer from Ibbs & Tillett the following year. Ibbs & Tillett wrote again in 1928, inviting Sibelius to accept engagements at that November's Eastbourne Festival, as well as at Queen's Hall (Ibbs & Tillett, 26 June 1928), although once again, nothing came of such plans.

4 Michael Musgrave's entry in *The Oxford Dictionary of National Biography* reveals that Newman died 'on 4 November 1926 at a nursing home at 40 Belsize Grove, Hampstead, of acute entero-colitis (from which he had suffered for three months)' ('Newman, Robert', in *Oxford Dictionary of National Biography*, ed. H. C. G. Matthew and Brian Harrison, 60 vols (Oxford, 2004), vol. 40, pp. 658–9).

5 Newman's pronunciation of Sibelius's name coincidentally recalls the misspelling of it as 'Siebelius' in a review of the concert at which the Suite from *King Christian II* was performed at the Proms on 26 October 1901, the first occasion when any work by Sibelius appears to have been given in Britain (see 'London Concerts', *Musical Times* 42 (1901), 819–20 (819)).

6 In 1925, Boosey hinted that Queen's Hall could be turned into 'a picture house' (Leanne Langley, 'Building an Orchestra, Creating an Audience: Robert Newman and the Queen's Hall Promenade Concerts, 1895–1926', in *The Proms: A New History*, ed. Jenny Doctor and David Wright (London, 2007), pp. 32–73 (p. 64)). The following year, as Elkin relates: 'Messrs. Chappell, taking the view that broadcasting constituted a deadly danger to public concerts, had decided that after the 1926–27 season the New Queen's Hall Orchestra must be disbanded, and it was even doubtful whether the Hall would be preserved for music at all' (Elkin, *Queen's Hall*, p. 33). On 7 March 1927, Chappell officially announced that it 'would no longer be able to support the Promenade and Symphony Concerts at Queen's Hall' (Cox, *The Henry Wood Proms*, p. 83). However, after considerable negotiation and despite Boosey's animosity towards the BBC, the corporation took over the running of the Proms that summer, thus securing the continuation of the tradition.

7 See, for instance, a review in *The Times*, where the performance of the symphony was described as 'the outstanding event of the concert', and comparisons were made with 'Vaughan Williams, whose "Pastoral Symphony" and whose suite, "Flos Campi," exhibit something of the same aloof and abstracted attitude of mind' ('New Queen's Hall Orchestra: Sibelius's Sixth Symphony', *The Times*, 22 November 1926, 19).

120 JEAN SIBELIUS TO ROSA NEWMARCH
[ORIGINAL IN FRENCH][1]

Paris, 5 February 1927.
Hôtel de Quai Voltaire,
19 Quai Voltaire.

Chère Madame,

Your very welcome letter gave me great pleasure, especially your views about my sixth symphony.

My wife and I are now in Paris for a few weeks and it is not impossible that we shall return home by way of England.[2] In which case it will be a great joy to see you and talk to you about all manner of things. Have not things changed greatly since we last met, above all the art of music? Most of the novelties of those days are now old-fashioned.

I have written a new symphony (No. 7, in one movement), and also a symphonic poem entitled 'Tapiola'.[3]

My thoughts often turn to you, and I remember everything we used to discuss together.

Best wishes to you, chère Madame, from my wife and myself.

Your ever devoted and grateful

Jean Sibelius

[1] Translation cited in Newmarch, *Jean Sibelius*, p. 66/p. 45.
[2] Sibelius and his wife visited Paris from January to April 1927.
[3] The Seventh Symphony, Op. 105, was completed on 2 March 1924 (*Dagbok*, p. 321) and first performed (under its original title of *Fantasia sinfonica*) in Stockholm on 24 March that year. *Tapiola*, Op. 122, was completed in September 1926 (*Dagbok*, p. 326) and first performed in New York (conducted by Walter Damrosch) on 26 December.

121 ROSA NEWMARCH TO JEAN SIBELIUS
[TELEGRAM, ORIGINAL IN ENGLISH]

London
9/12/1927

Best wishes symphony great success
Newmarch[1]

[1] The first British performance of Sibelius's Seventh Symphony was given by Henry Wood at a concert of the Royal Philharmonic Society at Queen's Hall

on 8 December 1927, at which Casals also performed the Dvořák Cello Concerto ('New Symphony by Sibelius: Philharmonic Concert', *The Times*, 9 December 1927, 12). The reviewer for *The Musical Times* wrote that for the audience, 'the Sibelius was plainly hard fare', and that despite an excellent performance, 'its reception indicated puzzlement, politely expressed' (H. G., 'Royal Philharmonic Society', *Musical Times* 68 (1927), 68–9). Sibelius's association with the Philharmonic Society went back to 1906, but this performance of the Seventh Symphony initiated a period in which the composer was extensively courted by the society, which hoped – along with many others – to secure the first European performance of the Eighth Symphony. *Tapiola* – the other recent work mentioned by Sibelius in his letter to Newmarch of 5 February 1927 – received its first British performance at the Proms on 1 September 1928. In *The Musical Times*, it was described as 'a strong, rugged work, thoroughly characteristic of the composer's later style, which gripped the attention from the start' ('Promenade Concert Novelties', *Musical Times* 69 (1928), 932–3 (933)).

122 ROSA NEWMARCH TO JEAN SIBELIUS [ORIGINAL IN FRENCH]

London
1A BELSIZE PARK,
N.W.3.

3 March, 1930

Dearest and most honoured friend,

I hear from Basil Cameron that you are still alive,[1] and that you often remember me, although I have no reason to doubt it – can I? But such is life! I know that I too, in my 72nd year, find it daily more difficult to <u>write</u> to than to <u>think</u> of my friends. I still have a lot of writing to do, and it would be easier to travel for two days than to write a letter. It is my hand that has grown old and not my heart!

I came back yesterday from Hastings where I had gone especially to hear 'The Tempest' and 'Night Ride and Sunrise'.[2] The first was superbly played, and was received with great enthusiasm. The second interested me greatly, since I remember that you spoke to me about it long, long ago, during a long car journey, but heaven knows where. The public seemed to like it too, although it is a very intimate work, and one should know it by heart before hearing it. I can reassure you that young Cameron has studied both very well. The performance of my beloved 4th Symphony a few weeks ago under his direction was also very poetic, very cared for and well thought through.³ He interprets your music well because he is not yet spoiled; he still has time to ponder a little before playing a score. He is the best of our 'young' musicians; but like the others, he will probably go to America and will come back quite altered. These American fairy godmothers spoil our young people! How the world of music is changed here! The word 'music' is the same for me as the word 'nightmare'. Thanks to the radio, the likes of Béla Bartók,⁴ Toch,⁵ Křenek,⁶ Haba,⁷ and many other evil little demons haunt our lives. Music today reminds me of Orcagna's scenes of 'hell' in the Campo Santo at Pisa.⁸

I should like to see you again very much, dear friend, but I fear that I shall never travel to Helsingfors again. I am almost obliged to go each year to Karlsbad, as I am very diabetic, and the waters do me much good. After the death of my husband (tragic but not sad) in 1927,⁹ Elsie and I live all alone in a pretty little house. John and his family are not far away, in Kensington. A few weeks ago I saw the Bantocks, who are thinking of setting up home soon in London.

Are you spending all the summer in Finland? If you ever come nearer to England, send me a wire, and I could perhaps come and meet you. I greet you, as well as dear Madame Sibelius, very affectionately. What is little Katarina doing, she who would call me simply 'Rosa', and who would send me the flowers that you always lost on the journey between Jarvenpää and Helsingfors?

à vous de cœur,
    Rosa Newmarch

1   Basil Cameron (1884–1975), British conductor. In a letter to Sibelius, Cameron recalled having played the violin under Sibelius's direction in 1910 (Cameron to Sibelius, 16 September 1929, NAF SFP Box 17).
2   Cameron performed *Night Ride and Sunrise* and the Prelude from *The Tempest*, Op. 109, at the Hastings Festival on 26 February 1930. Writing of these performances (for which Newmarch wrote the programme notes), *The Musical Times* noted that 'Mr. Cameron, like the rest of us, finds the personality of Sibelius refreshingly different from that of any contemporary composer', and wrote admiringly of 'how completely individual is Sibelius and how obstinately he remains in a category of his own, the shyest and most baffling of contemporary composers' (F. H., 'Hastings Festival', *Musical Times* 71 (1930), 363). In the early 1930s, there was considerable interest in Sibelius's music for *The Tempest*, which had been written for a production of the play at the Royal Theatre in Copenhagen in 1926. Bantock wrote in late 1932 and early 1933, giving details of plans for a gala performance of *The Tempest* with Sibelius's incidental music, first at Covent Garden and then at His Majesty's Theatre (Bantock to Sibelius, 20 November 1932, 15 February 1933, NAF SFP

> Londres
> le 3 mars, 1930   1ª BELSIZE PARK,
>   N.W.3.
>
> Très-cher et très-honoré ami,
>
> J'ai appris par Basil Cameron que vous existez toujours, et que vous vous souvenez toujours de moi, quoique j'ai un peu raison de m'en douter – n'est-ce pas ? Mais voilà la vie ! Je sais que, moi aussi dans ma 72ième année, trouve, de jour en jour, plus difficile d'écrire que de penser à mes amis. C'est que j'ai toujours beaucoup d'écriture et qu'il serait plus facile de voyager deux fois que d'écrire une lettre.

9. Rosa Newmarch to Jean Sibelius, 3 March 1930. (courtesy of the National Archives of Finland)

Box 16), although nothing appears to have come of this proposal, not least because Sibelius was reluctant to accept a conducting engagement (Sibelius to Bantock, 28 November 1932, BL Add Ms 64961, fols 17–18). In the end, the music was premiered in October 1934, first at the Leeds Festival ('Leeds Musical Festival', *The Times*, 10 July 1934, 14), and then in London ('Royal Philharmonic Society', *The Times*, 25 August 1934, 8).

3 Cameron conducted the Fourth Symphony on 16 January 1930 with the Royal Philharmonic Society (Arthur Schnabel also performed Mozart's Piano Concerto in A major, No. 23). Although *The Musical Times* reported that 'Mr. Cameron had given the work all his care and devotion' (C., 'Royal Philharmonic Society', *Musical Times* 71 (1930), 166), *The Musical Mirror* thought that he 'gave us everything except the imagination and depth of thought underlying this great symphony' (R. H., 'Concert Notes', *Musical Mirror* 10 (1930), 60).

4 Béla Bartók (1881–1945), Hungarian composer. A number of Bartók's works were performed by the composer himself at a concert broadcast by the BBC on 6 January 1930 (M-.D. C. [Michel Dmitri Calvocoressi], 'B.B.C. Chamber Concert: Works by Bela Bartók', *Musical Times* 71 (1930), 167). Under the patronage of the newly founded BBC, contemporary avant-garde music enjoyed increasing prominence in concert programmes during the 1920s. Broadcasts of works by Bartók seem to have provoked a particularly unenthusiastic reaction on the part of some listeners, prompting Percy Scholes to write a lead article in the *Radio Times* for 9 December 1927 ('Is Bartok Mad – or are We?'), in which he both defended Bartók's music (and that of other modern composers) and encouraged listeners to approach it with an open mind (see Jennifer Doctor, *The BBC and Ultra-Modern Music, 1922–1936: Shaping a Nation's Tastes* (Cambridge, 1999), pp. 122–5). For a detailed survey of Bartók's visits to and reception in Britain, see Malcolm Gillies, *Bartók in Britain: A Guided Tour* (Oxford, 1989).

5 Ernst Toch (1887–1964), Austrian composer. His piano concerto was broadcast by the BBC on 21 February (Auribus, 'Wireless Notes', *Musical Times* 71 (1930), 332–4 (334)).

6 Ernst Křenek (1900–91), Austrian composer. His *Kleine Symphonie*, Op. 58, was broadcast on 2 March 1930 (E. H., 'Radio Notes and Reflections', *Musical Mirror* 10 (1930), 114).

7 Alois Hába (1893–1973), Czech composer. Newmarch's antipathy to Hába's music can perhaps be seen in the fact that she did not provide the entry on him in the third edition of *Grove's Dictionary of Music and Musicians* in 1927 (it was written instead by Edwin Evans). In *The Music of Czechoslovakia*, Newmarch briefly refers to Hába as being 'well known in international circles as the exponent of the "quarter-tone" system' (p. 236).

8 Orcagna (Andrea di Cione di Arcangelo, c.1308–68), Italian painter and sculptor. The Campo Santo in Pisa contains a number of frescoes depicting the Last Judgment, Hell and the Triumph of Death that were traditionally attributed to him. In particular, the fresco of The Triumph of Death is said to have inspired Liszt's *Totentanz*.

9 Newmarch's husband went missing on Exmoor during a family holiday in Porlock in late July 1927. His body was discovered a few days later; he was reported as having fallen and broken his neck. ('Death of Mr. H.C. Newmarch', *The Times*, 3 August 1927, 12).

123 JEAN SIBELIUS TO ROSA NEWMARCH
[ORIGINAL IN FRENCH][1]

Järvenpää 10 March, 1930

Chère Madame,

You cannot imagine what a great joy came over me on receiving your letter. I felt as though I had retrieved something infinitely precious.

I was very much interested to hear that Basil Cameron had conducted my music so well. He came here to see me and we talked of England.[2]

I still go on composing but I feel very much alone. There is so much in the music of the present day that I cannot accept. For example, that one should be able to make for oneself an ideal by reflexion (a reflected ideal). Also it seems to me that modern music does not progress, that it marks time without getting a step further. It is the urgent need for progress which lacks when the architectural form is neglected.[3]

'Little' Katarina has been married for years to a judge, named Ilves, and has two children – a daughter and a son.[4] Our fourth daughter is also married,[5] so only the younger remains at home. She is studying 'applied art' in Helsingfors.[6]

My wife was delighted to receive your greetings and sends you, chère Madame, her kindest remembrances.

I have a great wish to come to England to see you again. I am afraid it will not come off this spring, but during the summer perhaps I might manage to meet you in Karlsbad. It would be a great, great pleasure to continue our interesting talks of old.

With all my heart, chère Madame,
 Your grateful,
 Jean Sibelius

[1] Translation cited in Newmarch, *Jean Sibelius*, pp. 66–7/p. 46. The letter is also reproduced in *Letters of Composers: An Anthology, 1603–1945*, ed. Gertrude Norman and Mirian Lubell Shrifte (New York, 1945), p. 325.
[2] Cameron flew to Finland to visit Sibelius in October 1929, when they discussed his interpretation of the Fourth Symphony (Cameron to Sibelius, 16 and 24 September, 16 October 1929, NAF SFP Box 17). Cameron then invited Sibelius to conduct at the Hastings Festival (25 November 1929, 1 January 1930, NAF SFP Box 17).
[3] Sibelius's seemingly frank comments give the impression that he shared Newmarch's aversion to modern music, but as Santeri Levas argues, Sibelius's

attitude was more complex than his rather unspecific remarks here suggest. Levas records, for instance, that amongst the 'senior moderns' (a group also including Hindemith, Schoenberg, Stravinsky and Berg), it was Bartók he admired most: 'Bartók was a great genius, but he died in poverty in America. I don't know what he thought about my music, but I always had the highest regard for his.' Hába, however, found Newmarch and Sibelius in complete agreement: 'I can't stand Alois Haba: it sounds all wrong to my ears', he is reported as saying to a journalist in 1951 (cited in Santeri Levas, *Sibelius: A Personal Portrait*, trans. Percy M. Young (London, 1972), pp. 73 and 74–5). British readers would have the chance to read Sibelius's views on some of these same composers as reported in Cecil Gray, *Sibelius* (London, 1931), pp. 59–60, and Walter Legge, 'Conversations with Sibelius', *Musical Times* 76 (1935), 218–20.

4 Merike Ilves (b. 1925) and Jan Ilves (b. 1927). By now, Sibelius's eldest daughter, Eva, had also had another son, Janne Paloheimo (1922–89).
5 Margareta married the conductor Jussi Jalas (1908–85).
6 'Applied art' in English in the original. Heidi later married the architect Aulis Blomstedt (1906–79) and became a noted Finish ceramicist.

124 ROSA NEWMARCH TO JEAN SIBELIUS [ORIGINAL IN FRENCH]

1a Belsize Park,
London N.W.3

22 July. 1930

Dearest and most honoured friend,

You will be – or perhaps already have been – visited by Petr Křička of Prague.¹ I would ask you to welcome him as one of my best friends. I always call him 'my son', and indeed he has treated me for nearly ten years with an utterly filial affection. Pierre is a man of most distinguished taste, a national poet, and a fearless patriot. All in all, a quite superior being. He will let you have my latest news, as he saw me during my convalescence in Karlsbad. A little after receiving your letter in May (?), I fell very ill. The doctors did not make a very good diagnosis of my illness, which was finally declared to be an abscess of the parotid gland. I had to undergo a fairly serious operation at my age, since I had suffered so much beforehand. But everything went well and I was sent to Karlsbad as soon as possible.² It was probably all down to a diabetic condition. I am well now, and I am beginning to regain my customary energy.

All my best wishes to you and to Madame,
   à vous de cœur,
   <u>Rosa Newmarch.</u>

[1] Petr Křička (1884–1949), Czech poet and translator, brother of the composer Jaroslav Křička (1882–1969).
[2] In a letter to Jessie Wood, Newmarch recalled that the surgeon was not very optimistic about her chances of survival: '"I've had 17 cases of removal of the parotid gland, they all died." I roared with laughter and said: "No. 18 has proved too tough for you"' (undated letter from Newmarch to Jessie Wood, BL Add Ms 56421, fol. 43).

125 ROSA NEWMARCH TO JEAN SIBELIUS [TELEGRAM, ORIGINAL IN ENGLISH]

London
8/12/1930

All affectionate good wishes
　Roosa [sic] Newmarch

126 ROSA NEWMARCH TO JEAN SIBELIUS [ORIGINAL IN FRENCH]

St. Hostyns,
Chorley Wood Road,
Rickmansworth.

3 December, 1935.[1]

Dearest and most honoured friend,

　Must I really congratulate you on your 70th birthday? What a funny convention! But I do so with all my heart if it means something for your honour and your happiness. For me you are still the young and romantic musical Viking whom I met at Bantock's centuries and centuries ago! Accept from your old friend all best wishes for 8 December, and for all the days that are left to you here on earth. It is dear Madame Aino who will be most proud on your birthday. Give her my most affectionate greetings, won't you?*

　I have followed everything you have written since those far-off days – symphonies No. 1 and 4 still remain in my life and in my soul; I adore your 'Tempest' and the songs. I preserve the selfish weakness to believe that no one understands this music better than I do. But it is time for the young to have their day. (I am celebrating my 80th birthday on 18 December).² I am well enough and still at work. Like you and your dear wife, my daughter and I live in a modest house in the country.³

Dear old friend, I embrace you cordially, and I never forget you,
Rosa Newmarch.

*I still have the photograph that I took of the both of you in your garden.

---

1. Although this appears to be Newmarch's first letter to Sibelius since the end of 1930, they had in fact remained in touch through a number of intermediaries in the intervening years. Harriet Cohen and Arnold Bax visited Sibelius in Finland in 1932 (a postcard sent from Helsinki on 5 July 1932 to Newmarch and signed by Cohen, Bax and Sibelius – who described Newmarch in it as 'une femme inoubliable' – was sold at Sotheby's in 2003). Newmarch sent her greetings to Sibelius in a collective postcard also signed by Henry Wood and the Hungarian violinist Emil Telmányi (1892–1988) (postmarked 16 February 1931, NAF SFP Box 24), and jokingly described herself to be 'Still alive age 97½' in a later note to Sibelius signed by various correspondents (9 June 1933, NAF SFP Box 24).
2. Newmarch is incorrect here, as she turned only seventy-eight that December.
3. Newmarch moved to a cottage in Hertfordshire, named after the pilgrimage site of Svatý Hostýn in Moravia, in the early 1930s.

---

127 JEAN SIBELIUS TO ROSA NEWMARCH [TYPED, ORIGINAL IN FRENCH]¹

Järvenpää,
14 Dec. 1935

Chère Madame,

I congratulate you with all my heart.

You can hardly imagine the joy that your welcome letter brought to me. It was like a tender memory of old and precious days and, thanks to you, of so much importance to my music.

In imagination I see you with your dear daughter in the charming English countryside. It pleases me to fancy you in your study just like the one you used to have in London. But it makes me yet happier to know that you are always working.

Personally I hardly feel the weight of my 70 years, but my claims on quietude in order to compose have grown immense. As to tranquillity, here I am in the very heart of it; I dwell in the very heart of solitude; but this autumn has been very odd: Interviews – often rather stupid – photographers, visitors, etc.

But the live wire of my life is composition as you know, and it is the only joy I possess.

I am still thinking of a journey to England to see you and talk together as we did in the days gone by.

Yours, in all friendship,
Jean Sibelius

---

[1] Translation cited in Newmarch, *Jean Sibelius*, pp. 69–70/pp. 46–7, where she misreads 'photographes' ('photographers') as 'photographies' ('photographs').

128 AINO SIBELIUS TO ROSA NEWMARCH [ORIGINAL IN FRENCH][1]

Järvenpää, 15 December 1935.

Chère Madame,

Allow me to join cordially in my husband's thanks to you for your congratulations on the anniversary of his birthday.

I send you affectionate greetings from our family from the house where we have been living alone for the last four years. All our five daughters are married and living in Helsingfors (not so very far away) which means a great deal to me. I missed them very much, especially at first, but now I have grown accustomed to it, and our life side by side is very pleasant and happy. If it does not tire you I should like to tell you about the great celebrations which our country offered to my husband on his birthday.

The government organized a concert in his honour at which seven thousand people were present. My brother, Armas Järnefelt, conducted. It was splendid; nothing like it has ever been known here. The President of the Finnish Republic presented my husband with a huge crown of laurels on behalf of the Finnish nation. The programme contained his First Symphony – the one you used to like best. It was well played and well accepted. All the great outside world sent thousands of letters, telegrams, congratulations and medals, etc. It was a great day. You can imagine how happy I felt, chère Madame!

We stayed a few days with our eldest daughter in town, but now we are at home again amid our big trees and the white snow.

Always yours, chère Madame,

Aino Sibelius.

Our sincere greetings to dear Elsie.

I am sending you a picture of the concert and the photograph of my husband taken this autumn.[2]

[1] Cited in Newmarch, *Jean Sibelius*, pp. 70–71/pp. 48–51.
[2] Reproduced in the American edition of *Jean Sibelius*, between pages 71 and 72.

129 ROSA NEWMARCH TO JEAN SIBELIUS [ORIGINAL IN FRENCH]

11 September 1937
53, CIRCUS ROAD MANSIONS,
N.W.8.

Dear and most honoured friend,

Henry Wood tells me that he received a telegram from you several days ago. My letter is the assurance that your symphonies and 'Les Océanides', which I adore, have been very successful, perhaps more so than for many years now. Last Thursday the Queen's Hall was crowded – especially by young people – for the second of the concerts devoted entirely to your music.[1]

I am sending you the programme. Please forgive me, dear old comrade, for breaking the silence of many years ago to write the short memoir which comes before the 'analytical notes'.[2] It gave me the greatest of pleasure to bring back the wonderful days that we spent together. And if I have written anything foolish, at least it is not as foolish as what is normally written in such programmes![3]

Forgive me, please, for such a short letter; but my eyes are no longer as effective as they once were. I shall be 80 in 3 months!

Give my affectionate best wishes to dear Madame Aïno, and believe always in my tender and faithful friendship –

to you, dear Janne,

Rosa Newmarch.

[1] Although there had been an annual 'Sibelius Concert' in each season of the Promenade Concerts from 1933 to 1936, 1937 witnessed what amounted to a

Sibelius festival, with two concerts devoted to his works on 26 August (*Festivo* from *Scènes historiques*, the Third and Fourth Symphonies, the Violin Concerto, *The Swan of Tuonela* and *Lemminkäinen's Return*) and 9 September (*The Oceanides*, the Second and Sixth Symphonies, *The Ferryman's Brides*, alongside Respighi's *The Fountains of Rome* and Warlock's *Capriol Suite*), and a number of other compositions – the Seventh Symphony (9 August), *En Saga* (21 August), *Finlandia* (24 August), the First Symphony (2 September), the Fifth Symphony (18 September) – performed throughout the remainder of the season (BBC Written Archive Centre R79/117/1). Of the first concert, *The Times* wrote: 'This concentrated programme . . . revealed more of Sibelius than any other single occasion before or after is likely to do outside Finland, and it showed that the riddle of his mind is not unreadable' ('Promenade Concert: An Evening with Sibelius', *The Times*, 27 August 1937, 10).

2   English in the original.
3   Newmarch no longer provided the analytical notes for the Promenade Concerts (those on Sibelius were written by D. Millar Craig), but her 'Introduction' (really a brief memoir of her relationship with Sibelius) was included in the programme for the Sibelius Concert of 9 September 1937 (pp. 7–10, reproduced in the programme for a similar Sibelius concert on 20 September 1938). The material in Newmarch's introductory note was subsequently incorporated into her longer book-length memoir of the composer.

130   ROSA NEWMARCH TO JEAN SIBELIUS
      [ORIGINAL IN FRENCH IN ELSIE
      NEWMARCH'S HAND]

53, Circus Road Mansions,
N.W.8.
21 February 1939

Dearest and most honoured friend,

Perhaps I shall surprise you with this letter. Before I became so blind, I very much wanted to write a memoir of our friendship – a book based on my memories and, of course, on our correspondence which has lasted for so long. Reading your letters again, I have realised that this book could be short, intimate and charming if it were handled in a delicate and discrete manner.

But I have discovered that in England people were always asking me for a long biography, in the tradition of the legends that the English always want to preserve about you: that's to say the portrait of a man as solemn as the Finnish forests; neglected in his youth and only discovered these last years by the critics of today! Whereas I wanted to show in miniature quite a different Sibelius: something more true – the composer who was so appreciated before the war, the comrade of Bantock, of Ernest Newman, of Henry Wood, and of myself.

So, I asked Bantock to find me a publisher in America (where he is travelling at the moment). Not long ago he found in Birchard (Boston) a publisher who has warmly welcomed my manuscript. I should add that Bantock has written a very interesting 'Foreword' to my little opus.[1]

I should like to have sent you the manuscript at the same time as my letter, but it is in America.

It remains for me to ask your permission to publish the passages taken from your letters. You can count on my discretion! But if you prefer to see the material, I shall send you the proofs. Only do not leave me too long without an answer, I beg you, since at my age one must finish without delay any work one undertakes.

The title of this very small book will be:
 Part I Jean Sibelius – a Memoir
 Part II The Seven Symphonies
 (It is not a very strict analysis, with examples from the scores, but only my personal impressions which perhaps no one will care for.)

I don't have any more room for all that I should like to tell you. All my affectionate greetings
 Rosa Newmarch
It is Elsie to whom I have dictated this letter.

[1] 'Foreword' in English in the original.

131   JEAN SIBELIUS TO ROSA NEWMARCH
[ORIGINAL IN FRENCH]

Järvenpää, 1, III, -39

Chère Madame,

Many thanks for your friendly letter, so dear to my heart.

You can cite my letters as you wish, because I know your discretion very well.

I was so happy to hear your news and everything that Eva told me on her return from London. I thank you from all my heart for your great friendliness to her.[1]

Accept, chère Madame, the most cordial wishes of my wife and myself, and do not forget your old
   Jean Sibelius

[1] Between 27 October and 11 November, four concerts of Sibelius's orchestral works were given by the Royal Philharmonic Society (conducted by Thomas Beecham), as well as two recitals of his chamber and vocal works. The festival was widely discussed and reviewed in the press (see, for instance, 'The Music of Sibelius: Plans for London Festival', *The Times*, 10 October 1938, 12; 'A Sibelius Festival: Royal Philharmonic Society', *The Times*, 28 October 1938, 12; 'The Sibelius Festival: An Elusive Work', *The Times*, 2 November 1938, 12; 'Sibelius Festival: Fourth Concert at Queen's Hall', *The Times*, 7 November 1938, 18; 'Queen's Hall: Sibelius Festival Concert', 12 November 1938, 10). Sibelius's daughter Eva Paloheimo attended (Stephen Williams, 'Sibelius's Daughter Comes for Festival of Her Father's Music', *Evening Standard*, 27 October 1938, 3), and was even quoted as saying 'I think . . . that he has finished his Eighth Symphony' (Stuart Fletcher, 'Sibelius Sends Daughter as Envoy', *Daily Herald*, 28 October 1938, 3).

132 ROSA NEWMARCH TO JEAN SIBELIUS
[ORIGINAL IN ENGLISH AND FRENCH]

53, Circus Road Mansions,
London. N.W.8.
March 26. 1939

Dear Friend,

Forgive my long delay in answering your letter of March 1st, but I have had a great sorrow since I received it in the death of my last remaining sister – the one who lived in Leamington. She was in her 89th year, so it was not unexpected, but it leaves me the last of my generation. It has also left me with a good deal of business to attend to.[1]

I thank you with all my heart for your kind and friendly letter. You can count on my discretion as in the past. I am very busy at the moment correcting the proofs of my little book about 'Jean Sibelius'. I hope to send you a first copy during the summer.

We have had the experience of a very long and sad winter. I think a lot of my good friends in Prague.[2]

My affectionate wishes to you and to Madame Aino,
   Your friend,
      Rosa Newmarch

¹ This paragraph is in English in the original; the remainder of the letter is in French. Newmarch's last remaining sister was Caroline Georgiana.

² In the wake of the Munich Agreement of September 1938, Czechoslovakia was forced to cede a large part of its territory to Nazi Germany. Germany finally invaded on 15 March, establishing a German Protectorate of Bohemia and Moravia, and a separate Slovak Republic. In the aftermath of the Munich Agreement, Newmarch commented privately to Wood: 'The events of the last two or three months bowled me over terribly at first, and the face of the whole world is changed for me' (Newmarch to Wood, 17 November 1938, BL Add Ms 56421, fols 47–8). In her posthumously published *The Music of Czechoslovakia* (p. 3), she angrily declared that:

> The work of emancipation, political and social, begun by President Masaryk, with all the *naïvités* and deficiencies which stamp a young generation not yet completely educated for the democracy bestowed upon it, and the difficulty of a swift transformation of ideals into action, have, as evinced by the Munich Four-Power Agreement, been totally and shamefully ignored.

133 ROSA NEWMARCH TO JEAN SIBELIUS [ORIGINAL IN FRENCH]

53, Circus Road Mansions,
N.W.8.
20 June 1939

Dearest and most honoured friend,

I am sending you the little book which I mentioned in my letter of February.¹ I think that the American publishers have taken a lot of effort to make the exterior attractive to the public. As far as the interior is concerned, I can only hope that you will find therein a few reflections of a past that is very dear to me, and that I have said nothing in my book that might detract from the ideal nature of this long friendship.

As for what I have said about your music, these are only the opinions of an old woman, who perhaps no longer has the surety of judgment that she had thirty years ago. But what difference does it make! Your art will always remain your own, and the opinions of men and women are not made to last.

I hope that it will bring a little pleasure to dear Madame Aino, to whom I send my fond wishes.

Bantock has taken a huge amount of interest in this little opus, like a true brother and comrade. Let me know if there is anything that brings you pleasure in this short essay.

À vous toujours de cœur,
>Your very old,
>>Rosa Newmarch

---

[1] Newmarch's memoir – *Jean Sibelius: A Short Story of a Long Friendship* – was published in Boston by C. C. Birchard in 1939. The copy in Sibelius's library is inscribed: 'To my very dear old friends Jean & Aino Sibelius from Rosa Newmarch. June 1939' (*Catalogue of the Library of Jean Sibelius*, p. 92). It was eventually published in Britain in 1944 by Goodwin & Tabb, simply entitled *Jean Sibelius*, with a different series of photographs and the addition of a number of facsimiles of Sibelius's letters to Bantock.

---

134 JEAN SIBELIUS TO ROSA NEWMARCH
[ORIGINAL IN ENGLISH, TYPED]

Järvenpää, July 24th 1939.

Dear Madam,

Many cordial thanks for your kind letter of June 20th and the splendid booklet about our friendship. Unfortunately I have not been able to answer it before.

There are not many things in life that count more than real good friendship and I feel very happy that you have put up a monument to a long amity which has been so very important to me and my art. So, dear Madam, please accept my deeply felt thanks for the great kindness you always have shown to me and my family. I would like to tell you my gratitude in my own handwriting but my nervous hand makes it difficult to me to write. And, alas, a short letter can not tell all that I would like to express.

Most cordial greetings to you and your charming daughter from Aino and the children who all of them master your beautiful language.

Always yours
>Jean Sibelius

135 ROSA NEWMARCH TO JEAN SIBELIUS
[ORIGINAL IN FRENCH]

Kingsway Hotel
Worthing
Oct. 13, 1939

Dear and most honoured friend,

My thoughts are with you and your family.[1] You see that we are near my son, and we shall stay here for some time. No point in writing you a long letter,[2] but all my best hopes are with you and your dear family,

À vous de cœur,

Rosa Newmarch

---

[1] In the wake of the Molotov-Ribbentrop Pact of August 1939, Estonia, Latvia and Lithuania had been forced to allow Soviet troops onto their territory. Throughout the autumn of 1939, Finland waged a diplomatic campaign aimed at enlisting international support for the defence of its independence and neutrality and for its resistance to Soviet pressure. On the day that she wrote to Sibelius, Newmarch could have seen pictures of the evacuation of Finland's major cities in *The Times* ('Precautions in Finland: Towns Being Evacuated', *The Times*, 13 October 1939, 12). On 30 November, the Soviet Union invaded Finland, inaugurating the so-called 'Winter War' that lasted until 13 March 1940.

[2] This was to be Newmarch's last letter to Sibelius; she died in Worthing on 9 April 1940. Sibelius does not appear to have been informed about her death until after the war, when he received the following letter from Elsie Newmarch (NAF SFP Box 24):

> 53 Circus Road Mansions
> N.W.8
>
> September 8th, 1945
>
> Dear Mr. Sibelius,
>
> Often in these last years would I have liked to write to you and Madame Sibelius to tell you of the death of my mother, Rosa Newmarch, in April, 1940, but it has not been possible till recently. As you may have realized my mother's health was not too good in 1939, and with her many friends and interests in the musical and literary life of other countries, she felt too very deeply the terrible possibilities of the war, especially since failing health and sight curtailed her activities. We spent the winter of 1939/40 at Worthing to be near my brother and his family, and it was just when we were thinking of coming back to our flat in London that she died after a few days illness, on April 10th [*sic*].
>
> Just recently Messrs. Goodwin & Tabb at last managed to bring out the English edition of the little book about you, (and the seven symphonies) which Mother published with Birchard & Co. in Boston, America, just

before the war, a copy of which I hope reached you. It has been difficult to get the American edition over here, so I think this English reprint will be very welcome, especially now, and I feel sure will find a ready sale among our young people from whom there is a great demand for good orchestral music.

I grieve to say that last summer brought another great loss to our musical life, as well as to me personally, in the death of Sir Henry Wood. He was still carrying on his great work for orchestral and choral music in spite of the difficulties of the war and the loss of his beloved Queen's Hall. Unfortunately the flying-bomb raids made it impossible to carry through the Jubilee Season of Promenade Concerts, and after three wonderful weeks with the usual large and enthusiastic audiences at the Albert Hall, it was deemed unwise to continue them in that hall with its immense glass-domed roof, and they were transferred to the B.B.C. studio outside London and partially broadcast. But all this meant great disappointment, problems and anxieties for Sir Henry, and the conditions under which he conducted the final concerts of the season were too much even for his wonderful vitality.

But the 'Henry Wood Proms' are still carried on, and the Jubilee Fund which was started last year and which he wished devoted to the building of a new Concert Hall to replace the old Queen's Hall, is now carried on as the Henry Wood Memorial Fund. This season's concerts are conducted by Sir Adrian Boult, Conductor of the B.B.C. Symphony Orchestra, and Basil Cameron, who was chosen a few years ago by Sir Henry as his associated conductor for these concerts, and I should like to tell you of the splendid way in which he is carrying on the Henry Wood tradition in conducting. All your symphonies are being performed this season, following Sir Henry's custom of former years, and I enclose you one recent programme when Basil Cameron gave outstanding renderings of these works to a crowded and enthusiastic audience (some five to six thousand people fill the Albert Hall every night for these Promenade Concerts). I wonder if you are yet able to get reception on the Radio?

We are all working very hard for this Memorial Fund to carry out Sir Henry's great wish for a fine, modern Concert Hall in London, where we can maintain the great work for music which he has built up in the last fifty years; and it is the devoted energy and inspiration of Lady Jessie Wood, whose help and devoted care meant so much to Sir Henry in these last years, which also helps us, his friends, to carry on his great work for the cause of music.

I hope some day it may be possible to publish a memoir of my mother, or complete her own book of memories and letters of which she left several chapters, but in these years of war strain such things have been very difficult. You, too, I am sure have had your trials and difficulties, and I hope you and Madame Sibelius have had health and strength to carry you through these sad and troubled times.

With kindest remembrances and best of wishes, to you and Madame Sibelius,

    Believe me,
        Yours sincerely,
            Elsie Newmarch

Please excuse a typewritten letter, but it is better for airmail. E. N.

APPENDIX

A. Bibliography of publications by Rosa Newmarch pertaining to Jean Sibelius

1906 *Jean Sibelius: A Finnish Composer* (Leipzig, 1906), trans. Ludmille Kirschbaum as *Jean Sibelius: ein finnländischer Komponist* (Leipzig, 1906)

1907 Translation of Jean Sibelius, *6 Songs*, Op. 50 (1. 'A Song of Spring', 2. 'Longing', 3. 'A Maiden yonder sings', 4. 'O, wert thou here', 5. 'The Silent Town', 6. 'The Song of the Roses') (Berlin and London, 1907)

Translation of Jean Sibelius, 'Hail O Moon!', Op. 18, No. 8, 'Sailing Seawards', Op. 18, No. 9, and 'The Song now stilled', Op. 18, No. 7 (Leipzig, 1907)

Translation of Jean Sibelius, *The Captive Queen*, Op. 48 (Moscow and Berlin, 1907)

1908 Translation of Jean Sibelius, 'Autumn Night', Op. 38, No. 1, 'A Dragon-Fly', Op. 17, No. 5, 'Driftwood', Op. 17, No. 7, 'The Harper and his Son', Op. 38, No. 4, 'The Heart's Morning', Op. 13, No. 3, 'I would I were dwelling', Op. 38, No. 5, 'In the Night', Op. 38, No. 3, 'A kiss's hope', Op. 13, No. 2, ''Neath the fir-trees', Op. 13, No. 1, 'On a Balcony by the Sea', Op. 38, No. 2, and 'To Evening', Op. 17, No. 6 (Leipzig, 1908)

1910 Translation of Jean Sibelius, 'Jubal', Op. 35, No. 1, and 'Theodora', Op. 35, No. 2 (Leipzig, 1910)

Translation of Jean Sibelius, *Impromptu*, Op. 19 (Leipzig, 1910)

1911 Translation of Jean Sibelius, *8 Songs*, Op. 61 (1. 'Shall I forget thee?', 2. 'Lapping Waters', 3. 'When I Dream', 4. 'Romeo', 5. 'Romance', 6. 'Dolce far niente', 7. 'Idle Wishes', 8. 'The Spell of Springtide') (Leipzig, 1911)

Translation of Jean Sibelius, *Ukko the Fire-Maker*, Op. 32 (Leipzig, 1911)

1912 'Chauvinism in Music', *Edinburgh Review* 216 (1912), 95–116

1913 *Jean Sibelius: Symphony No. 4 in A minor, Op. 63: Analytical Notes* (London, [1913]), trans. Ludmille Kirschbaum as *Vierte Sinfonie von Jean Sibelius (A moll, op. 63): Kleiner Konzertführer* (Leipzig, [1913])

1914 Translation of Jean Sibelius, 'The Bells of Berghall', Op. 65b (Leipzig, 1914)

1920 'Jean Sibelius, a Finnish Composer', *Musical Observer* 19/4 (1920), 27–31

1921 'Sibelius', *The Chesterian* n. s. no. 14 (April 1921), 417–21

1923 'Jean Sibelius, Finnish Composer', *Musical Observer* 23/9 (1923), 26, 55–7

1929 'Tone Poem, "En Saga". Sibelius' and 'Symphonic Poem, "Finlandia" (Op. 27). Sibelius', in *The Concert-goer's Library of Descriptive Notes*, 6 vols (London, 1928–48), vol. 2, pp. 66–9

1930 'Suite, "Karelia". Sibelius' and 'Valse Triste for Small Orchestra. Sibelius', in *The Concert-goer's Library of Descriptive Notes*, 6 vols (London, 1928–48), vol. 3., pp. 56–7 and 139–40

1937 'Introduction', in programme booklet for the 'Sibelius Concert' at Queen's Hall, Thursday 9 September 1937, pp. 7–10

1938 'Legends for Orchestra – *(a)* The Swan of Tuonela, *(b)* The Return of Lemminkainen. Sibelius', 'Prelude, "The Tempest" (Op. 109). Sibelius', 'Suite, "King Christian II". Sibelius', 'Suite for Orchestra (Op. 54), "Swan-White". Sibelius', 'Tone Poem, "Night-Ride and Sunrise" (Op. 55). Sibelius', and 'Tone Poem, "The Oceanides" (Op. 73). Sibelius', in *The Concert-goer's Library of Descriptive Notes*, 6 vols (London, 1938), vol. 5, pp. 78–91

1939 *Jean Sibelius: A Short Story of a Long Friendship* (Boston, 1939)

1944 *Jean Sibelius* (London, 1944)

Appendix

B. Rosa Newmarch, *Jean Sibelius: Symphony No. 4 in A minor, Op. 63: Analytical Notes* (London, [1913])

Newmarch's principal published writings on Sibelius – *Jean Sibelius: A Finnish Composer* (1906) and *Jean Sibelius: A Short Story of a Long Friendship* (1939, published in Britain in 1944 simply as *Jean Sibelius*) – are widely available in libraries around the world and have long been cited in the secondary literature on the composer. Although less easily accessible as individual documents, both her 'Sibelius' (published in *The Chesterian*, the house magazine of the publisher J. & W. Chester, in April 1921) and the introduction she wrote for the Sibelius Concert at Queen's Hall on 9 September 1937 were subsequently incorporated almost verbatim into *Jean Sibelius: A Short Story of a Long Friendship*. The articles published in 1920 and 1923 in the New York journal *The Musical Observer* are simply reprints of extracts from *Jean Sibelius: A Finnish Composer*. (The passages relating to Sibelius in her 1912 *Edinburgh Review* article, 'Chauvinism in Music', are cited in the notes to letter 66, written June 1912.) However, the 'analytical note' that Newmarch was commissioned to write for the first British performance of Sibelius's Fourth Symphony at the 1912 Birmingham Festival remains a bibliographical rarity. A copy of the note as it originally appeared in the programme booklet for the festival can be found at the Centre for Performance Studies of the Royal College of Music; copies of the revised and expanded version that was published the following year by Breitkopf & Härtel are in Sibelius's library and amongst Newmarch's own papers, and Ludmille Kirschbaum's German translation can be found in university libraries in Berlin and Leipzig.

Newmarch's published programme notes tended to be relatively brief, often blending summaries of the main musical themes and ideas with her own often poetic interpretation of a particular composition. However, when dealing with British premières of new orchestral works, she often wrote at greater length and with greater technical sophistication (see for instance, her analysis of Scriabin's *Prometheus* published in *The Musical Times* in April 1914).[1] In both its original and published variants, Newmarch's note on Sibelius's Fourth Symphony stands as her most serious and extended piece of writing about a single musical work; moreover, with its short examples (sixteen in the original note, twenty-six in its revised version), it constitutes one of the earliest attempts to produce an analysis of the symphony's formal and thematic characteristics. As to her sources of information about such a recent and challenging work, then Newmarch refers in her memoir to receiving 'a certain number of articles, mostly in Swedish, and much of the information contained in them went

---

[1] Rosa Newmarch, '"Prometheus": The Poem of Fire', *Musical Times* 55 (1914), 227–31.

into my analytical notes for the Fourth Symphony'.[2] By the time that Newmarch began work on her analysis, the only significant critical works to have been published in Swedish (or, indeed, in any language) were two articles by Otto Andersson that appeared in *Tydning för musik* in 1911.[3] A close comparison between these texts reveals that Newmarch drew, without explicit acknowledgement, on aspects of Andersson's work. Her interpretation of the symphony as a work rooted in the natural world, yet without a programme and avoiding explicit landscape-painting, and which combined a simplicity and brevity of expression with great originality of thought and orchestral detail, closely accords with that of Andersson (although there is much that is uniquely her own too). Furthermore, she employs an almost identical set of musical examples, although her actual commentary is considerably more detailed and poetic than Andersson's.

Andersson was later to claim that his published analysis of the symphony had been seen and authorised by the composer himself.[4] Sibelius, however, declined to provide Newmarch with any commentary on the work, reacting with trepidation to news that she had been asked to provide an annotation for its performance at Birmingham. His reticence may well be traced to the reception of the Fourth Symphony after its first performance in Helsinki on 3 April 1911. In a review in *Hufvudstadsbladet*, the critic Emil Wasenius had given details of a supposed programme to this otherwise abstract and ascetic work:

> The theme of the Symphony is a journey to the celebrated Koli (Kolivaara) near Lake Pielinen from whose height one has a superb view over the neighbouring countryside from the beauties of Hersjärvi in west Höytiänen while to the east there is Pielisjärvi and on the otherside of the lake the Russian border.[5]

Sibelius wrote to the newspaper to refute Wasenius's analysis, but his irritation may well have been related to the fact that the initial inspiration for the work that was to become the Fourth Symphony had indeed come during a trip to Koli in September 1909. This was not the first time that

---

[2] Rosa Newmarch, *Jean Sibelius: A Short Story of a Long Friendship* (Boston, 1939), p. 43 and Jean Sibelius (London, 1944) p. 29.

[3] Otto Andersson, 'Sibelius' fjärde symfoni', *Tydning för musik* 1 (1910–11), 171–3 and 'Sibelius' symfoni IV, op. 63', *Tydning för musik* 2 (1911–12), 201–7, collated and reprinted as 'Kring Sibelius fjärde symfoni', in Otto Andersson, *Studier i musik och folklore*, 2 vols (Åbo, 1964–69), vol. 1, pp. 101–10. Newmarch may also have been familiar with Axel Carpelan's, 'Sibelius' nya symfoni', *Göteborgs Handels- och Sjöfartstidning*, 11 April 1911. Of other early responses to the work, Evert Katila's 'Sibeliuksen neljäs sinfonia' (*Uusi Suomi*, 31 March 1912) was written in Finnish and hence unlikely to have been familiar to her.

[4] Andersson, 'Kring Sibelius fjärde symfoni', p. 101.

[5] Cited in Erik Tawaststjerna, *Sibelius*, trans. Robert Layton, 3 vols (London, 1976–97), vol. 2, pp. 170–71.

Appendix

critics had attempted to discern extra-musical programmes in Sibelius's symphonies. After the first performance of the Second Symphony in March 1901, for instance, Robert Kajanus published an interpretation of the work as a reflection of anti-Russian sentiment in Finland and of the journey towards freedom and independence. Despite a number of denials on the part of the composer, the myth persisted.[6]

Nonetheless, Newmarch seems to have been confident of her commentary on the Fourth Symphony and singled it out as one of her best essays in the genre:

> Of all her analytical notes, she herself prefers the notes upon the Symphony No. 4, in A minor, of Jean Sibelius. It is a work which she particularly admires, and her description of the musician and the music alike are laden with keen appreciation for the inner meaning of the great composer's mission. Admirers of the Finnish composer will do well to obtain these notes and the valuable information which they contain.[7]

As is argued in the introduction, Newmarch's interpretation of the symphony constituted an important modification of her earlier view of Sibelius as a nationalist; now, rather than being rooted in the mythic past of Finland's folklore and history, Sibelius promised a new direction for modern European symphonic music. Newmarch's contribution to the debate about the nature of modernism and the development of the symphony in both Finland and Britain seems to have gone largely unnoticed, leaving later generations of Sibelius scholars with an outdated and incomplete sense of her views.[8] After the Birmingham Festival, the Fourth Symphony received relatively few performances in Britain: Dan Godfrey conducted it at Bournemouth on 18 December 1913, and it was first heard at Queen's Hall in London on 20 March 1920, under the direction of Henry Wood (long after Edgar Speyer had first proposed to include it there).[9] Sibelius himself then performed it on 26 February 1921,

---

[6] Ibid., vol. 1, pp. 243–4.
[7] 'The Work of Mrs. Rosa Newmarch', *Musical Standard*, 4 March 1916, 174–6 (175).
[8] It is not included, for instance, in Glenda D. Goss, *Jean Sibelius: A Guide to Research* (New York and London, 1998). Ernest Newman was, however, aware of it, writing that 'the publishers were sufficiently confident . . . to bring out a brochure of fifteen pages, by Mrs Newmarch, dealing in considerable detail with the composer in general and the new work in particular' (Ernest Newman, 'Sibelius No. 4: Its English History', in *From the World of Music: Essays from 'The Sunday Times'*, ed. Felix Aprahamian (London, 1956), pp. 127–32 (p.127)). The presence of the German translation in a number of German university libraries means that it does figure in a number of bibliographies (i.e., Fred Blum, *Jean Sibelius: An International Bibliography on the Occasion of the Centennial Celebrations*, 1965, Detroit Studies in Music Bibliography 8 (Detroit, 1965), and Fabian Dahlström, *Jean Sibelius: Thematisch-bibliographisches Verzeichnis seiner Werke* (Wiesbaden, 2003)).

during his final trip to Britain (it was this occasion that inspired Newmarch's 1921 article in *The Chesterian*).

The musical examples are presented here as they are in Newmarch's revised and expanded booklet, other than to correct the few direct mistranscriptions from Breitkopf & Härtel's published score (1912). Typographical errors have been noted, but not corrected. Italics have been used to indicate words given in bold in the original. All notes are editorial.

Symphony, No. 4 in A minor, Op. 63

SIBELIUS

I. Tempo molto moderato, quasi adagio. III. Il tempo largo.
II. Allegro molto vivace.   IV. Allegro.

The name of Jean Sibelius first became a little known to German and English audiences about ten years ago. In Germany, his short tone-poem 'The Swan of Tuonela' – 111 bars of tensely emotional and strangely coloured music – was the first to attract the attention of the conductors. In England, Sir Henry Wood gave his Symphony No. 1, in E minor, at the Promenade Concerts in October, 1903, and Professor Granville Bantock introduced several of his compositions at the Concerts of the Liverpool Orchestral Society. But his more important works did not immediately leap into favour, because they followed none of the main currents of musical tendency, and could not be referred to the familiar origins of a good deal of contemporary music. They exact attentive study, independence of judgment and some exercise of the imagination; for whether we like his art or not, we have to confess that it is very different from that of other people. There are two reasons for this particular sense of aloofness which Sibelius's music seems to inspire in those who hear it for the first time: first, as already asserted, it is much less derivative than that of many present-day composers; secondly, it is representative of an ancient and somewhat mysterious race, and of a culture which, in spite of its veneer of Swedish influence, remains at its base, quite remote from most of us. But although some of Sibelius's works can only make their fullest appeal to his own race, it is an exaggeration to say his music is in any way unintelligible to those who will take the trouble to study it. We need know nothing of Finnish language or history to be moved by his sincere love of nature, his lofty idealism and intensity of emotion – an emotion which is always curbed by a noble respect for his art. In short, Sibelius is Sibelius, and from the outset of his career his independent judgment has saved him from being swept off his feet by passing waves of musical tendency. His music is stamped with his own image and not with that of Wagner,

---

[9] Speyer to Newmarch, 26 May 1913, BL Ms Mus 1117, fol. 54.

Appendix

Brahms, Tschaikowsky, Strauss, or any of the great overshadowing personalities of the time.

For a musician who from the beginning of his creative activity has been dubbed 'a national poet' Sibelius is singularly human and many-sided. His music is no mere folk-song echo, but contains what the life of his nation contains: much sorrow, a little gaiety – fleeting as a Northern summer; hopes perhaps too vast to be realized by a small people; a profound mysticism, and a Berserker power of indignation which makes the Finns terrible in their anger, and to which they owe the very fact of their existence. The popularity of his early work 'Finlandia' has been rather detrimental than otherwise to the appreciation of his more important compositions. Smetana, contemplating his fine series of unplayed symphonic poems and neglected operas, regretted bitterly that he had ever endowed his country with 'The Bartered Bride'; and for the same reason Sibelius's admirers are often tempted to wish that 'Finlandia' had been made *taboo* in other lands than its own.

Dr. George Göhler, in an article on Sibelius, published in the 'Kunstwart' in 1908, had already observed that the immense success of the composer's lesser works such as 'Valse Triste', and the Elegy and Minuet from the incidental music to Adolf Paul's tragedy 'King Christian II', had proved rather inimical than otherwise to the appreciation of his greater and more sustained efforts. Those who know Brahms by his Hungarian Dances only, or the Serenade in D (Op. 11), have explored but a small corner of a great soul; and those who only know Sibelius by his 'Valse Triste' are missing something valuable in contemporary music: a new note of strong, impassioned idealism which a future generation will assuredly begin to enjoy.

Not that there is seriously anything to be said against the miniature side of Sibelius's art. The 'Valse Triste', the Romance for Strings, the 'Valse Mélancolique', the melodious Sonatinas for piano, and all the rest of these highly finished, delicately wrought trifles, are perfectly genuine expressions of one side of his culture; for Sibelius is a complex psychological and musical problem. On the one hand is the rugged strength, the grim will power, the rare, shy tenderness and quick decisive thought that are the inheritance of a long line of free, sportloving, adventurous ancestors, violent in action, laconic in speech, stubborn in resistance; while contrasted with these qualities we find a traditional refinement of a type that would not have ill-become the ladies of 'Cranford'.[10] Sibelius's mother came from one of those quiet, cultured, clerical households such as existed – and probably still exist – like oases of refinement in the wilderness of a wholesome, but uncouth, northern life. The very fact of their isolation caused the inmates of such homes to set an immense value not only on all art and learning, but even upon trifling domestic elegancies. Sibelius has a tendency to this fastidious refinement in the

---

[10] A reference to *Cranford* (1851), a novel by Elizabeth Gaskell (1810–65), dealing with the lives of a group of genteel ladies in the fictional town of the work's title.

small details of life; and it is strongly evident in his art, disconcerting those who only care for music in its larger forms and more sensational aspects – 'Armies of angels that soar, legions of demons that lurk.'[11] The terse and lightly woven pianoforte pieces, the miniature compositions for strings – all the 'Sibeliana' that seem in such curious contrast to the large sculptural lines and powerful, pithy inspiration of the big orchestral works, and the restrained concentrated emotionalism of the songs, are probably sub-consciously reminiscent of that old-world culture. It is as though a sculptor amused himself from time to time by cutting out a delicate silhouette, or modelling small elegancies in wax, and, secure in the sense of his creative strength, took a whimsical pleasure in displaying these things side by side with his massive figures in bronze and marble. At first sight we might condemn the small finished objects as incongruous and trivial; but a moment's reflection would surely show us that while the great works were the outcome of an urgent irresistible impulse, the small ones were the result of moods no less personal and sincere. There is, of course, in almost all the northern composers a love of such small and delicate forms. Gade had it, and Grieg – to mention only two of the most familiar names. Perhaps the tendency came to them by way of Mendelssohn and Schumann. With Sibelius, who is certainly not influenced by either of these composers, we must set down the liking for these short forms to an inherent affection and admiration for articles of *virtu*, provided they fulfil their definition of 'excellence and rarity in art', and spring from a genuinely artistic *Stimmung*. The small pieces have undoubtedly a charm and aroma all their own; nevertheless we lose by the fact that we have been content, so far, to know Sibelius as an artificer and embroiderer, rather than as a hewer and shaper, of musical material.

Profiting by the example of his immediate predecessors, Tschaikowsky, César Franck and others, Sibelius throughout his career has written both 'absolute' and 'programme' music. Side by side with his first three Symphonies we find a series of works founded on episodes from the Finnish epic the 'Kalevala', such as 'The Swan of Tuonela' and 'Lemminkainen's Home-faring'; others are inspired by some unavowed poetic basis, like 'En Saga', and the later compositions 'In Memoriam' and 'Night-ride and Sunrise'. He has also written incidental music to Adolf Paul's tragedy 'King Christian II', Maeterlinck's 'Pelleas and Melisande', Järnefelt's 'Kuolema' (Death) – which contains the 'Valse Triste' – and Strindberg's fairy play 'Swan-White'. Of late years, dating from the appearance of 'Night-ride and Sunrise', his music shows a tendency to increased subjectivism. He seeks his ideals less in the historic past and more within himself. At the same time he has developed a ruthless determination to refine and clarify every musical thought; to prune and concentrate; to avoid all useless display of orchestral luxury; all garrulous emotionalism – in a word 'to cut the cackle' and deal only with essentials. Besides the

---

[11] A quotation from the opening stanza of 'Abt Vogler' (1864), a dramatic monologue by Robert Browning (1812–89) about the eighteenth-century organist Georg Vogler.

Appendix

hour-long symphonies of the present day, Sibelius's modest forty-minute works may deceive some people into the belief that paucity of inspiration rather than intense concentration accounts for their 'heavenly' brevity.[12]

The A minor Symphony has had three predecessors. The first, in E minor, a work of astonishing freshness of inspiration, bearing witness on every page to an intimate communion with nature, and reflecting the poetical pantheism which is inherent in the Finnish race. The second, in D major, more structurally developed, the movements more closely interrelated, and approaching more nearly to the classical model, while remaining entirely modern in spirit. The third, performed at a Philharmonic Concert four or five years ago, and summarily dismissed from our concert programmes, has only three movements, but those who know it well realize that it was so planned in the composer's mind and feel no sense of incompleteness.

The Fourth Symphony, like the earlier ones, is music of an intimate nature, and much of it was thought out and written in the isolation of hoary forests, by rushing rapids, or wind-lashed lakes. There are moments – especially in the first movement – when we feel ourselves 'alone with nature's breathing things'.[13] It has, however, no programme that could, or should, be expressed in literary terms. Undoubtedly Sibelius reflects in his music many impressions received directly from nature, and he is almost uncannily familiar with those aspects and undertones of outdoor life which so very few of us know, for the simple reason that unless we are sportsmen, shepherds, game-keepers, or poets, we are careful never to spend long hours alone with nature in all her moods. But to admit this is not – as superficial critics of his work seem to suppose – the equivalent of disposing of his music as landscape-painting pure and simple. Even when we have realised the setting of many of his thoughts and emotions, the work of comprehending them is only begun. Making every allowance for essential differences of nationality and temperament, we must listen to Sibelius's later music in something of the same spirit in which we listen to that of Brahms. Neither of these composers has the knack of projecting upon the world his emotional messages in glaring and unmistakable signs, after the fashion of the illuminated advertisement. The light burns all the same in the temple of their art for those who care to pursue it, but, as Browning says,

> 'whoso desires to penetrate
> Deeper, must dive by the spirit-sense'[14]

and that is what the public, and the critics too, so seldom bring to bear upon a new musical apparition. Our imaginations have grown so

---

[12] An inverted allusion to Robert Schumann's famous description of the 'heavenly length' of Schubert's Ninth Symphony ('The Great').

[13] The opening line of 'The Royal Aspects of the Earth', by John Byrne Leicester Warren, Baron de Tabley (1835–95).

[14] A quotation from the penultimate stanza of Browning's 'House' (1876).

indolent for want of use that we are disposed to resent the lack of a programme whenever the idiom departs from the familiar and the obvious. To those whose perversity is always demanding a sign, it may be said that no programme, short of vivisecting the composer and drawing charts of the inner workings of his heart and brain, could help us to understand music so deeply-brooded and closely knit up with the personality of its author as Sibelius's later string quartet ('Voces Intimae Op. 56') and the four Symphonies. In listening to this kind of music we experience the same sense of baffled enquiry that creeps over us after long contemplation of Michelangelo's Duke of Urbino, in the Chapel of the Medici Monuments at Florence. To fathom the thoughts and feelings at work behind Lorenzo's shadow-eclipsed brow is a riddle unsolved by generations of intelligent gazers; yet the impassioned concentration of the figure compels us to wonder and question. And although intellectually we find no answer to the problem, yet emotionally each one may, after patient scrutiny, realise the joy of coming near to a personal solution of it. Are there really, people – intelligent, art-loving people – who would refuse to contemplate this master-piece because Michelangelo has carved no explanatory scroll to destroy the eternal, intolerable mystery which enshrouds his Thinker? We would prefer to believe that people so devoid of imagination do not exist. But undoubtedly taking the body of criticism which has so far appeared in connection with Sibelius's Fourth Symphonys [*sic*] a good deal of unreasoning irritation has been shown because the composer has vouchsafed no official guide to the deeper thoughts which underlie the comparatively simple structure of the work.

For in its external presentment the work is extraordinarily simple, and set beside much contemporary music it affects us as might a nude statue planted amid an assemblage of sumptuously attired wax models. This affection for bare and primitive things is innate in Sibelius. The Chinese, it is said, like to have big slabs of rock, huge rugged boulders, disposed amid the luxuriant beauty of their parks and gardens; they find a certain moral strength and restfulness in letting their eyes rest upon such rudimentary things. In Sibelius's music, among much that is very modern and subtle, we are constantly coming upon such outcroppings of elemental bed-rock.

In the first place, there is simplicity of means. The Beethoven orchestra practically suffices to Sibelius's needs, but he puts it to new uses and knows how to extract the fullest individual value from each instrument. He is absolutely sure of his colour effects, although his instrumentation is subtle and low-toned as the landscape which surrounds him. It is, indeed, rather of light and shade than of colour that we think in connection with Sibelius's orchestration. Although colour is not actually wanting in some of his works, yet, on the whole, his music has affinities with Rembrandt rather than with Giorgione; and still more with that quality of deep-chiselled shadow and contrasting salience which Rodin describes as taking the place of colour in a sculptured design. There is quite an individual mastery in his power of making passages which look very simple on paper tell in a most arresting way when we hear them in the orchestra. They do not show like a splash of intensely vivid colour; they are rather projected in a clear light from out a sombre and mystical depth of shadow.

It is a mistake to judge Sibelius's art, and above all the later works, as purely 'impressionist' music. In common with most of the composers of northern Europe he values form for its own sake. It is true that we see in his compositions a growing tendency towards the continuous and uninterrupted development of his ideas, and the old formalism of the symphony suffers ellipsis, curtailment and condensation whenever close conformity with it would delay too long the progress of his main thought or emotion; but the architectural and sculptural requirements are not forgotten. When we have grown accustomed to its disconcerting directness of utterance we shall see that the structure of the Fourth Symphony, with all its telescoping of formal divisions, remains strong and clear.

Another point in which it differs from a great deal of the Symphonic music of the day is in the presentation of the thematic material. Too often in the work of the 'modernists' the short-winded, scrappy motives which serve as 'subjects' have to be disguised from their first appearance under some elaborate garb. They remind us of puny babies decked out in imposing christening robes; for they are often merely dwarfed and abortive ideas, disguised under brilliant orchestral tissues. But Sibelius undoubtedly retains an old-fashioned respect for the theme and regards the melodic material as the inspired word on which the whole message of the music depends. The design is a matter which concerns the composer's capacity for selection and his workmanship; the themes are the divine element. They come, at their best, from some source to which we give many names, but which remains beyond our control; which ebbs and flows at some will that is not wholly man's own. It is more than doubtful if themes can really be 'invented'; they certainly cannot be forced into existence. When they emerge from their mysterious birthplace they often make their appearance in small scintillating fragments; then, 'like nebula condensing to an orb',[15] they need time to coagulate and form an organic whole; finally they will become the guiding stars by which the musician steers his course when he embarks on the calm or troubled seas of creative activity. The presentation of the theme, the 'word of origin', to quote a term from the Finnish mythology, is clearly of the greatest importance to Sibelius, who proceeds very tactfully in apportioning each melodic rôle to the right exponent, so that an individual theme acquires a real and unforgettable personality. Many of his subjects are born, as it were, for the wood-wind; the oboe with its sense of melancholy remoteness; the cor anglais with its penetrating, unearthly loneliness, and the more human sadness of the clarinet – he uses them all, not merely with a sure sense of effect, but as the inevitable mediums of his ideas.

But now to turn from these general characteristics of Sibelius's style to

---

[15] A slightly misquoted line from scene 6 of the dramatic poem 'A Life-Drama' by the Scots poet Alexander Smith (1829–67) (the original reads: 'As nebula condenses to an orb').

the work in which he has recently condensed the mature experiences and ideals of middle age – the Fourth Symphony.

I. *Tempo molto moderato, quasi adagio* (A minor, 3–4 and 2–4).[16] Like some of Haydn's early symphonies, the present example opens with a slow movement. An introductory theme of considerable importance is given out immediately in syncopated rhythm by muted 'cellos, double-basses and bassoons, and quickly dies away pianissimo:

No. 1.

The progression of the first three notes should be particularly observed. A solo 'cello then presents the first true principal subject:

No. 2.

This results in some development, during which the F sharps and E naturals in No. 1 are repeatedly heard in the basses. Presently the bassoons and horns start this episode (*Adagio*):

No. 3.

A *crescendo* leads up to a forcible passage for brass, and this strenuous climax is succeeded by two tranquil calls from muted horns over a soft tremolo in the strings. (Sudden contrasts in the volume of tone will be noticed as a characteristic feature of the music both here and elsewhere). Then the chords in the brass return in this form:

No. 4.

Further developments of No. 2 are carried on in the strings, with tender, reassuring replies from solo clarinet and solo oboe:

No. 5.

---

[16] The German edition of the note correctly gives the time signatures of this movement as 'C and 3/2'.

At length in the dominant minor a solo 'cello presents the passage quoted below:

No. 6.

The other strings respond with swift transitions from loud to soft, and a phrase from the third bar of No. 6 comes into prominence. At first the wood-wind give out sustained, swelling phrases which end abruptly, *rinforzando*, like a cry uttered over the brooding, misty tremolo of the strings. But by and bye [*sic*] a little speaking figure, which seems to have something significant to tell us, is whispered from solo clarinet to solo flute and back again:

No. 7. Clar. solo.

The movement goes its quiet way, gradually gathering force for the next climax. An *allargando* phrase leads to the repetition of the stirring chords for brass, and the horns are heard once more calling over the prolonged drum roll, followed by references to No. 2. But this recapitulation is of the tersest and most concentrated description, and the only allusion to No. 1 comes at the close, in the strings, where it starts in the 'cellos and dies away in the first violins.

II. *Allegro molto vivace* (F major, 3–4).[17] The movement approaches, perhaps, as nearly to gaiety as anything that Sibelius has ever written; for though there are flashes of humour and moments of philosophical serenity in his music, the true sportive, *scherzando* mood is almost unknown to him. The opening is in a cheerful vein and speaks of sylvan surroundings in this pastoral theme, announced by a solo oboe, accompanied by violas:

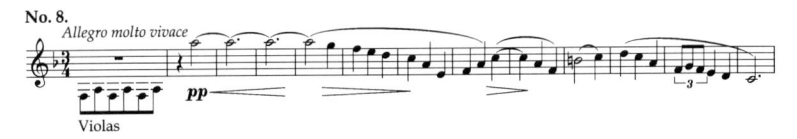

No. 8.

The violins reply with:

No. 9.

---

[17] The German edition of the note gives the time signatures of this movement as '3/4 and 2/4', although the only part of the movement in 2/4 is the thirty-two bar section from rehearsal letter B to four bars before rehearsal letter C.

and continue as follows:

No. 10.

[musical notation]

After this brief dialogue, the time changes to 2–4 and the strings introduce a strongly accentuated theme:

No. 11.

[musical notation]

The development of the above subject is presently interrupted by chords in the brass, answered by wood-wind, leading to a repetition of the dialogue-phrase over a pedal on B flat. After some strange harmonies in the strings, we hear this graceful passage in thirds, given by the flutes *tranquillo*, and at a more deliberate pace:

No. 12. *tranquillo*

[musical notation]

This passage, which looks like a reminiscence of No. 8, may be regarded as a truncated – or rather an extremely compressed – trio. It is heard thrice before the return of the first section of the *Scherzo* (No. 8) given by the oboe as before, but now accompanied by the 'cellos with a *pizzicato* passage in contrary motion. An expressive phrase for first violins and 'cellos precedes the re-entry of the dialogue, and this brings us to a section marked *Doppio più lento*. Here solo oboe and clarinets enter with this new motive:

No. 13.

[musical notation]

Unobtrusive as it appears to the eye, this theme, with its characteristic interval of a diminished fifth, stands out in a very striking way against sombre, tremulous accompaniment for divided strings, and is a good instance of what I have said about Sibelius's powers of setting a simple theme in relief, like a luminous object reflected in dark waters.

Considerable use is now made of the short but vividly expressive figure for violin shown above, which passes from the higher to the lower strings, while bassoons and muted horns have sustained notes in octaves. From the beginning of the *doppio più lento* to the end of this extended Coda, the second violins are occupied continuously with a figured pedal (alternations of F and E). Restatements of the whole of No. 13 are heard from the first violins, joined by violas, and from the oboes and clarinets. But the short, eloquent, answering figure dominates the whole concluding section, until we are penetrated by its strange persistence. In the final climax it is heard *fortissimo* from the wood-wind, and is answered with emotional intensity by the opening bars of No. 13. Then with a sudden drop to *ppp* the movement ends quite abruptly with an octave figure for drums. We think of many characteristic endings, some formal and courtly, others too long delayed, some brought about with carefully prepared eccentricity; but probably no one ever left off speaking so naturally and unconcernedly as Sibelius does here, with the very slightest gesture of dismissal.

III. *Il tempo largo* (C sharp minor).[18] This is a movement which, inspite [*sic*] of much that is beautiful and appealing in the music, hugs its emotional secret closely and jealously. It has that unity of idea and continuous structure which, failing a more accurate terminology, we must describe as characteristic of the Lied-form.

In the beginning some preliminary matter is distributed more or less between solo flute and solo clarinet:

No. 14. Flutes

The advent of the chief theme, round which revolve all the leading ideas and emotions contained in the movement, is long held back. We hear a suggestion of it in the passages for strings which precede the entry in four-part harmony of the horns; and they in their turn are made to be the heralds of it in this beautiful phrase:

No. 15. Horns

---

[18] The German edition of the note adds the time signature 'C' here.

Then the 'cellos, *con sordini*, foreshadow it once again just before the repetition of No. 14. At last, its evolution being completed, it is presented, with its bell-like figure of accompaniment in the violins:

When the theme has been dwelt upon for a moment, a dialogue is started between solo instruments of the wood-wind group, over a dominant pedal in the second violins:

and

This brings back No. 16 which is restated by the strings in unison and octaves, against a passage in the wood-wind descending from oboes to basses. Then No. 4 returns again; and after that No. 16, accompanied by a dark and heavy passage for basses, wood-wind and trombones. The rest is full of tender gravity. Snatches of dialogue pass from wood-wind to strings over a tonic pedal in the violas, and a sustained A in the horns, the last of the dialogue phrase being heard pizzicato from the basses, after which the movement comes to an end.

IV. *Allegro* (A major, ending in A minor).[19] While with many modern symphonies the *Finale* is the least satisfactory part of the work, Sibelius comes to his last movement with unimpaired vitality and a good reserve of thematic material. It might perhaps be possible to refer this *Allegro* structurally to a free Rondo-form, but I am not going to attempt this unnecessary task. The opening subject rings with franker gladness than

---

[19] The German edition of the note adds the time signature 'C' here, although according to the published score of the symphony, the final movement is in *alla breve* rather than in common time.

Appendix

that of the so-called *Scherzo* movement (No. 8). The outdoor feeling returns and a breadth and breeziness is noticeable in the theme, which is given out immediately by the first violins:

No. 19.

On repetition, the D sharp and E in the second bar of the foregoing quotation give rise to this emphatic confirmation in the violas:

No. 20.

a figure which plays its part in the subsequent development of the movement. The Glockenspiel replies with this motive:

No. 21.

We now have a second strain of the subject, heard against a syncopated accompaniment in the 'cellos:

No. 22.

A rather declamatory quaver theme, introduced by solo 'cello and afterwards taken over by the solo violin imparts a touch of agitation to the music:

No. 23.

This leads to the reappearance of No. 20 in various parts of the orchestra. Another figure expressive of motion is announced by the 'cellos, afterwards doubled by first violins in octaves:

No. 24.

All is now kept in a soft shimmer of movement. No. 22 reappears presently, first in the clarinet, then in the violas; No. 20 re-enters, to alternate with sweeping upward passages for wood-wind; and eventually we reach some chords, given successively by strings and wood-wind, belonging to different keys which contradict each other. After this the following occurs in the wood-wind:

No. 25.

poco f

and a figure of a falling fifth now appears in the strings and accompanies both the above passage and a syncopated figure that presently succeeds it:

No. 26. 1st V. divisi.

p

A middle section, in C, brings sustained chords for wood-wind, with a reference to No. 24, while the strings rush up and down in *pianissimo* scale-passages. A long drum-roll swells louder and louder, and presently the glockenspiel is heard above the rising and falling of the strings. This is a descriptive episode which must surely stir the imagination and set us seeking for the poetic purpose which underlies is. When the winnowing of the strings has ceased, a pizzicato figure, of ascending and descending fifths, is worked for a time against quiet sustained phrases in the wood-wind. The key then changes back to A major, and over the persistent accompaniment of fifths, passages are heard from the wood-wind similar to those shown in No. 25; but here the horns hold a pedal on B.

The Glockenspiel announces the beginning of the recapitulation, in which the orchestration is even more strikingly original than before. After a time the syncopated figure (No. 26) becomes very prominent, giving a solemn, almost religious feeling to the piece. A great sonorous climax is built up, and at its height the strings are heard proclaiming this motive (No. 26) *fff* against powerful, sustained chords in the wind, the clear silvery tones of the bells just piercing through the volume of sound. The climax subsides as the trombone gives one last forcible utterance. The mood now becomes quieter. The strings carry on the syncopated figure interrupted by the persistent calling of the wood-wind. Twice these plaintive octaves are answered by the muted horns; then the brass is heard no more. The strings continue the dominating thought (No. 26) until they, too, are extinguished in a faint misty tremolo. A solo flute is still left calling in a strange solitude, and three times a solo oboe – 'a still small voice'[20] – returns a tranquil but firm reply. Finally the strings revert for

[20] 1 Kings 19:12.

the last time to No. 26, and with these minor harmonies the Symphony comes to an end.

This modest and deeply-felt conclusion is like nothing else in all symphonic literature. It seems to be the final consecration and elucidation of a work which with all its architectural simplicity of expression, takes us at times into shadowy regions of mystical idealism. The music seems to have caught something of the religious spirit which is working in so many different directions at the present moment; which is in fact the moving undercurrent in art and literature, as well as in philosophy. We have always been accustomed to look for a certain pantheistic mysticism in Sibelius's music; but in listening to the close of this work we feel ourselves face to face with something quite different from the vague Nature-worship – the 'delirious animism' of the 'Kalevala' – which is the inheritance of the essential Finn. We are surely justified in thinking that here we catch the echo of an unsectarian, unobtrusive, but clearly spoken, *Credo*.

Rosa Newmarch

SELECT BIBLIOGRAPHY

Archival sources

BBC Written Archive Centre, Caversham:
R79/117/1 (Concert Organisers Office, Prospectuses and Handbills, Promenades)

British Library (BL), London:
Additional Manuscript 56421 (Correspondence of Sir Henry Joseph Wood)
Additional Manuscript 57786 (Cecil Gray Papers)
Additional Manuscript 64961 (Letters from Jean Sibelius to Sir Granville Bantock)
Music Manuscript 1117, fols 130–227 (Rosa Newmarch Papers)
Music Manuscript 1641 (Harriet Cohen Papers)
Royal Philharmonic Society Manuscripts (RPS) 337 and 363

Centre for Performance History of the Royal College of Music:
Concert programmes for the 1912 Birmingham Festival

Elgar Birthplace Museum:
Letters exchanged between Newmarch and Elgar

Harry Ransom Humanities Research Center, University of Texas at Austin:
John Lane Company Papers

National Archives of Finland (NAF), Helsinki:
Sibelius Family Papers (SFP)

National Library of Finland (NLF):
Coll.206 (Sibelius Papers)

Newspapers, journals and periodicals

The Athenaeum
The Birmingham Daily Post
The Chesterian
The Daily Herald
The Evening Standard
The Illustrated London News
The Manchester Guardian
The Morning Post
The Musical Herald
The Musical Mirror
The Musical Opinion and Trade Review
The Musical Standard
The Musical Times
The Nation
The Standard
The Times
The Violin and String World
The Yorkshire Post

Bibliography

Published sources

Adams, Byron, ed., *British Modernism*, special issue of *The Musical Quarterly* 91 (2008)

Andersson, Otto, 'Sibelius' fjärde symfoni', *Tydning för musik* 1 (1910–11), 171–3, reprinted in 'Kring Sibelius fjärde symfoni', in Otto Andersson, *Studier i musik och folklore*, 2 vols (Åbo, 1964–9), vol. 1, pp. 101–10 (pp. 101–3)

—, 'Sibelius' symfoni IV, op. 63', *Tydning för musik* 2 (1911–12), 201–7, reprinted in 'Kring Sibelius fjärde symfoni', in Otto Andersson, *Studier i musik och folklore*, 2 vols (Åbo, 1964–69), vol. 1, pp. 101–10 (pp. 103–10)

Bantock, Granville, 'Foreword', in Rosa Newmarch, *Jean Sibelius: A Short History of a Long Friendship* (Boston, 1939), pp. 7–11, reprinted in Rosa Newmarch, *Jean Sibelius* (London, 1944), pp. 5–7

Bantock, Helena [as Helen F. Schweitzer], *The Love-Philtre, and Other Poems* (London, 1897)

—, *A Woman's Love, and Other Poems* (London, 1911)

Bax, Arnold, *Farewell, My Youth* (London, 1943)

Beecham, Thomas, *A Mingled Chime: Leaves from an Autobiography* (London, 1944)

Blom, Eric, 'A Bibliography of Works by Jean Sibelius', *Dominant* 1 (1928), 33–5

—, 'Kuula, Toivo', in *Cobbett's Cyclopedic Survey of Chamber Music*, ed. Walter Willson Cobbett, 2 vols (London, 1929–30), vol. 2, pp. 83–4

—, 'Sibelius, Jean', in *Cobbett's Cyclopedic Survey of Chamber Music*, ed. Walter Willson Cobbett, 2 vols (London, 1929–30), vol. 2, pp. 416–17

—, 'Sibelius, Jean', in *Grove's Dictionary of Music and Musicians*, ed. H. C. Colles, 5 vols (London, 1927–28), vol. 4, pp. 748–51

Blum, Fred, *Jean Sibelius: An International Bibliography on the Occasion of the Centennial Celebrations, 1965*, Detroit Studies in Music Bibliography 8 (Detroit, 1965)

Boos, Florence S., 'Dante Gabriel Rossetti's Poetic Daughters: *Fin de siècle* Women Poets and the Sonnet', in *Outsiders Looking In: The Rossettis Then and Now*, ed. David Clifford and Laurence Roussillon (London, 2004), pp. 253–81

Boosey, William, *Fifty Years of Music* (London, 1931)

Brown, John Croumbie, ed., *People of Finland in Archaic Terms, Being Sketches of Them Given in the Kalevala and in Other National Works* (London, 1892)

Buckley, R. J., *Sir Edward Elgar* (London, 1905)

Bullock, Philip Ross, '"Lessons in Sensibility": Rosa Newmarch, Music Appreciation and the Aesthetic Cultivation of the Self', *Yearbook of English Studies* 40 (2010), 295–318

—, *Rosa Newmarch and Russian Music in Late Nineteenth and Early Twentieth-Century England*, Royal Musical Association Monographs 18 (Farnham, 2009)

Bibliography

Carley, Lionel, *Delius: A Life in Letters*, 2 vols (Aldershot, 1983–8)
Catalogue of the Library of Jean Sibelius (Helsinki, 1973)
Cobbett, Walter Willson, ed., *Cobbett's Cyclopedic Survey of Chamber Music*, 2 vols (London, 1929–30)
Cohen, Harriet, *A Bundle of Time: The Memoirs of Harriet Cohen* (London, 1969)
Colles, H. C., ed., *Grove's Dictionary of Music and Musicians*, 5 vols (London, 1927–28)
—, 'Jean Sibelius', in *Great Contemporaries: Essays by Various Hands* (London, 1935), pp. 396–407
—, *Walford Davies: A Biography* (London, 1942)
Comparetti, Domenico Pietro Antonio, *The Traditional Poetry of the Finns*, trans. Isabella M. Anderton (London, 1898)
Cox, David, *The Henry Wood Proms* (London, 1980)
Dahlhaus, Carl, *Nineteenth-Century Music*, trans. J. Bradford Robinson (Berkeley, Los Angeles and London, 1989)
Dahlström, Fabian, ed., *Högtärade Maestro! Högtärade Herr Baron! Korrespondensen mellan Axel Carpelan och Jean Sibelius 1900–1919* (Helsinki and Stockholm, 2010)
—, ed., *Jean Sibelius: Dagbok 1909–1944* (Helsinki and Stockholm, 2005)
—, *Jean Sibelius: Thematisch-bibliographisches Verzeichnis seiner Werke* (Wiesbaden, 2003)
Dangerfield, George, *The Strange Death of Liberal England* (London, 1936)
Distiller, Natasha, *Desire and Gender in the Sonnet Tradition* (Basingstoke and New York, 2008)
Doctor, Jennifer, *The BBC and Ultra-Modern Music, 1922–1936: Shaping a Nation's Tastes* (Cambridge, 1999)
—, and David Wright, eds, *The Proms: A New History* (London, 2007)
Ekman, Karl, *Jean Sibelius: His Life and Personality*, trans. Edward Birse (London, 1936)
Elkin, Robert, *Queen's Hall, 1893–1941* (London, 1944)
Fischmann, Zdenka E., ed., *Janáček–Newmarch Correspondence* (Rockville, 1986)
Fisher, Joseph R., *Finland and the Tsars, 1809–1899*, 2nd edn (London, 1901)
Flodin, Karl, 'Die Erweckung des nationalen Tones in der finnischen Musik', *Die Musik* 3 (1903–04), 287–9
—, 'Die Entwicklung der Musik in Finnland', *Die Musik* 2 (1902–03), 355–62
—, *Die Musik in Finnland* (Helsinki, 1900), trans. H. Biaudet as *La Musique en Finlande* (Paris, 1900)
Foreman, Lewis, ed., *From Parry to Britten: British Music in Letters 1900–1945* (London, 1987)
Franklin, Peter, 'Sibelius in Britain', in *The Cambridge Companion to Sibelius*, ed. Daniel M. Grimley (Cambridge, 2004), pp. 182–95
Garafola, Lynn, *Diaghilev's Ballets Russes* (New York and Oxford, 1989)
Gillies, Malcolm, *Bartók in Britain: A Guided Tour* (Oxford, 1989)

Bibliography

Godonhjelm, Bernard Fredrik, *Handbook of the History of Finnish Literature*, trans. E. D. Butler, 2nd edn (London, 1896)
Goss, Glenda Dawn, *Jean Sibelius: A Guide to Research* (New York and London, 1998)
—, *Jean Sibelius and Olin Downes: Music, Friendship, Criticism* (Boston, 1995)
—, ed., *Jean Sibelius: The Hämeenlinna*, ed., *Letters: Scenes from a Musical Life, 1874–1895* (Esbo, 1997)
—, *Sibelius: A Composer's Life and the Awakening of Finland* (Chicago and London, 2009)
—, ed., *The Sibelius Companion* (Westport and London, 1996)
Gray, Cecil, *Sibelius* (London, 1931)
Gray, Laura, 'Sibelius and England', in *The Sibelius Companion*, ed. Glenda Dawn Goss (Westport and London, 1996), pp. 281–95
—, '"The Symphonic Problem": Sibelius Reception in England Prior to 1950' (Unpublished PhD thesis, Yale University, 1997)
—, '"The Symphony in the Mind of God": Sibelius Reception and English Symphonic Theory', in *Sibelius Forum: Proceedings from the Second International Jean Sibelius Conference, Helsinki, 25–29 November, 1995*, ed. Veijo Murtomäki, Kari Kilpeläinen and Risto Väisänen (Helsinki, 1998), pp. 62–72
Grimley, Daniel M., ed., *The Cambridge Companion to Sibelius* (Cambridge, 2004)
—, 'Music, Ice, and the "Geometry of Fear": The Landscapes of Vaughan Williams's *Sinfonia Antartica*', *Musical Quarterly* 91 (2008), 116–50
Harper-Scott, J. P. E., '"Our True North": Walton's First Symphony, Sibelianism, and the Nationalization of Modernism in England', *Music and Letters* 89 (2008), 562–89
Hepokoski, James, 'Structural Tensions in Sibelius's Fifth Symphony: Circular Stasis, Linear Progression, and the Problem of "Traditional" Form', in *Sibelius Forum: Proceedings from the Second International Jean Sibelius Conference, Helsinki, 25–29 November, 1995*, ed. Veijo Murtomäki, Kari Kilpeläinen and Risto Väisänen (Helsinki, 1998), pp. 213–36
Hillila, Ruth-Esther, and Barbara Blanchard Hong, eds, *Historical Dictionary of the Music and Musicians of Finland* (Westport and London, 1997)
Holmes, John, *Dante Gabriel Rossetti and the Late Victorian Sonnet-Sequence: Sexuality, Belief and the Self* (Aldershot, 2005)
—, and Natasha Distiller, eds, *Horae Amoris: The Collected Poems of Rosa Newmarch* (High Wycombe, 2010)
Huttunen, Matti, 'How Sibelius Became a Classic in Finland', in *Sibelius Forum: Proceedings from the Second International Jean Sibelius Conference, Helsinki, 25–29 November, 1995*, ed. Veijo Murtomäki, Kari Kilpeläinen and Risto Väisänen (Helsinki, 1998), pp. 73–81
Irving, John, 'Schönberg in the News: The London Performances of 1912–1914', *Music Review* 48 (1988), 52–70
Jacobs, Arthur, *Henry J. Wood: Maker of the Proms* (London, 1994)

Jeaffreson, M. T., *Pedigree of the Jeaffreson Family with Notes and Memoirs* (London, 1922)
Jean-Aubry, Georges, 'Otto Kling', *Chesterian* n. s. no. 39 (May 1924), 209–10
Johnson, Harold E., *Sibelius* (London, 1960)
The Kalevala, the Epic Poem of Finland, trans. John Martin Crawford, 2 vols (New York, 1888)
Keeton, A. E., 'The Music of Finland', *Leisure Hour* 48 (1900), 1079–80
Kling, Otto, 'A Voyage to Russia in War Time', *Chesterian* no. 1 (November 1915), 3–8
Krohn, Ilmari, 'De la mesure à 5 temps dans la musique populaire finnoise', *Sammelbände der Internationalen Musikgesellschaft* 2 (1900), 142–6
—, 'La Chanson populaire en Finlande', in *The International Folk-Lore Congress 1891: Papers and Transactions*, ed. Joseph Jacobs and Alfred Nutt (London, 1892), pp. 135–9
Lahor, Jean, *Le Bréviaire d'un panthéiste et le pessimisme* (Paris, 1906)
—, *Histoire de la littérature hindoue* (Paris, 1888)
—, *L'Illusion* (Paris, 1888)
Lambourn, David, 'Henry Wood and Schoenberg', *Musical Times* 128 (1987), 422–7
Langley, Leanne, 'Building an Orchestra, Creating an Audience: Robert Newman and the Queen's Hall Promenade Concerts, 1895–1926', in *The Proms: A New History*, ed. Jenny Doctor and David Wright (London, 2007), pp. 32–73
Lee, Vernon, *Music and its Lovers: An Empirical Study of Emotion and Imaginative Responses to Music* (London, 1932)
Legge, Walter, 'Conversations with Sibelius', *Musical Times* 76 (1935), 218–20
Levas, Santeri, *Sibelius: A Personal Portrait*, trans. Percy M. Young (London, 1972)
Liebich, Mrs Franz, *Claude-Achille Debussy* (London, 1908)
M., 'Mrs. Rosa Newmarch', *Musical Times* 52 (1911), 225–9
MacLean, Charles, 'Chauvinism in British Music', *Musical Times* 53 (1912), 520
—, 'Sibelius in England', *Zeitschrift der internationalen Musikgesellschaft* 9 (1907–08), 271–3
Mäkelä, Tomi, 'Sibelius and Germany, *Wahrhaftigkeit* beyond *Allnatur*', in *The Cambridge Companion to Sibelius*, ed. Daniel M. Grimley (Cambridge, 2004), pp. 169–81
—, 'Towards a Theory of Internationalism, Europeanism, Nationalism and "Co-Nationalism" in 20th-Century Music', in *Music and Nationalism in 20th-Century Great Britain and Finland*, ed. Tomi Mäkelä (Hamburg, 1997), pp. 9–16
Maynard, Lee Anna, 'Rosa Harriet Newmarch', in *Late Nineteenth- and Early Twentieth-Century British Women Poets*, ed. William B. Thesing, Dictionary of Literary Biography 240 (Detroit and London, 2001), pp. 164–71

Bibliography

Moore, Jerrold Northrop, *Edward Elgar: A Creative Life* (Oxford, 1984)

Murtomäki, Veijo, 'Sibelius and Finnish-Karelian Folk Music', *Finnish Music Quarterly* 3 (2005), 32–7

Musgrave, Michael, 'Newman, Robert', in *Oxford Dictionary of National Biography*, ed. H. C. G. Matthew and Brian Harrison, 60 vols (Oxford, 2004), vol. 40, pp. 658–9

Newman, Ernest, 'Sibelius No. 4: Its English History', in *From the World of Music: Essays from 'The Sunday Times'*, ed. Felix Aprahamian (London, 1956), pp. 127–32

—, 'The Birmingham Musical Festival', *Nation*, 12 October 1912, 100–01

Newmarch, Rosa, 'Anton Dvořák: A Plea for Remembrance', *Chesterian* n. s. no. 28 (January 1923), 97–100

—, 'Chauvinism in Music', *Edinburgh Review* 216 (1912), 95–116

—, 'Chauvinism in Music', *Musical Times* 53 (1912), 594–5

—, *The Concert-Goer's Library of Descriptive Notes*, 6 vols (London, 1928–48)

—, 'Czechoslovakian Chamber Music', in *Cobbett's Cyclopedic Survey of Chamber Music*, ed. Walter Willson Cobbett, 2 vols (London, 1929–30), vol. 1, pp. 306–8

—, 'Czechoslovakian Performing Organizations' in *Cobbett's Cyclopedic Survey of Chamber Music*, ed. Walter Willson Cobbett, 2 vols (London, 1929–30), vol. 1, pp. 308–9

—, 'Debussy', *Contemporary Review* 113 (1918), 538–41

—, 'The Development of National Opera in Russia (Fourth Paper): Tchaikovsky', *Proceedings of the Musical Association* 30 (1903–04), 57–93

—, 'Edward Elgar: His Career and His Genius', *World's Work* 3 (1904), 547–9

—, 'Fedor Shalyapin', *Slavonic and East European Review* 17 (1938), 209–11

—, 'Feodor Ivanovich Shaliapin', *Musical Times* 55 (1914), 437–40

—, *Henry J. Wood* (London, 1904)

—, *Horae Amoris: Song and Sonnets* (London, 1903)

—, 'In the Russian Hospitals', *Outlook*, 24 July 1915, 108–9

—, *Jean Sibelius* (London, 1944)

—, *Jean Sibelius: A Finnish Composer* (Leipzig, 1906), trans. Ludmille Kirschbaum as *Jean Sibelius: ein finnländischer Komponist* (Leipzig, 1906)

—, *Jean Sibelius: A Short History of a Long Friendship* (Boston, 1939)

—, *Jean Sibelius: Symphony No. 4 in A minor, Op. 63: Analytical Notes* (London, [1913]), trans. Ludmille Kirschbaum as *Vierte Sinfonie von Jean Sibelius (A moll, op. 63): Kleiner Konzertführer* (Leipzig, [1913])

—, *Mary Wakefield: A Memoir* (Kendal, 1912)

—, 'Moussorgsky's Operas', *Musical Times* 54 (1913), 433–9

—, *The Music of Czechoslovakia* (London, 1942)

—, 'The Outlook in Russia', *Musical Times* 56 (1915), 521–3

—, *Poetry and Progress in Russia* (London, 1907)
—, 'Queen's Hall in 1914–15', *Monthly Musical Record* 62 (1932), 36–7
—, 'A Requiem for Allied Heroes', *Musical Times*, 58 (1917), 496–7
—, 'Rimsky-Korsakov: Personal Reminiscences', *Monthly Musical Record* 38 (1908), 172–3
—, *The Russian Arts* (London, 1916)
—, *The Russian Opera* (London, 1914)
—, 'Russian Opera in Paris: Moussorgsky's "Boris Godunov"', *Monthly Musical Record* 38 (1908), 147–9
—, 'Scryiabin and Contemporary Russian Music', *Russian Review* 2 (1913), 153–69
—, 'Sibelius', *Chesterian* n. s. no. 14 (April 1921), 417–21
—, 'Smetana, Bedřich', in *Cobbett's Cyclopedic Survey of Chamber Music*, ed. Walter Willson Cobbett, 2 vols (London, 1929–30), vol. 2, pp. 425–32
—, 'The Smetana Centenary: A National Festival', *The Times*, 8 March 1924, 8
—, 'The Smetana Centenary: Celebrations at Prague', *The Times*, 9 February 1924, 8
—, *Songs to a Singer and Other Verses* (London, 1906)
—, 'Stassov as Musical Critic', *Monthly Musical Record* 38 (1908), 31–2 and 51–2
—, 'Vospominaniya priyatel'nitsï-anglichanki', in *Nezabvennomu Vladimiru Vasil'evichu Stasovu: Sbornik vospominanii*, ed. S. Vengerov (St Petersburg, 1910), pp. 77–81
—, 'Wassily Safonoff', *Musical Times* 57 (1916), 9–12
—, 'Women's Musical Activities', *Time and Tide*, 4 January 1929, 19–20
Newnham-Davis, Nathaniel, *Dinners and Diners and How to Dine in London*, 2nd edn (London, 1901)
Niemann, Walter, *Jean Sibelius* (Leipzig, 1917)
—, 'Jean Sibelius und die finnische Musik', *Signale für die musikalische Welt* 62 (1904), 185–91
—, *Die Musik seit Richard Wagner* (Berlin and Leipzig, 1913)
—, *Die Musik Skandinaviens: Ein Führer durch die Volks- und Kunstmusik von Dänemark, Norwegen, Schweden und Finnland bis zur Gegenwart* (Leipzig, 1906)
Norman, Gertrude, and Mirian Lubell Shrifte, eds, *Letters of Composers: An Anthology, 1603–1945* (New York, 1945)
Payton, Robert, 'The Pagani Panels: The Conservation and Display of Painted Wall-Mounted Linoleum', *Conservator* 23 (1999), 3–10
Pollack, Howard, 'Samuel Barber, Jean Sibelius, and the Making of an American Romantic', *Musical Quarterly* 84 (2000), 175–205
Pound, Reginald, *Sir Henry Wood* (London, 1969)
Prins, Yopie, 'Sappho Recomposed: A Song Cycle by Granville and Helen Bantock', in *The Figure of Music in Nineteenth-Century British Poetry*, ed. Phyllis Weliver (Aldershot, 2005), pp. 230–58
Pudor, Heinrich, 'Zur Geschichte der Musik in Finnland', *Sammelbände der Internationalen Musikgesellschaft* 2 (1900), 147–57

Bibliography

Purkis, Charlotte, '"Leader of Fashion in Musical Thought"; The Importance of Rosa Newmarch in the Context of Turn-of-the-Century British Music Appreciation', in *Nineteenth-Century British Music Studies*, vol. 3, ed. Peter Horton and Bennett Zon (Aldershot, 2003), pp. 3–19

Report of the Fourth Congress of the International Musical Society, London, 29th May–3rd June 1911 (London, 1912)

Riley, Matthew, ed., *British Music and Modernism, 1895–1960* (Farnham, 2010)

Rudder, May de, 'Mélodies de Jean Sibelius', *Le guide musical*, 7 January 1906, 9–11

Sanders, Alan, ed., *Walter Legge: Words and Music* (London, 1998)

Scholes, Percy A., 'Stravinsky at Close Quarters', *Everyman*, 1 May 1914, 86–7

Scott, A. MacCallum, *Through Finland to St. Petersburg* (London, 1908)

Speyer, Edward, *My Life and Friends* (London, 1937)

Stephens, Anna Cox, 'Music in Finland', *Musical Standard*, 18 September 1897, 184–5

Stern, David, '"One Thought Grows out Another": Sibelius's Influence on Ralph Vaughan Williams's Fifth Symphony', in *Sibelius in the Old and New World: Aspects of His Music, its Interpretation, and Reception*, ed. Timothy L. Jackson et al., Interdisziplinäre Studien zur Musik 6 (Frankfurt, 2010), pp. 383–400

Stevens, Lewis, *An Unforgettable Woman: The Life and Times of Rosa Newmarch* (Leicester, 2011)

Stevenson, Alfred Boynton, 'Chaikovskii and Mrs Rosa Newmarch Revisited: A Contribution to the Composer's Centennial Commemoration', *Inter-American Music Review* 14 (1995), 63–78

Sundberg, Gunnar, 'National Parallels in the Orchestral Works of Jean Sibelius and Arnold Bax: Focusing on their Symphonic Language', in *Music and Nationalism in 20th-Century Great Britain and Finland*, ed. Tomi Mäkelä (Hamburg, 1997), pp. 59–66

Suomen laulu: juhlajulkaisu, 1900–1920 (Helsinki, 1920)

Talas, SuviSirkku, ed., *Aino Sibeliuksen kirjeitä Järnefelt-suvun jäsenille* (Helsinki, 1999)

—, ed., *Elisabeth Järnefeltin kirjeitä, 1881–1929* (Helsinki, 1996)

—, ed., *Sydämen aamu: Aino Järnefeltin ja Jean Sibeliuksen kihlausajan kirjeitä*, trans. Oili Souminen (Helsinki, 2001)

—, ed., *Syysilta: Aino ja Jean Sibeliuksen kirjeenvaihtoa, 1905–1931*, trans. Oili Suominen (Helsinki, 2007)

—, ed., *Tulen synty: Aino ja Jean Sibeliuksen kirjeenvaihtoa, 1892–1904*, trans. Oili Suominen (Helsinki, 2003)

Tawaststjerna, Erik, *Sibelius*, trans. Robert Layton, 3 vols (London, 1976–97)

—, 'Über Adornos Sibelius-Kritik', in *Adorno und die Musik*, ed. Otto Kolleritsch (Graz, 1979), pp. 112–24

Törne, Bengt de, *Sibelius: A Close-Up* (London, 1937)

Touchard, Maurice, 'Un musicien finlandais', *La Nouvelle Revue*, 1 January 1914, 55–65

Tracey, Minnie, 'Music Masters of Scandinavia', *Musical America*, 26 October 1912, 5
Tsuzuki Chushichi, *Edward Carpenter, 1844–1929: Prophet of Human Fellowship* (Cambridge, 1980)
Vahtola, Vesa, *Sibeliuksen konserttimatkat Englantiin* ([Tampere], 2008)
Vaughan Williams, Ursula, *R. V. W.: A Biography of Ralph Vaughan Williams* (London, 1964)
Vignal, Marc, *Jean Sibelius* (Paris, 2004)
Watkins, Hadley, ed., *The Bournemouth Municipal Orchestra: Twenty-One Years of Municipal Music, 1893–1914* (Bournemouth, 1914)
Wood, Henry J., *My Life of Music* (London, 1938)
Wright, Donald, ed., *Cardus on Music: A Centenary Collection* (London, 1988)
'Z hudebního života', *Listy hudební matice* 4 (1924), 121–33

INDEX

Ackté, Aino 118, 119, 120–24, 134, 145, 146, 167, 176, 176–80
Adler, Guido 148
Adorno, Theodor 33
d'Albert, Eugen 115
   Tiefland 115
Allan, Maud 103–4
Allen, Hugh 208, 210–11, 212
Alyabiev, Aleksandr 14
Andersson, Otto 127, 249–50
Apostol 188
Arensky, Anton 123
Augener 197
Austin, Ernest 67
   'A Shepherd's Love-Song' 67

Bach, Johann Sebastian 65, 85, 94, 161, 180, 194
   St Matthew Passion 85, 161
Balakirev, Mily 60
Ballets Russes 26–7, 116, 168, 171–2
Balling, Michael 5, 178, 180
Bantock, Granville 1, 2, 3, 4, 5, 7, 31, 34–5, 36, 37, 40, 48, 56–9, 60, 61, 74, 78, 79, 81, 84–5, 86, 96, 97, 99, 101, 102, 104, 114, 118, 119, 123, 142, 143, 144–5, 151, 152, 153–4, 159, 160, 162, 174, 176, 190–91, 193, 194, 201–2, 203–4, 206, 208, 221, 223–4, 226–7, 230–32, 235, 240, 242–3, 252
   Atalanta in Calydon 142, 143, 144–5

   Dante 119
   Dante and Beatrice 118, 119
   Fifine at the Fair 151, 152, 159
   Hebridean Symphony 31
   Old English Suite 99, 101
   Omar Khayyám 48, 58–9, 60, 78, 79, 86, 96, 97, 154
   Pierrot of the Minute 81
Bantock, Helena 56, 57, 74, 208, 230
Bartók, Béla 230, 232, 233–4
Bath, Hubert 67–8
   'Evoë' 67
   'Heart o' Beauty' 68
   'Now' 68
Battell-Stoeckel, Ellen 185
Bauer, Harold 99, 101
Bax, Arnold 67–8, 78, 236
Beck, Ellen 67–8
Bective, Lady 86
Beecham, Thomas 32, 33–4, 35, 36, 37, 113, 114–6, 119, 140, 169, 241
Beethoven, Ludwig van 17, 18–19, 32, 100, 116, 145, 156, 161, 163, 194, 256
   Fidelio 116
   Fifth Symphony 156
   Violin Concerto 145
Berg, Alban 234
Berger, Francesco 59
Bessel & Co. 109, 171
Birmingham, performances of Sibelius's works at 1, 10, 20, 21–3, 25, 26, 32, 84–5, 102, 104, 105, 109, 114, 150–52,

Index

153, 155, 156–8, 160, 161–2, 165, 201–2, 203–4, 208, 209, 210, 249–65
Bizet, Georges 114, 116
  Carmen 114, 116
Blom, Eric 206, 214, 217, 221, 225, 226
Blomstedt, Aulis 234
Blomstedt, Heidi 85, 194, 234
Bobrikov, Nikolay 104
Bodley Head *see* Lane, John
Boosey, William 193–4, 214, 224, 227
Borodin, Aleksandr 14–15, 60, 171, 175
  First Symphony 15
  Prince Igor 171, 175
Boughton, Rutland 194
Boult, Adrian 212, 245
Bournemouth, performances of Sibelius's works at 31, 32, 36, 182–4, 205, 208, 209, 210, 224, 251
Bowen, York 67
Brahms, Johannes 15, 16, 18–19, 145, 159–60, 180, 194, 253, 255
  Ein deutsches Requiem 159–60
  Hungarian Dances 253
  Serenade in D 253
  Violin Concerto 145
Breitkopf & Härtel 1, 3, 8, 22, 41, 44, 51, 52, 54, 57–8, 59, 60, 81, 87, 97, 100, 103, 103, 104, 109, 119, 128, 132, 135, 160, 162, 167, 171, 177, 189–90, 206, 249, 252
Brewer, Herbert 162, 176–7, 223–4
  Sir Patrick Spens 176
British Broadcasting Company (later Corporation) 31, 224, 227, 232, 245
British Women's Symphony Orchestra 31–2
Brooke, Harold 67

Browning, Robert 254, 255
Bruch, Max 147
  Violin Concerto 147
Bruneau, Alfred 194
Brussels Quartet 98, 100
Burton, Lady 76
Busoni, Ferruccio 4, 163, 209, 220, 221
  Indian Fantasy 209
Bussine, Romain 146

Cambridge University 210
Cameron, Basil 32, 34, 37, 97, 229–30, 232, 233, 245
Cardus, Neville 29
Carpelan, Axel 42, 43, 47, 53, 58, 86, 122, 131, 250
Carpenter, Edward 62
Casals, Pablo 141, 180, 214, 229
Cathie, Philip 67
Cazalis, Henri *see* Lahor, Jean
Chaliapin, Fyodor 174, 175, 188
Chappell & Company 193, 198, 214, 215, 217, 222–3, 224, 227
Chausson, Ernest 19
Cheltenham, performances of Sibelius's works at 65, 66, 71, 75, 162
Chemet, Renée 138–9
Chester, J. & W. 120, 187–8, 190, 196, 197, 204, 206, 220, 249
Chopin, Fryderyk 23
Clutsam, George 116
  A Summer Night 116
Cobbett's Cyclopedic Survey of Chamber Music 221
Cohen, Harriet 34, 211, 236
Colles, Henry 119–20, 179
Colonne, Edouard 97
Concert Goers' Club 51–2, 54, 65–8, 78, 95, 140
Cooke, Arthur 168
Corder, Paul 68
  Two Preludes 68
Cortot, Alfred 214, 215
Cowen, Frederic 128

· 278 ·

Cui, César 60

Dahlhaus, Carl 30
Dahlström, Fabian 42–3, 169
Dale, Benjamin 67, 140, 141
 'Romance' from *Suite for Viola* 67, 140, 141
Damrosch, Walter 228
Darmesteter, James 135
Darmesteter, Mary *see* Robinson, Mary
Debussy, Claude 23, 48, 77–8, 81, 104, 114, 116, 123, 125, 149, 166, 167, 168, 176, 194
 Danse sacré et danse profane 176
 L'Enfant prodigue 114
 Khamma 104
 Nocturnes 48, 77
 Pelléas et Mélisande 116
 Prélude à l'après-midi d'un faune 77, 166, 168
 String Quartet 123
Deiters, Herman 15
Delius, Frederick 84–5, 114
 A Village Romeo and Juliet 114
Desmond, Astra 203
Diaghilev, Sergey 116, 168, 172, 175
Dostoevsky, Fyodor 126
Downes, Olin 43
Duclaux, Emile 135
Duclaux, Mary *see* Robinson, Mary
Dukas, Paul 19, 194
Dvořák, Antonín 46, 97, 100, 160, 162, 180, 194, 209, 229
 Carnival 97
 Cello Concerto 180, 229
 Requiem 162

Ehrström, Fredrik 14
Ekman, Karl 4, 34, 164, 186, 211
Elgar, Edward 5, 17–21, 48, 78, 80–81, 85, 86, 101, 118, 119, 124, 128, 151, 152, 156, 158, 160, 161, 167, 194, 206

 The Apostles 20, 161
 'Death on the Hills' 80
 The Dream of Gerontius 20, 161
 First Symphony 17–20, 48, 78, 85, 86, 101
 The Kingdom 20
 'A Modern Greek Song' 80–81
 The Music Makers 20–21, 85, 151, 152
 Second Symphony 20
 'Serenade' 80
 Violin Concerto 20, 118, 119, 124
Elwes, Gervase 159, 161, 181
Elwes, Winifred 159
Enckell, Laura 202
Epstein, Julius 52
Epstein, Richard 51–2, 53, 54, 147

Fazer 188, 217
Finnish Literature Society 43
Flaubert, Gustave 126
Flodin, Karl 142, 143
Ford, John 21
Forsyth, Cecil 148
France, Anatole 126
Francis of Assisi 160
Franck, César 19, 87, 98, 194, 254
Fränkel, Professor 92
Fuchs, Robert 146
Furuhjelm, Erik 221

Gade, Niels 254
Gaskell, Elizabeth 253
Giorgione 256
Gladstone, William 132, 133
Glazunov, Aleksandr 100
Glinka, Mikhail 14–15, 55
Gloucester, performances of Sibelius's works at 4, 31, 160, 162, 165, 176–80, 222, 223–4, 226
Godfrey, Dan 31, 182–4, 213, 251
Goethe, Johann Wolfgang von 72, 159, 160, 161, 164
Göhler, George 253

Index

Goossens, Eugene 194
Goss, Glenda Dawn 43
Gounod, Charles 115–6
   Faust 115–6
Grainger, Percy 167
Grainger Kerr, Elizabeth Mary 51, 53, 54, 56, 57, 67
Gray, Cecil 25, 32–5, 37
Gray, Laura 17, 33
Grieg, Edvard 23, 64, 68, 190, 254
   'A Dream' 68
   'A Mother's Grief' 68
   'Ragnhild' 68
Grieg, Nina 190
Gripenberg, Bertel 126, 128
Grove's Dictionary of Music and Musicians 9, 206, 221, 232
Gutmann, Emil 122

Hába, Alois 230, 232, 234
Habets, Alfred 9
Hagberg Wright, Charles Theodore 144
Handel, George 20–21, 149, 161
   Messiah 161
Hannikainen, Ilmari 199, 200
Hansen, Wilhelm 190, 200, 217
Hardie, James Kier 132, 133
Harris, Frederick 60
Harty, Hamilton 31, 86
   Violin Concerto 86
Hase, Oskar von 81, 87, 160, 162
Hastings, performances of Sibelius's music at 97, 229, 230, 233
Hawkes, Ralph 197
Haydn, Joseph 120, 161, 180, 200, 258
Hess, Myra 67–8
Hindemith, Paul 234
Holbrooke, Joseph 67
   'A Winter Night' 67
Hugo, Victor 112
Humperdinck, Engelbert 114–6
   Hänsel und Gretel 114–6
Huttunen, Matti 32

Ibbs & Tillett 226–7
Ilves, Eero 222, 233
Ilves, Jan 234
Ilves, Katarina 83, 85, 95, 193, 194, 208–9, 221, 222, 230, 233
Ilves, Merike 234
d'Indy, Vincent 19, 78, 87, 98
Ingelius, Axel 14
International Congress of Music 127–8, 150

Jalas, Jussi 33, 234
Jalas, Margareta 83, 85, 95, 111, 194, 234
Janáček, Leoš 9, 161, 197
   Glagolitic Mass 161
Järnefelt, Armas 172, 182, 190, 237
   Praeludium 182
Järnefelt, Arvid 62, 254
Järnefelt, Elisabeth 44, 62
Järnefelt, Maikki 172, 172, 174, 175, 180
Jeaffreson, Caroline Georgiana 135, 145, 146, 178, 180, 241, 242
Jeaffreson, Louisa Sophia 145, 146
Jeaffreson, Marie Thérèse 145, 146, 164, 165, 170, 174, 178, 179, 180
Johnson, Elisabeth 91, 100, 101, 105, 108, 110, 112, 113–4, 117, 148
Johnson, Harold 48
Jürgensburg, Elena Clodt von 62

Kajanus, Robert 32, 199, 251
Kalevala 4, 22, 52, 55, 58, 72, 73, 149, 169, 254, 265
Kalisch, Alfred 66–7, 200–01
Kastalsky, Aleksandr 161
   Requiem for Allied Heroes 161
Katila, Evert 131, 143–6, 250
Kling, Otto 1, 51, 52, 54, 59, 61, 74, 81, 88, 103, 105, 106, 113,

132, 156, 187–8, 190, 193, 205, 221
Klingenberg, Alf 211
Kodály, Zoltán 161
  Psalmus Hungaricus 161
Koussevitzky, Serge 106
Kranz, Naum *see* Petersburg Quartet
Kreisler, Fritz 119
Křenek, Ernst 230, 232
  Kleine Symphonie 232
Křička, Jaroslav 235
Křička, Petr 234, 235
Krohn, Ilmari 127
Kullak, Theodor 146
Kuula, Toivo 199, 221, 221

Lahor, Jean 164, 165, 167, 169
Lalo, Edouard 101
Lambert, Constant 32, 35, 37
Lamoureux, Charles 97
Lane, Brand 179, 180, 210, 212, 213, 226
Lane, John 10, 78, 87, 98, 126, 151–2
Launis, Armas 127
Layton, Robert 45–7
Lee, Vernon 172
Leeds, performance of Sibelius's music at 100–01, 232
Legge, Walter 32, 37
Leino, Eino 218
Leroux, Xavier 115
  Le Chemineau 115
Levas, Santeri 40–41, 233–4
Liebich, Louise 78
Lienau, Robert 60, 96, 97, 100
Lindgren, Axel 188, 190
Linton, Jessie *see* Wood, Jessie
Liszt, Franz 101, 232
Liukkonen, Helmi 34
Liverpool, performances of Sibelius's works at 1, 2, 3, 6–8, 10–11, 32, 52, 57, 194, 224, 252
Lloyd George, David 132, 133

MacDowell, Edward 148
Mackenzie, Alexander 128, 160
Maclean, Alec 205
MacLean, Charles 27, 150
Madetoja, Leevi 199
Maeterlinck, Maurice 3, 254
Mahler, Gustav 33, 122, 166, 168, 178, 181, 184
  Eighth Symphony 122
  Kindertotenlieder 184
  Das klagende Lied 184
  Das Lied von der Erde 178, 181
  Seventh Symphony 166, 168
Maikov, Apollon 80–81
Mallarmé, Stéphane 164
Manchester, performances of Sibelius's works at 4, 31, 32, 75, 97–8, 178, 208, 210, 213, 217, 225, 226
Marcus Aurelius 160
Massenet, Jules 115
  Werther 115
Matthay, Tobias 68
  Love Phases 68
Matthews, Appleby 203
Melartin, Erkki 194, 199, 221
Mendelssohn, Felix 21, 254
Merikanto, Oskar 150
  'Finnish Cradle Song' 150
Michelangelo 79, 100, 101, 127, 256
Minsky, Nikolay 80
Missa, Edmond 115
  Muguette 115
Molière (Jean-Baptiste Poquelin) 169
Mozart, Wolfgang Amadeus 15, 100, 115–6, 137, 176, 209, 232
  Così fan tutte 115
  Don Giovanni 116, 137
  Die Entführung aus dem Serail 115
  Le Nozze di Figaro 115, 116
  Piano Concerto No. 22 209
  Piano Concerto No. 23 223
  Piano Concerto No. 27 176

Index

Müller, Max 169
Munsterhjelm, Ester 56, 57
Munsterhjelm, Hjalmar 57
Munsterhjelm, John 57
Musical Association 9, 175
Musorgsky, Modest 60, 109, 170, 171–2, 175, 194
   Boris Godunov 109, 171–2, 175
   Khovanshchina 171, 175
   The Musician's Peepshow 171
   Songs and Dances of Death 171
   Yeremoushka's Lullaby 171

Newman, Ernest 1, 7, 37, 119, 144–5, 151–2, 159, 160, 161–2, 240, 251
Newman, Robert 34, 64, 193, 196, 202, 210, 214, 218, 223, 225, 227
Newmarch, Elizabeth ('Elsie') 42, 47, 74, 109, 110, 139, 181, 190, 192, 216, 230, 236, 238, 239–40, 243, 244–5
Newmarch, Gwendoline 202
Newmarch, Henry ('Harry') 58, 74, 117, 132, 191, 230, 232
Newmarch, John 47, 74, 77, 88–90, 91, 117, 132, 139, 145, 171, 187, 191, 192, 202, 225, 230, 244
Newmarch, Rosa
   attitude to modernism 25–30, 124–5, 126, 230, 251, 257
   correspondence with Aino Sibelius 45–6, 73–4, 79–81, 82–5, 208–11, 237–8
   editorship of *Living Masters of Music* 10, 78, 151–2, 158
   first meeting with Sibelius 2–3, 8
   interest in Czechoslovakia 9–10, 196, 197, 221, 241, 242
   interest in nationalism 9, 10–16, 251
   interest in oriental philosophy 58–9, 160, 167, 169
   interest in Russian music 9, 14–16, 17, 26–8
   involvement in the 'English Musical Renaissance' 5, 15–20, 39
   lectures on Sibelius 1, 8–9, 11–16, 22, 24, 35, 51–2, 54, 55–6, 57–8, 97, 169
   poetry 79–80, 80–81, 81, 83, 85
   president of Society of Women Musicians 35, 180–81
   programme notes 10, 15, 21–23, 26, 36, 94, 96, 97, 112, 151, 152, 153, 167, 171, 173, 178–9, 200, 230, 238, 239, 248, 249–65
   translations of texts by Sibelius 58, 60, 67, 96, 97, 98, 119, 126, 127, 128, 144, 189, 217, 218, 247–8
   views on German culture 15–16, 18–20, 27, 44, 75, 94, 124–5, 186, 190
   visits Sibelius in Finland 24, 37–8, 103–13, 188, 190–91, 192
   visits Sibelius in Paris 24–5, 133–7, 140, 193
   visits to Karlsbad 31, 225, 230, 233, 234
   visits to Russia 103, 105–10, 188, 190, 191
   works
      'Chauvinism in Music' 142, 143, 147, 148–50, 248, 249
      'The Development of National Opera in Russia' 9
      The Devout Russian 9, 190
      Henry J. Wood 53
      Horae Amoris: Songs and Sonnets 10, 79, 80–81, 83
      Jean Sibelius: A Finnish Composer 1, 8–9, 11–16, 22, 24, 35, 51–2, 54, 55–8, 247, 249

Index

Jean Sibelius: A Short History of a Long Friendship 2, 37–8, 39, 41, 239–43, 244–5, 248, 249
Jean Sibelius: Symphony No. 4 in A Minor, Op. 63 1–2, 151, 152, 153, 167, 169, 248, 249–65
Mary Wakefield: A Memoir 10, 165
The Music of Czechoslovakia 10, 232, 242
Poetry and Progress in Russia 9
'"Prometheus": The Poem of Fire' 168
The Russian Arts 9, 190
The Russian Opera 9, 174–6, 179
'Sibelius' 210, 248, 249, 252
Songs to a Singer and Other Verses 10, 83, 85
Tchaikovsky: His Life and Works 9
Nicolai, Otto 86
   The Merry Wives of Windsor 86
Niemann, Walter 9, 23–4, 25
Nijinsky, Vaclav 166, 168
Nikisch, Arthur 18–9
Novello 81, 177
Nurmio, Heikki 187

Offenbach, Jacques 115–6
   Les Contes d'Hoffman 115–6
d'Oisly, Maurice 67–8
O'Neill, Norman 81, 194
   Two Songs 81
Orcagna 230, 232
O'Shaughnessy, Arthur 20
Oxford University 208, 210–11

Paderewski, Ignacy Jan 99, 101, 152
   Symphony in B Minor 99, 101
Pagani's Restaurant 40, 68, 69–70, 77, 85, 87

Paget, Violet *see* Lee, Vernon
Palmgren, Maikki *see* Järnefelt, Maikki
Palmgren, Selim 172, 174, 194, 199
   Second Piano Concerto ('The River') 199
Paloheimo, Arvi 132, 133, 173
Paloheimo, Eva 42, 83, 85, 131, 132, 171, 173, 194, 209, 234, 240, 241
Paloheimo, Janne 234
Paloheimo, Marjatta 194, 195
Paloheimo, Martii 194, 195
Parker, Horatio 185
Parker, Katie 53
Parry, Hubert 128, 148, 149, 160
Paul, Adolf 253, 254
Pawlo, George 191–2, 194, 195
Petersburg Quartet 98, 100
Philharmonic Society, performances of Sibelius's works by 37, 59, 61, 228–9, 232, 241, 255
Pitt, Percy 5
Poe, Edgar Allen 122
Prokofiev, Sergey 27
Promenade Concerts *see* Queen's Hall, London

Queen's Hall, London 1, 3–4, 5–7, 26–7, 31, 32, 33–6, 52, 53, 63–4, 65, 66, 68, 95, 116, 119, 148, 152, 168, 170, 172, 180, 181, 191, 192, 193, 196, 200–01, 203, 205, 206, 208, 209–10, 213, 214, 222–4, 225, 226, 227, 228–9, 238–9, 245, 249, 251, 252

Rachmaninov, Sergey 101, 118, 120, 123
   Aleko 120
   Second Piano Concerto 101, 120
   Second Symphony 120

Index

Rainger, C. E. 66
Ravel, Maurice 81, 157, 167, 194
Redesdale, Lord 127–8
Reed, William 176
   Will o' the Wisp 176
Reger, Max 93–4, 95, 123, 178, 181
   Konzert im alten Stil 178, 181
Rembrandt 256
Respighi, Ottorino 239
   The Fountains of Rome 239
Richter, Hans 4, 19, 96, 97–8, 99, 101, 180
Rimsky-Korsakov, Nikolay 28, 60, 171, 175
   Pskovityanka 171, 175
Robinson, A. Mary F. 135, 172
Robinson, Mabel 135, 172
Rodin, Auguste 256
Ronald, Landon 84, 85, 86, 91, 118, 119
Rosenthal, Moritz 214, 215
Rossini, Gioachino 116
   Il Barbiere di Siviglia 116
Royal Academy of Music 67–8, 95, 146, 205
Royal College of Music 204, 205, 208, 210, 212, 249
Royal Philharmonic Society *see* Philharmonic Society
Runeberg, Johan Ludvig 60, 126
Ruskin, John 64
Rydberg Viktor 126

Safonov, Vasily 15, 46, 57, 96–7, 209
Saint-Saëns, Camille 164, 176, 194
Sapelnikov, Vasily 99, 101
Saranchov, Dmitry 62
Saranchov, Konstantin 62
Savonlinna Festival 145, 146
Schauman, Eugen 104
Schlesinger'sche Buch- & Musikhandlung *see* Lienau, Robert
Schnabel, Arthur 232

Schnéevoigt, Georg 32, 36
Schoenberg, Arnold 25–6, 157, 178, 181, 184, 234
   Chamber Symphony 184
   Five Pieces for Orchestra 26, 178, 181
   Second String Quartet 184
Scholes, Percy 25, 232
Schubert, Franz 15, 255
   Ninth Symphony 255
Schumann, Robert 80, 81, 254, 255
Scriabin, Aleksandr 25–6, 151, 152, 164, 166–70, 178, 180, 181, 249
   Piano Concerto in F sharp minor 181
   The Poem of Ecstasy 169
   Prometheus 26, 151, 152, 164, 166–7, 168, 169, 178, 181, 249
   Third Symphony ('The Divine Poem') 26, 178, 180
Scott, Cyril 67
   'Lullaby' 67
Shakespeare, William 21, 58, 60, 146, 160
Sibelius, Aino 43–4, 45–6, 47, 61, 62, 63, 64, 65, 66, 68, 72–4, 76, 77, 79–81, 82–4, 86, 87, 93–95, 96, 100, 103, 104, 105, 106, 108, 109, 111, 113–4, 117, 119, 123, 124, 127, 131, 132, 134, 142, 146, 151, 152, 153, 157, 160, 167, 173, 179, 188, 191, 193, 194, 200, 208–9, 214, 216, 221, 223, 226, 230, 235, 236, 237–8, 241, 242, 243, 245
Sibelius, Christian 217, 218
Sibelius, Eva *see* Paloheimo, Eva
Sibelius, Heidi *see* Blomstedt, Heidi
Sibelius, Jean
   anxieties about health 47–8, 73–4, 76–7, 80, 82, 84, 91–2, 101, 121, 124

Index

attitude to modernism 25, 39, 122–3, 128–31, 175, 184, 228, 233, 234
critical reception in Britain 4–7, 10–12, 22, 61, 68, 69, 97–8, 133, 134, 138, 157–8, 176–7, 200–01, 209–11, 227, 229, 230, 252
critical reception in France 4
critical reception in Germany 4–5, 23–4, 252
fifth visit to Britain (1921) 26–7, 30, 62, 196, 197–8, 200, 201–13, 216, 251–2
first visit to Britain (1905) 1, 2–4, 7–8, 10, 52
fourth visit to Britain (1912) 102, 150–61
meeting with Debussy 77–8
offer of chair in composition in America 209, 211, 212, 213
offer of chair in composition in Vienna 145, 146
second visit to Britain (1908) 24, 60–62
third visit to Britain (1909) 47–8, 63–90
unrealised invitations to visit Britain 58, 59, 102, 104, 105, 109, 114, 222, 223–4, 225, 226, 227
visit to America 45–6, 164–5, 184–6, 189
visits to Berlin 54, 92, 112, 122, 123, 124, 134, 184
visits to Paris 1, 31, 51–2, 53, 74, 78, 83, 90–91, 133–7, 140, 193, 228
works
    2 *Songs*, Op. 35 96, 97, 98, 247
    5 *Songs*, Op. 38 60, 133, 134, 247
    6 *Partsongs for Male Chorus*, Op. 18 60
    6 *Songs*, Op. 50 60, 67, 247
    6 *Songs*, Op. 72 189
    7 *Songs*, Op. 17 60, 247
    7 *Songs of J. L. Runeberg*, Op. 13 60, 67, 247
    8 *Short Pieces*, Op. 99 216–7
    8 *Songs*, Op. 61 126–8, 247
    Aallottaret, Op. 73 see *The Oceanides*, Op. 73
    'Autumn Night', Op. 38, No.1 see 5 *Songs*, Op. 38
    'Berceuse', Op. 37, No. 2 67
    'Black Roses', Op. 36, No. 1 67
    'But My Bird is Long in Homing', Op. 36, No. 2 67
    Canzonetta, Op. 62a 138, 139
    'Caprice', Op. 24, No. 3 67
    The Captive Queen, Op. 48 60, 64–5, 247
    The Dryad, Op. 45, No.1 104, 123
    Eighth Symphony 37–8, 41, 229, 241
    En Saga, Op. 9 14, 55–6, 68, 69, 157, 191, 203, 210, 239, 248, 254
    'Farewell', Op. 72, No. 1 see 6 *Songs*, Op. 72
    The Ferryman's Brides, Op. 33 239
    'Festivo' see *Scènes historiques*, Op. 25
    Finlandia, Op. 26 3, 4, 8, 10–11, 13, 15, 32, 55, 56, 61, 66, 68–9, 157, 182, 187, 199, 203, 210, 223, 224, 239, 248, 253
    Fifth Symphony, Op. 82 29, 30, 31, 32, 156, 194, 196, 200, 202, 203, 205, 208, 209, 213, 239
    'The First Kiss', Op. 37, No.1 67
    First Symphony, Op. 39 3–4, 6, 8, 10–11, 52, 54, 55, 223, 235, 237, 239, 252, 254, 255

· 285 ·

Index

Fourth Symphony, Op. 63 20–23, 24–5, 26, 28, 30, 35, 38–9, 84–5, 112, 116, 119–20, 123, 127, 128–30, 146, 150–51 152, 153, 156–8, 161–2, 163, 170, 182–4, 200–01, 202, 204, 208, 209, 210, 223, 225, 226, 220, 232, 233, 235, 239, 248, 249–65
'Herbstabend', Op. 38, No.1 see *5 Songs*, Op. 38
'Höstkväll', Op. 38, No.1 see *5 Songs*, Op. 38
Hymn till jorden, Op.95 see *Hymn to the Earth*, Op. 95
Hymn to the Earth, Op. 95 217–20
'Impromptu', Op. 5, No. 5 67
Impromptu, Op. 19 117, 119, 247
'Ingalill', Op. 36, No. 4 67
In memoriam, Op. 59 103, 104, 117, 123, 254
'Jäger March', Op. 91a 187
Karelia Suite, Op. 11 15, 75, 210, 248
King Christian II, Op. 27 3, 4, 5–6, 210, 227, 248, 253, 254
Kullervo, Op. 7 54, 55, 56
'Lemminkäinen and the Maidens of the Island', Op. 22, No. 1 see *Lemminkäinen Suite*, Op. 22
'Lemminkäinen in Tuonela', Op. 22, No. 3 see *Lemminkäinen Suite*, Op. 22
Lemminkäinen Suite, Op. 22 6–7, 11, 36, 55, 199, 210, 239, 248, 252, 254
'Lemminkäinen's Home-faring' see 'Lemminkäinen's Return', Op. 22, No. 4
'Lemminkäinen's Return', Op. 22, No. 4 see *Lemminkäinen Suite*, Op. 22
'Lever de Soleil', Op. 37, No. 3 67
Luonnotar, Op. 70 34, 122, 176–80
Maan virsi, Op. 95 see *Hymn to the Earth*, Op. 95
The Maiden in the Tower 55
'A Maiden Yonder Sings', Op. 50, No. 3 see *6 Songs*, Op. 50
'Minun kultani' 139
Night Ride and Sunrise, Op. 55 96, 97, 123, 170, 229, 230, 248, 254
The Oceanides, Op. 73 184, 185, 199, 210, 238, 239, 248
The Origin of Fire, Op. 32 see *Ukko the Fire-Maker*, Op. 32
'Orion's Belt', Op. 72, No.2 see *6 Songs*, Op. 72
Pelléas et Mélisande, Op. 46 3, 53, 139, 254
Pohjola's Daughter, Op. 49 32, 58, 59, 60
The Raven 122, 123
'Rêve', Op. 13, No. 5 see *7 Songs of J. L. Runeberg*, Op. 13
'Romance', Op. 24, No. 9 67, 139
Romance in C, Op. 42 98, 100, 103, 210, 253
Scènes historiques, Op. 25 178, 210, 239
Scènes historiques II, Op. 66 170, 178
Second Symphony, Op. 43 4,

8, 54, 55, 97–8, 123, 239, 251, 254, 255
Seventh Symphony, Op. 105 29, 31, 223, 224, 228–9, 239
Sixth Symphony, Op. 104 31, 212, 220, 221, 223, 225, 226, 228, 239
'The Song of the Roses', Op. 50, No. 6 *see 6 Songs*, Op. 50
'The Spell of Springtide', Op. 61, No. 8 *see 8 Songs*, Op. 61
Three Sonatinas, Op. 67 150, 168, 169, 253
String Quartet, Op. 56 ('Voces intimae') 72, 78, 79, 82, 84, 92, 95, 98, 100–01, 204, 221, 256
Suite champêtre, Op. 98b 217
Suite mignonne, Op. 98a 214–7
'The Swan of Tuonela', Op. 22, No. 2 *see Lemminkäinen Suite*, Op. 22
Swanwhite, Op. 54 94–5, 96, 97, 123, 248, 254
Tapiola, Op. 112 31, 32, 228, 229
The Tempest, Op. 109 229, 230–32, 235, 248
'Theodora', Op. 35, No. 2 *see 2 Songs*, Op. 35
Third Symphony, Op.52 24, 32, 59, 61, 186, 190, 199, 203, 208, 209, 210, 239, 254, 255
'The Tryst', Op. 37, No.5 67
Three Songs for American Schools 185
Ukko the Fire-Maker, Op. 32 128, 248
Valse lyrique, Op. 96a 197, 210

Valse mélancolique 253
Valse romantique, Op. 62b 138, 139
Valse triste, Op. 44, No.1 66, 120, 182, 187, 203, 204, 210, 223, 224, 248, 253, 254
Violin Concerto, Op. 47 51, 53, 54, 67, 138–9, 145–6, 147, 210, 239
Sibelius, Katarina *see* Ilves, Katarina
Sibelius, Kirsti 85
Sibelius, Magareta *see* Jalas, Margareta
Sibelius, Ruth *see* Snellman, Ruth
Simpson, Elizabeth ('Bella') 91, 225
Sjögren, Emil 137, 186
Skandinavisk Musikförlag 189
Smetana, Bedřich 221, 253
  The Bartered Bride 253
Smith, Alexander 257
Smyth, Ethel 114
  The Wreckers 114
Snellman, Jussi 195
Snellman, Ruth 85, 95, 194, 195, 208
Speyer, Edgar *see also* Stosch, Leonora von 78, 79, 167, 169, 193–4, 224, 251
Speyer, Edward 224
Stanford, Charles 115, 160
  Shamus O'Brien 115
Stasov, Vladimir 12, 58, 60, 127, 128, 142, 174, 175
Stoeckel, Carl 185
Stosch, Leonora von *see also* Speyer, Edgar 78–9, 167
Strauss, Johann 115
  Die Fledermaus 115
Strauss, Richard 17, 97, 111, 112, 114–6, 119, 124, 125, 149, 152, 167, 169, 176, 180, 184, 253
  Ariadne auf Naxos 167, 169

Index

Le bourgeois gentilhomme 167, 169
Don Juan 112
Elektra 114, 116, 184
Feuersnot 115
Salome 116, 119, 176, 180
Sinfonia Domestica 17, 111, 112
Till Eulenspiegel 97
Stravinsky, Igor 25–7, 157, 234
   The Firebird 26
   Petrushka 26
   The Rite of Spring 26
Strindberg, August 95, 96, 254
Sullivan, Arthur 114
   Ivanhoe 114
Suomen Laulu 170–71, 172, 173–5, 179–80, 196–7, 218, 223, 224
Suominen, Oili 43–4
Szigeti, Joska 86

Talas, SuviSirrku 43–4
Taneev, Sergey 100
Tavaststjerna, Karl August 126
Tawaststjerna, Erik 2, 39, 45–7, 56, 211
Tchaikovsky, Modest 9, 114
Tchaikosky, Pyotr 14–5, 17, 18, 23, 27–8, 100, 101, 113, 114, 145, 149, 162, 253, 254
   First Piano Concerto 101
   Queen of Spades 113, 114
   Violin Concerto 145
Telmámyi, Emil 236
Tennyson, Alfred 112, 118
Tertis, Lionel 67, 140–41
Thibaud, Jacques 99, 101
Thomas, Ambroise 115
   Hamlet 115
Thompson, Margareta Örtenblad 43
Toch, Ernst 230, 232
   Piano Concerto 232
Tolstoy, Lev 62, 144
Törne, Bengt von 33, 218–9
Touchard, Maurice 185–6

Tovey, Donald Francis 31, 32
Tracey, Minnie 136–7, 185–6
Tree, Herbert Beerbohm 169
Turner, Eva 34

Vaughan Williams, Ralph 161, 194, 206–7, 227
   Flos Campi 227
   On Wenlock Edge 161
   A Pastoral Symphony 227
Vaughan Williams, Ursula 206–7
Vecsey, Franz von 145–6, 147
Verbrugghen, Henri 53
Verdi, Giuseppe 116, 160, 161
   Missa di requiem 160
   Rigoletto 116
Verstovsky, Aleksandr 14
Viebig, Clara 126
Vignal, Marc 44
Virkkunen, Erkki 195

Wagner, Richard 19, 114, 116, 119, 124, 149, 175, 193, 252
   Der fliegende Holländer 116, 119
   Tannhäuser 116
   Tristan und Isolde 114, 116
Wakefield, Mary 10, 64–5, 76, 86, 118, 119, 165
Walford Davies, Henry 118, 119–20, 151, 152, 194
   Festal Overture 119
   Solemn Melody 119–20
   Song of St Francis 119, 151, 152
Wallace, William 67
Walter, Bruno 101
Warlock, Peter 239
   Capriol Suite 239
Warren, John (Baron de Tabley) 255
Wasenius, Emil 250
Webster, John 21
Westerlund, R. E. 188, 190
Westmorland Festival 64–5

Index

Wieniawski, Henryk 53
    Second Violin Concerto 53
Wilde, Oscar 119
Williams, Fred 146
Williams, Joseph 216–7
Wood, Henry 1, 3, 8, 10, 31, 35–6, 37, 52, 53, 61, 63, 64, 68, 71, 74, 78–9, 84, 96, 103, 116, 126, 134, 138, 150, 151, 152, 166, 170, 178, 179, 181, 192, 199, 200–01, 205, 206, 223, 225, 226, 236, 238, 240, 245, 251, 252
Wood, Jessie 181, 235, 245
Wood, Muriel 179, 181
Wood, Olga 61, 64, 68, 71, 74, 78–9, 86, 87–8, 102–3
Wood, Tania 152
Woodall, Doris 181
Wordsworth, William 112, 118

Ysaÿe, Eugène 141, 164